W0091393

Advance Praise

'We are constantly told that in understanding radicalization, the context and deep knowledge of local dynamics is crucial. That is why this book is such an important contribution. It will be a must read for anyone looking to understand the complex dynamics of radicalization and extremism in South Asia.'

—Dr Andrew Blum,
Executive Director, Kroc Institute for Peace and Justice,
University of San Diego, USA

'The literature on radicalization focuses mostly on the Middle East and Europe. The editors of the present volume have rightly pointed to the multifaceted scene of radicalization in South Asia and put together a fascinating collection of case studies. The chapters add new perspectives on the cause and context of radicalization, from the local and psychological to the global and structural, perspectives that will add value not only to the literature on radicalization as such but also to the literature on South Asia.'

—Dr Arild Engelsen Ruud,
Professor, South Asia Studies,
University of Oslo, Norway

'This book is a South–South effort, a fact that increases its relevance and importance. Its context-specific recommendations in several cases offer guidance to policymakers and practitioners, directly from the coalface. As such, this book is an important contribution to both the literature and practice.'

—Dr Des Molloy,
Senior Programme Director,
The Nippon Foundation, Japan

Radicalization *in* South Asia

Thank you for choosing a SAGE product!
If you have any comment, observation or feedback,
I would like to personally hear from you.

Please write to me at **contactceo@sagepub.in**

Vivek Mehra, Managing Director and CEO, SAGE India.

Bulk Sales

SAGE India offers special discounts
for purchase of books in bulk.
We also make available special imprints
and excerpts from our books on demand.

For orders and enquiries, write to us at

Marketing Department
SAGE Publications India Pvt Ltd
B1/I-1, Mohan Cooperative Industrial Area
Mathura Road, Post Bag 7
New Delhi 110044, India

E-mail us at **marketing@sagepub.in**

Subscribe to our mailing list
Write to **marketing@sagepub.in**

This book is also available as an e-book.

Radicalization *in* South Asia

Context, Trajectories and Implications

Edited by
Mubashar Hasan
Kenji Isezaki
Sameer Yasir

Los Angeles | London | New Delhi
Singapore | Washington DC | Melbourne

First published in 2019 by

SAGE Publications India Pvt Ltd
B1/I-1 Mohan Cooperative Industrial Area
Mathura Road, New Delhi 110 044, India
www.sagepub.in

SAGE Publications Inc
2455 Teller Road
Thousand Oaks, California 91320, USA

SAGE Publications Ltd
1 Oliver's Yard, 55 City Road
London EC1Y 1SP, United Kingdom

SAGE Publications Asia-Pacific Pte Ltd
18 Cross Street #10-10/11/12
China Square Central
Singapore 048423

Published by Vivek Mehra for SAGE Publications India Pvt Ltd. Typeset in 10.5/13 pt Bembo by Zaza Eunice, Hosur, Tamil Nadu, India.

Library of Congress Cataloging-in-Publication Data Available

ISBN: 978-93-532-8548-7 (HB)

SAGE Team: Rajesh Dey, Guneet Kaur Gulati, Mahira Chadha and Ritu Chopra

Contents

List of Abbreviations

AL	Awami League
AP	Adhaalath Party
AQ	Al-Qaeda
AQIS	Al Qaeda in the Indian Subcontinent
ASP	Ansarul Sharia Pakistan
BBS	Bodu Bala Sena
BIISS	Bangladesh Institute of International and Strategic Studies
BIMSTEC	Bay of Bengal Initiative for Multi-Sectoral Technical and Economic Cooperation
BNP	Bangladesh Nationalist Party
HT	Hizb ut-Tahrir
MC	Muslim Conference
COIN	counter-insurgency
CPI (M)	Communist Party of India (Marxist)
CPI (Maoists)	The Communist Party of India (Maoist)
CPI (M–L)	Communist Party of India (Marxist–Leninist)
CPP	Communist Party of the Philippines
CTTC	Counter Terrorism and Transnational Crime Unit
CUNY	City University of New York
CVE	Countering Violent Extremism
JMB	Jamaat-ul-Muslimeen Bangladesh
DDR	Disarmament, Demobilization and Reintegration
DfID	Department for International Development
DQP	Dhivehi Qaumee Party
DRP	Dhivehi Rayyithunge Party
DW	Dark web
ESR	Education Sector Reform

EU	European Union
FARC	Revolutionary Armed Forces of Colombia
FGDs	focus group discussions
FUVs	follow-up visits
GI	Gaumee Iththihaadh (National Unity Alliance)
GRAIR	Guideline for Risk Assessment, Intervention and Reintegration
GSDRC	Governance, Social Development, Conflict and Humanitarian Knowledge Services
HEC	Higher Education Commission
HEMIS	Higher Education Management Information System
HuJI-B	Harkat-ul-Jihad-al-Islami Bangladesh
ICPVTR	International Centre for Political Violence and Terrorism Research
IDP	Islamic Democratic Party
IFAD	International Fund for Agricultural Development
ILO	International Labour Organization
IMF	International Monetary Fund
LMS	learning management system
IORA	Indian Ocean Rim Association
IS	Islamic State
ISAS	Institute of South Asian Studies
ISD	Institute for Strategic Dialogue
ISI	Inter-Services Intelligence
ISIL	Islamic State of Iraq and the Levant
ISIS	Islamic State of Iraq and Syria
IUCN	International Union for Conservation of Nature
JeM	Jaish-e-Mohammed
JKLF	Jammu Kashmir Liberation Front
JMB	Jamaat-ul-Mujahideen Bangladesh
JMJB	Jagrata Muslim Janata Bangladesh
JP	Jumhooree Party
JS	Jamiyatul Salaf
JVP	Janatha Vimukthi Peramuna
KII	key informant interviews

KITE	Khyber Institute of Technical Education
KPK	Khyber Pakhtunkhwa
LeT	Lashkar-e-Taiba
LKI	Lakshman Kadirgamar Institute
LoC	Line of Control
LTTE	Liberation Tigers of Tamil Eelam
MC	Monitoring Centre
MCCI	Maoist Communist Centre of India
MDP	Maldivian Democratic Party
MHT	Mental Health Team
MNC	Maldivian National Congress
MORENA	National Regeneration Movement
MSDP	Maldivian Social Democratic Party
MUF	Muslim United Front
NC	National Conference
NCTC	National Counter Terrorism Centre
NESA	Near East South Asia
NUS	National University of Singapore
OJT	on-the-job training
OPEC	Organization of the Petroleum Exporting Countries
OSCE	Organization for Security and Co-operation in Europe
PA	People's Alliance
PATA	Provincially Administered Tribal Areas
PDP	People's Democratic Party
PP	People's Party
PRP	Poverty Reduction Party
PVE	Preventing Violent Extremism
PWG	People's War Group
RAB	Rapid Action Battalion
RAN	Radicalization Awareness Network
RSS	Rashtriya Swayamsevak Sangh
RUSI	Royal United Services Institute
SAARC	South Asian Association for Regional Cooperation

SAH	Shahadat-e al Hikma
SAIS	School of Advanced International Studies
SAVRY	Structured Assessment of Violence Risk in Youth
SIMI	Students' Islamic Movement of India
SLFP	Sri Lanka Freedom Party
SLP	Social Liberal Party
SSR	Security Sector Reform
SWAaT	Social Welfare, Academics and Training
SYRIZA	Coalition of Radical Left
TNSM	Tehreek e Nafasat e Shariat e Muhammadi
TTP	Tehreek-e-Taliban Pakistan
TUFS	Tokyo University of Foreign Studies
UMT	University of Management and Technology
UNAMSIL	United Nations Mission in Sierra Leone
UNCIP	United Nations Commission for India and Pakistan
UNDP	United Nations Development Programme
UNTAET	United Nations Transitional Administration in East Timor
USAID	United States Agency for International Development
WWF	World Wide Fund for Nature

Foreword

The South Asian region has witnessed radicalization around diverse extreme ideologies. This includes both the political extremism and radicalization through religious and cultural differences. This important volume covers most of these radicalizations in the South Asian countries. It is a handy book to understand the phenomenon at one place. This volume, based on case studies, will also help to comprehend the malaise in its local context, as the contributions are based on the dynamics of the specific regions. The project began as a conference theme in Japan in 2018, which later concretized as a volume.

While discussing radicalization, we normally imagine and talk about Europe and the Middle East, with little emphasis on the South Asian region. And South Asia is also not a monolith; it is extremely diverse on several counts, including language, religion, culture and politics.

The book also acknowledges the emergence of political leaders, of course through democratic processes, holding radical views. Mostly, this sort of extremism is not identified as radicalization but visualized merely as a political shift. Commenting on the issue in the first chapter, it says, 'With the existing threats from religious radicalism, the recent rise of nationalist strongman leaders in key countries (such as the U.S. and India) have complicated the scene.'

We generally tend to deal with violence and bloodshed after radicalization as a law and order issue, which actually is a mere consequence of extremism of thought process. The radicalization of the mind complicates the politics if it is allowed to grow unabated and unchecked, many times patronized by powerful and popular demagogues. Pakistan under Zia-ul-Haq is one apt example in the region. Pakistan did emerge as a sovereign nation after millions died in the name of religion, which again happened because minds were poisoned for decades. However, it continued as an Islamic nation till the 1980s, with little societal and religious discomfort, but Zia-ul-Haq unleashed an era that almost defaced Islam through radicalization. The nexus between the radical Islamist groups and Pakistan's intelligence agency ISI got almost formalized as State patronage to violent radical Islam. Its ugliest manifestation is terrorism, which has gripped Pakistan. It even uses terrorism as a weapon to fight against its neighbours such as India and Afghanistan. The perversion Zia brought about cannot be reversed and Pakistan and South Asia will continue to bear the consequences for a long time to come.

It is true of political radical ideologies as well, and the case study of Maoist violence in India is one apt example. One can debate and discuss the relevance or failure of Maoism globally, but its acceptability among the poor and deprived sections cannot be ignored. In a country like India, where economic and social disparities abound and most of the governments do not seem to respond to the challenge empathetically, such radical political groups do find some space. However, with the increase in mindless violence, the cause they rightly espoused is almost a lost one now.

Sri Lanka went through a terrible consequence of the toxic mix of religion and nationalism when Sinhala Buddhist radicalization polarized the majority population against the fellow ethnic Tamils. The civil war that ensued between the two radical groups cost many lives as well as displacement of a large population. This ethnic war has ended, but the emerging Buddhist nationalism has found a new enemy in the local Muslim population. The Bodu Bala Sena (BBL) has radicalized Buddhism, using it as an exclusive nationalism, where the 'other' is the enemy of the nation. This othering of Muslims has resulted in violence and destruction of their business and property. A sense of alienation has crept in with the increase in Islamophobic and divisive politics of the BBL. Unfortunately, it has led to the emergence of radicalization among quite a few Muslim youth, who seem to have joined the despicable ISIS. Not a good development for Sri Lanka or for South Asia.

Bangladesh is facing a curious position in the context of radicalization. The two mainstream political parties use Islamic radicalism as a binary with ruling Awami League espousing secularism while the Bangladesh Nationalist Party embracing the radical (Salafi/Wahabi) Islam. However, the ground realities expose the binary itself as we find secular Awami League seeking support of 63 out of 70 Islamist groups active in Bangladesh. Thus, the acceptability and legitimacy of these radical factions are alarming and a challenge for all those who valorize liberal/secular politics.

One of the smallest island nations like Maldives is also in the grip of rising Islamic radicalism. Here again, the Salafi/Wahabi imams have indoctrinated the unemployed youth with their perverted/vulgarized Islam, which is a toxic combination and the consequences are there for all of us to see.

Radicalization in South Asia: Context, Trajectories and Implications is an insightful collection of case studies on most of the South Asian countries. It unravels the context of radicalization in each country, emphasizing on the specificities of local politics and thus avoiding the sweeping generalizations. The book could not have come at a better time, as the region is confronting challenges of diverse radicalizations.

S. Irfan Habib
New Delhi

Acknowledgements

We acknowledge the global programme of Tokyo University of Foreign Studies (TUFS) in Japan for supporting us to conceptualize this book in Tokyo, Japan. We also thank our contributors for working under a tight deadline to produce thought-provoking and empirically grounded chapters. Our further gratitude goes to Dr Simon Leitch in Brisbane, Mrs Marit Egner in Oslo, Mr Monishankar Prasad, Aya Fukuda and Vivian Turk at TUFS, and Jehangir Ali and Rajesh Venugopal at the London School of Economic and Political Science, University of London, for contributing in various capacities to complete this project. Last but not least, we warmly acknowledge Mr Rajesh Dey, commissioning editor at SAGE, for guiding us towards the completion of this project.

Introduction to Radicalization in South Asia
Context, Trajectories and Implications

Mubashar Hasan, Kenji Isezaki and Sameer Yasir

This book is being published in an extraordinary time in world history, when democracies across the world are facing challenges from radicalism and extremism. With the existing threats from religious radicalism, the recent rise of nationalist strongman leaders in key countries (such as the United States and India) has complicated the scene. Although much and due attention is paid to groups such as the al-Qaeda, the Islamic State of Iraq and the Levant (ISIL), the Taliban and Lashkar-e-Taiba, more attention is needed for local radical, violent and terrorist groups. This is because the roots, medium and implications for the radical ideologies that feed violence and terrorism are complex, context specific and diverse. This book presents and analyses the context-specific and diverse modes of radicalism which feed into violence and terrorism in five South Asian countries: India, Maldives, Sri Lanka, Pakistan and Bangladesh. Its unique contribution is not into the theoretical discussion on radicalization, violence and terrorism, as these concepts have context-specific meaning and ramifications. Rather, this book adds invaluable theoretical and practical insights into case-specific contemporary trajectories and implications of radicalization, violence and terrorism in the featured countries. In order to understand the rationale behind our approach to addressing the problems of radicalization, violence and terrorism on case-by-case basis, it is pertinent to revisit the contemporary context of radicalism in South Asia.

THE CONTEXT: RISING TIDE OF RADICALISM IN SOUTH ASIA

There is little doubt that South Asia is at a crossroad. Democracy in South Asia has never been stronger, but history shows that countries such as Pakistan, Bangladesh, Sri Lanka, Nepal and Maldives have been swinging between illiberal democracy, autocracy and military-backed dictatorships. In recent times, however, with the rise of Hindu nationalism and such phenomena as 'the cow vigilantes', even India's pluralist, democratic sociopolitical fabric—once a beacon of light in the region—is under serious pressure too.

It is a very interesting time in South Asian history for three main reasons. First, the region is going through a youth bulge. According to an estimate, 26 per cent of the global total of youth are now living in South Asia. Among them, India has the world's highest number of 10–24-year-olds at 356 million, followed by Pakistan with 59 million and Bangladesh with 48 million.[1] Second, South Asian economic growth is slowing down. Although the region is still in the second place for growth after Asia–Pacific, it is the leading centre for economic growth.[2] Generally, employment is high in South Asia; however, as the International Labour Organization (ILO) pointed out, 72 per cent of the labour force in South Asia is engaged in poor-quality jobs, with income inequality in this region reaching staggering heights.[3] Consequently, the quality of life in South Asia is poor for many of its inhabitants who labour away in economies better serving the rich. Third, and most important, a wave of illiberalism and radicalism is sweeping over South Asia. This point requires further elaboration and contextualization for the countries featured in this book.

[1] Monica Das Gupta et al., *The Power of 1.8 Billion* (New York, NY: UNFPA, State of The World Population, 2014). Available at: https://www.unfpa.org/sites/default/files/pub-pdf/EN-SWOP14-Report_FINAL-web.pdf (accessed on 23 July 2018).

[2] Joe Qian, 'South Asia Loses Growth Lead, Can Regain through Action', *The World Bank*, 8 October 2017. Available at: http://www.worldbank.org/en/news/press-release/2017/10/08/right-policies-south-asia-potential-growth-lead-saef (accessed on 15 June 2018).

[3] *ILO*, 'Employment in Asia-Pacific Continues to Grow but Often Remains of Poor Quality', 22 January 2018. Available at: https://www.ilo.org/asia/media-centre/news/WCMS_615872/lang–en/index.htm (accessed on 23 May 2018).

Although the foundations of democratic institutes in India are solid, and perhaps the strongest in South Asia, the country is not immune to the challenges of radicalism, violence and terrorism. Three major types of radicalism dominate the discussion on radicalization in India. They are as follows: Muslim radicalism, Hindu radicalism and leftist radicalism. In the view of B. Raman,[4] a respected Indian analyst and ex-civil servant, contemporary Muslim radicalism is the result of Hindu radicalism in India, and Raman refers to the specific trigger points in Indian history which drove Indian Muslims to radicalism, violence and terrorism. In the view of Raman,[5] these triggering points were as follows: (a) the demolition of the Babri Mosque in 1992 by radical Hindus, (b) allegation of excessive force against Muslims by the Mumbai police to quash Muslim violence after the demolition of the mosque and (c) the anti-Muslim massacres in Gujarat in 2002.[6] In Raman's view, these events provoked Muslim youths to join the Students' Islamic Movement of India (SIMI) and Al Umma, and to carry out a series of terrorist attacks on Indian soil. While at present the scenario seems to be under control, the rise of transnational terrorist groups such as the al-Qaeda and ISIL seem to continue inspiring occasional lone wolves.[7]

Kashmir is another triggering point of Muslim radicalism and terrorism in India. In a recent column by Barkha Dutt published in *The Washington Post*, titled 'Why the World No Longer Cares about Kashmir', Dutt[8] opines that India's Kashmir problem is now 'probably the worst' it has been in the past two decades. She outlines multiple

---

[4] B. Raman, 'Reasons for Radicalization', *Outlook*, 20 July 2011. Available at: https://www.outlookindia.com/website/story/reasons-for-radicalisation/277735 (accessed on 4 May 2019).

[5] Ibid.

[6] Ibid.

[7] P. S. Gopikrishnan Unnithan and Jacob Jeemon, 'ISIS Operative Yasmin Mohammed Gets 7 Years in Jail for Recruiting 15 Indians', *India Today*, 24 March 2018. Available at: https://www.indiatoday.in/india/story/nia-sentences-yasmin-mohammed-to-7-years-in-jail-for-recruiting-15-indians-for-isis-1196974-2018-03-24 (accessed on 15 April 2018).

[8] Barkha Dutt, 'Why the World No Longer Cares about Kashmir', *The Washington Post*, 6 June 2017. Available at: https://www.washingtonpost.com/news/global-opinions/wp/2017/06/06/why-the-world-no-longer-cares-about-kashmir/?utm_term=.a0a97dd6ea5c (accessed on 23 May 2018).

factors behind the current problem of Muslim radicalization in Kashmir. These are as follows: (a) Pakistan-backed militancy and a spate of terrorist attacks matched with unrelenting civilian protests, (b) heavy-handed responses by Indian anti-terrorism security forces and (c) the sense of injustice regarding the operation of the Indian security forces. These factors have made some young, educated men in Kashmir to pick up guns against the Indian State.[9] Nevertheless, the problems of radicalization in Kashmir are not new. The current crisis has entered into a newer phase with new dimensions.

One should note, however, that Muslim radicalism in India is not disconnected from radicalization of the wider Hindu population. The advent of communication technologies and widespread use of social media platforms have fuelled contemporary Hindu radicalization against the backdrop of the rise of the strongman leader Narendra Modi. Critics of Modi have argued that Modi and his support base, RSS, are slowly undermining the pluralist and secular social fabrics of India and shifting towards radical Hinduism.[10] Social media platforms have facilitated this idea of 'Hindu India' further. A 2018 report of the Observer Research Foundation found a link among online hate speech, real-life violence and radicalization in India. In this ground-breaking report, researcher Maya Mirchandani[11] found that social issues that would otherwise have been considered as apolitical by nature in other parts of the word have become highly politicized in India.

In contemporary India, Mirchandani observes that subjects of online hate speech range from 'opposition to interfaith marriage between Hindus and Muslims, positions on universal human rights, and the contentious issues of cow protection and beef consumption'.[12] Such

[9] Ibid.

[10] Hartosh Singh Bal, 'India's Embattled Democracy', *The New York Times*, 30 May 2018. Available at: https://www.nytimes.com/2018/05/30/opinion/india-democracy.html (accessed on 13 December 2018).

[11] Maya Mirchandani, 'Digital Hatred, Real Violence: Majoritarian Radicalisation and Social Media in India' (Occasional paper no. 167, Observer Research Foundation, New Delhi, 2018). Available at: https://www.orfonline.org/wp-content/uploads/2018/08/ORF_OccasionalPaper_167_DigitalHatred.pdf (accessed on 3 November 2018).

[12] Ibid.

hatred towards Muslims contradicts India's Constitution which gives every Indian citizen equality, irrespective of their faith or cultural background. A grizzly example of the use of technology is a much-circulated 2017 internet video containing the grisly murder of a Muslim labourer, Mohammad Afrazul. He was killed by a Hindu fanatic to deter 'love Jihad', a term used by Hindu nationalists to describe a practice in which Muslim men feign love to draw Hindu women away from their faith. The popularity and controversy around the video showed how the BJP-led Hindu nationalist religious, political climate feeds radicalization and violence, which is spread by technology.[13]

The third source of radicalization in India is from Maoism. Maoists want to establish communism in India through 'a new democratic revolution by overthrowing imperialism, feudalism and comprador bureaucratic capitalism through people's War'.[14] While the neoliberal Indian State has managed to contain the Maoists threat, critics argue that the issue of tackling Maoist radicalism in India is not immune from controversy. In 2018, police raids led to the arrest of a half-dozen activists, writers and lawyers known for supporting 'resistance movements and marginalized groups, or for speaking out against the Modi government'. They were accused of being involved with Maoism, a charge they deny. Critics are quick to point out that these arrests fit an ongoing pattern of divisive politics under Modi, who uses the 'Indian State to suppress dissents'.[15] However, police in reply said, 'They were arrested based on incriminating evidence of their elaborate communication with members of the armed banned Communist Party of India (Maoist) or CPI(M)'.[16]

---

[13] Ibid.

[14] *Al Jazeera*, 'India's Maoist Rebels: An Explainer,' 26 April 2017, https://www.aljazeera.com/indepth/features/2017/04/india-maoist-rebels-explainer-170426132812114.html (accessed on 4 May 2019).

[15] Schultz and Raz, 'Activists in Shackles: Indians Denounce Arrests as Crackdown on Dissent', *The New York Times*, 30 August 2018, https://www.nytimes.com/2018/08/30/world/asia/india-activists-arrests.html (acccessed on 4 May 2019).

[16] *BBC News*, 'Why India Activist Arrests Have Kicked Up a Storm,' *BBC News*, 31 August 2018. Available at: https://www.bbc.com/news/world-asia-india-45294286 (accessed on 4 December 2018).

India's most trusted neighbour in the contemporary period, Bangladesh, is truly at a crossroad in 2018. Before summarizing the contemporary situation of the country, it should be noted that the stability of domestic politics and the democratic environment in Bangladesh is of great significance to India because Bangladesh and India share a 4,000 km land border. Instability and conflict in Bangladesh affect India deeply. For example, during Bangladesh's Independence war against Pakistan in 1971, 'more than 10 million Bengali refugees sheltered in India'.[17] Apart from providing shelter and support to Bengalis, India had to mobilize its military and diplomacy to help Bengalis establish self-determination. It is against this backdrop that Bangladesh was born on 16 December 1971 as an independent country.

Presently, Bangladesh is facing crisis of; democracy on three fronts. First, its domestic politics is marred by authoritarianism, State repression of free speech, political equality and human rights, extra judicial killings, and enforced disappearances of regime critics by the law enforcement and intelligence agencies supported by the ruling party, the Awami League.[18] Although human rights organizations and Western democracies have repeatedly voiced concerns about these practices and pointed fingers to law enforcement agencies, the government of the Awami League has denied these allegations.[19] In addition to these arbitrary

---

[17] Martland Jha, 'India's Refugee Saga, from 1947 to 2017', *Live Mint*, 9 January 2018. Available at: https://www.livemint.com/Sundayapp/clQnX60MIR2L-hCitpMmMWO/Indias-refugee-saga-from-1947-to-2017.html (accessed on 8 November 2018).

[18] Faisal Mahmud, 'Is Bangladesh Moving towards One-Party State?' *Al Jazeera*, 4 April 2018. Available at: https://www.aljazeera.com/indepth/features/sheikh-hasina-turning-bangladesh-party-state-180404082024893.html (accessed on 7 July 2018); Salil Tripathi, 'Bangladesh's Authoritarian Turn', *The New York Review of Books*, 15 August 2018. Available at: https://www.nybooks.com/daily/2018/08/15/bangladeshs-authoritarian-turn/ (accessed on 18 August 2018); Robert Schwarz, 'Democracy under Pressure: Polarization and Repression Are Increasing Worldwide', Bertelsmann Stiftung, 22 March 2018. Available at: https://www.bertelsmann-stiftung.de/en/press/press-releases/press-release/pid/democracy-under-pressure-polarization-and-repression-are-increasing-worldwide/ (accessed on 5 April 2018).

[19] Gabriela Guzman, 'UN Expert Group Urges Bangladesh to Stop Enforced Disappearances', United Nations Human Rights: Office of the High Commissioner,

violations of rights and liberties, the government has been heavily criticized for executing anti-free speech laws (such as Section 57 of the Information and Communication Technology Act and the Digital Security Act) to put critics behind bars. According to these laws, anyone deemed as offending the State or religion could be jailed for up to 14 years.[20] Two examples of such cases came in 2018, when a world-renowned Bangladeshi photographer, Shahidul Alam, and a sociology professor at Chittagong University, Maidul Islam, were imprisoned on these grounds and later released, with pending charges.[21]

Second, in recent years, we have seen mainstreaming of Islamist forces into politics. Bangladesh's main opposition party, the Bangladesh Nationalist Party (BNP), and its Islamist ally, Jamaat-e-Islami, try to portray the Awami League as a party against Islam, and the Awami League claims to be the secular force in Bangladesh. However, out of 70 registered and unregistered Islamist parties in the 2018 election, 63 were in direct and indirect electoral alliances with the so-called secular Awami League.[22] Moreover, in a public event held in 2018 which saw hard-line Islamists demand a ban on public mixing of women and men

---

24 February 2017. Available at: https://www.ohchr.org/EN/NewsEvents/Pages/DisplayNews.aspx?NewsID=21220&LangID= (accessed on 12 April 2018); Human Rights Watch, 'Bangladesh: End Disappearances and Secret Detentions', 6 July 2017. Available at: https://www.hrw.org/news/2017/07/06/bangladesh-end-disappearances-and-secret-detentions (accessed on 24 May 2018); Justin Rowlatt, 'Fears over Bangladesh's "Disappeared"', *BBC News*, 13 October 2016. Available at: https://www.bbc.com/news/world-asia-37618205 (accessed on 1 July 2018).

[20] Mubashar Hasan, 'Rock "n" Roll Is Dying Bangladesh', *The Conversation*, 21 November 2018. Available at: https://theconversation.com/rock-n-roll-is-dying-in-bangladesh-106967 (accessed on 23 December 2018).

[21] Shafquat Rabbee, 'Bangladesh: Shahidul Alam Is Back, Free Speech Is Not', *Al Jazeera*, 25 November 2018. Available at: https://www.aljazeera.com/indepth/opinion/bangladesh-shahidul-alam-free-speech-181123112844245.html (accessed on 28 November 2018).

[22] Salim Zahid, 'Most Islamist Parties Are with Awami League', *Prothom Alo,* 20 November 2018. Available at: https://www.prothomalo.com/bangladesh/article/1565953/%E0%A6%86.%E0%A6%B2%E0%A7%80%E0%A6%97%E0%A7%87%E0%A6%B0-%E0%A6%B8%E0%A6%99%E0%A7%8D%E0%A6%97%E0%A7%87-%E0%A6%87%E0%A6%B8%E0%A6%B2-%E0%A6%BE%E0%A6%AE%E0%A6%BF-%E0%A6%A6%E0%A6%B2-%E0%A6%AC%E0%A7%87%E0%A6%B6%E0%A6%BF (accessed on 1 December 2018).

and capital punishment of writers who offend Islam, Sheikh Hasina, the prime minister of Bangladesh, announced a further Islamization of the public sphere by building over 550 mosques across the country and an Islamic university with Saudi funding.[23] With this mix of political and religio-social ground, security officials, bureaucrats, party members and affiliates with the Awami League have strengthened their grip over a State that supports radical mullahs over liberal civil society. Consequently, the space for political opposition has reduced significantly.

Third, Islamist terrorism remains a credible threat to Bangladesh. Recently, over 40 Bangladeshis, including secular and atheist bloggers, writers, publishers, moderate Muslims and members from minorities, were killed by Islamist terrorists.[24] The killing campaigned has accelerated, and it reached a high on the night of 1 July 2016, when five young local men armed with blades, guns and bombs stormed a restaurant in the neighbourhood of Gulshan in the capital Dhaka and took foreigners who were dining there as hostage.[25] The siege resulted in the death of 22 people in all, including 9 Italians, 7 Japanese, a US citizen and an Indian. Following hours of stand-off, a military raid saw all but one of the attackers being killed.

As a whole, the current crisis of Bangladesh is rooted in the crisis of democracy, state support for radical mullahs and threats from diverse groups of a new, younger generation of Islamists. The stability of

---

[23] Pulack Ghatack, 'Bangladesh PM's Moves toward Powerful Muslim Group Raises Eyebrows', *Benar News*, 21 April 2017. Available at: https://www.benarnews.org/english/news/bengali/hasina-hefazat-04212017154204.html (accessed on 12 April 2018); PTI, 'Sheikh Hasina Announces to Build 560 Model Mosques, Islamic University in Bangladesh', *The New Indian Express*, 4 November 2018. Available at: http://www.newindianexpress.com/world/2018/nov/04/sheikh-hasina-announces-to-build-560-model-mosques-islamic-university-in-bangladesh-1894224.html (accessed on 5 November 2018).

[24] Mubashar Hasan, 'Threats of Violent Extremism in Bangladesh Are a Symptom of Deeper Social and Political Problems', *The Conversation*, 11 January 2018. Available at: https://theconversation.com/threats-of-violent-extremism-in-bangladesh-are-a-symptom-of-deeper-social-and-political-problems-70420 (accessed on 4 December 2018).

[25] Ibid.

this nation with a larger 'Muslim population than Saudi Arabia, Iran and Egypt combined' will depend on the nature of its democratic transition.[26]

India's arch-rival (and neighbour) is Pakistan. It is no stranger to radicalization, violence and terrorism. According to the 2014 report by the United States Institute of Peace, within the past decade, more than 47,000 people had lost their lives in terrorist-related events in Pakistan.[27] Stanford University's mapping of militant groups in Pakistan identifies at least 12 active militant organizations in Pakistan. There are also numerous other political groups operational in the country that support radical views (but not necessarily terrorism). Pakistan's 'unequal economic class, poor education system and suppressed economic opportunities across the Pakistani society against the backdrop of an organised extremist structure' make the country's youth vulnerable to radicalization, violence and terrorism.[28]

The Pakistani State also plays a tacit or active role in radicalizing its own population. Haque[29] opines that the Pakistani State has fostered an enabling environment for radicalization and, at times, violent action where 'some groups provide forums for interaction and connections with more militant actors, while others carry out the whole range of social, political and violent activity'.[30] That said, Pakistan's problem of radicalization and violent extremism is not entirely domestic. The country has been an active partner of the United States in its War on Terror in Afghanistan. Despite that, Pakistan has faced a lot of criticism

---

[26] C. Christine Fair, Ali Hamza, and Rebecca Heller, 'Who Supports Suicide Terrorism in Bangladesh? What the Data Say', *Politics and Religion* 10, no. 3 (2017): 622–661.

[27] Raheem ul Haque, 'Youth Radicalization in Pakistan' (Peace brief 167, United States Institute of Peace, 26 February 2014). Available at: https://www.usip.org/sites/default/files/PB%20167_Youth_Radicalization_in_Pakistan.pdf (accessed on 4 December 2018).

[28] Moeed Yusuf, 'Prospects of Youth Radicalization in Pakistan: Implications for US Policy' (Analysis paper no. 14, the Brookings Institution, Washington, DC, 2008). Available at: https://www.brookings.edu/wp-content/uploads/2016/06/10_pakistan_yusuf.pdf (accessed on 1 December 2018).

[29] Haque, 'Youth Radicalization in Pakistan'.

[30] Ibid., 1.

for its 'dual role' in combatting terrorism. For example, in 2011, a US admiral Mike Mullen, the then chairman of the Joint Chiefs of Staff, accused Pakistan's spy agency (Inter-Services Intelligence Directorate) of covertly supporting terrorist networks.[31]

Pakistan's neighbour, India, also accused Pakistan of sponsoring terrorist activities in India. In the aftermath of the deplorable Mumbai attack, India's allegations against Pakistan received much attention, although Pakistan always denied involvement.[32] Similarly, US President Donald Trump has withdrawn hundreds of millions of dollars of security aid to Pakistan and accused it of not assisting its anti-terrorism efforts. In an interview with Fox News, Mr Trump said, 'I ended it because they don't do anything for us, they don't do a damn thing for us'.[33]

President Trump also accused Pakistan of withholding information about Osama bin Laden hiding in Pakistan. In addition, the United States has recently placed Pakistan on its terror-financing watch list.[34] In reply to the US policy steps and criticisms, Pakistan's newly elected prime minister, Imran Khan, has reportedly 'lashed out' at Trump's 'tirade against Pakistan'. Khan said, 'No Pakistani was involved in 9/11 but Pak decided to participate in the U.S. War on Terror.... Pakistan suffered 75,000 casualties in this war and over $123 billion was lost to the economy.' He added, 'U.S. aid was a minuscule and Taliban

---

[31] Fair, Hamza and Heller, 'Who Supports Suicide Terrorism'.

[32] *TimesNowNews*, '26/11 Mumbai Attacks: India Slams Pakistan for "Showing Little Sincerity" in Bringing Perpetrators to Justice', 26 November 2018. Available at: https://www.timesnownews.com/india/article/2611-mumbai-terror-attacks-india-slams-pakistan-terrorists-november-united-states-of-america-mike-pompeo-un-security-council-taj-mahal-hotel-cst/321065 (accessed on 12 December 2018).

[33] Salman Masood, 'Pakistan Angered by Trump's Claim That It Does "Nothing" for US', *The New York Times*, 19 November 2018. Available at: https://www.nytimes.com/2018/11/19/world/asia/pakistan-trump-imran-khan.html (accessed on 27 November 2018).

[34] Madeeha Anwar, 'Pakistan Confirms Place on Terror-Financing Watch List', *Voice of America*, 28 June 2018. Available at: https://www.voanews.com/a/pakistan-confirms-it-s-on-terror-financing-watch-list/4459625.html (accessed on 2 December 2018).

are stronger than before.'[35] Whatever Pakistan's anti-terrorism efforts are, the country remains vulnerable from radicalization, violence and terrorism.

Sri Lanka shares a maritime boundary with India. Its long history of radicalization is reflected in the political rivalry between the Sinhala and Tamil ethnic groups.[36] The country was plagued by the Civil War between Sinhala and Tamil ethnic groups from 1983 to 2009. Johansson[37] argues that the roots of the Civil War were numerous, but a key trigger point was the Sri Lankan government's move to embrace religious (Buddhist) nationalism. This had angered the Tamil-speaking minority, who then formed militant student organizations, assassinated military personnel and aimed to establish a new Tamil homeland through an armed revolution.[38] In reply, Sinhala people justified the war against Tamils using Buddhism nationalism. In Johansson's observation, it was not just the army but everyday people and monks who used 'military metaphors and Buddhist texts' to legitimize the war.[39] Since the Civil War ended in 2009, Muslims have been deemed the new enemies of Sri Lanka. Viswanathan[40] opines that the entrance of Bodu Bala Sena (BBS) or the 'Buddhist Power Force' into Sri Lankan politics has complicated the contemporary phase of radicalism in Sri Lanka.

---

[35] Drazen Jorgic, 'Pakistan PM Imran Khan Lashes Out at Trump "Tirade"', *Reuters*, 19 November 2018. Available at: https://www.reuters.com/article/us-pakistan-usa/pakistan-pm-imran-khan-lashes-out-at-trump-tirade-idUSKCN1NO1J9 (accessed on 23 November 2018).

[36] Ranga Kalansooriya, *Radicalization in Sri Lanka* (Islamabad: Pakistan Institute for Peace Studies, 2009). Available at: https://www.pakpips.com/web/wp-content/uploads/2017/11/128.pdf (accessed on 8 December 2018).

[37] Andreas Johansson, 'Violent Buddhist Extremists Are Targeting Muslims in Sri Lanka', *The Conversation*, 26 April 2018. Available at: https://theconversation.com/violent-buddhist-extremists-are-targeting-muslims-in-sri-lanka-92951 (accessed on 3 December 2018).

[38] *BBC News*, 'Remembering Sri Lanka's Black July', 23 July 2013. Available at: https://www.bbc.com/news/world-asia-23402727 (accessed on 14 November 2018).

[39] Johansson, 'Violent Buddhist Extremists'.

[40] Balasubramaniyan Viswanathan, 'Islamic State in Sri Lanka: Situation Report', *Geopolitical Monitor*, 12 July 2016. Available at: https://www.geopoliticalmonitor.com/islamic-state-in-sri-lanka/ (accessed on 1 November 2018).

BBS has voiced concern that Sri Lanka has turned away from the morality of Buddhism, and Muslims are one of the reasons behind that, as they are Islamizing Buddhist Sri Lanka.[41] Such a provocative narrative has two implications in contemporary Sri Lankan society. First, there has been a rise of Islamophobic violent attacks against Sri Lankan Muslims. According to media reports, 'Mosques and Muslim-owned businesses have come under attack and women have been forced to remove their head scarves in some parts of the country.'[42] BBS has also called for a 'complete boycott of Muslim institutions and shops', and a 2014 anti-Muslim protest rally of BBS organized in Aluthgama and Beruwala gutted many Muslim houses and shops. At least three Muslims were killed.

Second, such radical politics professed by some members of the Sinhala community have strengthened identity politics among Sri Lankan Muslims who feel alienated from mainstream Sri Lankan society.[43] However, Muslim society in Sri Lanka is deeply divisive as well. Division within the community and alienation have created 'a perfect ecosystem for radicalization of Muslim youngsters'.[44] It was reported that recruiters from ISIL were operational in Sri Lanka and at least 32 Sri Lankan Muslims have joined the notorious terrorist outfit.[45]

---

[41] Dayan Jayatilleka, 'The Instrumentalization of Islamophobia Provoking Islamist Terrorism: Who Benefits?' *The Island*, 7 March 2018. Available at: http://www.island.lk/index.php?page_cat=article-details&page=article-details&code_title=181061 (accessed on 23 November 2018).

[42] Shihar Aneez and Ranga Sirilal, 'Sri Lankan Muslim Leader Warns of Radicalization after Clashes', *Reuters*, 11 July 2014. Available at: https://www.reuters.com/article/us-sri-lanka-muslims-violence-idUSKBN0FG25L20140711 (accessed on 1 December 2018).

[43] Debobrat Ghose, 'How Sri Lanka's Sinhala Supremacists Are Helping ISI's War against India', *First Post*, 16 September 2014. Available at: https://www.firstpost.com/world/how-sri-lankas-sinhala-supremacists-are-helping-isis-war-against-india-1714787.html (accessed on 23 November 2018).

[44] Viswanathan, 'Islamic State in Sri Lanka'.

[45] Shihar Aneez, 'Sri Lanka Says 32 "Elite" Muslims Have Joined Islamic State in Syria', *Reuters*, 18 November 2016. Available at: https://www.reuters.com/article/us-mideast-crisis-syria-sri-lanka-idUSKBN13D1EE (accessed on 12 December 2018); Sunday Times, 'ISIS Indian Chief Recruiter Targets Youth from Sri Lanka, Bangladesh', *Times Online*, 16 June 2017. Available at: http://www.sundaytimes.lk/article/1023772/

Finally, South Asia's small island, the Maldives, also has a radicalization problem. This has recently caught wider attention among researchers and policymakers since the 2017 murder of the prominent Maldivian liberal blogger Yameen Rasheed. He was stabbed to death in his apartment. The Maldives, long known as an attractive tourist destination, has shown a dark face to the world.[46] The State's autocracy transitioned to democracy in 2008 after 30 years of rule by Maumoon Abdul Gayoom, but it entered political turmoil in 2012 when President Mohamed Nasheed was forcefully ousted from the presidency. Against the backdrop of political instability, other social factors such as 'radical preaching by Salafi–Wahabi imams and community leaders, organized crime by youth gangs, unemployment and drug use' have created a toxic environment for society.

Liberals have alleged that the State and hard-line Islamists in the Maldives have suppressed and intimidated critics such as journalists and bloggers, and have used methods including 'kidnapping, enforced disappearance, indefinite detention in secret prisons, extra judicial killing and so forth'.[47] Burke[48] argues that many of youth gang members of the Maldives are radicalized through the preaching of Wahabi and Salafi preachers, who denounce and despise defenders of liberal values. Critics have further argued that the Maldivian authorities (who position themselves as defenders of a moderate Islam) have tolerated assaults on liberal bloggers and writers by radical youths.[49] Some have argued that those liberal writers and bloggers were very offensive to Islam in

---

isis-indian-chief-recruiter-targets-youth-from-sri-lanka-bangladesh (accessed on 25 July 2018).

[46] Hassan Moosa and Kai Schultz, 'Outspoken Maldives Blogger Who Challenged Radical Islamists Is Killed,' *The New York Times*, 23 April 2017. Available at: https://www.nytimes.com/2017/04/23/world/asia/yameen-rasheed-dead-maldives-blogger-dead.html (accessed on 27 May 2018).

[47] Aaquib Khan, 'Free Speech Murdered in Maldives', *The Diplomat*, 4 January 2018. Available at: https://thediplomat.com/2018/01/free-speech-murdered-in-maldives/ (accessed on 3 December 2018).

[48] Jason Burke, 'Paradise Jihadis: Maldives Sees Surge in Young Muslims Leaving for Syria', *The Guardian*, 26 February 2015. Available at: https://www.theguardian.com/world/2015/feb/26/paradise-jihadis-maldives-islamic-extremism-syria (accessed on 2 December 2018).

[49] Khan, 'Free Speech Murdered in Maldives'.

their writings, and violent extremists have used this as a rationale to kill or hurt them.

According to a 2015 report, Maldives has become a country that supplies world's highest per capita number of foreign fighters to extremist outfits in Islamic State of Iraq and Syria (ISIS).[50] The government of the Maldives has, however, taken steps to counter radicalization, violence and terrorism. These steps include the following: the adoption of the Prevention of Terrorism Act 2015; the adoption of the Prevention of Money Laundering and Terrorist Financing Act; State intervention into religious lives through training of imams and State approval of Friday sermons; the establishment of an Islamic university to promote the academic study of religion and moderate Islam to counter preaching of radical and extremist Muslims.[51]

Given the state of democracy and radicalization in South Asia, it is an appropriate and exciting time to shed light on the contexts of radicalization, violence, terrorism and de-radicalization in India, Bangladesh, Pakistan, Sri Lanka and the Maldives.

THE BOOK: RADICALIZATION AND ITS MANY FACES IN SOUTH ASIA

The original idea for this book was conceived at a conference held at TUFS in Japan in 2018, when the Department of Peace and Conflict brought together a team of highly trained local experts and practitioners on radicalism from South Asian countries to understand why a wave of illiberalism is sweeping over South Asian nation states. The core goal of the programme was to bring in context-specific local knowledge to enhance our understanding on radicalization in South Asia. Later, in the course of executing this project, we added few more experts.

The book makes a unique contribution to the field of South Asian radicalization for a number of reasons. First, this might be the only

---

[50] The Soufan Group, *Foreign Fighters* (2015). Available at: http://soufangroup.com/wp-content/uploads/2015/12/TSG_ForeignFightersUpdate3.pdf (accessed on 13 September 2018).

[51] The US Department of State, *Country Reports on Terrorism 2016*. Available at: https://mv.usmission.gov/wp-content/uploads/sites/212/2017/07/Country-Reports-on-Terrorism-2016-Maldives.pdf (accessed on 23 July 2018).

book available that sheds light on the diverse trajectories of radicalization in South Asian countries. During the initial conception and the process of executing this book, we have found that only a few isolated chapters, commentaries and policy papers are available on addressing radicalization, violence and terrorism in individual South Asian countries. No single volume features a collection of expert analysis and research on several South Asian countries as case studies. Such scarcity is understandable since the sources of radicalism and violent extremism in South Asia (as mentioned above) are diverse, dynamic and context specific. In South Asia, radicalism, violence and terrorism have thrived on nationalism, religion, securitization, poor governance and even as a challenge to capitalism in some cases. Therefore, it is a hard and time-consuming task to pull together such a volume. This book brings together researchers based in 10 institutes located in 4 continents to understand the many faces of radicalism and its connection with violence and terrorism in South Asia. In that sense, this book is a trendsetter. Problems of radicalization and understanding the implications of ideologies and human behaviours associated with radicalization are matters of concerns for policymakers, practitioners and academics. For that reason, we included some chapters with policy implications.

Before presenting the summary of each chapter, we want to clarify how this book defines radicalization, since there is no shortage of debate, discussion and disagreement on what radicalism is and whether it is the same as extremism.[52] Bötticher[53] identified nine key distinctions

---

[52] For example, see Porta (1995); Bruce Hoffman and Fernando Reinares, eds., *The Evolution of the Global Terrorist Threat: From 9/11 to Osama Bin Laden's Death* (New York, NY: Columbia University Press, 2014); Lorenzo Vidino, *Radicalization, Linkage, and Diversity: Current Trends in Terrorism in Europe.* (Santa Monica, CA: RAND, 2011); Clark McCauley and Sophia Moskalenko, 'Mechanisms of Political Radicalization: Pathways toward Terrorism', *Terrorism and Political Violence* 20, no. 3 (2008): 415–433; Astrid Bötticher, 'Towards Academic Consensus Definitions of Radicalism and Extremism', *Perspectives on Terrorism* 11, no. 4 (2017): 73–77; Randy Borum, 'Radicalization into Violent Extremism II: A Review of Conceptual Models and Empirical Research', *Journal of Strategic Security* 4, no. 4 (2011): 37–62.

[53] Bötticher, 'Towards Academic Consensus Definitions of Radicalism and Extremism'.

between radicalism and extremism.[54] It is beyond the scope of this book to delve into theoretical discussions of radicalism and extremism, since contributing authors of this volume have clarified how these two concepts intersect or remain separate. However, the general theme of this book is to unpack the puzzle of radicalization, and its relationship with violence and terrorism in South Asian societies. We follow Hafez and Mullins,[55] who argue that 'radicalization involves adopting an extremist worldview'.[56] They argue that radicalization includes 'a gradual process that entails socialization into an extremist belief system that sets the stage for violence even if does not make it inevitable'.[57] In short, this book explains how radicalism feeds into violence and terrorism. Although Hafez and Mullins's study was conducted in the context of Muslim radicalization in Western societies, we find that our case studies support their terminology and paradigm.

Moreover, findings of this book show that there is no straightforward way to explain radicalism as purported by experts such as Borum[58] who coined in a 'four stage model',[59] or Moghaddam[60] who developed a 'staircase to terrorism' or Precht's 'typical radicalization pattern'.[61] Rather, our case studies found that multiple factors such as grievances, networks, ideologies and support structure are at play.

---

[54] Ibid., 75–76.

[55] Mohammed Hafez and Creighton Mullins, 'The Radicalization Puzzle: A Theoretical Synthesis of Empirical Approaches to Homegrown Extremism', *Studies in Conflict & Terrorism* 38, no. 1 (2015): 958–975.

[56] Ibid., 960.

[57] Ibid.

[58] Randy Borum, 'Understanding the Terrorist Mindset', *FBI Law Enforcement Bulletin* 72, no. 7 (2003): 7–10.

[59] Ibid.

[60] Fathali M. Moghaddam, 'The Staircase to Terrorism: A Psychological Exploration', *American Psychologist* 60 (2005): 161–169.

[61] Tomas Precht, *Home Grown Terrorism and Islamist Radicalization in Europe: From Conversion to Terrorism* (Danish Ministry of Defense, 2007). Available at: http://www.justitsministeriet.dk/sites/default/files/media/Arbejdsomraader/Forskning/Forskningspuljen/2011/2007/Home_grown_terrorism_and_Islamist_radicalisation_in_Europe-_an_assessment_of_influencing_factors__2_.pdf (accessed on 2 July 2018).

We open the book with three cases from India. In Chapter One, Maidul Islam assesses the radical political project of the Indian Maoists at a time when the Maoists were celebrating the golden jubilee of the Naxalite movement. His chapter analyses whether the Indian Maoists have any real military and political strength to combat the Indian State. Four principal arguments are made. First, the ideology of Indian Maoists has little grasp of the fast-changing, contemporary reality of Indian capitalism or the dynamism of the Indian State. As a result, it lacks innovative political strategies and tactics to ensure mass mobilization behind its radical project. Second, the military strategy of the Maoists has become obsolete. The failure of the Maoists to capture political power through an armed insurrection is real not only in India but also in other parts of the world. Examples of Maoist military failures can be found across Asia and Latin America, and the Maoist victory in China appears more and more an isolated case. Third, and related, it has become nearly impossible to enlist average people for a high-risk, dangerous war against a technologically superior neoliberal State. People are not interested in joining the Maoist's radical project because the practices and norms of electoral democracy have generated widespread participation. The legitimacy of the high-participation democratic process is such that is difficult to bypass. As Maidul Islam observes, Maoists must now engage with the new political subject of the citizen voter, who is very much entrenched within the massive architecture of neoliberal governmentality. Herein, the calculative entrepreneurial citizen voter is increasingly individualized and dependent on the doles, subsidies and various forms of welfare schemes of the modern State, and had little interest in violent and disruptive Maoist revolution.

Finally, Maoist military has primarily fought against the exploitation of mines and forests, thus spatially restricting its operations. Their hideouts and bases are mostly located in the forests of central and eastern India. Their restricted territorial locality has alienated them from vast sections of the people and kept them separated from everyday struggles against capitalist exploitation and forms of non-class oppression. Using discourse analysis of pamphlets, press releases, Maoist organizational reports, Indian government's reports, media reports and the existing academic literature, Maidul's chapter is a unique contribution in the field of South Asian radicalism. Maidul analyses how the radical transformation caused by capitalism in India has exposed the limits of the revolutionary promise of the Maoists. Extant academic literature and security agencies tend to overemphasize the Maoist threat, and Maidul explains the Maoist failure in combating the Indian State and living up to their promise of social revolution.

In Chapter Two, Noor Ahmed Baba focuses on the vulnerability of Kashmiri people in general (and its youth in particular) to radical influences. For Baba, Kashmir has evolved as a syncretic society with a distinct identity, exhibiting civility in its conduct in relation to its internal plurality. In his opinion, the socialization process has been successfully imparting Kashmir's syncretic traits to most young Kashmiris, who rejected radical and violent extremist influences, even in trying situations. However, Baba suggests that since 2015, a small number of Kashmir's educated youth has been attracted to radical extremist ideologies. New social media tools have been undermining traditional social connections and patterns of socializations in Kashmir, exposing the local youth to various radical influences across physical and cultural borders. In addition to drawing on historical evidence, the chapter outlines qualitative arguments and discussions on the socio-psychological aspects of new technologies which are undermining interpersonal relationships in Kashmir. Baba further analyses the situation in the valley in relation to the larger context across Muslim-majority regions.

In Chapter Three, Nazneen Mohsina and Sinan Siyech discuss how terrorist groups in India's neighbouring States, especially those operating in Pakistan and Bangladesh, manipulate the meaning of Indian foreign and domestic policies to justify violence. India has been classified as part of the 'Crusader–Zionist–Hindu' conspiracy against Muslims by jihadists, including Osama bin Laden and Ayman Zawahiri. Mohsina and Siyech refer to what terrorist groups claim is India's interference in Bangladesh's domestic affairs, its constant skirmishes with Pakistan and India's treatment of Kashmiris. Mohsina and Siyech argue that the issues have bred varying levels of anti-Indian sentiment in South Asia and have been leveraged by jihadist groups to garner support and recruitment. There are two unique aspects to this chapter. First, the use of anti-Indian narratives by extremist groups in Pakistan is not new but Bangladeshi terrorists leveraging anti-India sentiments is. It is also unexpected given that the India–Bangladesh bilateral relationship is often criticized as biased towards the Awami League. Second, terrorist groups in Pakistan and Bangladesh are forming anti-Indian alliances; however, Mohsina and Siyech argue that while anti-Indian narratives are strengthening, these are still too weak to generate drastic outcomes. This chapter relies on the existing literature of terrorist propaganda, including primary material in English and Bengali. Another contribution of this chapter is its analysis of strategic communications around terrorism in India's foreign policy. The chapter's discussions of anti-Indian terrorist groups in both Pakistan and Bangladesh bring together a range of unexplored perspectives.

In Chapter Four, Azim Zahir examines the spread and escalation of religious radicalism in the Maldives. Zahir's chapter examines the key macro-level political, religious and ideological contexts for radicalization in the Maldives and the relationship between Salafism and radicalization. While Salafism and Salafi-jihadism are transnational ideologies, the local context matters for their relevance, spread and escalation. Radical ideas emerged in the Maldives under the harsh experience of authoritarian, State-led suppression of Salafism in the 1980s and the 1990s. Zahir argues that 'mainstream' contemporary Salafism does not have a unidirectional relationship with radicalization and violent extremism. Mainstream Salafism acts as both a discursive resource and constraint for radicalization.

The chapter argues that it is the larger political and religious transformations in the early 21st century that have created macro-level factors behind the rise of Salafi-jihadism and the escalation of radicalization. In this respect, the chapter identifies three major themes in the Maldives transformation. First, the escalation of religious radicalism is a product of the broader 'communicative abundance' that includes the rise of Western and even anti-religious, secular discourses. In the wake of unprecedented political liberalization and access to modern media technologies since approximately 2004, both liberal and radical religious ideas have spread. Radical Islamism has been positioned as an alternative to Westernization-liberalization, which are also presented as alternatives to the long-standing authoritarian politics in the Maldives.

Second, radicalization has escalated because of the fragmentation of the State's religious authority. Previously, the State's official religious authorities could control the discourse; however, this is no longer the case. The fragmentation of traditional religious authority and the processes of modernization are deeply linked to the spectacular rise of Salafism as the most dominant religious voice in the public sphere.

Finally, the deepening crises of Maldivian politics had caused some disillusionment. The Maldivian democracy has become more authoritarian and has failed to prioritize sound economic and social policies, leading to dissatisfaction with democracy and the search for alternatives. As people in Maldives have already experienced authoritarian rule, the Salafi alternative is appealing to many, leading to increased radicalization. Zahir concludes that domestic factors and how they are addressed will determine the future of the spread of Salafi-jihadism and associated radicalization in the Maldives.

In Chapter Five, Iraj De Alwis, Anishka De Zylva and Barana Waidyatilake offer a comprehensive policy plan to counter radicalization in Sri Lanka. They rightly argue that the problem of radicalization in Sri Lanka is based upon dual problems of majoritarianism and marginalization and, therefore, countering radicalization will require distinct and coordinated policy action. Such policy action should consist of both domestic reforms and regional and global engagement. In their view to effectively counter radicalization in Sri Lanka, at the domestic front, the State requires to generate more employment, reform the education and language sectors and initiate better urban planning. In regional and international forums, the authors have coined in four policy suggestions for Sri Lanka to counter the problem of radicalization. The chapter makes a unique contribution in the existing knowledge on radicalization in Sri Lanka by offering a concrete policy plan to counter it.

In Chapter Six, Raafia Raees Khan and Feriha N. Peracha present an interesting practical story of de-radicalization and rehabilitation of male youth extremists in northern Pakistan. The case demonstrates the work of the organization Social Welfare, Academics and Training (SWAaT) for Pakistan, which is working closely with Pakistan's military. Khan and Peracha shed valuable insights into the significance of psycho-social intervention and support as part of a holistic approach to the process of de-radicalization. That holistic approach includes corrective religious instruction, mainstream education, vocational training and recreation. They argue that post-reintegration and monitoring procedures are significant, as experience of their programme shows zero recidivism, since significant efforts are made to ensure that the transition from a controlled environment to mainstream society is successfully managed. Overall, the chapter outlines lessons learned in de-radicalization which may be replicated in other parts of the world, especially where recruitment of children to violent extremism is a concern. The chapter is full of ground-level insights into factors which push someone towards violent extremism and bring them back to normality.

While Khan and Peracha's chapter presents the operational aspect of de-radicalization process in Pakistan, in Chapter Seven, Fatima Waqi Sajjad highlights how education could act as a tool to prevent radicalization and violent extremism in Pakistan. Her chapter investigates radicalization among the well-educated individuals in Pakistan and explores how and why higher education systems are unable to prevent young people from embracing radical militant ideologies. This problem is pertinent in Pakistan, where, in recent times, security agencies have been perplexed to find well-educated individuals among militant radical networks. This link between education and radicalization in Pakistan has been a subject of much debate in academic and policy circles since 9/11. Despite receiving generous financial support from international donor agencies, the Pakistani government has been struggling to create educational reforms to counter radicalization.

In the first part of the chapter, Fatima criticizes fear-driven anti-radicalization policies and the market-driven neoliberal policies in higher education. In that process, Fatima reviews the post-9/11 policy literature on education and radicalization by exploring three questions: What is radicalization? What is it in education that counters radicalization? What kind of education exists on the ground?

Fatima argues that extremism in higher education institutions cannot be mitigated through surveillance or imposition of anti-radicalization policies from the top. Neither can the market-driven education policies counter radical ideologies. The only effective way to counter dogmatic extremism is to open up spaces for critical dialogue in universities, including engagement with challenging ideas, rather than suppressing the ideas. Fatima offers a fresh, indigenous perspective on the problem of de-radicalization through education.

We conclude the book with four chapters on Bangladesh. To our knowledge, this is the most comprehensive analysis of Bangladesh's new trend of radicalism, violence and terrorism. In Chapter Eight, Asif bin Ali investigates the madrasa's role in radicalizing Bangladeshi youth, as well as Islamophobia and Bangladesh's own war on terror. Asif begins his investigation by comparing two—the arguments of those who blame madrasas for terrorism and those who doubt the madrasas' responsibility but seek secularization of madrasas as a critical part of anti-terrorism in Bangladesh. Asif argues that these apparently conflicting narratives on madrasas actually complement each other. Both views have contributed to an Islamophobic narrative regarding madrasas and have shaped their public image in the early days of the War on Terror. Asif uses Mahmood Mamdani's framework of 'cultural talk' to relate the approach of equating madrasa students to terrorists or potential terrorists. In that sense, this chapter contributes to the study of radicalization by critiquing the dominant claim that madrasas support terrorism in Bangladesh.

In Chapter Nine, Shahab Enam Khan explains why Bangladeshi women join terrorist outfits. The author reviews the literature and analyses reports, articles, public policy documents and his research experience for international organizations to illustrate the gendered dimensions of security. Khan has sought expert opinions—views of law enforcement agencies, civil society and academia—to understand this new, gendered security threat to Bangladesh. Khan has found that the main drivers behind women's involvement in terrorism are economic and sociopolitical grievances, strong personal relationships with religious radicals—family, kinship and romantic—and an indoctrinated belief system or oppression by the religious or political entities, among others. Khan argues that the interplay between these drivers is dependent on women's socio-economic profiles.

In Khan's opinion, extremist groups have increased their attention towards urban women through informal networks and social media. In the case of rural women, extremists focus on preaching a misrepresented version of Islam and deterring women from social activities and employment. In conclusion, Khan makes a series of policy suggestions including accelerated learning programmes regarding religion, strengthening the education and skills training, providing psycho-social support with qualified professionals and providing access to justice to unlock what Khan sees as the potential of women to be enablers for peace and stability in Bangladesh.

In Chapter Ten, Bulbul Siddiqi explores ways of exposure and expression of radicalization among urban Bangladeshi youth. Siddiqi begins by showing that the process of radicalization takes place in various forms in urban Bangladesh and it may begin very early or late in life. Siddiqi identifies several other push and pull factors behind radicalization including (a) gradual isolation or a feeling of alienation from family and society, (b) a crisis of identity that entices people to join globalized versions of Islam and move away from localized forms and (c) religious globalization, which brings new ways of knowing about 'authentic' forms and practices of Islam. These factors radicalize many urban youths in Bangladesh. Siddiqi's chapter is important because understanding the radicalization process is essential to prevent extremism in Bangladesh.

In Chapter Eleven, which is also the final chapter of the book, Mahbubur Rahman provides a critical overview of Bangladesh's responses to the recent increase of terrorism. He argues that while it is noticeable that Bangladesh has made a great deal of success in moment-to-moment counter-terrorism operations since the Dhaka café attack in 2016, the country's progress towards counter-narrative campaign and for that matter achieving its de-radicalization goals remains far away. In this context, he assesses Bangladesh's counter-radicalization policies, providing a detailed and 'anatomical examination' of its most important measures, such as the goal of the campaign—disengagement or de-radicalization—the message(s) it seeks to convey, the messenger(s) it has chosen to do this job and the medium(s) it is using for the counter-narrative purpose. While investigating the issues, he attempts to address the conceptual ambiguity which, as he says, not only works as a barrier to the nuanced understanding of this highly complicated and contested subject but also prevents from taking right policy measures. Pointing to the country's 'internationally publicized' and very well-meaning counter-narrative project like producing and disseminating a 'comprehensive fatwa (religious decree) against terrorism' by over 100,000 *ulema* (religious scholars), Rahman argues that due to poor planning (or an absence thereof) and lack of coordination, that excellent programme remains unnoticed and out of the reach of its audience. This, according to him, is not just a policy dilemma or a matter of policy preferences but more of a perceptual problem or lack of understanding on the part of the policymakers about the whole process of de-radicalization and counter-narrative. The principal arguments of his chapter are as follows: First, a true (and successful) de-radicalization programme should bring a change in a radical's underlying beliefs and ideology, not simply a change in behaviour. If a radical ideology is left unchallenged, it is more likely to continue attracting recruits. Citing example of 'changing platform' by the Jamaat-ul-Mujahideen (JMB) activists to Neo-JMB, which is more ferocious than the original JMB, Rahman argues that due to the lack of appropriate de-radicalization programme inside the prisons of Bangladesh, the released JMB detainees went back to the same radical path under the Neo-JMB, albeit with new zeal and commitment. Second, government actors or agencies are not well suited to act as a counter-narrative producer or messenger. The government, however, can play a valuable role by facilitating grass roots, and civil society actors, Rahman argues, are best placed to act as counter-narrative messengers. Third, it is extremely important to develop an in-depth understanding of the extremist narratives, their tones, styles and strategy of disseminating the poisonous materials. Fourth, at the outset of a campaign, goals and objectives of the campaign need to be delineated, and the channels and mediums of the campaign must be multiple, which should include but not be limited to offline, online, social media, Facebook, Twitter, etc. It is not only the text of the narrative that matters but also the messenger and medium that must be compatible and, if possible, superior to the extremist narrative. Finally, Rahman underscores the importance of formulating a concerted strategy, as opposed to the isolated and/or unidimensional approach that is at play in Bangladesh. Drawing on European and Southeast Asian examples, he specifically suggests for a 'National Action Plan' that would combine and mobilize various departments of the government, political parties, community organizations, and private and academic sectors, and help devise a comprehensive and effective counter-narrative campaign for Bangladesh.

In conclusion, in our view, the current wave of radicalism in these South Asian countries results from several common patterns concerning for policymakers, development partners, advocates of democracy and security practitioners. Radicalization in these countries has persisted against the backdrop of technological advancement, bad governance and economic inequality, where living standards of average citizens lag behind the liberal democracies of the West. In some instances, these case studies found that the State is less able to generate cohesion among people of different faiths, political beliefs and cultures to maintain peace and stability. There are also cases in which the State is complicit in supporting radicalization, whereas there are other cases which show that the State counters radicalization by curbing political pluralism and civil liberties. The increasing number of youths (including young women) joining radical groups and engaging in hate crimes and terrorist groups underpin something that has gone terribly wrong in the ongoing State-building process in South Asia. Only a collective effort, embedded in genuine desire for building peaceful South Asian societies, can reverse the ongoing trend of radicalization in South Asia, and counter-radicalization policy presented here in the case of Pakistan, Sri Lanka and Bangladesh should be considered seriously by the practitioners and policymakers.

Chapter 1

Fortunes of Radicalism
Indian Maoists and the Dead End of Politics

Maidul Islam

The materialist doctrine that men are products of circumstances and upbringing, and that, therefore, changed men are products of other circumstances and changed upbringing, forgets that it is men that change circumstances and that the educator himself needs educating. Hence, this doctrine necessarily arrives at dividing society into two parts, of which one is superior to society (in Robert Owen, for example). The coincidence of the changing of circumstances and of human activity can be conceived and rationally understood only as *revolutionising practice*.

—Karl Marx[1]

In April 2006, the then prime minister of India claimed that the Maoists are the greatest internal security threat to the country.[2] He reiterated

---

[1] Karl Marx, 'Theses on Feuerbach' (Third Thesis), in *Selected Works*, vol. 1, eds. Karl Marx and Frederick Engels (Moscow: Progress Publishers, 1969), 13–14 (emphasis in original).

[2] Siddharthya Roy, 'Half a Century of India's Maoist Insurgency: A Political Analysis of the Long-running Conflict', *The Diplomat*, 21 September 2017. Available at: https://thediplomat.com/2017/09/half-a-century-of-indias-maoist-insurgency/ (accessed on 24 November 2018).

that position later in a speech at the Chief Minister's Conference on Internal Security in New Delhi on 7 February 2010.[3] Who are these Maoists that are posing such a grave danger to the security and stability of the Indian nation-state? The Communist Party of India (Maoist) or CPI (Maoist) was formed by the merger of two Left-wing extremist parties, namely, the Communist Party of India (Marxist–Leninist) People's War Group, known as PWG, and the Maoist Communist Centre of India (MCCI) on 21 September 2004.[4] Both parties had their genealogical roots in the Naxalite movement of the late 1960s and cherished their Naxalite legacy. Thus, in May 2017, the Central Committee of the CPI (Maoist) issued a pamphlet that urged 'comrades' and 'friends' to celebrate the 50th year of Naxalbari armed rebellion from 23 May to 29 May.[5] The mission of the Naxalites has been the transformation of the existing socio–economic system. In other words, they believe in the radical restructuring of the society with the abolition of private property and along with it the dissolution of the remnants of feudalism and capitalism in socio–economic, political and cultural realms. Five decades later, in the aftermath of the golden jubilee celebration of the Naxalite uprising, and when India has gradually transformed from an old-order State-managed capitalism to corporate-led neoliberalism and, in effect, has further deepened the norms and practices of capitalist structures in everyday life of the people, what does it mean to be radical in contemporary India? Has the radical transformation of capitalism in India exposed the limit of the promise of the Maoists? Has the success story of Indian capitalism questioned the basic premise of the Maoists to fight the capitalist nation-state with its armed strategy? Do the Maoists need to learn from the global

---

[3] The full speech is available at: http://www.satp.org/document/paper-acts-and-oridinances/prime-minister-s-speech-at-the-chief-minister-s-conference-on-internal-security-february-27-2010 (accessed on 24 November 2018).

[4] Joint Press Statement by Kishan, General Secretary of MCCI and Ganapathy, General Secretary of CPI (M–L) [People's War] dated 14 October 2004. All primary materials in the form of party documents, pamphlets, press releases and statements of CPI (Maoist) used in writing this chapter have been taken from: http://www.bannedthought.net/India/CPI-Maoist-Docs/ (accessed on 31 October 2018).

[5] CPI (Maoist) Pamphlet on 50th anniversary of Naxalbari.

experiences of successes and failures of specific political strategies? Do they need to introspect their political tactics by seriously engaging with the failures of the armed strategy in fighting a neoliberal State and be open-minded to use electoral democracy and mass movements as sites of political struggles? This chapter will deal with such questions by analysing the ideological discourses of Maoism and examine the radical politics of the Maoists in contemporary India by assessing the extent of the Maoist influence and whether they pose any significant security threat to destabilize the Indian State. In order to do such an exercise, first, a brief exposition of the political ideology, strategy and tactics of the Indian Maoists is necessary.

IDEOLOGY, STRATEGY AND TACTICS OF THE INDIAN MAOISTS

The CPI (Maoist) considers the 1970 party programme of the Communist Party of India (Marxist–Leninist) or CPI (M–L) that broke away from the Communist Party of India (Marxist) or CPI (M) in 1969 and the MCC document of 1969 providing 'the correct revolutionary general line for the Indian revolution after breaking the decades-old entrenched revisionism in the Indian communist movement'. The Indian Maoists aim to 'apply Marxism–Leninism–Maoism to the concrete conditions of India and by fighting, exposing and breaking from the age-old revisionism of the CPI and CPI(M) brand'. They eulogize the Naxalbari revolt led by Charu Mazumdar in May 1967 in North Bengal.[6] The central task of the Indian revolution according to the Maoists is the seizure of political power by armed force or through protracted people's war.[7] In this respect, the Maoist party seeks to provide 'the much-needed leadership to the people's movement countrywide... to accelerate the armed agrarian revolutionary war throughout the country'.[8] The CPI (Maoist) identifies the 'imperialists, the comprador

---

[6] All quotes in the paragraph are from CPI (Maoist) Party Programme, 5.

[7] CPI (Maoist) Central Committee (P), 'Strategy and Tactics of the Indian Revolution', 21 September 2004, 36–48.

[8] CPI (Maoist) Party Programme, 5.

bureaucratic bourgeoisie and the big landlord classes' as the 'targets' of the revolution in order to

> overthrow the semi-colonial, semifeudal rule of the big landlord-comprador bureaucratic bourgeoisie classes, and imperialism that backs them, through armed struggle and to establish the people's democratic state under the leadership of proletariat—the new democratic state; in place of it by smashing the reactionary autocratic state.[9]

The Indian Maoists believe that to achieve victory in revolution, a strong revolutionary party must be ideologically guided by the principles of Marxism–Leninism–Maoism in all matters. Such a party should be

> well-disciplined and built up through revolutionary style and method; that is based on democratic centralism; that links the theory with practice; practises criticism and self-criticism; is closely integrated with the masses and relies firmly upon them; and stands firmly on the class line, mass line and armed struggle.[10]

In this regard, the Maoists in India identify specific classes who could be potential allies of a revolutionary strategic united front for carrying forward the task of the Indian revolutionary movement. This united front according to the Maoist party programme is a four-class alliance comprising 'the working class, peasantry, petty bourgeoisie and national bourgeoisie—under the leadership of working class based upon worker–peasant alliance'.[11] However, the Maoists describe the first three classes as 'the motive forces of the revolution', while the national bourgeoisie (middle traders, middle and small bourgeoisie) 'is a vacillating ally'.[12] In carrying forward the goal of the new democratic revolution in India, one primary task of the United Front is to 'unite all the oppressed nationalities, persecuted religious minorities and other

---

[9] Ibid., 23.

[10] Ibid., 29.

[11] Ibid., 28.

[12] CPI (Maoist) Central Committee (P), 'Strategy and Tactics of the Indian Revolution', 80; also see CPI (Maoist) Party Programme, 27–28.

oppressed social sections in the course of advancing the armed struggle for the seizure of political power'.[13]

Moreover, the Indian Maoists ascertain certain classes who could provide direct recruitment to the people's liberation army. Therefore, according to the Maoists, a strong and well-disciplined people's army under the leadership of a revolutionary party will be primarily built 'through the armed agrarian revolution mainly from among the landless poor peasants, agricultural labourers and the working class'.[14] The building of the people's liberation army is absolutely crucial for the Maoists as it signifies 'the armed power of the people', and it is by expanding and developing the guerrilla war that the Maoists 'can establish the guerrilla zones and the base areas in strategically favourable areas, where they aim 'to arouse, organise and arm the vast peasant masses on the basic slogan of the agrarian revolution, "Land to the tillers and political power to the revolutionary people's committees!"'[15] The Indian Maoists, thus, rely on the strategy of armed struggle to combat the State, and the road to political power through the electoral tactic is a closed option for them. As their party programme argues,

[T]he tactics of participation in the election in the name of using it is tantamount to abandoning the tasks of building and advancing the armed struggle. Reality is that without people's political power everything is illusion. The people's political power can be established and advanced only through the path of protracted people's war. Parliamentary path and participation in the elections are completely incompatible with Protracted peoples war in the concrete conditions of India. Even the advancement of real people's political consciousness is closely linked with it. More so, the accumulation of forces, including the development and Bolshevization of the party itself are inseparably linked with it. That is why the armed struggle is the 'centre of gravity' of the Party's work as comrade Mao stated. In this overall context, the slogan of 'Boycott Election', though a question of tactics, acquires the significance of strategy in the concrete conditions of India. It is also

---

[13] CPI (Maoist) Party Programme, 28.
[14] Ibid., 29.
[15] Ibid., 25.

correct to raise the slogan 'Boycott Election is a Democratic Right' on a mass scale'.[16]

In a Hindi pamphlet issued by the Dandakaranya Special Zonal Committee of the CPI (Maoist) dated 6 January 2015, the party gave a call to boycott the panchayat elections. Similarly, it regularly gives a call to poll boycott before assembly and parliamentary elections as well. A decade back, there was a sharp critique of the Maoist call of poll boycott and political violence by none other than a credible chronicler of the Naxalite movement.[17] The Maoists responded to such a critique by justifying the tactical line of poll boycott along with admitting the 'setback' in some states like Andhra Pradesh, where the voter turnout was high due to the high deployment of police.[18] However, the Maoists did experiment to participate in local rural bodies in Odisha in 2012 while winning more than 50 seats in the panchayat elections in Malkangiri and Koraput districts.[19] Such an experiment was not emulated elsewhere besides their reluctance to amend the party programme or change their strategy and political-tactical line regarding their general approach towards electoral participation. While carrying forward the armed struggle strategy, the Maoists identify certain strategic areas that need to be built as a core base for people's war.

> Basing on the laws of protracted people's war in India, in order to confront an enemy, who is far more superior in strength, the revolutionary forces will have to select areas, in which the enemy is relatively weaker and which are favourable to the revolutionary forces, and develop the revolutionary war there. Our country has many such areas that are strategically important for the people's war where Liberated Areas can be established. These Bases will act as the lever or fulcrum for coordinating

---

[16] Ibid., 25.

[17] Sumanta Banerjee, 'The Maoists, Elections, Boycotts and Violence', *Economic & Political Weekly* 44, no. 18 (2 May 2009): 8–10; Sumanta Banerjee, 'Critiquing the Programme of Action of the Maoists', *Economic & Political Weekly* 44, no. 46 (14 November 2009): 75–77.

[18] Spokesperson, CPI (Maoist), 'On the Election Boycott Tactic of the Maoists', *Economic & Political Weekly* 44, no. 38 (19 September 2009): 73–77.

[19] Ajay Gudavarthy, *Maoism, Democracy and Globalisation: Cross-currents in Indian Politics* (London: SAGE Publications, 2014), 61–66.

and advancing the people's war in the country and for seizing political power countrywide.[20]

There has been a recent change of guard in the CPI (Maoist) leadership with the replacement of the ideologue, Muppala Laxmana Rao, aka Ganapathy, as the general secretary of the party with Namballa Keshava Rao, aka Baswaraj, who was heading the Central Military Commission (CMC) of the party and is known to be an expert in fieldcraft, use of explosives and military tactics. According to a media report, the leadership change is for rejuvenating the fighting capabilities of the Maoist party, which has been in the 'setback' stage all over the country as several documents of the CPI (Maoist) point to the party's failure in attracting youth and the inability to spread the movement to urban areas.[21] However, replacing an ideologue with a military war specialist at the helm of the organizational leadership of the CPI (Maoist) means that the party will continue to follow the strategy of armed struggle. As part of the military strategy, the Maoists have chosen hilly and dense forest zones to combat the security apparatuses of the State.

These strategic areas are hilly regions with dense forest cover, have sufficient economic resources, a vast population, and a vast forest area spreading over thousands of square kilometres. In such areas the enemy is weak, and these areas are very favourable for the manoeuvres of the people's army. In these strategic areas we can defeat the enemy completely by fulfilling the tasks of building and consolidating a strong proletarian party and a strong people's army; procuring the people's support and economic resources, while developing the guerrilla war aiming at the building of liberated/base areas in these areas.[22]

At the operational level, the Maoists have mostly chosen the forests and hilly areas of the central-eastern provinces of India. They have preferred

---

[20] CPI (Maoist) Central Committee (P), 'Strategy and Tactics of the Indian Revolution', 50–51.

[21] K. Srinivas Reddy, 'Ganapathy Steps Down as Maoist Chief', *Telangana Today*, 6 November 2018. Available at: https://telanganatoday.com/ganapathy-steps-down-as-maoist-chief (accessed on 11 February 2019).

[22] CPI (Maoist) Central Committee (P), 'Strategy and Tactics of the Indian Revolution', 51.

such a zone in their party programme as well in the following manner: '[T]he waves of the new phase of the "spring thunder" are once again reverberating today in Andhra, Bihar–Jharkhand, Dandakaranya, and other areas of our country.'[23] According to an observer, the core areas of Maoist conflict is in the 'Chota Nagpur and Orissa plateaus—loaded with 93 percent of the country's iron ore, and 84 percent of its coal' that has a terrain of plateau hills, forests and rivers.[24] However, despite their ideological commitment, by sticking to the path of armed struggle while targeting certain geographical spaces as their core strategic base areas and giving the call to boycott elections, the Maoists have really shrunk in the form of organizational influence in recent years.

THE EXTENT OF THE MAOIST INFLUENCE

The leaders of the Maoist movement have expressed concerns about how the Maoists are weak in plains and urban areas while being confined to the most backward forest areas of the country.[25] According to a status paper on the problem of Left-wing extremism, tabled by a former home minister of India on 13 March 2006, Naxal violence was reported from 509 police stations in 11 provinces of India, which is 5.8 per cent of the total number of police stations in those Indian states.[26] However, from 2008 onwards there has been a steady decline of Left-wing radical activities and the quantum of violence. In reply to a question in the lower house of the Indian Parliament, the minister of state for home affairs replied that in 2008, Left-wing extremist activities were reported from 223 districts of India, while in 2009 it was 208, in 2010 it was 196 and by 2011 it was just 182. Out of 182 districts, only 83 districts were considered to be severely affected by Left-wing extremism.[27] Also, 2013 onwards, a shrink in the number of Maoist leaders at the middle and top can be witnessed due to killings,

---

[23] CPI (Maoist) Party Programme, 5.

[24] Roy, 'Half a Century of India's Maoist Insurgency'.

[25] Gudavarthy, *Maoism, Democracy and Globalisation*, 53.

[26] Available at: http://www.satp.org/document/paper-acts-and-oridinances/status-paper-on-the-naxal-problem (accessed on 24 November 2018).

[27] Ministry of Home Affairs, Government of India, 'Starred Question Number 1, Answered on 22nd November 2011' in Lok Sabha.

arrests and surrenders.[28] Based on the data available with the South Asia Terrorism Portal, an analyst has shown that by 2016, only 104 districts were affected by Left-wing extremism, and out of them, only 25 districts have been profoundly affected while another 31 are moderately affected.[29] Also, there has been a steep fall in the number of casualties (including civilians, security personnel and Maoists) driven by Left-wing extremists from 1,180 in 2010, the peak year of Maoist violence to 238 in 2017, the lowest since the formation of the CPI (Maoist) in 2004.[30] Recently, the home minister of India stated in May 2018 that 'casualties among security forces have declined by 53–55 per cent' and the 'geographical expanse of leftwing extremism affected areas has also decreased by 40–45 per cent.'[31]

In the 2018 Chhattisgarh assembly elections, the Maoists gave a poll boycott call, and according to the media reports, some districts such as Dantewada, Bijapur and Sukma had a tensed situation.[32] In fact, in the first phase of Chhattisgarh assembly elections, out of 18 assembly constituencies, 12 were in the Maoist heartland of Bastar.[33] However, the voter turnout in this phase was 70 per cent even as explosives were recovered in a couple of regions.[34] In 2008 assembly elections, in the

[28] N. Manoharan, 'Left-wing Extremism in 2013: A Mixed Bag', in *Armed Conflict, Peace Audit and Early Warning 2014: Stability and Instability in South Asia*, eds. D. Suba Chandran and P. R. Chari (New Delhi: SAGE Publications, 2015): 126.

[29] Roy, 'Half a Century of India's Maoist Insurgency'.

[30] Ibid.

[31] Shishir Tripathi, 'Red Corridor Is Shrinking', *Governance Now*, 15 July 2018. Available at: https://www.governancenow.com/news/regular-story/red-corridor-is-shrinking (accessed on 24 November 2018).

[32] Suvojit Bagchi, 'Chhattisgarh Assembly Elections 2018: Maoist Boycott Call Looms over Dantewada', *The Hindu*, 11 November 2018. Available at: https://www.thehindu.com/elections/chhattisgarh-assembly-elections-2018/maoist-poll-boycott-call-whose-election-is-it-anyway-in-chhattisgarh/article25469374.ece (accessed on 2 December 2018).

[33] Arunima, 'Bastar Votes Amid Fear That Leadership Change in CPI Maoist Could Mean More Violence', *CNN-News18*. Available at: https://www.news18.com/news/india/bastar-votes-amid-fear-that-change-in-guard-in-cpi-maoist-could-mean-more-violence-1936227.html (accessed on 2 December 2018).

[34] *The Hindu*, 'Chhattisgarh Assembly Elections 2018: 70% Turnout in Phase One of Polls', 12 November 2018. Available at: https://www.thehindu.com/

same 18 constituencies of Chhattisgarh, the voter turnout was 67.07 per cent, while in 2013 assembly elections, it was 75.86 per cent.[35] In the Maoist-affected areas in Chhattisgarh, barring just two tribal assembly constituencies of Bijapur and Konta, no assembly constituency reported a voter turnout less than 50 per cent in 2008 and 2013 Chhattisgarh assembly elections. In the first phase of 2018 Chhattisgarh assembly elections, 18 sensitive constituencies went to polls, which are regarded as Maoist affected zones. According to the Election Commission of India data, they recorded an average turn out of 76.46 per cent. In 2018, Konta witnessed a voter turnout of 55.30 per cent, Bastar, Dantewara and Bijapur noticed a turnout of 83.37 per cent, 60.64 per cent and 48.90 per cent respectively. In the last one decade, moderate to high voter turnout has been witnessed in the so-called Maoist-influenced districts in the states of Bihar, Jharkhand, Telangana (previously part of Andhra Pradesh), Odisha and West Bengal. Thus, there is ample evidence to argue that the Maoist influence has been dwindling in India as their organizational presence is shrinking on the one hand, while their poll boycott calls seem to be not working on the other hand. In this context, a pertinent question could be of the following: Why has the Maoist influence waned despite their rhetorical call to serve the interests of the poor and the most downtrodden sections of the Indian population? One can argue that the retreat of the Maoists in the recent past is because of their dated understanding of the dynamics of Indian capitalism and the neoliberal State, which has a bearing on their political-tactical line and the nature of mobilization behind their political project.

INDIAN CAPITALISM, THE NEOLIBERAL STATE AND THE CONSTRAINTS OF THE MAOISTS

The Maoists regard India as 'a semi-colonial, semi-feudal country with uneven development' and vast rural backward areas with sharp class contradictions. In such a context, the CPI (Maoist) argues that

---

elections/chhattisgarh-assembly-elections-2018/chhattisgarh-assembly-elections-2018-voting-live-updates/article25472703.ece (accessed on 2 December 2018).

[35] Computed from the Election Commission of India data.

The party of the proletariat has no other way but to take the path of protracted people's war, just as in China, to advance the revolution towards victory i.e. to liberate the rural areas first and then having expanded the base areas—the centre of democratic power in rural areas—advance towards countrywide victory through encircling and capturing the cities.[36]

In this respect, they also maintain that the 'urban petty-bourgeoisie class and middle class revolutionary intellectuals are revolutionary forces and their vast majority will become the faithful ally of the revolution'.[37] In this regard, commentators have questioned the Maoist understanding of India as a semi-colonial and semi-feudal country like China in the 1930s and their formulations of primary contradiction between feudalism and the broad masses that have been influenced by the programme of the Communist Party of China in the context of political economy transformations in India from late 1960s.[38] Moreover, can the Maoist analysis of the urban middle classes as a revolutionary force who could be an ally of the cause of revolution be taken seriously when India's middle classes have been the direct beneficiary of the neoliberal economic reforms with the gradual implementation of the policies of liberalization, privatization and globalization?

The political economy of contemporary India has been characterized by rapid economic growth as a result of the processes of primitive accumulation of capital, and the logic of profit primarily driving such an accumulation economy. However, the processes of primitive accumulation have simultaneously created a large redundant surplus population as a constitutive outside of capital who cannot be absorbed into the capitalist enterprises but must be supported through various forms of anti-poverty programmes and governmental welfare schemes because this surplus population in a post-colonial context has electoral power besides the consensus in the policymaking discourses about

---

[36] CPI (Maoist) Party Programme, 25.

[37] Ibid., 27.

[38] Deepankar Basu and Debarshi Das, 'The Maoist Movement in India: Some Political Economy Considerations', *Journal of Agrarian Change* 13, no. 3 (July 2013): 365–381.

taking care of such a population.[39] Thus, effects of the primitive accumulation on the vast number of peasants, artisans and petty producers in the informal sector need to be reversed in the form of providing livelihood needs of the poor to continue the growth of corporate capital under conditions of electoral democracy because leaving the marginalized groups without any governmental support system runs the risk of turning them into 'dangerous classes'.[40]

A decade back, noted social scientist Partha Chatterjee had correctly observed how peasant societies in India have dramatically changed in the aftermath of economic transformation from the 1980s onwards. He mentioned five prime changes of peasant societies in contemporary India. First, the spread of governmental technologies as a result of the deepening reach of the developmental State and electoral democracy has created a condition where the State is no longer an external entity to the peasant community. To quote him,

> Governmental agencies distributing education, health services, food, roadways, water, electricity, agricultural technology, emergency relief and dozens of other welfare services have penetrated deep into the interior of everyday peasant life. Not only are peasants dependent on state agencies for these services, but they have also acquired considerable skill, albeit to a different degree in different regions, in manipulating and pressurising these agencies to deliver these benefits.[41]

Second, even the gradual and piecemeal reforms since the 1950s in the domain of agrarian property have led to a situation where except in few isolated areas, 'for the first time in centuries, small peasants possessing land no longer directly confront an exploiting class within the village, as under feudal or semi-feudal conditions' which has far-reaching consequences at the level of inventing new strategies of peasant politics.[42] Third, according to Chatterjee,

---

[39] Kalyan Sanyal, *Rethinking Capitalist Development: Primitive Accumulation, Governmentality and Post-Colonial Capitalism* (New Delhi: Routledge, 2013[2007], paperback ed. with a Foreword by Partha Chatterjee).

[40] Partha Chatterjee, 'Democracy and Economic Transformation in India', *Economic &Political Weekly* 43, no. 16 (19 April 2008): 53–62.

[41] Ibid., 54.

[42] Ibid.

Since the tax on land or agricultural produce is no longer a significant source of revenue for the government, as in colonial or pre-colonial times, the relation of the state to the peasantry is no longer directly extractive, as it often was in the past.[43]

Fourth, the possibility of shifting from peasant occupation and peasant migration into new cities and industrial regions is 'no longer a function of their pauperisation and forcible separation from the land, but is often a voluntary choice, shaped by the perception of new opportunities and new desires'.[44] Finally, there is a new economy of desire among the younger members of peasant families not to opt for a life of a peasant anymore but to accept urban non-agricultural occupations even though moving to a new city or town might pose some hardships and uncertainties. This trend according to Chatterjee is due to 'the spread of school education and widespread exposure to modern communications media such as the cinema, television and advertising' along with the 'lure of anonymity and upward mobility' in city-based non-agricultural professions.[45]

In addition to the changing nature of contemporary peasant society in India, Chatterjee sharply points out the relative decline of the landed elites in comparison to the ascendancy of the power of corporate capital, and the hegemony of corporate capital over the space of civil society whose members are constituted by the urban middle classes. The educational, professional and social aspirations of the middle classes have now become tied with the fortunes of corporate capital along with an emergence of a vague belief among the urban middle classes that rapid economic growth will solve all problems of poverty and unequal opportunities.[46]

When one compares the contemporary reality of the fast-changing nature of Indian capitalism under conditions of neoliberal governmentality and electoral democracy, then one cannot but conclude that the Maoists in India have a dated understanding of

---

[43] Ibid.
[44] Ibid.
[45] Ibid.
[46] Ibid., 56–62.

the dynamism of Indian capitalism and the neoliberal State. Indian capitalism has fundamentally transformed from the early 1990s onwards while expanding the rural market and transforming peasant societies. Moreover, the inclusion of the agrarian economy within the neoliberal governmental strategies creates a significant impediment for the Maoists to mobilize the agrarian population. What is interesting to note is that under a neoliberal policy regime when farm incomes have been declining and issues of farmer suicides and demands for farm loan waiver have been emerging, the Maoists have been unable to mobilize the peasant population throughout India. Instead, new demands for reservation by landed castes in government jobs are emerging as agriculture has become economically unviable. Thus, the agrarian revolution that the Indian Maoists aspire to achieve, in effect, has been mostly symptomatic of emotionally charged fetishes than a serious strategy of political mobilization. At the same time, when the hegemony of corporate capital has swayed an overwhelming majority of the urban middle classes in India at a time when neoliberal capitalism has directly benefited the urban petty bourgeoisie, the Maoist assessment of the urban petty bourgeoisie as a 'revolutionary force' which will 'become the faithful ally of the revolution' is nothing short of wishful thinking. In the context of the aforementioned critical evaluation of the Maoist movement, a critical examination of the responses by the Parliamentary Left towards the Maoists is relevant.

The standard critique of the Maoists by the ideologues of the Parliamentary Left has been that the Maoists have a confused understanding of the world situation, an incorrect analysis of the Indian State, an artificial theoretical construct like the 'Chinese path', ignorance about the element of class struggle within the parliamentary system, distance from everyday political struggles of the people and distortion of Mao Zedong's thought by putting Mao out of context to seek justification for guerrilla warfare and, in effect, represent an ideological strand of violent anarchism.[47] Such analyses of the Maoists had their genealogy

---

[47] Anil Biswas, '"Maoism": An Exercise in Anarchism', *The Marxist* 21, no. 4 (October–December 2005): 1–15. A similar kind of response by challenging and critiquing the politics and ideology of the Indian Maoists was later articulated by two more ideologues of the CPI (M). See Pushpendra Grewal, 'Indian Maoists: Flawed Strategy and Perverted Praxis', in *Maoism: A Critique from the Left,* ed.

in the ideological critique by the CPI (M) ideologues towards the Naxalites in the late 1960s, 1970s and 1980s with particular reference to their wrong analysis about the nature of Indian big bourgeoisie, incorrect understanding about India's independence, factional fights within the Naxalite movement and subsequent splintering of several Naxalite groups.[48] What is remarkably similar in all polemical critique of the CPI (M) ideologues towards the Maoists is that of copious quotes from Lenin's *Leftwing Communism: An Infantile Disorder*. The point is that while the Maoists have been correctly understood by the CPI (M) ideologues as an anarchist force with a warped ideological path, the CPI (M) ideologues' copious quote of Lenin's pamphlet by locating the roots of Left-wing extremism cum adventurism as a petty bourgeois phenomena is a problematic formulation on four grounds. First, there is a subaltern base of the Indian Maoists, particularly among the poor Adivasis in parts of Chhattisgarh[49] and landless Dalits in parts of Bihar[50] who cannot be even remotely identified with the petty bourgeois strata.

Second, Lenin's analysis of the nature of petty-bourgeois adventurism and childishness, written between 1918 and 1920 in a specific context of the early days of the Soviet Union,[51] is wrong to be extrapolated and transplanted into Indian conditions. In other words, when the Government of India is not led by a revolutionary party unlike the post-revolutionary situation in the erstwhile Soviet Union, there is no point to mimic an argument that was put forward by Lenin in

---

Prasenjit Bose (New Delhi: LeftWord Books, 2010); Nilotpal Basu, 'The Tragedy of "Maoism"', in *Maoism: A Critique from the Left*, ed. Prasenjit Bose (New Delhi: LeftWord Books, 2010).

[48] See 'Ideological Debate Summed Up', Party Document issued by the Polit Bureau, CPI (M), June 1968; Biplab Dasgupta, *The Naxalite Movement* (New Delhi: Allied Publishers, 1974); Prakash Karat, 'Naxalism Today; At an Ideological Deadend', *The Marxist* 3, no. 1 (January–March, 1985), 42–65.

[49] Nandini Sundar, *The Burning Forest: India's War in Bastar* (New Delhi: Juggernaut Books, 2016).

[50] George J. Kunnath, *Rebels from the Mud Houses: Dalits and the Making of the Maoist Revolution in Bihar* (New Delhi: Social Science Press, 2012).

[51] See V. I. Lenin, '"Left-Wing" Childishness and the Petty-Bourgeois Mentality', in *Lenin: Selected Works*, vol. 2 (Moscow: Progress Publishers, 1968 [1918]), 429–451; V. I. Lenin, '"Left-Wing" Communism—An Infantile Disorder', in *Lenin: Selected Works*, vol. 3 (Moscow: Progress Publishers, 1968 [1920]), 512–585.

countering a specific adventurist trend in the aftermath of the Bolshevik revolution in Russia. Also, the socio-economic and political conditions along with the correlation of political actors in the form of specific class forces and non-class identitarian groups in contemporary India are different from that of the nascent stage of the former Soviet Union.

Third, since the petty bourgeois middle class is an ally of the CPI (M)'s own people's democratic front, it is somewhat disingenuous to only critique the Maoists as victims of petty-bourgeois deviations. In fact, there exists a compelling critique not by anyone less than a prominent party intellectual of the CPI (M) about how the Bengal unit of the CPI (M), governed by the demands of the urban middle classes, opted for a corporate capital-led industrialization with a neoliberal policy trajectory at the cost of the class interests of the peasants, rural poor, petty producers and small traders.[52] In other words, unlike the charge of petty-bourgeois anarchism in the case of Maoists, the CPI (M) has been trapped into petty bourgeois revisionism. Moreover, what the CPI (M)-led Left Front has been traditionally doing regarding political mobilization is nothing different from non-Left parties' adoption of populist rhetoric for mass mobilization. The political and ideological content of such populist rhetoric might be different in the cases of the big national parties, the regional parties and the communist Left. However, the logic of populism as a strategy to mobilize various sectors of the electorate cutting across caste, class, language and gender has been the aim of all major political parties in India.

Finally, the critique of the Maoists about their incorrect analysis of the world situation could also be directed against the CPI (M). The CPI (M) still believes that China, Vietnam and North Korea (DPRK) are 'socialist' countries.[53] However, there exists a credible

---

[52] See Prabhat Patnaik, 'Left in Government', *Frontline* 23, no. 10 (20 May–02 June 2006): 23–25; Prabhat Patnaik, 'In the Aftermath of Nandigram', *Economic & Political Weekly* 42, no. 21 (26 May 2007): 1893–1895; Prabhat Patnaik, 'The Left in Decline', *Economic & Political Weekly* 46, no. 29 (16 July 2011): 12–16.

[53] See the following documents of the CPI (M) in their party congresses in the last few years. Communist Party of India (Marxist), Paragraphs 6.1–6.32 of *Resolution on Some Ideological Issues* adopted at the 20th Party Congress (Kozhikode: 4–9 April 2012), 15–21; Communist Party of India (Marxist), Paragraph 1.35 of the *Political Resolution* adopted at the 21st Party Congress (Vishakhapatnam: 14–19

academic literature that convincingly demonstrates that China has been implementing a project of neoliberalism entirely different from the Anglo-American variant[54] while Vietnam is also reaching new heights of building capitalism[55] and North Korea looks like a monarchy with a dynastic rule.[56] While a detailed analysis of the ideological debates between the Maoists and the Marxists in India is beyond the scope of this chapter, one can safely argue that both the Maoists and the Marxists forget to acknowledge that the socialist experiments in the 20th century eventually built capitalism.[57] In this regard, the Indian Marxists are still to acknowledge that the Chinese and the Vietnamese have successfully built neoliberal capitalism in the 21st century. The Chinese experience has proved that neoliberalism as an economic doctrine has been a malleable technology of governance in different political regimes quite distinct from one another such as authoritarian, democratic and communist.[58] In the context of the aforementioned theoretical and ideological debates, can the Maoists learn from the *practice* of the Left in the 21st century?

CAN THE MAOISTS LEARN FROM 21ST-CENTURY INTERNATIONAL EXPERIENCE?

If one analyses the prospects of the international experience of Left-wing politics globally in the 21st century, then it is clear that traditional

---

April 2015), 9; Communist Party of India (Marxist), Paragraphs 1.56–1.68 of the *Political Resolution* adopted at the 22nd Party Congress (Hyderabad: 18–22 April 2018), 15–18.

[54] David Harvey, 'Neoliberalism "with Chinese Characteristics"', in *A Brief History of Neoliberalism* (Oxford: Oxford University Press, 2005), 120–151.

[55] Lan Nguyen, *Guerilla Capitalism: The State in the Market in Vietnam* (Oxford: Chandos Publishing, 2009); also see Christina Schwenkel and Ann Marie Leshkowich, eds., 'Neoliberalism in Vietnam', special issue, *Positions: Asia Critique* 20, no. 2 (May 2012): 379–670.

[56] Andrei Lankov, *The Real North Korea: Life and Politics in the Failed Stalinist Utopia*, fully updated and revised ed. (New York: Oxford University Press, 2015 [2013]).

[57] Aditya Nigam, 'Democracy, State and Capital: The "Unthought" of 20th Century Marxism', *Economic & Political Weekly* 44, no. 51 (19 December 2009): 35–39.

[58] See Aihwa Ong, *Neoliberalism as Exception: Mutations in Citizenship and Sovereignty* (Durham, NC: Duke University Press, 2006).

communist parties have not been much successful in the road to political power. Instead, various forms of socialist and Left-wing populists have been able to form governments through democratic political mobilization. It is in this regard that the Indian Maoists have severe limitations in championing and articulating a political project that could be appealing for a Left-wing populism in the 21st century. Apart from a conventional class-centric approach and the limitations in the class-centric formulation of the united front[59] like major communist parties in India, the Maoists have four additional problems. Firstly, the military strategy of the Maoists to combat the modern Indian State has become obsolete. It is because, now, it has become almost impossible to tackle the surveillance system and the humongous military strength of the neoliberal State.[60] The failure of the Maoists to capture political power through an armed strategy is real not only in India but also in other parts of the world. In the recent past, in Nepal, the Maoists did not opt for an armed seizure of political power and had chosen the route of electoral democracy. Revolutionary Armed Forces of Colombia (FARC), the Shining Path in Peru, the Maoist Communist Party of the Philippines (CPP) and several other Maoist groups in Latin America have been unsuccessful to capture political power through armed guerrilla warfare.[61] Many Maoist groups in these countries have been primarily restricted to specific zones of forests and mountains, much like the Indian Maoists.

The emergence of a progressive Left in an emerging world has already given signals of moving away from 'traditional ideas associated with socialist theory and practice' of the 20th century, although there are continuities with the socialist ideas of the 20th century concerning

---

[59] CPI (Maoist) Party Programme, 23, 27–29; CPI (Maoist) Central Committee (P), 'Strategy and Tactics of the Indian Revolution', 78–80. The limitations of the Maoists in championing the politics of left-wing populism has been argued by me in *Indian Muslim(s) after Liberalization* (New Delhi: Oxford University Press, 2019), pp. 249–253.

[60] The relevance of political violence or the revolutionary violence of the Maoists as a necessary condition for radical social and political change is well debated in Ajay Gudavarthy, ed., *Revolutionary Violence versus Democracy: Narratives from India* (New Delhi: SAGE Publications, 2017).

[61] Vijay Prashad, 'The Antinomies of "Maoism"', in *Maoism: A Critique from the Left*, ed. Prasenjit Bose (New Delhi: LeftWord Books, 2010), 70–88.

the role of the nation-state and the attitude towards imperialism.[62] Globally, it is the Left-wing populists, who have been able to capture political power while fighting neoliberalism. The 'pink tide' of Left-wing populism that swept several Latin American countries during the first one and a half decade of the 21st century is often anchored around the name and the figure of a charismatic leader. For example, democratic and Left-wing populist mobilization could be noticed with the popularity of Kirchnerism in Argentina in which both Néstor Kirchner and Cristina Fernández de Kirchner gave a Left-wing turn to the traditional Peronist populism of the Justicialist Party. Similarly, Left-wing populist leaders like Hugo Chavez came to power with the call for a Bolivarian revolution in Venezuela. Evo Morales in Bolivia and Rafael Correa in Ecuador are primarily charismatic populist Left leaders with massive support. The socialist Left in Venezuela, Ecuador and Bolivia or the Centre-Left populists in Nicaragua, Chile and the Workers Party in Brazil, the socialist Left in Portugal, the National Regeneration Movement (MORENA) in Mexico and the Coalition of Radical Left (SYRIZA) in Greece have been successful models of Left-wing populism. Similarly, the Left-wing populist articulations have helped to form strong opposition parties like the Labour Party under Jeremy Corbyn in the United Kingdom. The Left-wing populists have also been able to rally significant mass support as evident in the cases of the Podemos in Spain, the Die Linke in Germany, Jean Luc Melechon's Unsubmissive France or enthusiasm behind Bernie Sanders in the United States.

One could maintain that there are also limitations of these Left populists, as in the case of SYRIZA in Greece[63] and in some cases in Latin America, the Left populists have also lost power as in Brazil and Argentina or are under serious threat from the opposition in Venezuela. The achievements of the agrarian policies of the Left governments in Latin America concerning land redistribution and advancement in agribusiness were complemented by the long commodity boom in the first one and a half decade of the 21st century that helped to increase

---

[62] Jayati Ghosh, 'The Emerging Left in the "Emerging" World', *Economic & Political Weekly* 47, no. 24 (16 June 2012): 33–38.

[63] Cas Mudde, *SYRIZA: The Failure of the Populist Promise,* with a Foreword by Petros Papasarantopoulos (London: Palgrave Macmillan, 2017).

employment and reduce poverty among the rural subaltern classes. At the same time, the limitations of the transformative social project of the 'pink tide' were that the Left governments in South America got entangled within the logic of capitalist liberal representative democracy.[64] However, the road to power is not perpetual, and that contingency, uncertainty and indeterminacy are ineluctable part of politics. In other words, the permanent feature of human societies is that there is no end of politics and there is nothing outside politics. Thus, even if today there have been setbacks for the Left populists in some parts of Europe and Latin America, it does not mean that the possibility of building a new hegemony for the Left populists does not exist in future. However, what is interesting to note is that traditional communist parties lead none of those successful Left-wing populist mobilizations in Europe and Latin America. In such a global context, the Indian Maoists need to understand that today the practice and norm of electoral democracy has been so profound and instrumental in the making of widespread participation of the people in the democratic process that it is difficult to bypass electoral democracy. It has become nearly impossible to earn the consent of the Indian people for a high-risk political game of military fight against a technologically superior neoliberal State.

Second, the Maoist politics has increasingly exposed its limits at a time when a new political subject, namely the *homo œconomicus* (the individual rational and calculative entrepreneur),[65] has emerged under conditions of neoliberalism in India. This new subject is very much entrenched within the massive architecture of neoliberal governmentality in India where the calculative entrepreneurial 'citizen-voter' is increasingly becoming individualized and dependent on the doles and subsidies of the modern State.[66] This new citizen–voter is

---

[64] Leandro Vergara-Camus and Cristóbal Kay, 'New Agrarian Democracies: The Pink Tide's Lost Opportunity', in *Rethinking Democracy: Socialist Register 2018*, eds. Leo Panitch and Greg Albo (London: Merlin Books, 2017), 224–243.

[65] For a detailed analysis of such a concept and its evolution from the 18th century and its return under neoliberal conditions, see Michel Foucault, *The Birth of Biopolitics: Lectures at the Collège de France, 1978–1979*, ed. Michel Senellart, trans. Graham Burchell (Basingstoke: Palgrave Macmillan, 2008).

[66] Ranabir Samaddar, *Neo-Liberal Strategies of Governing India* (London: Routledge, 2016).

engaged in making Aadhaar cards, NREGA job cards, BPL cards, etc., which make them dependent on the neoliberal State. It is challenging for the Maoist politics to organize this new political subject for high-risk militarist war against the State when this new citizen-voter is so much dependent on the statist agencies. The only path that is open for any form of Left movement is then to use electoral democracy as a site of popular struggle against neoliberal policies of the Indian State. This electoral democracy, which has been given legitimacy by the Indian State is the only site to be subverted by the people. It is an electoral democracy that has been instrumental in the vote for Donald Trump. The Brexit episode also shows that substantial sections of people have voted against the agenda of the neoliberal establishment. If the alt-right can successfully use electoral politics, it is difficult to imagine that the Left cannot do when there are successful examples from Europe and Latin America.

Third, the Maoists have focused on the primacy of struggle against primitive accumulation in the domain of *jal* (water), *jangal* (forests) and *zamin* (land). Sometimes, their restricted spatial location as a hideout strategy hinders them from coming out in the villages and towns to initiate both economistic and political struggles. In effect, such an approach has alienated them from vast sections of workers and peasants in large parts of the country because their restricted territorial locality has kept them outside the domain of the struggles against capitalist exploitation and other forms of non-class oppression in hundreds of towns and cities, and thousands of villages and suburbs. Although the political activities of the Maoists in urban areas in India are clearly expressed in the party's document,[67] it is crystal clear that they have been unable to mobilize any significant sections of the urban population and have largely been trapped in the forest areas of central-eastern parts of India. The contradiction between their tactical target of liberating rural areas first and then 'advance towards countrywide victory through encircling and capturing the cities'[68] according to their party pro-gramme on the one hand and the emphasis on the Maoist organizational

---

[67] CPI (Maoist) Central Committee (P), 'Strategy and Tactics of the Indian Revolution', 135–144.

[68] CPI (Maoist) Party Programme, 25.

activities in urban areas on the other seems to be a significant hindrance in connecting with the people at large.

Finally, in an age of populist and horizontal mobilizations along different class and non-class lines, the Leninist model of vanguard party with the organizational principle of democratic centralism has reached its limits. Democratic centralism was adopted in a state of emergency in a war-like situation, more than a century back in Russia. Moreover, it has been suitable for and indeed served its purpose once for a militarist organization. However, it will not work under conditions of electoral democracies as evident from the experiences of the 20th century where the communist parties, guided by democratic centralism have been relatively more successful to capture political power against forms of monarchy, autocracy and military dictatorships but have been far less successful to gain power under parliamentary democracies. Moreover, what is the point of adopting a democratic centralist line if the military strategy has itself become obsolete at a time of great democratic upsurge?

CONCLUDING REMARKS

The Maoist politics in India, as we have seen in this chapter, welcomes political violence in the form of an armed struggle at the cost of vilifying participation in elections as a wrong tactic that would dissolve the radical character of a revolutionary party. However, one must understand that political violence threatens democratic politics, with increasing levels of political antagonism and enmity getting priority over democratic ways of political articulation. In this respect, according to noted political theorist Chantal Mouffe, the objective of democratic politics is to domesticate 'hostility' and try to defuse 'potential antagonism'[69] where the main objective of democratic politics is 'to transform antagonism into agonism'.[70] Here, one must understand that while antagonism is a friend/foe relation and a 'struggle between enemies, agonism is [a] struggle between adversaries'.[71] As Mouffe points out that while

---

[69] Chantal Mouffe, *The Democratic Paradox* (London: Verso, 2000), 101.

[70] Ibid., 103.

[71] Ibid., 102–103.

'antagonism is a we/they relation in which the two sides are enemies who do not share any common ground, agonism is a we/they relation where the conflicting parties...nevertheless recognize the legitimacy of their opponents. They are "adversaries" not enemies.'[72] In this regard, according to Mouffe, the aim of democratic politics

> is to construct the 'them' in such a way that it is no longer perceived as an enemy to be destroyed, but as an 'adversary', that is, somebody whose ideas we combat but whose right to defend those ideas we do not put into question.[73]

However, what is the condition of existence of such a violent politics which treats opponents as enemies? Here, Mouffe argues that 'when there is lack of democratic political struggles...the opponent cannot be perceived as an adversary to contend with, but only as an enemy to be destroyed.'[74]

Thus, taking refuge in physical violence and extermination is a result of perpetual depoliticization, which is again a by-product of lack of democratic political struggles in a given political context. The circularity of political violence of the Maoists is precisely a mirror image of the statist violence where the Maoists, much like the State, mimic the logic of annihilation of the political enemy. The ideological justification in favour of a politics of violence with its ideological roots in the classic Naxalite formulation of the annihilation of class enemy[75] is primarily a reflection of the crisis of political hegemony of the Maoists. A politics which cannot democratically mobilize people behind its project takes refuge to violence. It is true for any kind of extremist politics including religious extremism of various strands, which is fundamentally grounded on a politics of hatred and vindictive assaults. A politics of hatred, which takes refuge to violent elimination of political opponents than politically and ideologically combat the same is a reflection

---

[72] Chantal Mouffe, *On the Political* (London: Verso, 2005), 20.

[73] Mouffe, *The Democratic Paradox*, 101–102.

[74] Chantal Mouffe, *The Return of the Political* (London: Verso, 1993), 6.

[75] The annihilation campaign of the Naxalites in the early 1970s has been written by Sankar Ghosh, *The Naxalite Movement: A Maoist Experiment* (Calcutta: Firma K. L. Mukhopadhyay, 1974).

of deep-seated depoliticization. The frustrated violence of the Indian Maoists in that sense meets its political dead end, which closes down any scope of politics in general and undoubtedly democratic politics in particular. In such a context, the Maoist vision of the Indian revolution only becomes a utopia much like the utopia of the utopian socialists. Thus, the vanguard party of the Maoists, 'the educator', needs some 'educating' to quote Marx from the epigraph of this chapter. This educating is about updating the Maoist understanding of dynamism of neoliberal capitalism and the lessons from the international Left movement, which might help the Maoists to invent alternative strategies and tactics to transcend the neoliberal State with a vision of a post-neoliberal order. At present, the strategy and tactics of the Indian Maoists are warped, confused and flawed, the results of which are apparent in the form of the shrinking base of the Maoist party in India.

Before concluding, let me put forward the major arguments of this chapter. This chapter has tried to assess the radical political project of the Indian Maoists in the aftermath of the golden jubilee celebration of the Naxalite movement of the late 1960s. In effect, this chapter has analysed that the Indian Maoists have no real military and political strength to combat the Indian State and thus pose no great security threat to the Indian State. Such an argument was primarily based on the following. First, the ideological formulations of the Indian Maoists have no robust analysis of the fast-changing nature of Indian capitalism and the dynamism of the Indian State. As a result, it lacks innovative strategies and tactics of political practice that would ensure a sustained level of mass mobilization behind its political project. Second, the military strategy of the Maoists to combat the modern Indian State has become obsolete besides being escaping the strategy of democratic political mobilization. The failure of the Maoists to capture political power through an armed insurrection is real not only in India but also in other parts of the world as evident from the examples from contemporary Asia and Latin America. Third, it has become nearly impossible to earn the consent of the people for a high-risk military fight against a technologically superior neoliberal State. This is because the practice and norm of electoral democracy have been so profound along with the widespread participation of the people in the democratic process that it is difficult to bypass electoral democracy. Fourth, Maoist politics has to now engage with a new political subject of citizen-voter, who is very much entrenched within the massive architecture of neoliberal governmentality where the calculative entrepreneurial citizen-voter is increasingly becoming individualized and dependent on the doles, subsidies and various forms of welfare schemes of the modern State. Finally, the primacy of Maoist military struggle against primitive accumulation in the domain of mines and forests has restricted their spatial operation as a hideout strategy in the forests of central and eastern India. Their restricted territorial locality has alienated them from vast sections of the people and has kept them outside the domain of everyday struggles against capitalist exploitation and forms of non-class oppression.

The radical transformation of capitalism and neoliberal State in India has exposed the limits of the revolutionary promise of the Maoists. Extant academic literature and security agencies tend to overemphasize the threat of the Maoists[76] than their actual strength. In contrast, this chapter has pointed out the failure of the Maoists in combating the Indian State and living up to their promise of the social revolution. A more realistic assessment would be that the Maoists will continue to create some sensation with violent attacks here and there just like many armed militias have been doing in various parts of the world. However, they would be unable to create any major destabilizing situation for the Indian State. The redundant surplus population who have been the victims of primitive accumulation under conditions of neoliberal capitalism in India remains as the constitutive outside of capital in the domain of political economy. The Indian State has acquired the skills to accommodate those redundant surplus population by making them more participatory in everyday democratic exercise of demands and claims on the State, engaging them with the electoral process and offering various forms of doles and subsidies. Besides, the statist parties can deflect the attention of the very same population through caste and community-based assertions. In contrast, the

---

[76] One such glaring example of treating Maoists as 'a serious threat to India's stability and integrity' can be found in an essay published a few years back by Arvind Verma, 'The Police and India's Maoist Insurgency', in *Policing Insurgencies: Cops as Counterinsurgents*, eds. C. Christine Fair and Sumit Ganguly (New Delhi: Oxford University Press, 2014).

Maoists have not been able to invent any alternative strategy to rally the victims of the twin processes of primitive accumulation of capital and capitalist accumulation. Therefore, the Indian Maoists only remain as the constitutive outside of Indian democracy. However, remaining outside the domain of Indian democracy is a voluntary choice of the Maoists. It is not structurally bound as the redundant surplus population is with regards to the zone of the contemporary political economy of India. Unless the Indian Maoists change their course to use electoral democracy as a site of political struggle while learning from the practices of the Nepali Maoists and the Left populists from the international experience in the 21st century, it would eventually become an irrelevant political force, the symptoms of which are pretty clear at this moment.

Chapter 2

Kashmir's Syncretic Tradition and Challenges of Radicalization in a Raging Conflict

Noor Ahmed Baba

Kashmir has been unique in a number of respects. Its cultural personality is an outcome of its evolution as a community that runs into 5,000 years of history.[1] Its geophysical structure has reinforced its defined borders in ethnocultural terms as well. It is generally accepted that the geography and all that constitutes the physical environment of a place play a very significant role in shaping the social characteristics and cultural attitudes of people.[2] This could be no less true for Kashmir. Kashmir has been aptly described as a 'fertile plain embedded among high mountain ranges, a valley large enough to form a kingdom for itself and capable of supporting a highly developed civilization'.[3] The

---

[1] Balraj Puri, '5000 Years of Kashmir', *Early Times* (Jammu), 13 May 2009.

[2] Ibn Khaldun (1332–1406) has been an important propounder of this view. His methodology emphasizes the study of environmental impact on social organization and economic process that define values, prosperity and culture. See Muhsin Mahdi, *Ibn Khaldun's Philosophy of History: A Study in the Philosophical Foundation of the Science of Culture* (Chicago, IL: University of Chicago Press, 1964).

[3] M. A. Stein, *Kalhana's Rajtarangni: A Chronicle of Kings of Kashmir*, notes on translation (Westminster: Archibald Constable & Co., 1900), 388.

mountainous surrounding of Kashmir has helped it to shape up differently from its neighbouring areas. It is not only the borders but the nature of Kashmir's topography and divinely gifted natural assets that have helped to reinforce and strengthen this uniqueness of Kashmiri culture as reflected in the day-to-day idioms of common man, folklore evolved through centuries of living together in interface with serene natural surroundings, language and literature. It has all been influenced by the capitulating beauty of its meadows, mighty mountains, forests, water bodies and the general ambience of variety in changing seasons.[4] Kashmir has everything that can stimulate a creative mind and a compelling passion. There is a lot of variety in which there is something for everybody's interest. According to a 19th-century geologist and ethnographer Frederick Drew, who had stayed here for a decade-long service,

> The Kashmiri people are doubtless physically the finest of all the races that inhabit the territories we are dealing with and I have no much hesitation in saying that in size and in features they are the finest on the whole continent of India. Their physique, their character and their language are so marked as to produce a nationality different from all around as distinct from their neighbors as their country is geographically separated.[5]

Kashmir has remained the home of learning and creative art and literature from ancient times. It has contributed to the growth of philosophy, sciences, language, literature and discourses on religion.[6] Within the whole of the Indian subcontinent, Kashmir is the only region that can claim the distinction of possessing an uninterrupted record of history.[7] *Rajtarangni* of Kalhana Pandit is based on the works of historians who

---

[4] For a very good account of how Kashmir, its beauty and physical glory have been variously Described, see Walter Lawrence, *The Valley of Kashmir* (Srinagar: Kesar Publishers, 1967), 12–31.

[5] Frederic Dew, *The Northern Barriers of India and Jammu and Kashmir Territories* (Srinagar: City Book Centre, 2008 [1875]), 124.

[6] See Prem Nath Bazaz, *History of Struggle for Freedom in Kashmir* (Srinagar: Gulshan Publishers, 2003), 22–33.

[7] Stein as quoted in Lawrence, *The Valley of Kashmir*, 179.

were living much before the monumental work was undertaken in the 11th century.[8]

Another unique thing about Kashmir is its location in geo-civilizational terms. Kashmir for last 5,000 of its history has remained at the crossroads of civilizational interface and a meeting point of Chinese, Central Asian, Indian and Persian civilizations, cultures and economies.[9] All these civilizational traditions have had an enriching impact on Kashmir. In addition to its links with north, more particularly the north-western Indian subcontinent, it has had close trade and cultural relations with places in the present-day China, Greater Tibet, a number of cities in Central Asia, Afghanistan, Iran and, via Silk Route, even Europe. Traditionally, Kashmir remained connected to these places at different points through routes in different directions.[10] In addition, Kashmir to this day retains the imprints of influences of Hellenic and other civilizations borne out in far-off places in West Asia and beyond in Europe.[11] People have come and gone from here as travellers and missionaries and for learning and exchange of knowledge. In addition, Kashmir also has been at the crossroads of transition of many important spiritual and religious traditions such as Hinduism, Buddhism and Islam and must have also been impacted by other religious traditions that evolved in its proximity like that of Zoroastrianism in Iran and Confucianism in China. This impact has been a two-way give and take. In fact, one of the dimensions of Kashmir issue has been that the 1947 political development separated Kashmir from its natural surroundings and pushed it to a status of secluded periphery.[12]

---

[8] For a detailed account of its sources, etc., see ibid., 179–203.

[9] Noor Ahmad Baba, 'Cultural Contours of Kashmir's Identity', *Sheeraza: A Quarterly Journal of Culture and Literature* 12, no. 3 (July–September, 2016): 4–11.

[10] Noor Ahmad Baba, 'Reconnecting Kashmir: Need for Reopening Traditional Routes', *Epilogue* (September 2008): 39–40.

[11] Ajaz A. Banday, 'A Recent Discovery of Hellenistic Image of Gaja-Lakshmi From Kashmir: Style and development', *The Journal Of Central Asian Studies* 18, no. 1 (2009): 75–86.

[12] Noor Ahmad Baba, 'Reconnecting Kashmir: Need "Peace Process and Imperative of Resolving Kashmir Problem"', in *India & Pakistan: Pathways Ahead,* eds. Amitabh Mattoo, Kapil Kak and Happymon Jacob (New Delhi: Knowledge World, 2007), 209–218.

What has been unique about Kashmir is the variety and the richness of these surrounding traditions and the fact that in spite of being surrounded by a number of such rich and dominant civilizations it could retain the uniqueness of its cultural personality.[13] It did change with and in relation to changing times, challenges and incoming influences from its surroundings, but it absorbed these changes in a manner that did not fragment its social fabric and did not create cleavages that would distort its unique collective personality with which it is still identified. It has been strongly a consensual society that changed by and large together but without uprooting itself from its inherited socio-cultural possessions and legacy. Kashmir has been truly a melting pot that has absorbed various influences from its surroundings without being undermined or overtaken by any one of these dominant civilizations and instead formed its own uniqueness. The strength of Kashmiri personality has been that with all these influences coming from left and right, north and south, near and far, it has retained its personality as a distinct cultural community while being enriched in the process.[14]

The by and large peaceful and gradual transition of faiths without violent disruptions and enriching interface with many magnificent civilizational traditions has given its people a culture of inclusivity, a cosmopolitan outlook and creative ingenuity that is reflected in their approach to creative arts and crafts, literature and approach to politics even in very trying situations. Thus, as a society it formed its own uniqueness by absorbing the rich variety in its own history and its surroundings and forming a hybrid identity and a syncretic personality. This has promoted an intercommunity living with common cultural references. This composite living and social inclusivity continued even after Islam emerged as the dominant religion of its people and became a very important component of Kashmir's identity. Therefore, Kashmir continued to be defined by the culture of interfaith peace and understanding in which its own unique Rishi mystic tradition has played a very important role. The two persons who have approximated and symbolized the Kashmir's identity with

---

[13] It is manifested in uniqueness of its language, dress, food habits, social moorings, etc.

[14] Baba, 'Cultural Contours'.

all the richness of its cultural genius and spiritual ethos are Lalleshwari (Hindu) better known as Lal Ded (Mother Lala) and Sheikh-ul-Alam/ Sheikh Nuruddin Wali (Nund Rishi, Muslim), the most revered saint of Kashmir representing a composite legacy.[15] Historically speaking, both have occupied the cultural and literary imagination of people in Kashmir across religious lines. Both have had tremendous significance in shaping the socio-psychological consciousness and identity of the Kashmiri society and in symbolizing intercommunity harmony and tolerant character of its society. However, it has been Sheikh-ul-Alam/ Sheikh Nuruddin Wali who has more significantly approximated and symbolized Kashmir's identity with all its cultural genius and richness of spirituality. Historically speaking, he as the 'patron saint' has had tremendous significance in shaping the socio-psychological character of the Kashmiri society and in promoting its intercommunity harmony and the tolerant character.[16] He laid the foundation of the Rishi mystic tradition with syncretic attributes. Therefore, he became an epitome of Kashmir's cultural and spiritual personality.[17] He as a person and as an institution personifies Kashmir's national personality as well. He and his legacy continued to inspire the people of Kashmir for peace, reconciliation and harmony. Through all these influences, Kashmiri society in spite of various challenging situations it was faced with, by and large, remained pacifist and non-violent. These virtues remained intact and unchallenged till Kashmir remained independent.

Kashmir lost its political independence as a kingdom with it annexation by Akbar in 1586 and it was brought under the jurisdiction of the Mughal Empire. During the Mughal rule, Kashmir retained its status as a politico-administrative unit that of a province. The Mughal Empire, because of its enlightenment, prosperity, civilizational grandeur, syncretic policies and fascination of its rulers for the place, contributed to economic well-being, administrative reforms, architectural and landscape refinement, enriching art, culture, literary and intellectual life of the place that have left permanent and positive marks on its

---

[15] Chitralekha Zutshi, *Language of Belonging: Islam, Regional Identity and Making of Kashmir* (Delhi: Permanent Black, 2003), 18–19.

[16] Puri, '5000 Years of Kashmir'.

[17] Ibid.

identity.[18] With the weakening of the empire, the valley came under the Afghan rule from 1756. This in the words of Lawrence meant passing 'to a time of brutal tyranny, unrelieved by good works, chivalry, and honour'.[19] It remained under the Afghans till it was captured by Maharaja Ranjit Singh and annexed to the Sikh Kingdom of Punjab in 1819 and remained so till 1846. Sikh rule was no better. It was a very oppressive regime and 'looked upon Kashmiris as little better than cattle'.[20] Both Afghans and Sikhs were politically novice, culturally coarse, bereft of any refinement and notably oppressive, crudely partisan and extracting in their approach to people and the place. However, in spite of their oppressive and partisan character, the valley of Kashmir retained its identity as a politico-cultural unit. However, Kashmiris under the strangulating and oppressive nature of the Sikh regime were almost pushed to reconcile with tyranny and lost much of 'grandeur and heroism' that characterized them in earlier times.[21]

During the first Anglo-Sikh war (1846), the British East India Company defeated the Sikh state with the clandestine support from (till the then Raja of Jammu and the functioning prime minister of the Sikh state) Gulab Singh. After defeating the Sikhs, British connived in a manner that constrained the Sikh state to cede the control of Kashmir valley over to Gulab Singh through the Treaty of Amritsar mainly as a reward by the British for the clandestine help that he rendered to them to defeat Sikh state while being its prime minister.[22] The acquisition of Kashmir valley by Gulab Singh in 1846, under the British colonial design, and its incorporation in his Dogra Kingdom marked a major boost to his political fortunes. Kashmir represented a name, recognition and a long political and civilizational history, and gifted people

---

[18] For Mughal contributions to Kashmir, see Lawrence, *The Valley of Kashmir,* 194–197.

[19] Ibid., 197.

[20] For the nature of Sikh rule in Kashmir, see Bazaz, *Struggle for Freedom,* 113–117.

[21] Ibid., 115–116.

[22] For a comprehensive and lucid account of factors for British to transfer Kashmir to Gulab Singh, see Bawa Satinder Singh, *The Jammu Fox; A Biography of Maharaja Gulab Singh of Kashmir, 1792–1857* (New Delhi: Heritage Publishers, 1988), particularly see pages 105–122.

stable economy and recognition as a centre for learning, which no other unit of his kingdom could even come closer to. Acquisition of Kashmir transformed Raja Gulab Singh of Jammu to Maharaja Gulab Singh of a new construct called the Jammu & Kashmir state. It marked Kashmir's political and economic marginalization and beginning of a new and, from the point of view of the present study, crucial phase in its long and chequered contemporary history. Many of its present-day problems are borne out of this factor. In this process, the historically held Kashmir's position of centrality in relation to its surroundings was lost to a new political equation under which Jammu (a hilly terrain with little political history) because of ruling dynasty's ethnic, religious and political roots in the region emerged as a centre of power and parallel capital to Srinagar in Kashmir. As compared to Kashmir, Jammu considerably benefited within the new equation. From a small fiefdom confined to Jammu central hills, its provincial status was expanded to include a large number of newly conquered regions that were historically more significant than Jammu.

Under the new dispensation that lasted for more than a century, the Dogra dynasty, on account of the very nature of state formation and also because of the character of its politics, became partisan in favour of the Dogra community (that constituted less than 15% of the state's population), to which it belonged, in particular and Hindus in general. Dogra rulers designated the princely state as Hindu, giving it a partisan communal character in spite of the fact that Muslims overall constituted almost 80 per cent of its population while as in the Kashmir province Muslims constituted more than 95 per cent of the population.[23] Under this partisan arrangement, Muslims in general and Kashmiri Muslims in particular suffered a number of disadvantages, resulting in their alienation, deprivations and sufferings. They suffered these disadvantages on account of discrimination in services, heavy taxation on handicraft, forced labour, etc.[24] For Dogras in general, Kashmir was a conquered

---

[23] For a very comprehensive account of Hindu nature of Dogra state, see Mridu Rai, *Hindu Rulers, Muslim Subjects* (Princeton, NJ: Princeton University Press, 2004); for specifics references, see pages 7 and 80.

[24] See G. H. Khan, *Freedom Movement in Kashmir: 1931–1940* (New Delhi: Light & Life Publishers, 1980), 11–31.

and even a 'purchased territory' and therefore deserved neither empathy nor consideration. During the Dogra rule, the people of the state suffered hard because of the institution of Jagirdari system. The claim of the ruler that 'all lands in Kashmir belong to him' shows the feudal character of Jammu & Kashmir state.[25] The privileged class of Hindus, Dogra Rajputs, Kashmiri Pandits and Punjabi Hindus was very close to Dogra rulers and got the maximum benefits and *jagirs* from them. In fact, the majority of the higher posts were held by Dogra Rajputs themselves.[26] The aforementioned information clearly highlights that the condition of the common masses comprised mainly of Muslims was pathetic. Muslims were always discriminated against and were always kept out of power. Such policies had to have very serious implications in the light of increasing emancipating atmosphere developing around the state.[27]

These discriminative and oppressive policies against the Muslims of the state in general and of Kashmir valley in particular continued till the beginning of the 20th century that witnessed the emergence of a wave of emancipative and anti-colonial forces and movements across the colonized world. Looking from this perspective, the 1931 uprising was preceded by many important developments, which suggest that emancipative forces were already at work in Kashmir. The symptomatic of these included the Shawlbaf agitation in 1865, establishment of the first Muslim school in 1889 and the subsequent transformation of the initiative into a movement in the form of Anjumani Nusrat-ul-Islam (1905) with a reformist agenda and for providing Kashmiri Muslims leadership on a number of issues and problems concerning the community, the silk factory workers' agitation (1924) and other such developments that became reflective of the growing awakening and agitation of Kashmiri Muslim masses against the policies of personalized and discriminative feudal order. One of the important developments of the time included the submission of memorandum to the

---

[25] Ibid., 11–17.

[26] P. S. Verma, *Jammu and Kashmir at the Political Crossroads* (New Delhi: Vikas Publications, 1994), 12.

[27] Ibid., 11.

Viceroy of India in 1924 by some concerned and prominent Kashmiris highlighting the problems and disadvantages suffered by Kashmiri Muslims and soliciting their redress. The focus of the memorandum was on extension of rights on land for peasants, greater representation for Muslims in the state services and steps to be taken for improving their educational status. This all reflected growing awareness and assertion of Muslims of their rights, who in spite of constituting an overwhelming majority in the state population were marginalized in almost all walks of life. It also demonstrated their growing willingness to stand up and strive for their rightful place. One important factor that we need to take note of in the context of Kashmir is the impact of the Punjab Press and more particularly the concern of the Kashmiri (mainly Muslim) diaspora settled across northern India in general and Punjab in particular that included some of its eminent members such as Allama Muhammad Iqbal, Sanaullah Amritsari, Muhammad Din Fauq and Saifuddin Kitchlew. This diaspora did its utmost for alleviating the plight of what it called Kashmiri nation. A number of periodicals/ papers were published from Lahore solely devoted to the awakening of the Kashmiri Muslims and focusing on their plight. Primarily, the Kashmir Muslim diaspora focused on the awakening of neglected Muslims of the state by invoking their Muslim consciousness as a community of deprivation.

In spite of promotion of Muslim consciousness, the freedom movement that emerged in the state remained committed to secular demands for education, employment, representation in governance process and government services, taxation reforms, land rights for peasants, etc. The agitation was also joined by the Muslims of Jammu. However, in the context of the time, and in response to the nature of regime and of problem that Muslims confronted, the political movement that was formed to pursue the grievances or demands of people was named as the Muslim Conference (MC), as it worked for the empowerment of Muslims who had remained marginalized within the state. But just within less than a decade of its formation, the organization reflecting the Kashmir's inclusive, composite ethos was renamed as National Conference (NC) with commitment of secular values of national emancipation, democracy, inclusiveness and progressive empowerment of all sections of society irrespective of cast and creed. Soon after this change in 1949, the Jammu chapter of the organization resurrected the MC to suit the orientation in the Jammu region. This division subsequently had a far-reaching impact on the politics of the state and that of subcontinent as a whole.

Difference in orientation in the context of a larger polarization in mainland India between the Muslim League and Indian National Congress had a serious bearing on the politics of the state with far-reaching implications. Gradually, the two branches of the freedom movement in the state, MC and NC, developed political proximity with rival political forces in mainland Indian depending on their politico-ideological orientations. That meant that NC developed closer proximity with the Indian National Congress and its leadership particularly with Jawaharlal Nehru and Mahatma Gandhi. Most important, during the crucial year of 1947 at the time of the British withdrawal and partition that resulted in the division of the subcontinent into India and Pakistan when all border regions were overtaken by violence and bloodshed, Kashmir remained peaceful. Even when the state's Jammu region saw violence and killing of a large number of Muslims, the Muslim majority in Kashmir remained calm and peaceful. Thereafter, at the crucial juncture of a challenging situation that emerged, Kashmir rooted NC leadership and supported and endorsed Maharaja Hari Singh's belated accession with India on 27 October 1947. It supported accession with India on assumption of its democratic and secular credentials and retaining substantial powers to the state on lines of terms of the accession deed signed by Maharaja Hari Singh. Maharaja through the instrument of accession surrendered his jurisdiction on defence, foreign affairs and communication towards the dominion government.

Subsequently, when the question of defining the state's relationship with the Union of India was taken up within the Constituent Assembly of India, the interim government of the state led by Sheikh Mohammad Abdullah pressed for a special position for the state. It sought that the state's relationship with the centre be restricted to only three subjects indicated in the instrument of accession.[28] The leadership that represented the state in spite of having supported the accession with India strongly wanted Kashmir's special identity to be preserved and safeguarded and have enough powers to implement the progressive socially emancipative agenda for social engineering that it had adopted in 1944 as an instrument of social change in Kashmir. There were several rounds of discussions and a number of drafts exchanged between the state representatives and the Government of India before the two parties came to agree on what became Article 370 of the Indian Constitution on its adoption in November 1949.[29] The agreed draft was prepared by Ayyanger, who had taken over as minister of Kashmir affairs in consultations with Mirza Afzal Beg and other NC members nominated for the Constituent Assembly of India.[30] In retrospect, it seems that it was because of the international dimension of the issue that the leadership in Delhi was constrained to agree to such a position because it could not afford to alienate the local leadership completely at the critical time.[31] Therefore, on the promulgation of the Constitution on 26 January 1950, it became clear that only two of its articles, namely Article 1, declaring India as the union of state, and Article 370, which defined the relationship of the state with the Indian union, became applicable to the state directly and completely.[32] Under Article 370, Jammu & Kashmir was made an exception to the

---

[28] In October 1947 as emergency administrator, changed to prime minister in March 1948; A. S. Anand, *The Constitution of Jammu and Kashmir* (New Delhi: Universal, 1994), 117–118.

[29] For a detailed account of the process through which Article 370 was evolved and divergent perceptions on the issue, see M. K. Teng, *Kashmir's Special Status* (New Delhi: Orient Publishers, 1975).

[30] Noor Ahmad Baba, 'Kashmir Special Status: Myth and Reality', in *Conflict in Jammu and Kashmir*, ed. V. R. Raghavan (New Delhi: Vij Books, 2012), 191–208.

[31] For assimilationist mind set in Delhi, see Ashok Behuria, 'Demands for Autonomy; Internal Weaknesses of a Multiethnic, Multicultural, and Multinational State', in *Searching Peace for Central and South Asia*, eds. Monique Mekenkamp, Paul Van Tongeren and Hans Van de Veen (Colorado: Lynne Rienner publishers Inc., 2002), 348.

[32] Enumerated Jammu & Kashmir within the list of such states in the Schedule 1 of the Constitution Of India.

application of Article 238, which regulated relations between Group 'B' of the Indian states and the Union government.[33] It explained that the power of Parliament to make laws for the said state shall be limited to the subjects mentioned in the instrument of accession, that is, defence, foreign affairs and communication. The president of India had to identify matters in the central and the concurrent list 'in consultation with the government of the state' which corresponds with those specified in the instrument of accession.[34] Thus, as per the democratic aspirations of its people, articulated by its leadership, the state was able to secure a special position within the Constitution of India.

So far so good, but Kashmir's assertion of a progressive, secular and inclusive identity that seemed to be going well came to face serious external and internal challenges. Pakistan had assumed that as per the partition framework Kashmir will accede to it because of its Muslim character and greater geographical proximity with it. Therefore, the conflict that had begun in Jammu with the revolt of Muslims in its Poonch district and the tribal invasion subsequently supported by the Pakistan's regular army culminated in the effective division of the state between what became as Indian and Pakistani controlled parts of Jammu & Kashmir.[35] In addition, Pakistani contestation of Maharaja's accession, Indian commitment to referring the issue of final dispensation of the state to its people, internationalization of the issue and the UN

---

[33] This Group (B) of states included former princely states that included Jammu & Kashmir. Jammu & Kashmir in other words even though a princely state was to be governed differently from the rest under Article 370.

[34] S. P. Sathe, 'Art 370 and Jammu and Kashmir: For a Future Federalisation of Polity', *Mainstream, 25* July 1992, 14.

[35] As a result of the Karachi Agreement of 1949 that created a ceasefire between India and Pakistan under the supervision of the United Nations Commission for India and Pakistan (UNCIP), the former princely state of Jammu & Kashmir got divided in de facto terms between what is known as Indian- and Pakistani-controlled Kashmirs. As a result of this, out of the total area of 222,236 sq. km of what constituted Jammu & Kashmir, 36 per cent came, and is, under the control of Pakistan and the rest, about 64 per cent, remained under the control of India till 1963 when the Chinese, through aggression, occupied about 18 per cent of the state's territory leaving only about 46 per cent under Indian control. 'Some Facts and Figures about Jammu and Kashmir', *Manthan*, New Delhi, October 1991.

endorsement of the right to self-determination of the people combined together to make Kashmir an international dispute that continued to strain the identity of Kashmir.[36]

All this caused a serious challenge for Kashmir's political identity and predicaments for the leadership that had a vision for its future development. Even though the national movement rooted in Kashmir valley after having lost the option for an independent state envisioned in its Naya Kashmir (New Kashmir) Manifesto in the complex context of politics created by the decision of the division with independence of the subcontinent on religious lines, it had demonstrated preference in favour of what it assumed to be a secular democratic India.[37] It was able to secure a special status within the Indian Constitution that allowed security to the Muslim-majority character of the state and to secure sufficient powers for implementing the progressive vision it had for the state. In the changed context, the progressive and emancipative outlook of the secular democratic leadership of NC had a very long-term impact on the Kashmiri society. One of it was the land reforms that were initiated in 1950, whereby landless peasant gained land ownership. It contributed to long-term empowering of most of the so far disposed peasantry who in the context of Kashmir were Muslims. Other measures that further reinforced this emancipative trend were measures such as free universal education and health care. These measures with the passing of time produced a new generation of educated Muslim youth with claim for government services which till then was almost the sole prerogative of the minuscule Kashmiri Pandit community. This process of equalizing was with time being resented by the Pandits who traditionally enjoyed a sort of monopoly of government jobs because of the low education levels among Muslims who otherwise constituted more than 95 per cent of the population

---

[36] For a comprehensive account of all these aspects, see Sisir Gupta, *Kashmir: A Study in India Pakistan Relations* (New Delhi: Asian Publishing House, 1966), 110–139.

[37] Andrew Whitehead, 'The Rise & Fall of New Kashmir' in *Kashmir, History, Politics, Representation*, ed. Chitralekha Zutshi (Cambridge: Cambridge University Press, 2018), 70–88.

in the valley. But in spite of this emerging competitiveness between Pandits and Muslims in the valley, their social equation continued to be cordial and harmonious. However, greater challenge that was caused to community relationships and regional equation came mainly from the following two counts.

1. As stated earlier that within the political construct of multi-ethno-regional Jammu & Kashmir, Kashmir had lost geopolitical eminence and autonomy as an identity that it enjoyed historically as a result of Gulab Singh's taking over its possession in 1846 when British facilitated its transfer to him as part of their own colonial political project. After 1947, because of the effective division of the state, the regional polarization on its Indian side was further reinforced because in the changed situation, the three regions of Jammu, Kashmir and Ladakh got a distinct majority religious character.[38] In this situation, the progressive nationalist vision of the NC leadership (that was mainly rooted in the valley) was being resented by the dominant elite in Jammu and Ladakh (that because of the division were changed into Muslim minority parts of the state). These created internal fissures within the state, facilitating external intervention and subsequently undermining of the whole autonomy project.[39]

2. The NC leadership in its visualization had seen India through the prism of Nehru and Gandhi, and their secular and pluralist plan for the country. However, the leadership soon after accession and more after drafting of the Indian Constitution began to see alternative non-secular forces asserting assimilationist agenda for the country and pressurizing for undoing of Kashmir's autonomy. These forces even supported/promoted communal polarization within the state.[40] That resulted in bringing in greater strains in the relationship between the governments in Kashmir and that of Indian

---

[38] In the united Jammu & Kashmir till 1947, all the three regions were with Muslim majority. But with the division, Jammu and Ladakh of the state on the Indian side became Muslim minority regions. Jammu turned to be a Hindu majority and Ladakh was being identified as a Buddhist majority region.

[39] Baba, 'Kashmir Special Status'.

[40] Ibid.

union resulting in 1953 dismissal of Sheikh's government and his being sent behind the bars. This further complicated the Kashmir politics by undermining people's trust in secular democratic credential of the Indian State. After having dismissed the most popular leader whose endorsement of accession was considered essential by the Indian leadership during 1947, the Government of India had to depend on unpopular leadership to run the state that required elections to be manipulated.[41]

The combination of these dimensions continued to complicate Kashmir politics and considerably strained its inclusive and syncretic character. This undermined the faith that the secular democratic leadership had placed in India's secularist and pluralist vision and weakened their influence.[42] In a way it vindicated the protagonists of the two-nation theory in the state. This strengthened the Pakistani case and its ideological underpinnings for the two-nation theory that by implication meant that the Muslim identity of Kashmir cannot be secured within what it said was primarily a 'Hindu' India with a secular facade. In this context, within the state and valley dormant supporters of the two-nation theory gained a new lease of life as the contention of secular Muslim leadership had been considerably weakened. However, the movement for self-determination that was launched in 1955 under the leadership of Sheikh Abdullah continued to be committed to secular, pluralistic and non-violent values and methodology.[43] But it began to be undermined because of number of factors. Internally, Sheikh's compromise in 1975 accord whereby he regained power without having been able to undo the erosion to the state's autonomy carried out between his dismissal in 1953 and assumption of power in 1975. It undermined him and his brand of secular politics. So the Islamist forces committed to self-determination of state with accession to Pakistan as a preference began to assert as soon as the towering person of Sheikh

---

[41] Ibid.

[42] A. G. Noorani, *Article 370: A Constitutional History of Kashmir* (New Delhi: Oxford University Press, 2011), 9–10.

[43] The movement for self-determination that was launched in 1955 under the banner of Plebiscite Front by Mirza Afzal Beg under the patronage of Sheikh Abdullah.

got removed from the state with his death in 1982. Then Mrs Gandhi's personalized government at the Centre pushed for undemocratically engineering the dismissal of Farooq Abdullah's popularly elected government. This further undermined the people's faith in democratic credentials of the Indian State in relation to Jammu & Kashmir. More importantly, it encouraged the traditional leadership—inclined towards a more Islamist agenda—to get activated and become assertive within a globally facilitating context. It began with a number of developments within the Muslim world that saw assertion of political Islam particularly in and after the 1970s with impact on South Asia. It happened along with technological changes that brought in television transmissions to the global stage as an effective transmission of news, ideas and influences across countries and regions. This facilitated an effective news interface between the Muslim lands and Kashmir. These developments that created a facilitating context for political Islam to emerge were as follows:

1. After 1967 Arab's defeat with Israel, the secular forces within the Arab world led by President Nasser of Egypt declined considerably, and conservative Gulf regimes led by Saudi Arabia gained ascendancy within the Arab Muslim world. It was more particularly in the 1970s that some new development in the vicinity of Southwest Asia began to have a very profound impact all across Muslim Southwest Asian region. It began with conservative monarchies in the Gulf led by Saudi Arabia with largest discovered oil reserves gaining financial clout as a result of soaring oil prices because the Organization of the Petroleum Exporting Countries (OPEC) was able to push for increasing prices for oil.[44]

2. It was then followed by the Iranian Revolution of 1978–1979 that generated revolutionary appeal across the Muslim world. Its revolutionary rhetoric message for and of revolutionary Islam, democracy and republicanism had a destabilizing impact on conservative and hereditary regimes in the Gulf region. It prompted these

---

[44] Noor Ahmad Baba, 'Nasser's Pan-Arab Radicalism and the Saudi Drive for Islamic Solidarity: A Response for Security', *India Quarterly: A Journal of International Affairs 48,* nos. 1 and 2 (January–June, 1992): 3–22.

conservatory regimes with their growing financial clout to counter Iran by invoking Sunni consciousness among Muslims. This began to polarize Muslim societies including in South Asia on sectarian lines. It particularly had impact on vulnerable Pakistani society that had begun to get polarized under these external stimulus with a facilitating regime under Zia-ul-Haq (1977–1988) who had his own project of Islamization. This polarization along Shia–Sunni sectarian lines was further reinforced after the Iran–Iraq war that began in the early 1980s as both sides in the war began to invoke support within their side of the fault lines. In this, Saudi Arabia began to push for and promote a more literal and hard-line interpretation of its own Wahhabi brand of Islam with its growing resources. With this, the Muslim societies were not only divided on Shia–Sunni lines, but it also led to Sunni fragmentation on various *maslaki* (sub-sectarian) lines. The worst case of this extreme multi-level fragmentation of Muslim society happened in Pakistan where violent attacks led to mass killings in mosques and other shrines of various historically revered saints. Such sectarian sentiment did impact Kashmir to the extent that a host of new mosques started coming up with sectarian identification, more prominently Salafi mosques, reflecting the Saudi influence and funding.[45] But probably because of the character of Kashmiri society it did not lead to the significant levels of social fragmentation and violence on sectarian lines of the kind that was witnessed elsewhere in various Muslim societies.

3. Third development that had very serious impact on the region was the Soviet invasion of Afghanistan in 1979 that continued for about a decade and plunged Afghanistan in an unending turmoil. It brought in a number of politically motivated powers led by the United States together to prop up a new crop of conservative and radical jihadis (fighters) in defence of 'Muslim Afghanistan' in resisting to the atheistic communist power, the Soviet Union. This development further impacted Pakistan that was used as a frontline

---

[45] According to one estimate, during the reign of King Fahd (1982–2005), over $75 billion was spent in efforts to spread Wahhabi Islam. The money was used to establish 200 Islamic colleges, 210 Islamic centres, 1,500 mosques and 2,000 schools for Muslim children in Muslim- and non-Muslim-majority countries.

state against the Soviet occupation that radicalized sections within its society and granted legitimacy to non-state violence and facilitated flow of weapons. This at one level undermined the Pakistani State and liberal sections within its society. In spite of various efforts, Pakistani State has not been able to overcome this problem completely so far. This impacted Kashmir situation more directly because of existence of the political problem, resentment caused by its non-resolution and growing alienation of its society during the 1980s, particularly after the emergence of the militancy.

Because of these influences combined with growing communalization of the Indian politics, idiom of politics in Kashmir began to draw increasingly Islamist that was gaining ground in Pakistan. Such trends gained strength with weakening of secular, democratic and nationalist elements in Kashmir politics. Major turning point in this connection can be to a great extent traced back to unjustified and even 'unconstitutional' dismissal of Farooq Abdullah's government in July 1984 and installation of a regime which for its survival had to impose curfew for about 70 days of its initial 90 days existence to pre-empt any protest demonstrations in the valley.[46] This exposed the hollowness of the Indira–Abdullah accord that had brought NC back to power with the promise of restoring the autonomous position to the state lost since 1953.[47] It was during the subsequent Governor's/President's Rule in 1986–1987 that extremist trends in Kashmir politics started emerging and gaining strength. Parties with proved secular, nationalist credentials like NC started losing ground and new forces with more radical non-secular Islamist tinge started gaining ground in the valley. These forces grouped together under the name of the Muslim United Front (MUF).

This situation prompted Farooq Abdullah to enter into an alliance with the Congress party that was in power at Delhi. This alliance totally undermined him and his capacity of representing the

---

[46] For a comprehensive background and the fraudulent nature of the dismissal, see B. K. Nehru, *Nice Guys Finish Second* (New Delhi: Viking, 1997), 609–641.

[47] Noor Ahmad Baba, 'Democracy & Governance in Kashmir', in *The Parchment of Kashmir, History, Society and Politics*, ed. Nyla Ali Khan (New York, NY: Palgrave Macmillan, 2012), 111–112.

distinctive Kashmiri aspirations and identifying with the identity urges of the people. In other words, it blocked the normal and moderate channels of expression of Kashmiri sentiments, thereby paving the way for extremist/more radical forces to replace them as vanguards of the people and their interests in the state. This situation helped in strengthening the MUF to make it a major force in Kashmir politics. So much so that NC–Congress alliance had to resort to a large-scale rigging in order to secure a clear majority in the state assembly and prevented the MUF from winning a respectable number of seats in the state assembly. By doing so, an opportunity of exercising an influence of moderation on the MUF was missed by denying it an opportunity of participation in the democratic process and thereby co-opting it into the system. Instead, this exposed the NC–Congress alliance further. The people lost faith in democracy and the younger elements felt that in order to get justice the only alternative left for them was to resort to armed violence. More significantly it marked the resurgence of a separatist movement in the valley with vigour never witnessed earlier.[48] So we need to note that the present problem in Kashmir has not been the problem born out of militancy. In fact, the militancy was the outcome of the Kashmir problem. Because of the regional and international atmosphere, it began to draw from the support from Pakistan and the Islamist idiom growing in that country due to factors indicated earlier.

After 1987, the situation in Kashmir went beyond the normal political discourse in which predominant majority of people lost faith in the electoral process. The situation in the state became worse since 1989 when there was a popular uprising combined with the beginning of militant activities. First group of young men who took to violence comprised mostly those who had actually worked on the side of the MUF during the 1987 elections. These people were subjected to severe torture for their association with the opposition alliance. The objective situation thus created provided a good opportunity for Pakistan to

---

[48] In the words of Sumantra Bose, 'I stress that the roots of the crisis that erupted in 1989–90 lie in a post-1947 history of denial of democratic rights and institutions to the people of J&K, particularly those of IJK'. Sumantra Bose, *Kashmir: Roots of Conflict, Pathways to Peace* (New Delhi: Vistaar Publications, 203), 7.

get involved in Kashmir as never before. The experts have almost unanimously held the view that one of the most important factors contributing to the post–1989 turmoil in Kashmir has been the total incredibility of its electoral practice.[49]

Factors that also helped in strengthening a new hope in the success of the movement were as follows:

1. Soviet withdrawal (1989) from Afghanistan had symbolic significance. A small country defeating a superpower became a big inspiration. This also meant that Pakistan's security establishment that had gained expertise and experience in Afghanistan would have confidence to focus on Jammu & Kashmir.
2. The breakdown of the Soviet Union (1991) that followed the Soviet withdrawal from Afghanistan resulted in the independence of six Muslim states in Central Asia and Caucasus also became a big inspiration for people in Kashmir.

So the context was quite encouraging and gave a hope to militants, their supporters in Pakistan and general masses in Kashmir. It needs to be noted that militancy in the early 1990s as it emerged was mainly symbolic and nominal. It was the wholehearted massive support from general masses all across in the valley that made the movement a major challenge for the Indian State to deal with. Massive public demonstrations with over million people's participation became a regular feature in the valley in 1990.[50] The all-out mobilization of the repressive machinery by the Indian State gave rise to the issue of human rights violations. So much so that it is generally admitted that Kashmir began to earn the dubious distinction of having the heaviest

---

[49] For a more detailed account of the democratic deficit in the state, see Sumantra Bose, *The Challenge in Kashmir* (New Delhi: SAGE Publications, 1997), 23–54; Sten Widmalm, *Democracy and Violent Separatism in India: Kashmir in a Comparative Perspective* (Uppsala: Uppsala University, 1997).

[50] Over million people's participation became a regular feature in the valley in 1990.

military presence within a civilian area in the world.[51] This was also the time when Hindutva forces began to gain greater ground within mainland India. The increasing mobilization of these forces culminated in the demolition of the Babri Masjid in Ayodhya by the Hindu mobs in 1992.[52] This not only led to the communal polarization in India but also had bearing on the balance of forces in Kashmir. It was within this overall atmosphere of the communal polarization that Islamist pro-Pakistan Hizbul Mujahideen began to gain ascendancy over otherwise secular nationalist Jammu Kashmir Liberation Front (JKLF) that had initiated the armed resistance in Kashmir. Thus, Islamism did increasingly become the idiom of politics but it still by and large continued to espouse political objectives like *azadi* (freedom)/accession with Pakistan without mixing it with much of pan-Islamic aspirations. However, Islamic slogans combined with demand for *azadi* were a factor in scaring pro-India Kashmiri Pandits and even many Muslims. Their migration from the valley in large numbers has been a major setback to Kashmir's syncretic and pluralist identity with far-reaching implications.[53]

The militant movement getting divided broadly into pro-independence and pro-accession (to Pakistan) groups resulted in a series of group clashes. However, in spite of this premature division in the militant ranks, they continued to receive popular support and approval. The gun in hand raised the social position of even those who otherwise belonged to a very humble background. As a result, more and more young men started joining the militancy. Many of them hardly shared any commitment to the cause for which the militancy had earlier been initiated. But the greater pressure from security forces pushed many

---

[51] Shubh Mathur, 'Life and Death in the Borderlands: Indian Sovereignty and Military Impunity', *Race & Class* 54, no. 1 (2012): 42. She says that according to conservative estimates there are about 500,000 military/paramilitary personnel present in the state.

[52] A. K. Pasha, 'Communal Revivalism in India: Its Impact on Ties with West Asia and North Africa', *in Communal Revivalism in India: A Study of External Implications*, ed. Muchkund Dubey (New Delhi: Har Anand, 1994).

[53] See Ankur Datta, *On Uncertain Ground: Displaced Kashmiri Pandits in Jammu & Kashmir* (Oxford: Oxford University Press, 2016).

such elements to change their side to what came to be known as pro-government/renegade militants. These so-called reformed militants operating in liaison with or on behalf of the army and paramilitary forces 'emerged as a major menace in many areas of the valley' by getting involved into a number of criminal activities. They did help to weaken and contain militancy for some time. But in the process they further alienated people. However, the increasingly coercive response to the state and its success against militancy was temporary as it re-emerged with greater vengeance and sophistication. In the changed situation towards the latter part of the 1990s, we saw the militancy getting confined to people with higher degree of motivation, dedication and skill drawn both from within and without. In the process, the militancy also gained the pan-Islamic dimension, and non-local groups such as Lashkar-e-Taiba and Harkatul Ansar gained ascendancy over the local groups like Hizbul Mujahideen. In spite of the very difficult situation, the militants continued to find the recruits from within, in addition to contingents of support that were drawing from outside. The state authority in Kashmir largely depended on coercive and repressive agencies. It became a reflection of its weakness rather than strength. It was in this context that the then Army Chief Mr S. Padmanabhan and the Defence Minister of India Mr George Fernandes echoed the considered view that Kashmir is fundamentally a political problem and requires a political settlement.[54] This was the view that was also shared by then Prime Minister of India Atal Bihari Vajpayee. Even the people in Kashmir who have been historically used to living a peaceful life within the comfort of the serene surroundings could not sustain violence for long and have always responded positively to the call for peace in a situation of hope.

Along with this realization it was the changing international situation in the context of 9/11 that became the basis for an initiative for dialogue. Kashmir began to change for better on account of these two following factors:

---

[54] See *Greater Kashmir*, 'Fernandes Echoes Padmanabhan', Srinagar, 24 October 2000.

1. One of these was delegitimization of violence as a means of political objectives in which even Pakistan found it more difficult to support the cross-border militancy.
2. The positive context was further strengthened because of the peace process that began to consolidate particularly after 2003–2004.

In this context of evolving peace process that significant initiatives such as Cross LoC (Line of Control) bus service, opening of trade points across the LoC in Jammu & Kashmir were taken.[55] It was in addition to the Indo–Pak agreement on ceasefire across the LoC. These steps were viewed positively by people not only in Kashmir but also across the subcontinent. It was in this situation of overall hope that significant efforts were made to resolve Kashmir issue on the permanent basis through a very creative approach. Musharraf's four-point proposal to resolve the Kashmir was seen as the realistic option to resolve the issue on permanent basis. In this situation, militancy got considerably weakened across Kashmir and in words of a well-grounded Kashmiri journalist it was being assumed that 'Kashmir is the first conflict-ridden Muslim region in the world where people have consciously made a transition from violence to non-violence, and this includes the staunch Islamists too.'[56]

However, this hope for peace was short-lived. A series of developments and a combination of factors further aggravated the situation. It began with the collapse of the peace process. By 2007, Musharraf, as a result of lawyers' agitation against him, began to lose grip on the power. After 26/11 (2008) Mumbai attack, India suspended all peace talks with Pakistan. The ceasefire agreement that was reached in 2003 began to be breached thereafter. Internal situation in Kashmir began to worsen as a result of the changed policies. Then we witnessed a series of summer unrests in Kashmir beginning in 2008 and continuing in 2009. It was prolonged public protests and a chain of *hartals* (strikes) combined with stone pelting defining a new mode of agitation. The

---

[55] Noor Ahmad Baba, 'Kashmir Bus: Small but a Step in the Right Direction', *Peace & Conflict*, April 2005 (New Delhi: Institute of Peace and Conflict Studies).
[56] Muzamil Jaleel, 'Unarmed Freedom Fighters', *The Guardian,* 31 August 2008.

major setback came in June 2010 with news of fake encounter killing of three Kashmiri youths by army at Macchil (a village in Kupwara district in Kashmir, which it initially had claimed to be were 'Pakistani infiltrators') leading to prolonged agitation that saw more than 100 youths being killed during public demonstrations that continued for a number of months. It was followed by the execution of M. Afzal Guru in February 2013, the Parliament attack accused about whom general impression in Kashmir was that he did not get a fair trial.[57] The secretive manner in which he was executed even not allowing his family to meet him and not handing over his dead body to his family for proper burial added to the mass anger.[58] Non-empathetic and non-responsive nature of the Indian State and its purely coercive handling of the situation angered Kashmiri youth marking the emergence of a new phase of militancy that was rooted locally drawing mainly from the educated young that used the new media to connect to people in general and youth in particular. The typical representative of this phase of militancy was Burhan Wani from South Kashmir. He became popular, and through his proficient use of social media there was greater interface with the common masses. It began appealing more Kashmiri youth for joining the militancy. Burhan quickly rose to become the commander of a Kashmiri militant group Hizbul Mujahideen. Rather than being involved in violent actions, he emerged as a greater challenge to the Indian State for his increasing popularity as a symbol of political defiance of the state.[59]

But instead of redressing the situation by creative responses, the state continued with its repressive policies of using disproportional coercion even against peaceful and stone-pelting protests that began to gain increasing currency with the growing alienation. The new militancy continued to be rooted locally mostly as part of the Hizbul Mujahideen that kept a conscious distance from the emerging radical

---

[57] Even many others in India and across the globe shared this view. Arundhati Roy said, 'The hanging of Afzal Guru is a stain on India's democracy'.

[58] Shujaat Bukhari, 'How Dead Butt, Guru Help Militancy to Live and Survive' (editorial), *Rising Kashmir*, 16 February 2018.

[59] There was no significant evidence of his participating in any encounter with security agencies.

Islamist trends that began to emerge and operate in the Muslim West Asia. However, the situation began to worsen after Hindu nationalist BJP, wedded to more muscular and assimilationist policy in relation to Kashmir, took over power in Delhi in 2014. The situation took a turn to the worse in 2015 after BJP became a coalition partner of the Peoples Democratic Party (PDP) in the formation of the government in the state. PDP aligned with the BJP in spite of the fact that it had been completely rejected by voters within the valley. BJP's ascendancy increasingly began to create apprehensions about undermining of political identity, autonomy that was incorporated within the Indian Constitution to safeguard the special character of the state. The situation deteriorated further in 2016 when Burhan Wani, who had gained considerable popularity as a symbol of resistance, was killed along with his colleagues in a trap on 8 July that year. This led to massive protests particularly in South Kashmir. The state handling of these protests resulted in a heavy loss of life, resulting in the agitation that broke all records of the past in terms of longevity, expanse of areas affected and civilian casualties. There were protests all across Kashmir that even extended to Muslim districts of Jammu and Ladakh. The State as usual used coercion in dealing with the protests that led to prolonged shutdowns, hundred plus casualties, thousands injured and maiming that included blinding (full and partial) of more than 100 children/youth (including girls) across Kashmir. As a result of all this, public anger has continued because of which public protests and stone pelting encounters with the security forces have become a regular feature more particularly in South Kashmir that had remained relatively peaceful even during the heyday of militancy.[60] The pronounced use of muscular policy in dealing with Kashmir bereft of any initiative for meaningful dialogue and peace has resulted in further alienation of

---

[60] Hundreds of our bright children have lost their eyesight, shattering their dreams in life. Thousands are maimed and grievously injured. Many of our civil and political leaders and youth are being detained under various repressive laws. Noor Ahmad Baba, 'Kashmir Protests: Case for a Critical Reflection', *Greater Kashmir*, 25 October 2016.

the Kashmiri youth and many of them mostly educated ones joining militancy in recent years.[61]

Thus, as stated earlier, Kashmir militancy had remained by and large immune to ultra-radical ideologies with pan-Islamist agenda even when there was a dramatic rise of groups like ISIS/Daesh destabilizing the entire Arab-Muslim West Asian region, sending alarm bells across the globe. So far, Kashmir in spite of the abnormal politics, violence, repression and vulnerability has not seen serious inroads of religious extremism because of its ethos. That is why groups like ISIS have not found much appeal among angry youth in a big way.[62] It is because the social evolution of people in Kashmir is different from places like Afghanistan because of which it cannot sustain violence beyond a point where it becomes a mass phenomenon. But that should not make us complacent to such possibilities. There is a need to be cautious against such trends. There is evidence that suggests that during the past year or two, a small number of Kashmiri youth has been attracted to such radical extremist ideologies.[63] If immediate redressive measures are not taken, the vulnerability is likely to grow because of the following factors.

1. Kashmir is predominantly a Muslim society that is undergoing a raging conflict as a result of which its youth are caught in situation of suffocation and hopelessness.
2. The use of hard-line muscular approach to the situation in Kashmir and absence of hope for a dialogue and peace have increased the vulnerability to such influences as we witnessed during past year or two. Growing religious intolerance and obscurantist forces ruling India also add to such vulnerabilities.
3. Because of recent technological developments, there has been social erosion in Kashmir as elsewhere in the world. The process

---

[61] *The Economic Times*, 'Spurt in Kashmiris Joining militancy in 2017', 25 December 2017; see also Mudasir Ahmad, 'Why Educated Kashmiri Youth Continue to Join Militancy', *The Wire*, 16 October 2018.

[62] Zafar Meraj, 'Groups Like ISIS Have Got No Public Support in Kashmir', *Multimedia*, 15 July 2018.

[63] Bharat Bhushan, 'Waiting for Moderators: Kashmiri Youth Are No Longer Amenable to Sagacious Advice', *Outlook*, 16 April, 2018.

of socialization of younger generations in the age-old tradition and ethos through living and experiencing together has been undermined by the exposure to new social media. In the changing atmosphere, the new generations instead of being connected with society live in the virtual world devoid of the real-world society. Therefore, instead of being socialized in the syncretic social setting, they are prone to get exposed to all kinds of influences.[64] With this, their vulnerability to extraneous and mostly undesirable influences is growing.

4. The new generations remain connected mainly with technological gadgets, experiencing the outer world through it, and get into gaming through artificial characters and through these to a heartless competition in the virtual world where pain and suffering, life and death lose psychological value requiring empathy and compassion. The life and death are seen merely as winning and losing and not as pain and suffering. Such upbringing is more likely to dehumanize human conduct vis-à-vis others.

Thus, within the discourse of repression, violence and protests, there is a prevalence of hopelessness, psychological trauma and economic distrust. The daily scenes of death and destruction have become a common sight. All this has undermined many of the traditional attributes that defined the identity of Kashmir. Muslim identity is more pronounced than ever. This is so at a time when extremist radical ideologies globally are drawing impressionable minds within Muslim societies through social media. So, as said earlier, vulnerabilities are growing and youth in Kashmir even if in very small numbers have been drawn to groups like ISIS and to their ideological idiom. The Kashmiri society has already lost some of its inherited virtues. But still we have a reason to believe that Kashmir in spite of such an atmosphere still exhibits a situation of hope, as in spite of the vulnerabilities the Kashmiri youth broadly exhibited resistance to the temptation of joining global radical forces in spite of being caught with a raging violent conflict. There is strong case for building on the still persisting positive indicators of civility in interpersonal and intercommunity conduct of the Kashmiri society.

---

[64] Ibid.

The best way of doing it and meeting the challenge of vulnerabilities is to address the situation of conflict through a peaceful dialogue that generates a process of reconciliation and a situation of hope. Because once resolved, Kashmir, as seen earlier, has all human potential and natural resources that will generate prosperity and opportunities for youth to remain beneficially absorbed and creatively engaged.

Chapter 3

Terrorist Narratives and Recruitment in South Asia
The India Factor[1]

Nazneen Mohsina and Sinan Siyech

INTRODUCTION

South Asia, one of the most ethnically, culturally, linguistically diverse and most populous region in the world, has been host to a number of local, regional and transnational militant groups since the 1980s.[2] It has experienced deeply entrenched ethno-religious hostility, communal violence and numerous wars, both inter- and intra-State.[3] Numerous individuals have, thus, fallen victim to indiscriminate terrorism with strong religious overtones. The transition to modernity and the political culture in some of these States has led to identification with religion and ethno-linguistic solidarities.[4] For example, religious nationalism and

---

[1] Parts of this chapter have appeared in a previously written essay by the same authors.

[2] Niranjan Dass, *Terrorism and Militancy in South Asia* (New Delhi: MD Publishers, 2006).

[3] S. D. Muni, 'Conflicts in South Asia: Causes, Consequences, Prospects' (working paper, ISAS, Singapore, 2013).

[4] Ibid.

religion is proliferating exceedingly in the public sphere in countries such as India, Sri Lanka, Pakistan and Bangladesh. Sri Lanka's decision to become a Sinhala–Buddhist State in 1959 by disregarding the sensitivities of its minority communities has caused serious internal conflicts, especially in its Tamil-occupied areas.[5] Similarly, India is facing violent separatist movements in Assam, Kashmir and the tribal areas of its northeastern region.[6] Likewise, intra–Muslim sectarian divides continue to rise in Pakistan and are also spilling over to Bangladesh, fuelling conflicts and spurring violence.[7] Interference from external groups, powers and elements (both governments and independent organizations) has also given a dangerous tilt to this volatile state of affairs.[8]

While there are a variety of reasons behind the rise of extremism and terrorism in the region, in this chapter, we analyse the references made to the intertwined role of Indian foreign and domestic policies by various South Asian jihadist[9] groups. Specifically, we refer to India's interference in its neighbours' domestic affairs (Bangladesh, Nepal, Sri Lanka and Maldives), its constant skirmishes with Pakistan and its treatment of the Kashmiris as well as its wider Muslim population. These factors have, as we will demonstrate later on, bred varying levels of anti-Indian sentiments in South Asia and have consequently been leveraged by jihadist groups—especially those operating in Pakistan and Bangladesh, to garner support for themselves and recruit individuals.

---

[5] Ibid.

[6] A. Z. Hilali, 'Political and Ethnic Waves in South Asia', *Pakistan Institute of International Affairs* 58, no. 3 (2005): 55–75.

[7] Asma Khan Mahsood, 'History of Sectarianism in Pakistan: Implications for Lasting Peace', *Journal of Political Sciences & Public Affairs* 5, no. 4 (2017); International Crisis Group, 'Political Conflict, Extremism and Criminal Justice in Bangladesh', 2016. Available at: https://www.crisisgroup.org/asia/south-asia/bangladesh/political-conflict-extremism-and-criminal-justice-bangladesh (accessed on 18 July 2018).

[8] Sadia Nasir, *Rise of Extremism in South Asia* (Islamabad: Policy Research Institute, 2004).

[9] We have chosen to describe the groups as 'jihadist' principally because they have themselves defined their undertaking in this manner. It is not, however, intended as a judgement on the legitimacy of the use of this term. Scholars and theologians have vigorously disputed the degree of sanction Islam gives to the use of force, and indeed the very meaning of the term jihad itself, which this chapter does not delve into.

The chapter proceeds as follows: First, we explain the contours of Indian foreign policy over the last 50 years with a special focus on the 'Indira Doctrine' as a base for understanding India's regional ambitions. Within this section, we also incorporate how it has been perceived by its neighbours and the recent manifestations of antagonism towards its foreign policy. In the second and third sections, we seek to focus on India's relations with Pakistan and Bangladesh respectively, covering a brief history of both and highlighting how anti-Indian narratives have been employed by various political parties and their influence on the citizens of the countries. These sections also demonstrate how regional and transnational terrorist groups existing in the two countries use such sentiments to then try recruiting individuals to their cause via the propaganda issued by them.

In the fourth section, we shed some light on major underlying themes of terrorist propaganda especially with regard to solidarity with the *ummah*. In this section, we also draw on existing terrorist propaganda literature to assess the actual effectiveness of such propaganda. We conclude this chapter by noting that while there is a definite evolution in terrorist propaganda among South Asian groups, there is much lacking in the terrorist groups propaganda targeting India.

INDIAN FOREIGN POLICY

Owing to its structural dominance in South Asia and resultant policies in the region, India has been a natural target of resentment and suspicion, and has borne the brunt of varying degrees of anti-India sentiments across its neighbouring nations. Since its formation as an independent country in 1947, India had a mildly hegemonic strategy with regard to its neighbours in South Asia on account of its large size and dense population.[10] Nonetheless, subcontinental dominance became a goal of the Indian foreign policy after India's defeat in the 1962 Sino-Indian border war, which emphasized threats to India and

---

[10] Swaminathan S. Anklesarian Aiyar, 'Indian versus American Hegemony', *Times of India*, 9 September 2007. Available at: https://timesofindia.indiatimes.com/sa-aiyar/swaminomics/Indian-versus-American-hegemony/articleshow/2351533.cms (accessed on 18 July 2018).

precipitated a greater security consciousness.[11] This became much more pronounced during the reign of Indira Gandhi in the 1970s as it worked to expand India's influence in the region.[12] Three main principles enshrined in Indira Gandhi's foreign policy, informally known as the Indira Doctrine were: (a) no outside intervention by the great powers would be tolerated in South Asia, (b) the South Asian countries should not pursue any security agreements with outside powers that would threaten India's interests, and finally (c) that all South Asian countries would first ask Indian assistance for their domestic problems before asking external powers.[13]

India's strategic ambitions in South Asia prompted it to annex territory such as the kingdom of Mizoram[14] and interfere in the domestic affairs of some of its neighbouring countries such as Bangladesh and Sri Lanka for its own political gains.[15] In the process, it reaped much criticism for projecting a policy of anti-colonialism and non-alignment in the Cold War while simultaneously trying to establish its own dominance in South Asia.[16] India's overbearing conduct in dealing with its smaller neighbours (as shown further) due to its domestic political compulsions or in its own strategic interests has created the image of it acting like a 'big brother' among smaller countries such as Nepal, Bangladesh and Sri Lanka, who in turn have viewed India's advances and moves in the region with concern.

---

[11] Subrata K. Mitra, 'The Reluctant Hegemon: India's Self-Perception and the South Asian Strategic Environment', *Contemporary South Asia* 12, no. 3 (2003): 399–417.

[12] Missile programmes were initiated after 1983 and defence spending doubled from 1980 to 1989. Operations Siachen (1984) and Brasstacks (1986–1987) occurred. Support was lent to the Tamil Tigers (1987–1990) and an Indian intervention in Male took place in 1988.

[13] Surjit Mansingh, 'Indira Gandhi's Foreign Policy: Hard Realism', in *Oxford Handbook of Indian Foreign Policy*, eds. C. Raja Mohan, Srinath Raghavan and David M. Malone (Oxford: Oxford University Press, 2015).

[14] Aiyar, 'Indian versus American Hegemony'.

[15] Mitra, 'The Reluctant Hegemon'.

[16] C. Rajamohan, 'Burying the Indira Doctrine', *The Hindu*, 24 May 2001. Available at: https://www.thehindu.com/2001/05/24/stories/05242523.htm (accessed on 12 July 2018); Mansingh, 'Indira Gandhi's Foreign Policy'.

Beginning in 1987, India engaged in a three-year-long intervention in Sri Lanka's civil war at the latter's behest.[17] This move eventually elicited antagonism within the rebel factions towards India and led to the death of at least 2000 Indian soldiers and, ultimately, the assassination of Rajiv Gandhi—demonstrating how India's interference in the domestic issues of another country could have grave implications on itself.[18] In 1988, India was the only nation to offer military support to the then President of Maldives, Abdul Gayoom, to quell a coup attempt. In 2016, India was alleged to have attempted to topple the then incumbent government of Nepal.[19] South Asian nations have viewed these actions as an interventionist posture, leading to them perceiving India as a regional bully which has resulted in the fanning of anti-India sentiments.[20] Additionally, India's cultural, religious, ethnic and linguistic soft power dominates the entire South Asian region from Afghanistan in the west to Myanmar in the east and from Nepal in the north to Sri Lanka in the south. Consequently, smaller neighbours of India are wary of Indian domination subsuming their own identity. In fact, most of India's neighbouring States have incorporated India into the domestic political scenario with parties and political blocs from Pakistan, Bangladesh, Sri Lanka and Nepal often exploiting anti-India sentiments to bolster their nationalist credentials, shore up support and gain electoral victories.[21] Furthermore, authors like Dhruva Jaishankar

---

[17] Arijit Mazumdar, 'India's South Asia Policy in the Twenty-First Century: New approach, Old Strategy', *Contemporary Politics* 18, no. 3 (2012): 286–302.

[18] *Times of India*, February 2018. Available at: https://timesofindia.indiatimes.com/world/south-asia/operation-cactus-how-indian-troops-went-to-maldives-and-helped-quell-a-coup/articleshow/62816787.cms (accessed on 10 May 2019).

[19] Kamal Dev Bhattaria, 'Fresh Turmoil in Nepal–India Relations', *The Diplomat*, 14 May 2016. Available at: https://thediplomat.com/2016/05/fresh-turmoil-in-nepal-india-relations/ (accessed on 20 June 2018).

[20] Monalisa Adhikari, 'Politics and Perceptions of Indian Aid to Nepal', *Strategic Analysis* 38, no. 3 (2014): 325–340.

[21] Sushant Sareen, 'Why India Is a Big Factor in Pakistani Polls', *Scroll*, 8 June 2018. Available at: https://www.dailyo.in/politics/pakistan-polls-islamabad-nawaz-sharif-diplomacy/story/1/24725.html (accessed on 29 July 2018); Nadeem Qadir, 'BNP Raises Its Anti-India Card Again', *Dhaka Tribune*, 7 May 2018. Available at: https://www.dhakatribune.com/opinion/2018/05/06/bnp-raises-anti-india-card (accessed on 20 June 2018); MSM Ayub, 'Politics of India Bogey',

have pointed to the rising tide of nationalism in these countries, which often manifests itself as anti-Indianism in many of these countries.[22] Increasingly, as we show in the next few sections, jihadist groups in Pakistan and Bangladesh also exploit such sentiments to achieve their agenda. While this has existed among regional and some transnational terrorist groups for quite a while, we argue that there has been (a) an increased prominence of such rhetoric and (b) a nuanced shift in the discussions employed by terrorist groups.

We have specifically chosen to analyse anti-India sentiments in Pakistan and Bangladesh because we wanted to narrow the discussion on jihadist groups that target India externally, most of whom are largely present in these two countries.[23] We observed via propaganda materials from these groups that the messaging of terrorist groups in these two countries have tapped into the anti-India sentiments already existing in the country, something we will expound upon in the future sections. Other than Pakistan and Bangladesh, Maldives and Afghanistan are the other two nations with substantial Muslim populations that jihadist groups can draw on. However, Afghanistan generally has a favourable view of India and trusts the country, mainly as a response to the aids received from the Indian government in recent years and its assistance in the development of Afghanistan's economic, education and health sectors. Consequently, anti-India jihadist narratives barely gain traction among Afghanis. Similarly, India–Maldives relations have always been on an even keel, though of late there has been some friction between the two.

Daily Mirror, 19 May 2017. Available at: http://www.dailymirror.lk/article/Politics-of-India-bogey-129176.html (accessed on 19 June 2018); Debashish Roy Chowdhury, 'Driven By India into China's Arms, Is Nepal the New Sri Lanka?' *South China Morning Post*, 20 February 2018. Available at: https://www.scmp.com/week-asia/geopolitics/article/2134532/driven-india-chinas-arms-nepal-new-sri-lanka (accessed on 10 June 2018).

[22] Dhruva Jaishankar, 'Reports of India's Demise as a Regional Power Are Greatly Exaggerated', *The Print*, 20 February 2018. Available at: https://theprint.in/opinion/reports-indias-demise-regional-power-greatly-exaggerated/36699/ (accessed on 10 June 2018).

[23] Dass, *Terrorism and Militancy in South Asia*.

In the next two sections, we will discuss relations between India and the two countries in study—Pakistan and Bangladesh—separately. Within these two sections we also elaborate on how bilateral relations and Indian domestic policies led to an intense amount of anti-Indian activity that was cultivated by terrorist groups later.

INDIA AND PAKISTAN: PERENNIAL ENEMIES

India's relationship with Pakistan is the most intractable and intense out of all its neighbours. The very nature of their mutual animosity and hatred stems from the Partition and formation of the two nations in 1947. In the 1940s, Mohammad Ali Jinnah believed that the Muslims of India would be dominated by the majority Hindu community and hence fought for a separate nation under the banner of the Muslim League, a political party.[24] While these agitations finally paid off with the formation of Pakistan in 1947, the consequences were bloody. The two nations have subsequently fought two more major wars in 1965 and 1971 with the latter resulting in the breakup of Pakistan and the formation of Bangladesh.[25] They also engaged in several border skirmishes and military standoffs.

Another major after-effect of the Partition was the fight for Kashmir. In a sense, the Kashmir dispute can be attributed to Britain's failure to devise a feasible way to deal with the princely states in the region.[26] The Indian Independence Act merely declared that the princely states could accede to either India or Pakistan or consider some other arrangement. Hence, the status of Kashmir (along with Hyderabad and Junagadh), a

---

[24] Nisid Hajari, *Midnight's Furies: The Deadly Legacy of India's Partition* (Wilmington: Mariner Books, 2016).

[25] Victoria Schofield, *Kashmir in Conflict: India, Pakistan and the Unending War* (London: I.B. Taurus, 2010).

[26] Princely states in the Indian subcontinent during the British Raj were semi-sovereign political entities which were not directly governed by the British, but rather by a local ruler, subject to a form of indirect rule on some matters. Following British withdrawal from the subcontinent, almost all of the principalities had acceded or were forcefully annexed into either India or Pakistan by the 1950s.

Muslim majority state with a Hindu ruler, was undecided. However, the king soon acceded to India in 1948 in a bid to protect his legacy, resulting in conflicting claims to the state that has continued ever since.[27] While India took control of the state, Pakistan believed it to be its own on account of Kashmir's majority Muslim population. Over the years, the situation exacerbated due to political and administrative failures on India's part, gradually encompassing a major insurgency that began in 1989.[28]

Also, following Jinnah's death, the military established its dominance in Pakistan slowly wresting control away from the civilian government. One way it achieved this was to paint the looming presence of India as an existential threat to Pakistan.[29] The wars it engaged with India and the fact that India was holding on to Kashmir, made for easy fodder to feed Pakistani citizens and gain popularity, thereby increasing hatred against India. Moreover, Pakistani political figures also painted India as a Hindu dominated country that was anti-Islamic and hence a natural enemy of Pakistan. Similarly, Indian narratives consistently present antagonistic portrayals of Pakistan. In effect, both countries have created an identity that is in opposition to the other.[30]

The rise of Hindu nationalism has strengthened anti-Pakistan attitude in India. Furthermore, mainstream Indian media channels have constantly heralded a jingoistic approach towards Pakistan encouraging military retaliation when Pakistan-based militants launch incursions in India.[31] Gradually, the word 'Pakistan' has also become a slur in India,

---

[27] Victoria Schofield, *Kashmir in the Crossfire* (London: I.B. Tauris, 1996).

[28] Paul Staniland, *Networks of Rebellion: Explaining Insurgent Cohesion and Collapse* (New York, NY: Cornell University Press, 2014); Kunal Mukherjee, 'The Kashmir Conflict in South Asia: Voices from Srinagar', *Defence & Security Analysis* 30, no. 1 (2014): 44–54.

[29] Mazhar Aziz, *Military Control in Pakistan: The Parallel State* (New York, NY: Routledge, 2008).

[30] Marie Lall, 'Educate to Hate: The Use of Education in the Creation of Antagonistic National Identities in India and Pakistan', *Compare: A Journal of Comparative and International Education* 38, no. 1 (2008): 103–119.

[31] Harinder Baweja, 'Making of a Terrorist: Babri Demolition Triggered Masood Azhar's Jihad', *Hinudstan Times*, 14 January 2016. Available at: https://

whereby Muslim individuals dissenting with the Indian government are often asked to go to Pakistan.[32] This has had a mirror effect in Pakistan. Political blocs have used the country's Islamic identity to defend their own political position and interests, which have been conducive to the perpetuation of the rivalry.[33]

These incidents have pitted the two countries against each other and engendered hatred for each other among their respective populace.[34] Distaste towards each other has had far reaching consequences for both countries. However, in order to not diverge from the main theme of this chapter, we only look at the repercussions of the anti-India sentiments. The image of India as an eternal enemy is quite pervasive among a majority of the Pakistani population. For instance, research conducted has shown that more than 50 per cent of Pakistani respondents in surveys view India as an unfavourable threat.[35]

Additionally, given the amount of violence (leading to more than 40,000 deaths) in the state since 1989 insurgency, the Indian government has employed heavy-handed and often times problematic techniques in suppressing violence such as the use of pellet guns

---

www.hindustantimes.com/india/making-of-a-terrorist-babri-masjid-demolition-triggered-azhar-s-jihad/story-zg6YSKXSjxRk5xo3AlvdfM.html (accessed on 1 July 2001).

[32] *Times of India*, 'Muslims should not even be living in this country, they should go to Pakistan or Bangladesh' Says BJP MP Vinay Katiyar', February 2018. Available at: https://timesofindia.indiatimes.com/india/muslims-should-not-even-be-living-in-this-country-should-go-to-pakistan-bangladesh-says-bjp-mp-vinay-katiyar/articleshow/62815998.cms (accessed on 23 July 2018).

[33] Gitika Commuri, 'The Relevance of National Identity Narratives in Shaping Foreign Policy: The Case of India–Pakistan Relations', *Journal of South Asian Development* 4, no. 2 (2009): 2.

[34] Sarmad Iqbal, 'A Pakistani's Account of How Indophobia is a Part of Daily Life', *Quint*, 3 November 2017. Available at: https://www.thequint.com/voices/blogs/pakistani-on-indophobia-and-cultural-ties (accessed on 19 July 2018); *Dawn*, 'Minister Concerned over Rising Anti-Pakistan Sentiments in India', 19 October 2015. Available at: https://www.dawn.com/news/1214160 (accessed on 12 June 2018).

[35] Niloufer Siddiqui and Christopher Clary, 'Voters and Foreign Policy: Evidence from a Conjoint Experiment in Pakistan' (unpublished research paper, 2017).

on protesters, illegal arrests etc.[36] India's aggressive military action in Kashmir has generated acute anti–Indian sentiments among the Pakistani populace, who have much emotional attachment to the Kashmiri Muslims.[37]

Both these broad issues—the encouragement of anti–India sentiments by the Pakistani army and the issue of Kashmir—have helped the case of terrorist groups in the region. Pakistani terrorist groups have used these events to justify violence in India on many occasions. Consequently, terrorist violence has visited India from Pakistan numerous times, the most prominent recent incidents being the Pathankot and Uri attacks, two heavily militarized zones causing about 25 deaths.[38] Some other conspicuous incidents include: The hijack of an Indian Airlines flight by Pakistan-backed terrorists in December 1999 that compelled the Indian government to release three Islamist militants jailed in India;[39] the December 2001 terrorist attack on the Parliament of India;[40] a suicide car bomb attack on the Indian Embassy in Kabul in July 2008;[41] and the November 2008 and 2011 terrorist attacks in Mumbai among others.[42]

---

[36] Amnesty, *Denied: Failures in Accountablity for Human Rights by Security Force Personnel in Jammu and Kashmir* (London: Amnesty International, 2015).

[37] Munir Akram, 'Human Rights and Peace', *Dawn*, 24 June 2018. Available at: https://www.dawn.com/news/1415775 (accessed on 10 July 2018).

[38] Rezaul H. Laskar, 'How Pakistan's Response to Uri and Pathankot Attacks Differed', *Hindustan Times*, 19 September 2016. Available at: https://www.hindustantimes.com/india-news/how-pakistan-s-response-to-uri-and-pathankot-attacks-differs/story-NkUYYQVMvW4eutNg2FatcM.html (accessed on 29 May 2018).

[39] Aadil Ikram Zaki Iqbal, 'Kandahar Hijack: Revisit Story of Five Terrorists Bringing India on its Knees', *India*, 20 December 2015. Available at: http://www.india.com/news/india/kandahar-hijack-revisit-the-story-of-five-terrorists-bringing-india-on-its-knees-trading-176-lives-for-3-terrorists-810146/ (accessed on 4 June 2018).

[40] *India Today*, 'How 2001 Parliament attack allowed Osama bin Laden's escape from Tora Bora, 1 June 2017. Available at: https://www.indiatoday.in/magazine/books/story/20170529-india-parliament-attack-bin-laden-al-qaeda-tora-bora-986405-2017-05-20 (accessed on 20 July 2018).

[41] Abdul Waheed Wafa, 'Suicide Car Blast Kills 41 in Afghan Capital', *New York Times*, 8 July 2008. Available at: https://www.nytimes.com/2008/07/08/world/asia/08afghanistan.html (accessed on 18 July 2018).

[42] *Indian Express*, '26/11 Mumbai Terror Attacks: Here's What Happened at Taj Mahal Hotel, Trident-Oberoi, Nariman House', 12 November 2017. Available at:

While Pakistan is host to a large number of terrorist groups, objectives and targets are often varied. We look specifically at those groups that target India, the most prominent being Jaish-e-Mohammed (JeM) and Lashkar-e-Taiba (LeT; now Jamaat-ud-daawa). Both groups were formed in the late 1980s and early 1990s, and have launched multiple attacks both in Kashmir and the rest of India. While LeT was best known for launching the horrific Mumbai attacks in 2008 that killed more than 160 people, JeM too has launched a number of prominent attacks including a recent one on the Uri military air base in India.[43] Both groups were alleged to have enjoyed some funding and support from the Pakistani army and the Inter-Services Intelligence (ISI) until 2001, when the United States designated it as a foreign terrorist organization and Pakistan froze its assets.[44]

Both LeT and the JeM have made liberating Kashmir and Muslims in the rest of India as one of the objectives of their existence. As Fair has documented previously, preachers in Pakistani mosques have constantly cited instances of Indian abuse in Kashmir as a way to motivate and pull recruits to these groups.[45] It is also important to note that statistically, rhetorical statements in the press are normally followed up with violent attacks within one–three (average) months at least in the case of LeT, as was revealed in a big data analysis of the group's activities. This was best demonstrated in LeT leader Hafiz Saeed providing an interview on failed Kashmir policies in 2008 which was followed shortly after by the aforementioned Mumbai attacks.[46] Furthermore, Saeed has maintained

https://indianexpress.com/article/26–11/timeline/2611-mumbai-terror-attacks-heres-what-happened-at-taj-mahal-hotel-trident-oberoi-nariman-house/ (accessed on 12 June 2018); *The Guardian*, 'Mumbai Blasts', 13 July 2011. Available at: https://www.theguardian.com/world/blog/2011/jul/13/mumbai-blasts (accessed on 19 June 2018).

[43] Laskar, 'Pakistan's Response to Uri and Pathankot'; Stephen Tankel, *Storming the World Stage: The Story of Lashkar-e-Taiba* (Oxford: Oxford University Press, 2011).

[44] Tankel, *Storming the World Stage*.

[45] C. Christine Fair, 'Militant Recruitment in Pakistan: Implications for Al Qaeda and Other Organizations', *Studies in Conflict and Terrorism* 27, no. 6 (2010): 489–504.

[46] V. S. Subrahmanian, Aaron Mannes, Amy Sliva, Jana Shakarian, and John P. Dickerson, *Computational Analysis of Terrorist Groups* (New York, NY: Springer, 2013).

that if the Indian government were to deprive Kashmiris of freedom, then LeT would be forced to pursue the conquest of India.[47] In June 2017, LeT released statements in 2017 referring to India as a 'cancer to humanity' and a 'human rights violator'.[48] Similarly, the terrorist group JeM has held rallies where it advocated attacks against India. As recently as March 2018, the group declared that it would march to New Delhi, killing as many Indians as it could along the way.[49] Unsurprisingly, this perception and rhetoric has also trickled down to other, more visceral transnational terrorist groups. In the 13th issue of *Dabiq*, the Islamic State (IS) constantly alludes to the treatment of Kashmiris by the Indians and Pakistan's negligence of the Kashmiris as a reason to join the group.[50]

While jihadist groups use a variety of tactics to recruit, policies and events fuelling perceived and real oppression of fellow Muslims in India and resultant anti-India sentiment is perhaps among the strongest motivator used. A noteworthy example of this would be JeM's chief Masood Azhar who began to recruit members to fight in India after the demolition of the Babri Masjid in 1992 to seek revenge. According to some reports, Azhar would never have targeted India had it not been for this incident.[51] Correspondingly, journalists reported that the recruitment drives led by other terrorist groups in states like Gujarat and Maharashtra had peaked immediately after the Babri Masjid incident.[52] Another prominent incident that also worked in the terrorist

---

[47] Tankel, *Storming the World Stage*.

[48] *India Today*. 'India a cancer to humanity, will burn to ashes, Lashkar-e-Taiba says in statement', 16 June 2017. Available at:https://www.indiatoday.in/india/story/india-a-cancer-to-humanity-lashkar-e-taiba-says-983177-2017-06-16 (accessed on 15 August 2018).

[49] *Business Standard*, 'JeM Continuing to Threaten PM Modi, India at the Behest of Pakistan's ISI', 2 March 2018. Available at: https://www.business-standard.com/article/current-affairs/jem-continuing-to-threaten-pm-modi-india-at-the-behest-of-pakistan-s-isi-118030200094_1.html (accessed on 2 August 2018).

[50] Islamic State, 'Interview With the Amīr of the Khilāfah's Soldiers in Bengal Shaykh Abū Ibrāhīm Al-Hanīf.' *Dabiq*, 13 April 2016, 58–66.

[51] Baweja, 'Making of a Terrorist'.

[52] Praveen Swami, 'The Making of an Indian Terrorist', *The Hindu*, 10 July 2012. Available at: https://www.thehindu.com/opinion/op-ed/the-making-of-an-indian-terrorist/article3621200.ece (accessed on 13 July 2018).

group's favour were the Gujarat riots where hundreds of Muslims were killed in retaliation to a fire incident, allegedly caused by Muslims, in a train carrying Hindu pilgrims in Godhra. Many people considered the Gujarat state government complicit in the attacks against Muslims resulting in many Muslims joining terrorist groups.[53] Concurrently, the LeT displayed photos of the riot victims and called for a jihad to avenge the brutalities against the Muslims.[54] Both these events are significant since revenge sought for acts of repression have been a common motivation for many terrorist events.

Thus, as we can see, terrorist groups use the antagonism between India and Pakistan, which is further fanned by Pakistani figures as well as India's own mistreatment of minorities in both Kashmir and the rest of India, to work on recruiting and radicalizing Pakistani individuals. In the near future, India's path to completely depriving terrorist groups of propaganda material is clear, albeit highly unlikely. The easy answer would be peace with Pakistan resulting in a strong crackdown on India-focused groups. However, this path of action is besieged by lack of political will on both sides of the border, corruption, international stakes and domestic events.

When Modi assumed the mantle of prime minister, observers noted that his initial warmth accorded to Pakistan may be signs of a changing dynamic between the two nations.[55] However, the two major terrorist attacks in Uri and Pathankot, along with a slew of other attacks conducted by JeM and LeT proved otherwise. Given India's continued antagonism towards Pakistan and its policies in Kashmir, it would not be surprising to see continued attacks being launched on Indian military targets. In effect though, it remains to be seen when the next large terrorist attack on the Indian homeland (other than in Kashmir) may

---

[53] Ibid.

[54] Praveen Swami, 'Gujarat Riot Victims Look to the Lashkar-e-Taiba', *The Hindu*, 16 August 2003. Available at: https://www.thehindu.com/2003/08/16/stories/2003081601471200.htm. (accessed on 10 June 2018).

[55] Saeed Shah and Qasim Nauman, 'India's Narendra Modi Makes First Visit to Pakistan for Chat With Nawaz Sharif', *Wall Street Journal*, 25 December 2016. Available at: https://www.wsj.com/articles/indias-narendra-modi-to-make-first-visit-to-pakistan-for-chat-with-nawaz-sharif-1451037151 (accessed on 12 July 2018).

occur and, as the last section of this chapter will explain, needs much more fuel than what is presently occurring. In the next section, we begin with a detailed background and analysis of India–Bangladesh relations and similar trickledown effects among regional terrorist groups.

INDIA–BANGLADESH: DIVERGENT TRAJECTORIES, SIMILAR RESULTS

India–Bangladesh relations experienced ups and downs throughout history and have sometimes been defined as an 'enigma'.[56] According to Islam, it has 'often been complicated, challenging, tense and crisis-ridden and overwhelmed by accusations and counter accusations'.[57] Unlike Pakistan, Bangladesh had adopted a markedly pro-India stance in the immediate aftermath of its formation in 1971. This was largely because India had played a significant role in Bangladesh's war of liberation against Pakistan.[58] It was also the first country to recognize Bangladesh as a sovereign State. India and Bangladesh entered into The Treaty of Friendship, Cooperation and Peace for a term of 25 years based on mutual respect for each other's independence, sovereignty and territorial integrity while 'refraining from interfering in each other's internal affairs'.[59] However, this cordial relationship took a hostile turn following allegations that India had selectively aided groups close to the Awami League (AL) in order to serve its own political interests. Many Bangladeshis came to believe that India's real aim was to install a pro-India government in Bangladesh that would be subservient to its interests.[60] These suspicions were stimulated by India's refusal to share Pakistani arms and ammunition which were seized in the 1971

---

[56] Partha S. Ghosh, 'Changing Frontiers: Making Deeper Sense of India–Bangladesh Relations', *South Asia Research* 31, no. 3 (2011): 195–211.

[57] Shariful Islam, 'Dynamics, Challenges, and Future Prospects of Indo-Bangla Relations', *Daily Sun*, 2011. Available at: http://www.daily-sun.com/old_version/details_yes_02-07-2011_Dynamics-challenges-and-future-prospects-of-Indo-Bangla relations_268_2_17_1_1.html#sthash.ZYaRDyJp.dpuf

[58] Mansingh, 'Indira Gandhi's Foreign Policy'.

[59] Harsh V. Pant, 'India in the Asia-Pacific: Rising Ambitions with an Eye on China', *Asia Pacific Reveiw* 14, no. 1 (2007): 54–71.

[60] V. K. Vinayaraj, 'India as a Threat; Bangladeshi Perceptions', *South Asian Survey* 16, no. 1 (2009): 13.

war, the high-handed attitude of the Indian bureaucrats who reminded Bangladeshis of the preceding West Pakistani bureaucrats, the AL leaders' ostensible submissiveness to India, among others.[61] India's failure to realize the sensitivities of a society which had just emerged from a long history of colonial exploitation aroused psychological fear among many Bangladeshis. Moreover, India's administration of Kashmir, liberation of Goa in 1961–1962 via military means and annexation of Junagadh, Sikkim and Hyderabad aggravated Bangladeshi suspicion and mistrust towards India.[62]

This was exacerbated over the years by a number of reasons. This include the unresolved disputes regarding the sharing of common river waters; the Chittagong Hill Tracts issue whereby India harboured and armed dissidents to destabilize Bangladesh,[63] the killing of scores of unarmed Bangladeshis by the Indian Border Security Force, land and maritime border disputes, and bilateral trade imbalances.[64] Additionally, India's overbearing conduct and 'big brother' attitude while dealing with the smaller neighbour, due to its domestic political compulsions or in its own strategic interest, proved to be rather counterproductive and soured its relations with Bangladesh. These issues have been seen by some as a threat to Bangladesh's territorial integrity and political independence.

The core of much of the tension between the two nations can also be attributed to the big country/small country syndrome that exists between them. While dealing with bigger and more powerful states in the international sphere, small states are typically guided by comparative inferiority and resultant insecurity about its sovereignty

---

[61] Ibid.; Ishtiaq Hossain, 'Bangladesh–India Relations: Issues and Problems', *Asian Survey* 21, no. 11 (1981): 1115–1128.

[62] Vinayaraj, 'India as a Threat'.

[63] *Economic Times*, '2004 Chittagong Arms Haul Case Exposes Many Terror Links', 6 February 2014. Available at: https://economictimes.indiatimes.com/opinion/et-commentary/2004-chittagong-arms-haul-case-exposes-many-terror-links/articleshow/29918978.cms (accessed on 1 July 2018).

[64] *DW*, 'Bangladesh, India Resolve Border Issue', 20 April 2011. Available at: https://www.dw.com/en/bangladesh-india-resolve-border-issue/a-6508552 (accessed on 1 July 2018).

and territorial integrity.[65] This influenced both Bangladesh's foreign and domestic policies. India's power in the region in comparison to Bangladesh's limited military and economic potentiality has generated fear of its dominance in Bangladesh. Furthermore, its overwhelming presence on three sides constituting more than 4,000 kilometres of land boundary has rendered Bangladesh 'India locked', and thereby more vulnerable to coercion from India. To add on, India's cultural, ethnic and linguistic soft power in the country has made Bangladesh wary of Indian domination subsuming its own identity. These factors, coupled with the rising tide of nationalism in Bangladesh, often manifests itself as anti–Indianism.

Distrust and suspicion of India has also been fuelled by domestic politics in both the countries. Several Bangladeshis are 'anti-India' due to New Delhi's close ties with the ruling AL. The first generation AL leaders had received assistance and shelter from India during the Liberation War. Subsequently, AL-led administrations' foreign policies and local narratives have been pro-India and anti-Pakistan. Following the transition towards democratic governance in Bangladesh in 1991, India's overt prying into Bangladesh's domestic affairs, particularly when the AL-led government was in power, became an issue.[66] India's increasing and unwarranted interference in Bangladesh's political situation and its staunch support of the AL has created a scenario in which internal political chaos in Bangladesh invokes deep sensitivity among a large section of its citizens' opinion of India. For instance, the perception among many Bangladeshis that India had abetted anti–democratic actions by the AL government during the 2014 elections exacerbated anti–India sentiments. This discussion was furthered by one of the two major political parties, the Bangladesh Nationalist Party (BNP) led by Khaleda Zia, which repeatedly accused the AL of selling out Bangladesh to India.[67]

---

[65] Živilė Marija Vaicekauskaitė, 'Security Strategies of Small States in a Changing World', *Journal on Baltic Security* 3, no. 2 (2017).

[66] A. A. Hossain, 'Contested National Identity and Political Crisis in Bangladesh: Historical Analysis of the Dynamics of Bangladeshi Society and Politics', *Asian Journal of Political Science* 23, no. 3 (2015): 366–396.

[67] Prothom Alo, 'AL Silently Working to Sell Out Bangladesh: BNP', 23 June 2016. Available at: http://en.prothomalo.com/bangladesh/news/109387/

The AL is presented as pro-India/anti-Pakistan and pro-Hindu/anti-Islamic whereas BNP's ideology is implicitly anti-India. Consequently, the narrative where India is the aggressive Hindu neighbour and regional bully, has long been used by the BNP to endorse its religionationalist political goal. Playing on the Indophobic sentiments and the historical relationship of AL with India, the BNP's campaign against the AL has been on the latter's pro-India stance, which is depicted to be adversely affecting Bangladesh. This narrative gained further traction in 2016 when the Hasina regime signed the Rampal Energy project agreement, an India–Bangladesh joint venture near the Sundarbans, regardless of resistance at home due to the project's possible detrimental environmental impact on the Sundarbans.[68] Most recently, India deported Lord Alex Carlile, a member of the legal team of opposition BNP leader Khaleda Zia. This move has revived talks about Indian intrusion in the forthcoming Bangladesh election.[69]

Given the heightened anti-Indian sentiments among a segment of the Bangladeshi populace, terrorist groups are exploiting and using it as a recruitment tool. Such groups paint Indian policies as a neocolonialist scheme—an attempt by non-Muslims to subjugate Muslims. For instance, al-Qaeda in the Indian Subcontinent (AQIS), in its document 'the code of conduct', highlighted India's influence in 'secularizing' Bangladeshi domestic policy as a direct assault on Islam.[70] It also pointed out India's water-sharing practices as tantamount to depriving the Muslim population from their rights.[71]

AL-working-silently-to-sell-out-Bangladesh-BNP (accessed on 12 January 2018).

[68] Daily Star, 'Sundarbans Risks Being World Heritage in Danger', 20 October 2016. Available at: https://www.thedailystar.net/frontpage/unesco-firm-its-stance-against-rampal-project-1301380 (accessed on 9 July 2018).

[69] David Bergman, 'UK Lawyer Alleges India Deported Him under Bangladesh Pressure', *Al Jazeera*, 13 July 2018. Available at: https://www.aljazeera.com/news/2018/07/uk-lawyer-alleges-india-deported-bangladesh-pressure-180713094355772.html (accessed on 18 July 2018).

[70] As-Sahab Media Subcontinent, 'Code of Conduct', June 2017. Available at: https://azelin.files.wordpress.com/2017/06/al-qacc84_idah-in the-indian-subcontinent-22code-of-conduct22-en.pdf (accessed on 20 March 2018).

[71] Ibid.

Correspondingly, an issue of the AQIS Bengali language magazine, published by Ansar al-Islam stated, 'The war against Islam by the Western crusaders, Zionist Jews and the Hindus is not a simple war between two parties; it's between ideologies that cannot co-exist. It's the war between what's right and what needs to be overturned'. It also alleged that India's control on 'the *taghut* government of Bangladesh[72] and on the country's resources is a part of that war'. It went on to note: 'From Rampal to Rooppur, from tax-free transit to Indian television channels and movies, and propagation and expansion of the filthy *shirki* culture in Bangladesh, everything is tied to the same thread (of war against Islam)'.[73]

Similarly, in the 14th issue of *Dabiq*, the IS accused the Bangladeshi government of conspiring with the Indian government. Moreover, they also advocated—in couched language—for the genocide of Hindus in Bangladesh, on grounds of them colluding with Indian Hindus to attack Islam and Muslims in India.[74]

Terrorist groups constantly emphasize Bangladesh's Muslim identity, exploit anxieties over perceived threats from India to their values and ways of life, and justify their acts as retaliation for perceived attacks against Muslims. These anxieties are further aggravated by the increasing anti-Muslim Hindutva rhetoric in India and perpetration of human rights violations against its Muslim citizens, postulating Hinduism against Islam.[75] Being Muslims, some Bangladeshis view these aggressions as an attack on Islam, thus, a threat to their identity. Resentment towards India also deepened with the BJP's frequent references to illegal migration from Bangladesh during their various

---

[72] In Jihadist circles, *taghut* refers to Muslim governments who rule by other than laws of God, a vast definition that encompasses democratic, autocratic and monarchical systems of governance.

[73] Ansar al-Islam–AQIS, 'Muslim Ummahr Proti Ahoban', 15 December 2016.

[74] Islamic State, 'Interview with the Amīr of the Khilāfah'S Soldiers in Bengal Shaykh Abū Ibrāhīm Al-Hanīf,' *Dabiq*, (13 April 2016): 58–66.

[75] Maya Mirchandani, *Digital Hatred, Real Violence: Majoritarian Radicalisation and Social Media in India Delves into How Online Hate against Minorities Sanctions Real World Violence* (Delhi: ORF, 2018).

election campaigns.[76] In Narendra Modi's 2014 election manifesto, the BJP leaders cited dubious statistics and argued that border states such as West Bengal and Assam are bearing the brunt of illegal migration from Bangladesh—which according to them is a well-designed plan to Islamize these states and establish a large Muslim nation.[77] Hence, once the victory of BJP, known as the 'Hindu Nationalist' party, was confirmed in the last election, concern grew due to BJP's ideological predisposition towards 'Hindutva' and the 'hawkish/extremist' nature of Narendra Modi towards Muslims even among Bangladeshis.

Anti-Indian sentiments in Bangladesh have given rise to notable terrorists in the past, such as Babu Bhai, a madrasa-educated individual who joined the Harkat-ul-Jihad-al-Islami Bangladesh (HuJI-B) as its chief bomb specialist with the intention of avenging the demolition of the Babri Masjid by Hindu fundamentalists in 1992.[78] Furthermore, in December 2017, the neo-Jamaat-ul-Mujahideen Bangladesh (JMB) released India-centric literature encouraging attacks against the leadership of Rashtriya Swayamsevak Sangh (RSS), the Sangh Parivar and its affiliated organizations such as Durga Vahini and Vishwa Hindu Parishad.[79] Similarly, in AQIS' address to Muslims in South Asia, it justified attacks against heads of Hindu right-wing organizations who are alleged to be mistreating (Muslim) minorities.[80] It has also produced some videos that have tried to capitalize on the communal incidents taking place in India referring to Hindu extremism as 'Saffron

---

[76] Joyeeta Bhattacharjee, 'Bangladesh in Modi's Foreign Policy', Institute of Asia and Pacific Studies (IAPS), 21 September 2017. Available at: https://iapsdialogue. org/2017/09/21/bangladesh-in-modis-foreign-policy/ (accessed on 1 July 2018).

[77] While it is true that many Bangladeshis have illegally migrated to India, the statistics cited by BJP are blown out of proportion. Also, unlike what the BJP portrays, the refugees in West Bengal are predominantly (if not all) Hindus, not Muslims. As such, these refugees cannot 'Islamize' Bengal.

[78] Stephen Tankel, *Jihadist Violence: The Indian Threat* (Washington, DC: Woodrow Wilson Center, 2013).

[79] Ankit Kumar, 'RSS leadership on Bangla terror group's hit list' *India Today*, 13 June 2018. Available at: https://www.indiatoday.in/india/story/ rss-leadership-on-bangla-terror-group-s-hit-list-1147897-2018-01-17

[80] AQIS, 'Code of Conduct', *Azeline Press Files*, July 2017. Available at: https:// azelin.files.wordpress.com/2017/06/al-qacc84_idah-in-the-indian-subcontinent-22code-of-conduct22-en.pdf (accessed on 1 June 2018).

Terror'—a well-established term in Indian media.[81] Such narratives demonstrate how anti-Indian sentiments do not arise solely due to foreign policy but due to domestic policies as well.

These sentiments then translate to the formation of transnational militant networks based on shared resentment. For instance, various intelligences have disclosed Bangladeshi links to terrorist attacks in Bangalore and New Delhi.[82] Bangladeshi security forces have also arrested numerous Indian militants linked to LeT, the Pakistani militant group which was blamed for the 2008 Mumbai attack, thereby substantiating the presence of a transnational militant network operating in and through Bangladesh.[83] In October 2014, an accidental bomb blast (the Burdwan blast) in the Indian state of West Bengal was traced to JMB, which at that time was working with the AQIS.[84] Indian security forces in numerous instances arrested Bangladeshi militants belonging to both JMB and Ansarullah Bangla Team in different parts of India.[85]

Insurgent groups in India's north-eastern states also use Bangladesh as headquarters, sanctuaries, training camps, arms procurement and storage facilities and transit route. Correspondingly, the North Eastern region also serves as a transit route for Bangladeshi jihadists to infiltrate into Jammu & Kashmir. Stephen Tankel argues that external support from Pakistan and Bangladesh-based militant groups act as a force multiplier to the Indian jihadist movement—which form due to

---

[81] AQIS, 'Saffron Terror, Part–3', Jihadology, 26 December 2017. Available at: http://jihadology.net/2017/12/26/new-video-message-from-al-qaidah-in-the-indian-subcontinent-saffron-terror-part-3/ (accessed on 28 January 2018).

[82] Paul Cochrane, 'The Funding Methods of Bangladeshi Terrorist Groups', *Combatting Terrorism Center* 2, no. 5 (2009): 1.

[83] *The Daily Star*, 'Another Lashkar Man Captured', 21 July 2009. Available at: https://www.thedailystar.net/news-detail-98023 (accessed on 12 June 2018).

[84] Ali Riaz, 'Who Are the Bangladeshi "Islamist Militants"?' *A Journal of the Terrorism Research Initiative* 10, no. 1 (2016): 2.

[85] *Times of India*, 'Top leader of Bangaldesh-based militant outfit JMB held in Bengaluru', 7 August 2018. Available at: https://timesofindia.indiatimes.com/india/top-leader-of-bangaldesh-based-militant-outfit-jmb-held-in-bengaluru/articleshow/65307964.cms (accessed on 10 July 2018).

endogenous factors, specifically domestic communal grievances and consequential alienation and a desire for revenge.[86]

Thus, it is evident that both India's domestic and foreign affairs influence Bangladesh. As discussed earlier, India's interference in Bangladesh's domestic matters has spawned resentment among the latter's population. This is slightly different from the case of Pakistan in that, while India's enmity with Pakistan has generated hostility, it is India's cordial relations with the AL and its abuse of its power that has caused similar sentiments. However, similar to the case of Pakistan, the BNP turned a blind eye to some extremist groups, such as JMB,[87] which eventually trained their sights on Indian as well as Bangladeshi targets, denoting the possible risks of state support or at least, tolerance towards such groups.

To allay Bangladesh's concerns, India must come up with a more consistent Bangladesh policy, along the lines of greater people to people contact, enhanced economic assistance and keeping its domestic politics at an arm's length. Jihadist groups are bound to exploit anti-India sentiments to gain relevance. To win this battle, India will have to correct its historical faux pas and take on the role of a more benevolent regional power. However, as we explain in the concluding section, this is not a plausible path that India will take in the future.

In the next section, we look at the major themes that exist in terrorist propaganda relating to anti-India sentiments. In doing this, we also try to assess how effective such propaganda actually is using the existing literature.

PERCEIVED ATTACK ON ISLAM: ASSESSING THE EFFECTIVENESS

One of the main themes underlying the narratives used by South Asian jihadist groups seems to be that of Islam and by extension, a Muslim's very identity being under threat. Perceived threats to the in-group

---

[86] Tankel, *Storming the WorldStage.*
[87] Riaz, 'Who Are the Bangladeshi "Islamist Militants"?'

leads to increased group cohesion and creates an 'us' versus 'them' dichotomy.[88] This, in turn, motivates some to foster a political attachment to the global brotherhood of Muslims and trigger curiosity in the cultivation and support for Islamist movements (including violent ones) which engage in identity politics to mobilize individuals around strong in-group and out-group narratives.[89] Like other social movements, radical Islamist groups diagnose problems, attribute responsibility and offer solutions to mobilize support. They construct, produce, and disseminate meaning to frame narratives in ways that best resonate with the sentiments, interests and views of their potential recruits.[90] For instance, they constantly emphasize the Muslim identity and exploit anxieties over perceived threats to their values and ways of life. Their propaganda materials recurrently include troubling images of Muslim civilian deaths to foster righteous indignation among individuals. In their narrative as the self-appointed defenders of the *ummah*, they compel Muslims to avenge their co-religionists.

The key to radicalization and successful recruitment, though, is whether the movement's version of 'reality' resonates or can be brought to resonate with the movement's potential constituency. Some scholars have referred to this process as 'frame alignment'.[91] Radicalization then takes place as a response to 'proxy' subjugation, where group identity (as the global community of Muslims) is powerful enough to make people feel aggrieved and angry without undergoing the hostilities directly. By pointing out India's real and perceived hostilities towards its Muslim community, terrorist groups have managed to portray India as an enemy of Islam. Religion and ethnicity are widely acknowledged as powerful expressions of group and personal identity—which is a crucial factor in motivating and legitimizing appeal to violent

---

[88] Fathali M. Moghaddam, 'The Staircase to Terrorism: A Psychological Exploration', *American Psychologist* 60, no. 2 (2005): 162.

[89] Ibid.

[90] Quintan Wiktorowicz, 'Islamic Activism and Social Movement Theory: A New Direction for Research', *Mediterranean Politics* 7, no. 3 (2002): 187–211.

[91] Anja Dalgaard-Nielsen, 'Studying Violent Radicalization in Europe II: The Potential Contribution of Socio-psychological and Psycholigical Approaches' (working paper no 2008/3).

ideologies.[92] Furthermore, increasing Islamophobia in India has catalysed the racialization of Muslims as a monolithic category irrespective of national, ethnic and/or linguistic affiliations. Specifically, in the face of intensified hostility and scrutiny, many Muslims cultivate an increased self-conscious sense of collective identity as Muslims and a cemented sense of group solidarity.[93] Being Muslims, they view Indian aggression towards fellow Muslims as an attack on Islam, thus, a threat to their identity. This fear is exploited by jihadist groups. Indeed, in the second issue of an AQIS magazine, India's 'oppression' of Muslims, especially in Kashmir is stressed:

> The cow-worshipping Indian army is inhumanely torturing and killing the Muslims in Kashmir. It is our responsibility to help these people. They are being persecuted by the oppressors. Why aren't we following what the Quran prescribed for us? Why have we normalised the killings of the *ummah*? [94]

Similarly, the IS has highlighted extremist Hindutva actions including the lynching of various Muslims suspected of eating cows as reasons to attack Indian targets.[95] Nonetheless, this narrative or anti-India sentiments does not necessarily translate into radicalization. As asserted by most studies, although narratives do play a part, radicalization emerges from the interplay of different push and pull factors at various points. In other words, no single aspect suffices as an explanation for an individual's journey to radicalization.[96] This point can be elaborated more by examining the narratives from a strategic communications perspective.

---

[92] Harriet Allan, Andrew Glazzard, Sasha Jesperson, Sneha Reddy-Tumu and Emily Winterbotham, *Drivers of Violent Extremism: Hypotheses and Literature Review* (London: Royal United Services Institute, 2015).

[93] Ibid.

[94] Al-Balagh 1438, no. 2 (2017): 20.

[95] *International Business Times*, 'ISIS Terrorist Threatens to Avenge Lynching of Muslim Man over "Beef Eating" Rumour', 20 October 2015. Available at: https://www.ibtimes.co.in/isis-militant-threatens-avenge-lynching-muslim-man-over-beef-eating-6 (accessed on 5 June 2018).

[96] James Khalil, 'The Three Pathways (3P) Model of Violent Extremism', *The RUSI Journal* 162, no. 4 (2017): 40–48.

Groups like the IS that were particularly successful in creating successful propaganda had a few distinguishing characteristics embedded in their narratives. According to Fernandez, this encompassed authenticity, urgency, agency and victory. Authenticity means that narratives are based on real-world issues.[97] He refers to this as those steps taken by IS in Syria to build on its dream of bringing about a caliphate such as execution of criminals, providing services etc. In South Asia, the fact that terrorist groups have undertaken attacks in retaliation to oppression against Muslims, has lent a certain amount of authenticity to the image of these terrorist groups. Moreover, other studies also discuss the importance of reality of situations in providing fuel to terrorist propaganda which is a more fundamental concern.[98] The two examples discussed earlier—India's relationship with its neighbouring states and its poor treatment of Muslims are examples of this reality which is useful in further backing the narratives of such groups.

It is the next three themes that terrorist groups are still struggling to embed into their propaganda successfully.[99] Urgency refers to issues that are ongoing and necessitate an immediate response. For instance, the brutalities of the Bashar al-Assad regime was used by the IS and al-Qaeda (AQ) during the 2014–2018 period to gain popularity. Given the astounding crimes committed by Assad against Sunni Muslims, the groups found it easy to paint the toppling of Assad as an urgent task that Muslims should respond to.[100] Terrorist groups in South Asia would require a similar event to radicalize and recruit individuals. Although communal violence against Muslims is common in the Indian society (and in Kashmir), barring the demolition of the Babri masjid and the Godhra riots, there has not been an event tragic enough to trigger violent response.

Second, the issue of victory is another theme that terrorist groups have not been able to incorporate into their narrative. When the IS

---

[97] Alberto Fernandez, 'Here to Stay and Growing: Combating ISIS Propaganda Networks' (Washington, DC: Brookings Institution, 2015).

[98] Ariel Victoria Lieberman, 'Terrorism, the Internet, and Propaganda: A Deadly Combination', *Journal of National Security, Law and Policy* 9, no. 1 (2017): 95–124.

[99] Fernandez, 'Here to Stay and Growing'.

[100] John Cantile, 'The Meltdown', *Dabiq*, 15 February 2015, 58–63.

took over large swathes of territory in its military blitzkrieg in Iraq and Syria, they positioned their victories as divinely sanctioned, giving legitimacy to their position as the caliphate for all Muslims.[101] Such propaganda was also used by other groups such as AQ in the Arabian Peninsula when they acquired territory in Yemen.[102] However, in South Asia, this theme hardly finds adequate space to support itself given that groups (other than the Taliban who are not outward looking) are not in control of territory.[103] Nor have the regional terrorist groups such as LeT and JMB been able to make substantial progress in group strength or create strong impressions via major attacks against India.

Moreover, beyond just themes present in the narratives, analysts point out that propaganda has to be much more multifaceted and nuanced to achieve success. Ingram for example notes that three factors that make IS propaganda successful are: reach, resonance and relevance.[104] While the aforementioned factors (i.e., agency, urgency, victory and authenticity) would come under resonance and relevance, terrorist groups are yet to employ the same levels of sophistication in reach that IS did during its peak in 2014–2016.[105] For example, as Ingram qualifies, IS used multiple messages with various different topics as a way of attracting people towards its ideology.[106] These ranged from issues like safety and security in the caliphate, to menial issues like playing with cats and discussing products available in their lands. The range of topics gave it a good amount of diversity that appealed to people of various mindsets and psychological profiles.

---

[101] Fernandez, 'Here to Stay and Growing'.

[102] Michael Horton, 'Guns for Hire: How al-Qaeda in the Arabian Peninsula Is Securing Its Future in Yemen', *Jamestown Foundation*, 26 January 2018. Available at: https://jamestown.org/program/guns-hire-al-qaeda-arabian-peninsula-securing-future-yemen/ (accessed on 12 July 2018).

[103] Courtney Kube, 'The Taliban Is Gaining Strength and Territory in Afghanistan', *NBC News*, 31 January 2018. Available at: https://www.nbcnews.com/news/world/numbers-afghanistan-are-not-good-n842651 (accessed on 18 June 2018).

[104] Haroro J. Ingram, 'Three Traits of the Islamic State's Information Warfare', *RUSI Journal* 159, no. 6 (2014): 4–11.

[105] David Garrenstein Ross, 'The Islamic State's Global Propaganda Strategy' (research paper, International Center for Countering Terrorism, Hague, 2016).

[106] Ingram, 'Three Traits of the Islamic State's Information Warfare'.

Contrasting this with the propaganda in South Asia, while there is some nuance and depth in recent discussions among terrorist groups, the anti-India narrative is mostly centred on foreign policy and India's treatment of Muslims. While this may work alongside other narratives that are domestic oriented (for example AQIS' pointing to secular bloggers and their threat to Islam in Bangladesh) to enlist members,[107] it is not substantial enough to motivate many attacks against India specifically. A useful comparison point would be United States' actions in the Middle East countries, especially Iraq. The US invasion of Iraq under the flimsy pretext of removing chemical weapons led to the mushrooming of anti-American jihadist organizations globally,[108] just like its actions in South America during the 1960s and the 1970s led to the creation of various left-wing militant organizations locally.[109] Various studies have shown that the most compelling factor in directing jihadist attacks against the United States was its military presence and abject failure to maintain law and order in Iraq.[110] In this sense, India, while having interfered in other countries' domestic issues, has not conducted military operations recently (apart from Sri Lanka, which resulted in the eventual assassination of Rajiv Gandhi in 1991 by LTTE supporters).[111]

Importantly, the volume of terrorist group messaging concerning India is also another factor that plays a role in driving attacks against country. A thorough content analysis of IS' magazines, *Dabiq* (15

---

[107] Nathanel Barr, 'Diverging Trajectories in Bangladesh: Islamic State vs al-Qaeda', *Jamestown Foundation*, 9 December 2017. Available at: https://jamestown.org/program/diverging-trajectories-bangladesh-islamic-state-vs-al-qaeda/ (accessed on 28 May 2018).

[108] Peter Taylor, 'Iraq War: The Greatest Intelligence Failure in Living Memory', *The Telegraph*, 18 March 2013. Available at: https://www.telegraph.co.uk/news/worldnews/middleeast/iraq/9937516/Iraq-war-the-greatest-intelligence-failure-in-living-memory.html (accessed on 19 July 2018).

[109] Naomi Klein, *The Shock Doctrine: The Rise of Disaster Capitalism* (London: Picador, 2008).

[110] Thomas Hegghammer, 'Global Jihadism after the Iraq War', *Middle East Journal* 60, no. 1 (2006): 11–32.

[111] Pratyush, 'India and Sri Lanka's Civil War', *The Diplomat*, 29 December 2012. Available at: https://thediplomat.com/2012/12/india-and-sri-lankas-civil-war/ (accessed on 18 July 2018).

issues), *Rumiyah* (7 issues), as well as AQ's *Al-Balagh* (2 issues) and other Bengali magazines published by AQIS/Ansar al-Islam/JMB reveal less than five different references to India (each). Comparing it to the more than thousands of tweets per day released by IS at its peak in 2015[112] or the usage of bots by Qaeda in places like Yemen, it is quite likely that most of this propaganda is not reaching its intended target.[113] Moreover, in the whole of IS' existence since 2014, there have been less than two dedicated videos against India.[114] AQ did however produce more videos, but it still has not crossed more than 10 videos in the past few years.[115] Therefore, in our assessment, if terrorist groups in South Asia were to massively ramp up their tweets, references and official literature about India, there would be higher chances of inciting more attacks against India. However, with the limited propaganda churned out by groups on this issue, there are minimal fears of such events taking place.

CONCLUSION

In this chapter, we have explored how jihadist groups are exploiting anti-India sentiments in the South Asian region. We have argued that these sentiments stem from unhealed scars of partition in the Indian subcontinent, India's anti-Muslim attitudes and religious violence against its Muslim population, especially subsequent to the revival of right-wing Hindu nationalism in Indian politics, and its intrusion in

---

[112] J. M. Berger and Jonathon Morgan, *The ISIS Twitter Census: Defining and Describing the Populationof ISIS Supporters on Twitter* (Washington, DC: Brookings Institution, 2015).

[113] Jonathan M. Berger, 'The Evolution of Terrorist Propaganda: The Paris Attack and Social Media', Brookings Institution, 27 January 2015. Available at: https://www.brookings.edu/testimonies/the-evolution-of-terrorist-propaganda-the-paris-attack-and-social-media/ (accessed on 19 July 2018).

[114] Aishwarya Kumar 'Know Siddhartha Dhar, the Indian-origin ISIS Leader Designated Global Terrorist by US,' *News18*, 25 January 2018. Available at: https://www.news18.com/news/world/know-siddhartha-dhar-the-indian-origin-isis-leader-designated-global-terrorist-by-us-1641287.html (accessed on 19 September 2018).

[115] Animesh Roul, 'Saffron Scare: Al-Qaeda's Propaganda War in India', Jamestown Foundation, 23 March 2018. Available at: https://jamestown.org/program/saffron-scare-al-qaedas-propaganda-war-india/ (accessed on 19 July 2018).

neighbouring States' domestic issues. Should India stop interfering in its neighbours' affairs, there are lesser chances of these narratives taking root. However, given India's ambitions in the region and in Asia, it is unlikely that there will be a major change in its foreign policy trajectory, thereby always providing fuel to terrorist groups. Also, given the influence of the incumbent Hindu nationalist government, it is also unlikely that the treatment of India's Muslim community is going to get any better. While the general elections of 2019 may replace the government, the actual chances of this happening are low.[116] Thus, this factor will also be readily available for usage by terrorist groups. With the Indian government not delivering key economic promises, and the resultant potential for loss of support, the Modi government is increasingly relying on the politics of communal divide. This is also resulting in Hindus attacking minority communities in India, especially Muslims—who form 15 per cent of the country's population and are its largest minority group.

This may have an action–reaction effect and therefore result in radicalization of Muslims in India. All in all, the Modi government's legitimization of fanatical Hindu nationalism, endorsements and in some instances instigation of hate crimes against minorities will give rise to the insecuritization of the targeted minorities in India. By extension, any individual with a shared identity with these groups, in the immediate region beyond the Indian homeland, will be insecuritized to an extent, given Indian posturing in the region. Terrorist groups can easily capitalize on this heightened state of insecurity, as it would leave the individuals more susceptible to accept their ideological narratives, which are often clever manipulations of the original message formulated in ways that would resonate with the public and cater to their religio-political goals.

Mobilization would depend a lot on domestic environmental and personal factors as well. For example, individuals who have prior

---

[116] Milan Vaishnav, '2019 Election Won't Be a Cakewalk for BJP', Carnegie Endowment, 29 May 2018. Available at: https://carnegieendowment. org/2018/05/29/2019-election-won-t-be-cakewalk-for-bjp-pub-76465 (accessed on 10 July 2018).

experience with social rejection, family violence and so forth would be more predisposed to believe in an idea of collective rejection and negation. And if they feel negated, they would then take the actor by whom they feel they are insecuritized to be an existential threat. Violence to them would be justified at this point.

It is also clear that so far both global and regional terrorist groups have not been able to achieve a high-level of sophistication in their anti-India propaganda despite newer nuances. Operationally and experience wise terrorist groups are still struggling to present India as an attractive target. Security agencies may find it slightly reassuring to know that even if various groups restart propaganda efforts online, the anti-India sentiment will assume lesser priority as compared to other global issues.

It seems clear that the current circumstances will set the stage for further recruitment narratives in the future and with the help of a trigger event, provide impetus to a lot of groups outside and inside of India to enlist more individuals. The influence and significance of the jihadist groups will be dependent on both the domestic and global political developments. If global politics emboldens the reinforcement of the sense of Muslim victimhood, the jihadist's appeal to South Asians will plausibly strengthen. This dismal situation will also create fertile ground for radicalization of frustrated minds in South Asia and transnational Islamists can potentially utilize the region as a new battlefield in their battle against perceived exploitation and inequality.

Chapter 4

Religious and Political Transformations in the Maldives

The Macro-Level Contexts of Radicalization

Azim Zahir

INTRODUCTION

The tiny Indian Ocean nation of the Maldives, which claims to be a 100 per cent Muslim State, experienced an impressive political liberalization process from around 2003, transitioning to an electoral democracy in 2009 for the first time.[1] The political liberalization was by no means a smooth process. Deep political turmoil engulfed the country since 2003, constantly threatening the liberalization process and later the democratic transition. During this same period, religious radicalism and violent extremism became a major issue of concern for the Maldives. A steady flow of Maldivian foreign fighters joined jihadist groups in Syria and Iraq.

---

[1] Freedom House, 'Maldives', Freedom in the World 2010, 2010. Available at: https://freedomhouse.org/report/freedom–world/2010/maldives (accessed on 4 March 2019).

The rise of religious radicalism with the ideology of Salafi-jihadism is also striking given that the Maldivian State had attempted to maintain a 'moderate' and even a 'modernist' form of Sunni Islam throughout the 20th century. Multiple explanations exist as to why individuals undergo radicalization, emphasizing religious, ideological, economic and psychological factors.[2] In a wide-ranging review of the literature, Alex P. Schmid,[3] among others, has argued that the 'causes' of radicalization that can lead to violent extremism include not just the micro-level factors (e.g., identity problems, alienation, marginalization or discrimination) but also the meso-level ('wider radical milieu') and the macro-level factors (i.e., the role of government and society, the radicalization of public opinion and socio-economic problems).

This chapter aims to examine some of the key macro-level political, religious and ideological contexts for radicalization in the Maldives and the relationship between Salafism and radicalization. It shows that while Salafism and Salafi-jihadism are transnational ideologies,[4] the local matters[5] for their relevance, spread and escalation. Radical ideas 'emerged' in the Maldives under the harsh experience of authoritarian State suppression of Salafism in the 1980s and 1990s. However,

[2] H. Keiran, 'Comparing Theories of Radicalisation with Countering Violent Extremism Policy', *Journal for Deradicalization* 15 (2018): 76–110.

[3] A. P. Schmid, 'Radicalization, De-radicalization, Counter-radicalization: A Conceptual Discussion and Literature Review', International Centre for Counter Terrorism—Hague, 2013, 4. Available at: https://www.icct.nl/download/file/ICCT-Schmid-Radicalisation-De-Radicalisation-Counter-Radicalisation-March-2013.pdf (accessed on 4 March 2019).

[4] R. Meijer, *Global Salafism: Islam's New Religious Movement* (Oxford: Oxford University Press, 2014); Q. Wiktorowicz, 'A Genealogy of Radical Islam', *Studies in Conflict & Terrorism* 28, no. 2 (2005): 75–97. doi:10.1080/10576100590905057; Q. Wiktorowicz, 'Anatomy of the Salafi Movement', *Studies in Conflict & Terrorism* 29, no. 3 (2006): 207–239. doi:10.1080/10576100500497004

[5] M. Al-Rasheed, 'The Local and the Global in Saudi Salafi-Jihadi Discourse', in *Global Salafism: Islam's New Religious Movement*, ed. R. Meijer (Oxford: Oxford University Press, 2014); S. Ismail, *Rethinking Islamist Politics: Culture, the State and Islamism* (London: I. B.Tauris, 2006).

such connection between religious ideas and radicalization has to be unpacked.[6] Drawing from the discursive theoretical insights by scholars such as John Dryzek,[7] I argue that 'mainstream' contemporary Salafism does not have a unidirectional relationship with radicalization into violent extremism. Mainstream Salafism acts as both a discursive resource and a major discursive constraint for radicalization in a broader contestatory discursive field.

Instead, this chapter argues that it is the larger political and religious transformations since the early 21st century that have unleashed macro-level factors behind the rise of the minority ideology of Salafism—Salafi-jihadism—and the escalation of radicalization. First, the escalation of religious radicalism is an aspect of the broader 'communicative abundance'[8] that included the rise of Western and even anti-religious, secular discourses, in the wake of unprecedented political liberalization and access to modern media technologies since around 2004. Under the transformative discursive context, radical religious ideas also positioned as alternatives to the rapid rise of Western discourses, which themselves presented as alternatives to the long-standing authoritarian politics in the Maldives. Second, radicalization has escalated under unprecedented fragmentation of religious authority, long monopolized by the State. The escalation of radical ideas is also the effect of fragmentation of religious authority through general processes of modernization and the spectacular rise of Salafism as the most dominant religious voice in the public sphere. Finally, the deepening crises of politics and de-democratization that have failed to prioritize a sound policy have also contributed the escalation of radicalization.

This chapter consists of three sections. The first section schematically outlines a genealogy and background of radicalization in the

---

[6] P. R. Neumann, 'The Trouble with Radicalization', *International Affairs* 89, no. 4 (2013): 873–893. doi:10.1111/1468-2346.12049

[7] J. S. Dryzek, *Deliberative Global Politics: Discourse and Democracy in a Divided World* (Cambridge: Polity, 2006); J. S Dryzek and L. T. Holmes, *Post-Communist Democratization: Political Discourses across Thirteen Countries* (Cambridge: Cambridge University Press, 2002).

[8] J. Keane, *Democracy and Media Decadence* (Cambridge: Cambridge University Press, 2013).

Maldives. The second section explores the transformative political and religious contexts of radicalization. The third section examines how radicalism has escalated under the conditions unleashed through the transformative political and religious contexts and crises of politics and de-democratization.

RADICALIZATION AND VIOLENT EXTREMISM IN THE MALDIVES: AN OVERVIEW

On 29 September 2007, the 17th of the holy month of Ramadan—the anniversary of the Battle of Badr[9]—the Maldives experienced its first major terror attack. An improvised explosive device (IED) was exploded at the main public park, Sultan Park, in the capital Malé, injuring 12 foreign tourists. The attack was planned and executed by a group of Maldivians at the height of political liberalization in the Maldives.

In connection with the attack, the police travelled to Himandhoo Island, close to Malé, to arrest a suspect, but faced an unprecedented violent showdown with more than 70 armed 'radicalized' individuals who laid siege to a make-shift mosque where they had been having separate prayers.[10] Those islanders had been practising a radical version of Salafism for several years. Radical ideas especially emerged in the wake of the devastating Indian Ocean tsunami in 2004, which itself coincided with unpreceded political turmoil in the Maldives. Media reports, religious propaganda materials after the incident and statements by some of the suspects of the Sultan Park terrorist attack at the trial gave some clues about the ideological and operational links of those behind the attacks and individuals who confronted the police in Himandhoo.

---

[9] The Battle of Badr was a key battle by the Prophet Muhammad against his Meccan opponents fought on 17 Ramadan, 2 AH.

[10] R. Ramesh, '50 Held in Maldivian Mosque Siege', *The Guardian*, 9 October 2007. Available at: https://www.theguardian.com/world/2007/oct/09/randeep-ramesh (accessed on 4 March 2019).

Salafi-Jihadi Ideology, Roots and Its Linkages

In the broader radicalization research, ideology is taken to be crucial for justification of violence.[11] Several scholars have argued that there is no straightforward causal link between ideology and violent extremism.[12] While some have argued that religion plays a far lesser role in radicalization,[13] others have argued that 'Salafi-jihadi' ideology is the 'bedrock and catalyst' for violent extremism.[14]

Internet-based outlets and witness statements associated with Himandhoo episode and the Sultan Park attack suggest that those actors espouse what scholars[15] (have identified under the rubric of Salafi Jihadism.[16] They believe that Muslims and Islam are under attack by a 'Zionist-Crusader' conspiracy led by America. As such, the contemporary era fulfils the conditions of individual (*fard al-'ayn*) jihad. They believe that the concept of jihad has been distorted, as true jihad is physical fight against the enemies of Islam.[17] Similarly, they believe that the prevailing political systems are un-Islamic and *taghut* (idolatrous) and resort to *takfirism* (excommunication) against political leaders, judges, lawmakers, 'moderate' religious scholars and liberals. They, for example, declared President Gayoom as an apostate.[18]

---

[11] Schmid, *Radicalisation, De-radicalisation, Counter-Radicalisation*.

[12] Neumann, 'The Trouble with Radicalization'.

[13] A. Aly and J. L. Striegher, 'Examining the Role of Religion in Radicalization to Violent Islamist Extremism', *Studies in Conflict & Terrorism* 35, no. 12 (2012): 849–862. doi:10.1080/1057610X.2012.720243

[14] S. Maher, *Salafi-Jihadism: The History of an Idea* (Oxford: Oxford University Press, 2016); M. Silber and A. Bhatt, *Radicalization in the West: The Homegrown Threat* (New York Police Department, 2007), 16. Available at: https://sethgodin.typepad.com/seths_blog/files/NYPD_Report-Radicalization_in_the_West.pdf (accessed on 4 March 2019); Wiktorowicz, 'A Genealogy of Radical Islam'.

[15] Maher, *Salafi-Jihadism*; Wiktorowicz, 'A Genealogy of Radical Islam'; Wiktorowicz, 'Anatomy of the Salafi Movement'.

[16] 'Haqqu Forums' and its branch 'Jihadu ge Adu' (the Voice of Jihad) were the media brands used by Maldivian jihadists to identify themselves during this period. The leader and editor of Jihadu ge Adu was known by the alias, Abu Zubaida.

[17] Abdullah, *Abdullage Vaseeaiy* (Abdullah's Will), 2007. Available at: https://www.haqqubooks.com/single-post/2018/06/19/6784 (accessed on 4 March 2019).

[18] Haqqubas (Producer), *Muslim Ge Haalu* (Condition of the Muslim), 18 October 2007. Available at: https://www.youtube.com/watch?v=NUY90dma9ho

The elements of this ideology in the Maldives go back to the figure of Sheikh Muhammad bin Ibrahim, the Maldivian pioneer of Salafism. Ibrahim, perhaps the first Maldivian Medina University graduate, was persecuted by President Maumoon Abdul Gayoom's regime in the 1980s. He had worked for Gayoom regime but religious disagreements had soured his relationship with Gayoom. This included most famously the minor issue of *qunut* during the dawn prayer, which Ibrahim believed was a *bid'a* or religious innovation. He was imprisoned, tortured and sent on exile to Kalaidhoo Island in the 1980s and later house-arrested in the capital, Malé.

Only a few of his work and exchanges with his followers are publicly available.[19] However, sufficient evidence exists that Ibrahim had continued to spread a version of Salafism and for this purpose had established informal study circles. However, an informant (personal communication), who had been a member of his circle of followers, related to me that Sheikh Ibrahim sounded even more uncompromising than Muhammad ibn Abdul Wahhab when he interpreted the latter's work. It was possibly after his harsh experience under Gayoom regime, Ibrahim seemed to have started to propagate more radical ideas, including *takfirism* and radical interpretation of the concepts of *tawhid* and *hakimiyya* based on Salafi literature such as *Miraathul Anbiya*, a book by an al-Qaeda suspect, Abu Omar. While Ibrahim rejected *taqlid* to any *madhhab* or religious scholar, Ibrahim[20] had declared that President Gayoom had distorted even the Shafi'i *madhhab* and had created his own *madhhab* in the name of religious unity. Ibrahim propagated the view that the Maldivian regime was a *taghut* system and the political leaders, lawmakers and the judges were *taghut* rejecting *tawhid* and *hakimiyya*.[21]

(accessed on 4 March 2019).

[19] For example, https://www.facebook.com/bodusheikh/ (accessed on 4 March 2019).

[20] Sheikh Muhammad bin Ibrahim (Producer). *Islam kan* (Islam). 2 December 2016. Available at: https://www.facebook.com/bodusheikh/videos/1019074268202718/ (accessed on 4 March 2019).

[21] Abu Omar, 'Nabiyyunge Tharika' (Inheritance of the Prophets), n.d., 9, 26. Available at: https://www.haqqubooks.com/single-post/2018/06/19/6843 (accessed on 4 March 2019).

During his years of persecution, Ibrahim had attracted several followers in the island of Kalaidhoo, and in Malé. Ibrahim translated several Salafi literature and established a hand–written clandestine magazine, circulated by his followers. The venue his followers conducted their prayers and religious study circles in Malé was known as 'Dot' among his followers. 'Dot group' has therefore been used by the government authorities and others to refer to the network of individuals espousing Salafi-jihadi ideas in the Maldives.[22]

Those behind the 2007 Sultan Park attack and Himandhoo separatist mosque had ideological links to Ibrahim.[23] One piece of evidence that seems to link some of those who executed the 2007 Sultan Park attack to Ibrahim was the admission by one of the suspects, Ahmed Naseer, that he had sought religious advice from Ibrahim and had attended the 'Dot' prayer circle, where he also met individual supportive of jihadism.[24] A propaganda video released after the Himandhoo episode also referred to Ibrahim as '*bodu sheykh*' or 'big sheikh' and quoted him as having issued a fatwa declaring Gayoom was an apostate on 150 counts.[25] The Maldivian jihadi outlets supporting people from Himandhoo also have published work by Ibrahim.[26]

While some behind the Sultan Park attack and Himandhoo were religiously influenced by Muhammad bin Ibrahim, Maldivian jihadist figures also had ideological training and operational links to external radical groups. Several Maldivians who went to study in Pakistan in the

---

[22] There is some controversy over this name. Some claim 'Dot' stands for 'Defenders of Truth' and others suggest it comes from '.com' as the network became prominent through the internet. However, a figure, who had frequented Ibrahim's study circle, informed me in a personal communication that 'Dot' means simply the 'point' they met.

[23] Haveeru Media Group (Producer), *Religious Extremism in L. Gan—Maldives*, 2007. Available at: https://www.youtube.com/watch?v=ah4OKVtYXNU (accessed on 4 March 2019).

[24] A. Haleem, 'Bomuge Hamalaa Dhin Meehunge Shareeaiy' (The Trial of the Bomb Attackers), *Haveeru*, 2007. Available at: http://webcache.dhivehi.mv/ haveeru.com.mv/dhivehi/news/55065 (accessed on 4 March 2019).

[25] Haqqubas, *Muslim Ge Haalu*.

[26] Omar, *Nabiyyunge Tharika*.

1980s and 1990s were attracted to jihadist groups.[27] Since 9/11 and especially the US invasion of Iraq in 2003, those linkages intensified.[28] Some Maldivians had training and operational links to jihadist groups such as al-Qaeda and Lashkar-e-Taiba in Pakistan. Contemporary Maldivian online jihadist outlets (e.g., Al Bashaaraa Media, Thooba, Dar al-Arqam, Haqqu Books) propagate the Salafi-jihadi literature by key jihadist figures such as Abdullah Azzam, Osama bin Laden, Anwar al-Awlaki, Abu Musab al-Zarqawi and Omar Abdel Rahman. In 2009, a Maldivian by the name of Ali Jaleel, linked to al-Qaeda, carried out a suicide attack against Pakistan's Inter-Services Intelligence headquarters in Lahore[29] and in 2010, nine armed Maldivians, some with links to the Sultan Park attack, were arrested in North Waziristan by Pakistani authorities.

Evolution and Emergence of a New Type of Violence

With the rise of the Islamic State of Iraq and Syria (ISIS), there was a steady flow of Maldivian fighters joining jihadist groups in Syria and Iraq. Largely young and mostly male Maldivians joined the Islamic State (IS) and other jihadist groups in significant numbers. Based on some estimates the Maldives could be among the top per capita contributors of foreign fighters, with an estimated 200 fighters by December 2015.[30] While operational recruitment methods varied (e.g., mosques and internet), it was the rise of social media during this period that became the major conduit of jihadist literature.

Maldivian jihadists, like others, joined both IS and other jihadist groups in Syria. These divisions suggest that the Dot network is not the only Salafi-jihadist group in the Maldives or at least it has split in

---

[27] H. Amir, *Islamism and Radicalism in the Maldives* (Monterey, CA: Naval Postgraduate School, 2011).

[28] Ibid.; Haveeru Media Group, *Religious Extremism in L. Gan —Maldives.*

[29] A. Roul, 'The Threat from Rising Extremism in the Maldives', *CTC Sentinel* 6, no. 3 (2013): 24.

[30] The Soufan Group, '*Foreign Fighters: An Updated Assessment of the Flow of Foreign Fighters into Syria and Iraq,* 2015, 9. Available at: http://soufangroup.com/wp-content/uploads/2015/12/TSG_ForeignFightersUpdate4.pdf (accessed on 4 March 2019).

the wake of the rivalry between the IS and al-Qaeda. Reflective of these divisions, different internet-based outlets that support IS and other jihadist groups, respectively, have emerged.

The nature of violent extremism in the Maldives has also evolved: the target of violence now includes fellow Maldivians. The harassment and attacks against a vocal religious scholar affiliated with President Gayoom, Afrasheem Ali, since late 2007 marked the emergence of a new type of religion-based violence based on *takfirism*. Ali was excommunicated by jihadist elements in 2007 for his more liberal views, among other things, on music and dance. A jihadist outlet declared there was no 'response' to what Ali believed in, but there was a 'solution': to kill.[31]

Later in 2013, Ali was brutally murdered with multiple stabbings; but no jihadist outlet claimed responsibility. While the perpetrators are still unknown, the police arrested several who were supportive of jihadism in connection with the similar murder of the liberal blogger and human rights advocate, Yameen Rasheed, in 2017. Similarly, several other violent extremist incidents linked to jihadist elements targeting who they believe secularist and apostate Maldivians have also taken place. For example, Hilath Rasheed, who advocated religious tolerance, was near fatally attacked in 2012, and another liberal journalist and blogger, Ahmed Rilwan, has been missing since August 2014.

POLITICAL AND RELIGIOUS TRANSFORMATIONS: CONTEXTS FOR RADICALIZATION

While the genealogy of Salafi-jihadism goes back to the 1980s and 1990s, the public rise of radical religious ideas and escalation of radicalization are linked to the transformative political and religious contexts

---

[31] A. Zubaida, *Haqqu Forums in Afrasheem Ah Radhdheh Nudhenee Keevvetho?* (Why Doesn't Haqqu Forums Respond to Afrasheem?), 2007. Available at: https://fagudi.wordpress.com/2008/08/22/%DE%99%DE%A6%DE%87% DE%B0%DE%A4%DE%AA-%DE%8A%DE%AF%DE%83%DE%A6%DE %89%DE%B0%DE%90%DE%B0-%DE%87%DE%A8%DE%82%DE%B0- %DE%87%DE%A6%DE%8A%DE%B0%DE%83%DE%A7%DE%9D%DE%A 9%DE%82%DE%B0-%DE%87%DE%A6%DE%81%DE%B0/ (accessed on 1 May 2019).

in the country. As there is a dearth of scholarly literature on these dual transformations, this section explains these macro-level transformations in detail before exploring, in the next section, the specific factors they unleashed that were behind the escalation of religious radicalization.

Political Landscape: Sultanate to an Electoral Democracy to De-Democratization

Styled as a sultanate since adoption of Islam from around the 12th century and as a British-protected State since 1887, the Maldives began attempts at modern constitutional reforms from the early 1930s. A short-lived Republic was promulgated in 1953 and later again in 1968 after the Maldives gained full independence from the British in 1965.[32] Even though at least five key constitutions have been promulgated (1932, 1953, 1954, 1968 and 2008), which provide for certain civil and political rights, and certain electoral politics, in practice, deeply controlled and autocratic politics prevailed.[33]

Although President Maumoon Abdul Gayoom, a religious scholar educated at Sunni Islam's most prestigious university, Al-Azhar University in Egypt, came to power on a platform of reform and a rhetoric of democracy in 1978, his regime was also characterized by pervasive suppression of any form of dissent—political or religious.[34]

---

[32] U. Phadnis and E. D. Luithui, *Maldives: Winds of Change in an Atoll State* (New Delhi: South Asian Publishers, 1985).

[33] E. O. Colton, *The Elite of the Maldives: Sociopolitical Organisation and Change* (PhD dissertation, London: London School of Economics and Political Science, 1995); C. Maloney, *People of the Maldive Islands* (New Delhi: Orient BlackSwan, 2013); Phadnis and Luithui, *Maldives*; A. A. Rasheed, *Tourism, Economic Development and Governance in the Maldives: A Historical Institutional Evaluation* (PhD dissertation, Brisbane: The University of Queensland, 2013). Available at: https://espace. library.uq.edu.au/view/UQ:312716 (accessed on 4 March 2019); A. A. Rasheed, 'Historical Institutionalism in the Maldives: A Case of Governance Failure', *The Maldives National Journal of Research* 2, no. 1 (2014): 7–28.

[34] Amnesty International, *Republic of Maldives: Prisoners of Conscience and Unfair Trial Concerns, 1990–1993*, 1993. Available at: https://www.amnesty.org/en/documents/asa29/001/1993/en/ (accessed on 4 March 2019); Amnesty International, *Republic of Maldives: Repression of Peaceful Political Opposition (ASA 29/002/2003)*, 2003. Available at: https://www.amnesty.org/en/documents/asa29/002/2003/en/ (accessed on 4 March 2019); *The BBC*, 'Amnesty Blasts "Holiday Paradise"',

Political parties did not and were not allowed to exist in the Maldives. Similarly, although the minimal constitutional rights of freedoms of expression, the media, association and assembly were also generally provided in successive constitutions, the State dominated over society, blocking the emergence of a free public sphere.

However, Gayoom spearheaded rapid socio–economic modernization, a process which scholars link to liberalization and democratization.[35] Three specific modernization-related conditions together helped in rapid political liberalization from around 2003: (a) economic modernization; (b) high literacy rates and urbanized segments with modern education and (c) increased access to information and communications technologies and the internet. From the 1980s to the 2000s, GDP per capita in the Maldives increased substantially.[36] The per capita gross national income stood at $2,120 in 2002, the highest in South Asia.[37] In 2003, the adult literacy rate was more than 97 per cent. The primary and secondary education sector had also significantly expanded. By 2004, primary education was universally available in all 199 inhabited islands.[38] Similarly, while there were only 90 students studying abroad

---

2003. Available at: http://news.bbc.co.uk/2/hi/south_asia/3110425.stm (accessed on 4 March 2019).

[35] For example, S. M. Lipset, 'Some Social Requisites of Democracy: Economic Development and Political Legitimacy', *The American Political Science Review* 53, no. 1 (1959): 69–105. doi:10.2307/1951731; S. M. Lipset, 'The Social Requisites of Democracy Revisited: 1993 Presidential Address', *American Sociological Review* 59, no. 1 (1994): 1–22. doi:10.2307/2096130; S. P. Huntington, 'Will More Countries become Democratic?', *Political Science Quarterly* 99, no. 2 (1984): 193–218. doi:10.2307/2150402; S. P. Huntington, *The Third Wave: Democratization in the Late Twenieth Century* (Norman: Okalahoma Press, 1991); C. Boix and S. C. Stokes, 'Endogenous Democratization', *World Politics* 55, no. 4 (2003): 517–549; B. Geddes, 'What do we know about Democratization after Twenty Years?', *Annual Review of Political Science* 2, no. 1(1999): 115–144, doi:10.1146/annurev.polisci.2.1.115.

[36] A. A. Rasheed, *Tourism, Economic Development and Governance in the Maldive*, 33.

[37] The World Bank, *The World Bank in the Maldives: Country Report* (2004). Available at: http://siteresources.worldbank.org/INTMALDIVES/Resources/MV05.pdf (accessed on 4 March 2019).

[38] UNESCO, *World Data on Education: Maldives* (2011). Available at: http://www.ibe.unesco.org/sites/default/files/Maldives.pdf (accessed on 4 March 2019).

in 1971[39] and in 1977 there were only 56 university graduates,[40] by the early 2000s, at any given time, there were 1,000–1,500 Maldivian students seeking higher education abroad.[41] Most of them sought university education in the United Kingdom, Australia, Malaysia, India and Sri Lanka.[42] However, many also travelled to Middle Eastern countries. While these are still very low numbers, many key actors at the forefront of the oppositional public sphere came from the more highly educated and urbanized backgrounds. The 42 signatories to register the first political party in 2001 suggest this point: 16 people (35.7%) out of the 42 signatories had at least a university degree.[43] Similarly, high literacy rates facilitated communications and the spread of ideas through the various media outlets that sprang up since late 2003.

The expansion of electronic communications was as much an effect of liberalization as also a cause. Household access to television increased from 28 per cent in 2000 to 85 per cent by 2006. There was also a 45 per cent increase in the availability of satellite television between 2000 and 2006, with about 50 per cent of the households having access by 2006.[44] A 2013 survey showed television was the most popular means for political information, with 58 per cent saying television was their main source for information. Mobile phone penetration stood around 40 per cent of the population in 2004.[45] Internet was introduced in 1996, but by 2002, it penetrated more than 5 per cent of the popula-

---

[39] J. M. Ostheimer, *The Politics of the Western Indian Ocean Islands* (New York, NY: Praeger, 1975), 143.

[40] Phadnis and Luithui, *Maldives,* 51.

[41] A. Muhsin, *Country Report from the Maldives* (paper presented at the Eighth Session of the Regional Committee for the Regional Convention on Recognition of Qualification, Kunming, 2005).

[42] Ibid.

[43] See M. A. Shafeeg, *Dhivehi Raajje Democracy Ah Kuri Dhathuru* (Democratic Journey of Maldives; Male: Novelty Printers and Publishers, 2011), 22–23.

[44] MPND, *Population and Housing Census 2006,* (Male: Ministry of Planning and National Development, 2006). Available at: http://statisticsmaldives.gov.mv/nbs/wp-content/uploads/2006/12/Population&HousingCensus2006/graphs.htm (accessed on 4 March 2019).

[45] MPND. *Maldives: Key Indicators 2005* (Male: Ministry of Planning and National Development, 2005). Available at: http://statisticsmaldives.gov.mv/nbs/wp-content/uploads/2015/09/keyindicators-2005.pdf (accessed on 4 March 2019).

tion[46] that mostly included key urbanized segments in the capital, where the opposition operated. These numbers exponentially increased: in 2016 about 260,000 people (out of 372,000) had access to the internet.

The spark for major political liberalization began on 19 September 2003 when the security personnel in the Maldivian Maafushi island prison tortured to death a 19-year-old prisoner, Hassan Evan Naseem. Naseem's death triggered a prison riot. Security personnel opened fire on prisoners indiscriminately. A total of 20 people were shot. One prisoner died immediately. Two others died while being treated in Sri Lanka. Naseem's death also triggered spontaneous riots throughout the capital, Malé. Protesters damaged and torched several government buildings and vehicles. Such riots and violence were unprecedented in the tightly controlled regime of Gayoom. By then he had been in power for nearly 25 years. A deeply shocked government declared a state of emergency and arrested several people to bring the situation under control.

However, under both domestic and external pressure, the regime undertook major political liberalization measures. Political parties were allowed in 2005 for the first time and 13 political parties came into existence by 2008, having been so allowed since 2005 (see Table 4.1 for a list).

There was also an exponential growth of civil society organizations, with some estimating up to 700 registered between 2003 and 2008.[47] Based in these organizational nodes and enabled by modern media technologies, a vibrant and oftentimes a deeply contestatory public sphere emerged. The exponential growth of the Maldivian blogosphere during the period is one indicator of the emergent public sphere enabled by modern media technologies.

---

[46] I. Ahmed, *Statistics and Indicators on ICTs in the Maldives* (2004), 2. Available at: https://www.itu.int/ITU-D/ict/mexico04/doc/doc/42_mdv_e.pdf (accessed on 4 March 2019).

[47] Rajje Foundation, 'NGO Capacity and Needs Assessment' (2009). Available at: http://www.undp.org/content/dam/maldives/docs/Democratic%20 Governance/NGO%20Capacity%20&%20Needs%20Assessment%20-%20 Raajje%20Foundation.pdf.

Table 4.1 *Political Parties Registered between 2005 and 2008*

Political Party	Date
Maldivian Democratic Party (MDP)	June 2005
Dhivehi Rayyithunge Party (DRP)	July 2005
Adhaalath Party (AP)	August 2005
Islamic Democratic Party (IDP)	December 2005
Maldivian Social Democratic Party (MSDP)	December 2006
Maldivian National Congress (MNC)	December 2007
People's Party (PP)	December 2007
Social Liberal Party (SLP)	May 2008
Jumhooree Party (JP)	August 2008
People's Alliance (PA)	August 2008
National Unity Alliance (Gaumee Iththihaadh or GI)	September 2008
Poverty Reduction Party (PRP)	September 2008
Dhivehi Qaumee Party (DQP)	December 2008

Source: Compiled by the author based on data from Elections Commission of the Maldives.

On the back of the pressures from the emergence of an oppositional public sphere and scaled up by external transnational advocacy networks, political liberalization culminated in the adoption of a new constitution in 2008. Under the 2008 Constitution, multiparty presidential elections and parliamentary elections took place in 2008 and 2009, respectively. The presidential elections brought an end to the 30-year regime of Maumoon Abdul Gayoom on 11 November 2008. In 2010, the international democracy clearinghouse, Freedom House listed the Maldives as an electoral democracy for the first time.[48]

However, liberalization and democratization in the Maldives was from the beginning fraught with deep political unrest and societal polarization. The liberalization process was characterized by constant

---

[48] Freedom House, 'Freedom in the World 2010—Maldives (2010). Available at: https://freedomhouse.org/report/freedom-orld/2010/maldives

street protests and clashes between the security personnel and often-times supporters of the regime. Soon after coming to power, the first democratically elected President, Mohamed Nasheed, faced major challenges from former President Gayoom and Nasheed's own coalition parties. Nasheed resigned on 7 February 2012 after sections of the security services mutinied and demanded his resignation.

Nasheed's resignation led to political chaos and deep political polarization entangling all State institutions and every sector of the society. His party and supporters staged major protests and demonstrations throughout 2012–2013 until about new elections were announced. The elections, however, brought back former President Gayoom's party to power and his half-brother, Yameen Abdul Gayoom as the president. Since then, democratic and human rights violations have sharply increased, endangering any democratic gains that may have existed.[49] Freedom House has delisted it as an electoral democracy since its 2013 annual report.[50]

Religious Landscape: From Sufism to Salafism

Islam of the Maliki *madhhab* started to take root since the 12th century in the Maldives. However, Shafi'i *madhhab*, which had deep Sufism influences, replaced Maliki *madhhab* under the influence of a prominent Maldivian religious figure, Muhammad Jamaluddin, who had sought

---

[49] Amnesty International, *Maldives 2017/2018* (2018). Available at: https://www.amnesty.org/en/countries/asia-and-the-pacific/maldives/report-maldives/ (accessed on 4 March 2019); Freedom House, *Maldives Profile 2017* (2017). Available at: https://freedomhouse.org/report/freedom-world/2017/maldives (accessed on 4 March 2019); R. Sharma and A. Zahir, *A Troubled Future for Democracy: Results of the 2015 Maldives Democracy Survey* (2015). Available at: http://transparency.mv/files/media/6dca8a9f7beda482335bb654b88020f7.pdf (accessed on 4 March 2019); A. Zahir, *Does Islam Have a Problem with Democracy? The Maldivian Case* (2016). Available at: https://theconversation.com/does-islam-have-a-problem-with-democracy-the-case-of-the-maldives-58040 (accessed on 4 March 2019).

[50] Freedom House, *Freedom in the World 2013* (2013). Available at: https://freedomhouse.org/report/freedom-world/freedom-world-2013 (accessed on 4 March 2019).

religious knowledge in Yemen in the 16th century. Islam of the Shafi'i school of law had therefore existed as the sole recognized religion for more than 800 years in the Maldives. Yet, historical and ethnographic accounts suggest that a more relaxed, non-ostentatious and even syncretic orthopraxy had prevailed.[51] Similarly, while the State maintained a collective Islamic identity theoretically, a certain role differentiation regime had existed between religious functionaries, headed by the chief justice and the highest political authority, the sultan, until 1968. This arrangement was facilitated by the medieval pragmatic Muslim political thought that had influenced Maldivian chief justices. Such religious political theology stressed 'justice' and 'consultation' in State affairs, while accepting the prevailing political reality.

However from the 1930s, Islamic modernism, especially from the Indian subcontinent, influenced Maldivian religious and political thinking. South Asia and Egypt, among others, were the most important sites of Islamic modernism during the period.[52] Not surprisingly, some of the major educational institutions, journalism, literature and Islamic modernist intellectuals in these areas had direct influence on some key Maldivian elites such as Ahmed Kamil and the first President, Mohamed Amin, who were behind constitutional modernization in the 1930s. Amin, who was educated at Aligarh University founded by India's pre-eminent Islamic modernist, Sir Sayyid Ahmed Khan, laid down modern nation-state foundations in the 1940s and early 1950s. He sought Western-inspired 'civilization,' which he believed was largely compatible with the Islam of 'liberty, rationality and justice'.[53]

---

[51] Colton, *The Elite of the Maldives*; Maloney, *People of the Maldive Island*; F. O. Pyrard, *The Voyage of François Pyrard of Laval: To the East Indies, the Maldives, the Moluccas and Brazil* (London: Printed for the Hakluyt Society, 1887); X. Romero-Frías, *The Maldive Islanders: A Study of the Popular Culture of an Ancient Ocean Kingdom* (Indica: Nova Ethnographia, 2003).

[52] C. Kurzman, *Liberal Islam: A Source Book* (Oxford: Oxford University Press, 1998).

[53] M. Amin, *Kuriyah Dhivehi Qaum* ('onwards Maldives; Male: Novelty Printers and Publishers, 2007); M. Amin, 'Male Ge Muthaqbalaa Medhu Alhugan'duge Hiyaalu' ('My Dreams for the Future of Male'), In *Dhivehi adheebunge Dhuvasvee Liyunthah,* ed. A. Hussain (Male: Novelty Printers and Publishers, 2008), 27–37.

While their modernist ideology of civilization had influence among the elite, there was very limited societal modernization.

It was only in the 1960s and especially in the 1970s that the Maldives underwent rapid modernization and Westernization under President Ibrahim Nasir, who was educated in Ceylon. The participation in the global capitalist system with the introduction of tourism in 1972 and signing to the United Nations after gaining independence in 1965 facilitated this rapid modernization.[54] The real and perceived Westernization in this period created a context for resistance by a new wave of actors, who were educated in Egypt.

Headed by Maumoon Abdul Gayoom, who received a master's degree in Islamic sharia from Al-Azhar University, these new actors sought an Islamized modernity based on an exclusivist religious nationalism. Even though they were influenced by Muslim Brothers, they believed Islam endorsed modernization. As such, they were influenced by a certain Islamic modernism and Mu'tazilite theology. After coming to power in 1978, Gayoom however pursued paradoxical religious policies. As indicated, the 1968 Constitution ended the role differentiation regime between the president and the chief justice, which was ironically a secularist attempt to control religion by modernizing President Nasir. However, this created institutional space for Gayoom to extensively control religion.

On one hand, Gayoom maintained a rhetoric of Islamic identity, Islamic modernity and non-secular democracy. As part of promoting Islamic identity, there were extensive efforts to promote religious education and religious propagation to increase 'religious vitality' (i.e. individual beliefs and behaviour.[55] While a number of re-Islamization processes took place under Gayoom, he also paved way for societal modernization and even secularization. Hence, under Gayoom, there was significant economic and societal modernization as explained previously. He largely allowed the increased availability and consumption of Indian and Western popular cultural products. Western novels and literature, Hollywood and especially Bollywood

---

[54] Maloney, *People of the Maldive Islands*.

[55] See D. Herbert, *Religion and Civil Society: Rethinking Public Religion in the Contemporary World* (Aldershot, Hampshire; Burlington, VT: Ashgate, 2003).

films, Hindi television soap operas, Bollywood and Western music, songs and fashion became part and parcel of the Maldivian popular culture. Sports, Divehi cinema, music and song, drugs and other commodities of gratification also increased. Although two Arabic medium schools were opened, in line with his modernist Islam, Gayoom promoted the British curricula-based education and opened the first English-medium secondary school, Science Education Centre, in 1979.

On the other hand, Gayoom crushed both political and religious dissent of all hues except his 'moderate' statist Islam. As indicated, policies that suppressed religious opinions largely targeted Salafi fig-ures educated mainly in Saudi Arabia and Pakistan since especially the 1980s.[56] In the early 2000s the government and educational institutions seemed to have increased the suppressive measures against young people from both Salafi backgrounds and from more secular backgrounds. The outcome of these paradoxical policies was secularization of the 'real community' (in terms of differentiation of subsystems and discourses) and sacralization of the 'imagined community'. This context was not only ripe for push for greater political liberalization, as explored in the previous subsection. It also provided 'right' discursive conditions for the emergence of Salafism.

With political liberalization, just like other groups, Salafi figures also considered how to steer in the transformative political environment. Some pushed for a top-down approach of insertion into political society and the State. Others wanted a more bottom-up civil society-based approach. In the end, some decided to form a political party in the form

---

[56] See Declaration, 'Maumoon Abdul Gayoom Islam Dheenaa Khilaafu Vaahakathah Dhakkaifaivaathee Eynaa Aa Dhekolhah Raajjeyge Ilmuverin Nerenu Bayaan' (Declaration against Gayoom's Un-Islamic Views), 2008. Available at: https://immaadhil.wordpress.com/2008/09/28/%DE%87%DE%A6%DE%8D %DE%B0%DE%87%DE%AA%DE%90%DE%B0%DE%8C%DE%A7%DE%9B %DE%AA-%DE%89%DE%A6%DE%87%DE%AA%DE%89%DE%AB%DE%8 2%DE%AA-%DE%A2%DE%A6%DE%84%DE%B0%DE%8B%DE%AA%DE% 8D%DE%B0%DE%A4%DE%A6%DE%87%DE%B0%DE%94/ (accessed on 4 March 2019); I. H. Ibrahim, 'Raees Abdul Nasir Ge Dheenee Ingilaabaai Raees Maumoon Ge Dheenee Ingilaab' (Religious Revolutions by President Nasser [of Egypt] and President Gayoom), 2006. Available at: http://www.ilyashussainibra-him.com/?p=224 (accessed on 4 March 2019).

of AP, registered in 2006. Others decided to operate within the civil society. The most prominent example is the Salafi NGO, Jamiyatul Salaf (JS), registered in 2006. As stated, since especially 2007, Salafism, which had been hitherto suppressed, emerged as the most dominant religious voice in the public sphere. Since then by 2009, Salafism has spectacularly emerged as the most dominant religious voice in the public sphere using all the socialization processes. Through the coalition against Gayoom, Islamist AP, with a membership of less than 15,000, became part of the new government elected in 2008. The new government created a full-fledged cabinet ministry headed by AP figures, an unannounced political rise of Salafism in the State for the first time. Since then, the nature of majoritarian electoral politics has further favoured Salafi groups beyond the size of their political constituency. Similarly, while there were no more than two NGOs with religious objectives before 2004, there were 12 registered by 2010 (see Table 4.1).

The supply side of Salafism has exponentially grown via the mainstream media such as radio and television, social media such as Facebook and Twitter and platforms such as WhatsApp and Viber, within a very short span of time. Today, more than any other civil society sector, they are perhaps the most active in outreach activities in the communities.[57] Finally, the Islamic education outlets have increased too. From pre-schools to universities, a major change is visible. Now, at any given year about 15 new people are given permits to preach. Overall therefore the Salafism's supply side through socialization processes is now unmatched by any other religious voice.

MACRO-LEVEL FACTORS BEHIND ESCALATION OF RADICALIZATION

The spread of radical religious ideas and escalation of radicalization in the Maldives are no doubt in the context of globalization of jihadism

---

[57] See, for example, *Maldives Democracy Network*, 'Preliminary Assessment of Radicalisation in the Maldives' (2006). Available at: http://mdn.mv/wp-content/uploads/2016/09/Preliminary-Assessment-of-Radicalisation-in-the-Maldives-Final.pdf (accessed on 3 May 2019).

and the War on Terror. However, the global developments also coincided with the unprecedented transformative religious and political contexts in the Maldives that unleashed specific factors behind the escalation of radicalization in the same period. One outcome of political liberalization leading to an electoral democracy in the Maldives was the unprecedented communicative abundance—a dominant aspect of which was the rise of Western discourses as the basis for a new political order. Radical religious discourses, along with Salafism, present themselves as alternatives to those discourses. A second outcome of the general processes of modernization and rise of Salafism was the fragmentation of religious authority hitherto monopolized by the State. Religious radicalization has thrived under fragmentation of religious authority. Finally, radicalization has also thrived on the deepening crises of politics and de-democratization.

Radicalization as an Aspect of Communicative Abundance

Communicative abundance is a global phenomenon and is enabled by 'a new world system of overlapping and interlinked media devices'.[58] It enables 'messages to be sent and received through multiple user points, in chosen time, either real or delayed, within modularized and ultimately global networks'.[59] Hence, the broader communicative abundance in the Maldives in a globalized context was rapidly permeable to global discourses—both non-religious and religious discourses.

The rise of Salafi-jihadism and associated radicalization is a phenomenon of the broader communicative abundance that emerged since 2003 under political liberalization and positioned as an alternative to other discourses, especially those of Western origin, in this context. The global discourses of human rights and democracy emerged as the most dominant 'messages' in the rising communicative abundance in the Maldives since late 2003. In fact, the global human rights discourse, interpreted in secular terms in some political segments, was very much

---

[58] Keane, *Democracy and Media Decadence,* 1.
[59] Ibid., 2.

the basis of the new political order against the authoritarian regime.[60] The new constitution provided a sweeping Bill of Rights. Out of 46 Muslim States ranked by the number of rights in their constitutions in 2014, the Maldives was placed second, with 72 rights, second only to Albania with 75 rights.[61] This is not to say that the new constitution was secular (it established Islam as the State religion and sharia one main source of law) or that most people received the discourse based on secular liberal ideology.

Yet, human rights and democracy spread horizontally in a short period of time. Survey findings in the Maldives show that the mass support for democracy was fairly strong.[62] Sixty-two per cent believe democracy is the best system. Similarly, more than 75 per cent of the people believe that having a democratic political system is good.[63] Among the 77 per cent of Maldivians who stated democracy was good for their country (with only 15% saying it was bad), most associated democracy with certain freedoms and rights.[64]

Beyond these discourses, calls for outright secularism and anti-religious ideas also slowly emerged as an aspect of the communicative abundance. Such discourses have been largely confined to the margin, existed through Internet-based platforms such as blogs and became more prominent with the rise of new social media platforms such as Facebook. While a minority of Maldivians express these ideas, their reach became much wider through the rise of new social media. By 2016, for example, there were more than 270,000 Facebook users in the Maldives.

Religious discourses generally rose to prominence as an aspect of the communicative abundance by positioning themselves as alternatives to

---

[60] A. Shahid and H. Yerbury, 'A Case Study of the Socialization of Human Rights Language and Norms in Maldives: Process, Impact and Challenges', *Journal of Human Rights Practice* 6, no. 2 (2014): 281–305. doi:10.1093/jhuman/huu008.

[61] D. Ahmed and M. Gouda, 'Measuring Constitutional Islamization: The Islamic Constitutions Index', *Hastings International and Comparative Law Review* 38, no. 1 (2014): 60.

[62] Sharma and Zahir, *A Troubled Future for Democracy*.

[63] Ibid., 11.

[64] Ibid., 12.

the more dominant discourses of Western origin. As explained before, Salafi ideas emerged as the dominant religious voice. However, Salafism is not monolithic either in their discourse or practice and this is true in the Maldives too.[65] The 'mainstream' Salafism, that is, Salafism which operates in the open public sphere through registered outlets using mainstream media has two broad discursive and political tendencies. The first tendency denounces partisan politics, political factionalism and even other Salafi groups for their partaking in politics and organizations. Relatively less dominant, they emphasize on education as the appropriate means for the Salafi cause. Hence, they have opened educational centres in several areas. Those with this variety of Salafism are Wiktorowicz's 'purists'. They are known as 'Super Salafis' in the religious and political circles in the Maldives.

The second tendency of Salafism has unambiguously positioned onto the platform of politics and the State. While some Salafi figures operate through parties, others do so through civil society organizations. They believe that while societal Salafization is necessary, the political society and State constitute crucial arena for religion. They are Wiktorowicz's 'politicos'. Organizations such as JS and the political party AP have attracted these figures. The 'politicos' constitute the most dominant variety of Salafism and in fact the most dominant religious voice in the public sphere. Ideologically, some of the leading mainstream Salafi figures believe that democracy is a system of *kufr* because it is against God's *hakimiyya* (sovereignty). They are deeply critical of the circumscribed place for sharia in the State. However, in practice they work within the prevailing system towards a more comprehensive sharia. They have participated in the electoral field based on 'jurisprudence of balances' and selecting 'the lesser of the two evils'. Perhaps more than any ideological issue, secularism as 'the other' of Islam has become their defining discourse.[66]

---

[65] Maher, *Salafi-Jihadism;* Meijer, *Global Salafism;* Wiktorowicz, 'A Genealogy of Radical Islam';Wiktorowicz, 'Anatomy of the Salafi Movement'.

[66] A. Naseem, 'Dhawlathun Dheen Vakikohlumakee....' (Separation of Religion from the State Is....), *Dharuma* (2004): 3–12; M. Shaheem, *Islaam Dheenaai Democracy (Islam and Democracy;* Male: Noorul-Islam, 2006).

Salafi-jihadism—the third category of the broader Salafi movement according to Wiktorowicz's typology—that advocates violent means also positioned themselves as an alternative vision and escalated in this broader transformative contexts of communicative abundance, enabled by modern media technologies. Hence, while Salafi-jihadism concerns itself with the global, the local matters too. Locally, Salafi-jihadism found relevance by indicting the dominant discourses of democracy, which it portrayed as an idolatrous system, and through indictment and excommunication of political leaders, 'liberals' and 'moderate' scholars. However, a prominent theme of Salafi-jihadism has been the cause of global jihadism as an individual obligation on all Muslims, intensifying in the post-Arab Spring context. In this context, as explained, social media became widely available in Maldives, further increasing communicative abundance. Even then, however, the steady flow of Maldivians to Syria to join jihadist groups was linked to the local: jihadists spread the narratives of *hijra* (migration) and a possible caliphate and an Islamic system in Syria as an alternative to the idolatrous political system prevailing in the Maldives.

Relationship between Salafism and Radicalization

Even though Salafi-jihadism is, therefore, part of the broader movement of Salafism in the Maldives that positioned in a transformative discursive context, a question arises how mainstream Salafism is related to Salafi-jihadism. This is important given that the dominant media commentary on radicalization in the Maldives assumes that contemporary Salafism imported from Saudi Arabia is the key driver of religious radicalism in the Maldives.[67] However, this link between mainstream Salafism and radicalization into violent extremism based on Salafi-jihadism is more assumed than argued for in the Maldivian context. Taking 'ideas' or 'discourses' as resources and constraints existing in a broader discursive field,[68] I argue that mainstream Salafism has existed both as a resource

---

[67] I. Dharmawardhane, 'Maldives', in *Handbook of Terrorism in the Asia-Pacific*, eds. R. Gunaratna and S. Kam (London: Imperial College Press, 2016), 335–368.

[68] Dryzek and Holmes, *Post-Communist*.

and as a constraint for radicalization, rather than a unidirectional contributor of radicalization in the Maldives.

Mainstream Salafism has existed as a discursive resource by mainstreaming certain elements of the Salafi-jihadi ideology. It has vigorously promoted the discourse of a global conspiracy against Islam and existence of a 'clash of civilization' between Islam and the West. It is through this discursive framework and an existence of a global 'Zionist-Crusade' conspiracy against Islam they have analysed the conflicts and wars in the Middle East and elsewhere in Muslim lands. It therefore also promotes concepts such as *al-wala wal-bara* (loyalty/love and disavowal/hate) that reinforce the clash of civilizational discourse. As mentioned, many mainstream Salafi figures also see democracy as inappropriate for Muslims and even as a system of *kufr*. More crucially, while not a prominent theme, they also do promote jihad where the conditions prevail. Hence, for example, Palestine is a clear case where Muslims should organize jihad.[69] As the most dominant religious voice in the contemporary public sphere, their diagnosis of the contemporary global issues through a lens of clash of civilization, discourses against pluralism and mutual tolerance and calls for a comprehensive sharia State therefore aligns with elements that Salafi-jihadism also shares. If those elements are not positive discursive resources for radicalization, they cannot at least function as a deterrence against radicalization.

However, this positive or facilitative relationship is not straightforward. There has been major contestation between those subscribing to Salafi-jihadism and mainstream Salafism in the Maldives. Several mainstream Salafi figures have criticized Salafi-Jihadists as uneducated and ignorant of true Salafi methodology. In the wake of the Himandhoo episode and Sultan Park attack, leaders from AP publicly condemned violence, *takfirism* and jihadist interpretation of politics.[70] Similarly,

---

[69] The YouTube channel, DharusMV, https://www.youtube.com/channel/UCRDNN5KD3BljbhlvualpC_w, contains several speeches by mainstream Salafi figures focusing on these themes.

[70] Haveeru, 'Dr Majeed Bari Ge Interview' (Interview with Dr Abdul Majeed Bari), 2007. Available at: http://webcache.dhivehi.mv/haveeru.com.mv/dhivehi/news/53624 (accessed on 4 March 2019).

religious figures with the purist variety have vigorously criticized and condemned Salafi-jihadism. Mainstream figures have also condemned the ISIS. While some are sympathetic to the cause of jihad in Syria, mainstream figures have been critical of the actions of the various jihadist groups in Syria. Again as the dominant religious voice, and with religious educational credentials, the mainstream Salafi criticisms therefore undermine the religious credibility of Maldivian jihadists.

Fragmentation of Religious Authority

If radicalization has no unidirectional relationship to mainstream Salafism, Salafi-jihadist ideology has thrived under fragmentation of religious authority in no small measure due to the spectacular rise of Salafism. The fragmentation of religious authority was slow in coming but emerged through modernization and transformation of religious landscape.

Clarence Maloney and Elizabeth Colton both observed that even in the late 1970s, Islam in the Maldives was largely a matter of practice rather than a topic of philosophizing, debate or examination.[71] Such confinement of religion as largely a practice is not unique to the Maldives. However, a process of 'objectification' of Islam emerged since around the mid-1970s in Muslim societies.[72] Eickelman and Piscatori define objectification as the process whereby 'basic questions come to the fore in the consciousness of a large number of believers'.[73] The increased mobility, rise of mass media and communications and mass literacy are credited as enabling factors for this process.[74]

The rapid modernization in the Maldives as explained before provided these factors for objectification of Islam, and intensified through political liberalization and rise of Salafism. The emergence of Salafism

---

[71] Maloney, People of the Maldive Islands, 227; Colton, The Elite of the Maldives, 176–177.

[72] D. F. Eickelman and J. P. Piscatori, Muslim Politics (Princeton, N.J: Princeton University Press, 1996), 38.

[73] Ibid., 37–45.

[74] Ibid.

in the public sphere in particular led to a major shift in the State–society relationship with regard to religious authority. The religious authority that was monopolized by the State, under the chief executive, became publicly contested. Salafists and Islamists vigorously competed to claim authority on religious matters. A declaration signed by 44 oppositional religious figures in 2008 condemning President Gayoom spectacularly signalled the State–society shift with regard to religious authority, the fragmentation of religious authority, and the ever increasing pluralization of religious discourses. The declaration condemned Gayoom for his religious positions, among other things on death penalty, the veil and his methodological approach to understanding Qur'an.[75] Such a declaration would be unimaginable before political liberalization. It is not just the State monopoly on religious authority that was undermined. Salafi figures also contested the religious authority of those who follow more liberal and modernist line of religious thinking. A case that illustrates this is the book *Freedom of Religion, Apostasy and Islam*, co-authored by Abdullah Saeed, a Maldivian reformist Muslim scholar at the University of Melbourne, and his brother Hassan Saeed, a former Maldivian politician and judge. This scholarly work argued laws on apostasy and its punishment of death were untenable in the modern era. However, it was not specifically focused on the Maldives, but used mainly Malaysia as a case study. The book was presented to President Gayoom himself in 2004 by Hassan Saeed, who was a judge appointed by Gayoom at the time, which he reportedly praised at that time. However in 2008, JS issued a 15-page declaration condemning the book and its authors. Similarly in 2007, JS also issued a declaration against the relatively more liberal religious scholar, Dr Afrasheem Ali condemning his religious views and practices.

The general effects of objectification of and fragmentation of religious authority has been an ever more individualization of religious authority irrespective of the level of one's religious education. The Salafi-jihadist network of individuals in fact generally lacks formal religious educational credentials. The general Arabic and English linguistic literacy competencies have enabled individual readings of religious

---

[75] Declaration, 'Maumoon Abdul Gayoom'.

literature. They have therefore not only contested the State religious authority on Islam, but also the authority of religious scholars and organizations increasingly since 2007. Hence, whole pamphlets have been produced by them criticizing scholars belonging to JS and AP.[76] In the social media, they continue to portray these scholars as *murjiah* (*Murijites*)— that is, akin to those who fail to pass religious judgements on those who commit sins.

Crises of Politics and De-Democratization

A final factor that has escalated radicalization relates to the crises of politics and de-democratization in the Maldives that have constrained sound policymaking and devotion of relevant resources on counter-radicalization and de-radicalization. The security services in the Maldives have been deeply entangled in the larger political crises throughout the liberalization processes and later in the de-democratization. As indicated, police and military personnel were involved in the ouster of the first democratically elected government in 2012. These institutions have therefore become highly politicized.

As a consequence, a comparatively larger focus on politics has been prioritized over devotion of necessary resources for issues such as radicalization. Not surprisingly, jihadist online outlets had proliferated unabated especially since 2012 and the propagation of radical ideas had taken place in mosques for long periods of time without police action. The policy side is equally problematic: it was only in 2014, for instance, a special National Counter Terrorism Centre (NCTC) was established. The NCTC is under the Ministry of Defence and led by the military.

It was only in 2016 a policy on violent extremism was adopted and only in 2017 a national strategy on preventing and countering violent

---

[76] Haqqu Forums, 'Aadheyhaa Eku Jamiyyathul Salaf ah' (To Jamiyyathul Salaf; 2008). Available at: https://archive.org/details/Dhivehi (accessed on 3 May 2019); Haqqu Forums, 'Adhalaathu Paateege Riyaasathah Hulhuvifaivaa Sitee' (Open Letter to the Leadership of Adalath Party 2009). Available at: https://archive.org/details/HaqquForums (accessed on 2 May 2019).

extremism was adopted. Similarly, the policymaking has not been evidence-based. It was only with the establishment of NCTC that the State started even studying the phenomenon of radicalization.

Finally, where they have functioned, the security services had pursued a traditional intelligence approach to violent extremism. It was only in recent years that the State attempted counter-radicalization and de-radicalization efforts.

CONCLUSION

This chapter has argued that while transnational linkages existed, the Salafi-jihadi ideology behind radicalization in the Maldives had a local genealogy dating back to the emergence of Salafism in the 1980s and 1990s. However, contemporary mainstream Salafism is plural and acts as both a resource and major constraint for Salafi-jihadism. Instead, the macro-level conditions unleashed due to a rapidly transformative political and religious context explained the rise of Salafi-jihadism and associated radicalization: the general rise of communicative abundance, enabled by media technologies, that is home to a variety of discourses—most dominantly Western discourses; the fragmentation of religious authority under modernity and pluralization of religious discourses; and, the crises of politics that has failed to prioritize sound policy over partisan politics. These domestic factors and how they are addressed would, therefore largely determine the future of the spread of Salafi-jihadism and associated radicalization.

Chapter 5

Counter-Radicalization in Sri Lanka
A Blueprint for Action

Iraj De Alwis, Anishka De Zylva and
Barana Waidyatilake

INTRODUCTION

Sri Lanka is no stranger to the devastating impacts of radicalization. Since achieving independence in 1948, the country has suffered from two insurrections and a three-decade-long civil war, all of which were prompted by various processes of radicalization. Moreover, many of the factors that fuelled the various forms of radicalization in Sri Lanka remain unaddressed, or at best addressed through short-term measures that do not guarantee non-recurrence and lasting political and socio-economic stability. It is therefore necessary to undertake a systematic study of radicalization in Sri Lanka as well as the State's responses to such radicalization. Indeed, this study aims to contribute to that investigation and enable Sri Lankan policymakers to identify what more needs to be done to effectively address the issue of radicalization.

To begin the examination of radicalization in Sri Lanka, this chapter argues that in Sri Lanka radicalization is linked to two processes, majoritarianism and marginalization, which require distinct and coordinated policy action. Such policy action should consist of both domestic reforms and regional and global engagement. The case for such an initiative is made by examining the various instances of radicalization in Sri Lanka and their root causes, as well as the shortcomings in the current counter-radicalization measures adopted by the country. In outlining a blueprint for both domestic reform and global engagement on counter-radicalization, this chapter draws on several countries' experiences in tackling both radicalization and the root causes of it.

Through both its analysis and its policy prescriptions, this chapter makes a new contribution to the study of radicalization in Sri Lanka. Although there is some research on the various forms of radicalization in Sri Lanka, those studies have largely remained analytical and have not considered outlining a holistic policy plan for addressing the issue of radicalization. Sri Lanka's counter-radicalization efforts require a fundamental rethink, particularly at a 'macro level,' and this chapter will contribute to that need through policy-oriented research and analysis on the topic.

AN OVERVIEW OF RADICALIZATION IN SRI LANKA

According to the European Union (EU),[1] radicalization is a complex process whereby one embraces religious, political or social ideas and goals that inspire acts of violence or terror. This chapter considers two distinct processes of radicalization that are interlinked and often drive each other but require specific as well as coordinated policies: majoritarian and marginalized.

Radicalization driven by the process of majoritarianism is present in many Indian Ocean region countries, including Sri Lanka. In Sri Lanka religious, linguistic and ethnic markers have been used to create a Sinhala-Buddhist majority community that dominates the resources of the State. Following independence in 1948, through majoritarian discourse, political leaders in Sri Lanka have regularly mobilized citizens,

---

[1] European Commission, 'Radicalisation Awareness Network (RAN)', 2017. Available at: https://search.proquest.com/docview/1441429436?accountid=11752 (accessed on 5 March 2019).

in particular youth suffering from slim economic opportunities, political exclusion or social pressures, to gain power and dedicate the resources of the State entirely or overwhelmingly to the majority community.[2] Consequently, these actions have legitimized majoritarian discourse in the public sphere and in State institutions. Therefore, although most majoritarian views do not translate into violence, the normalization of majoritarianism provides the bedrock for more radical movements that lead to violence and terror.

Radicalization driven by the process of marginalization is also present in Sri Lanka. The Liberation Tigers of Tamil Eelam (LTTE), for example, emerged from this process of radicalization. This process of radicalization takes place when marginalized groups of people who suffer from economic and political pressures are exempted from the welfare system of the State apparatus, and denied access to opportunities and resources. These marginalized groups are not only often ignored by the government but also discriminated against by other communities in the public sphere. This has led to youth from these marginalized groups to become radicalized through various means that are often non-institutional and informal.[3]

Although there exists radicalization through the process of majoritarianism and radicalization through the process of marginalization, the two are co-dependent. A brief overview of radicalization in Sri Lanka illustrates this intertwined past and present of the two processes.

The Rise of Sinhala-Buddhist Ethnic Politics (1947–1980s)

The early calls for preferential treatment for Sri Lanka's Sinhala-speaking Buddhist majority came from rural youth, who were led

---

[2] N. Biziouras, 'The Political Economy of Ethnic Mobilisation: Comparing the Emergence, Consolidation, and Radicalisation of Ethnic Parties in Post-Colonial Sri Lanka and Malaysia', *Commonwealth & Comparative Politics* 51, no. 4 (2013): 479–502.

[3] Minority Rights Group International, *No War, No Peace: The Denial of Minority Rights and Justice in Sri Lanka* (London: Minority Rights Group International, 2011). Available at: http://www.worldcat.org/oclc/698586938 (accessed on 5 March 2019).

by a group of young monks in 1947.[4] Their grievances were against both the prosperous minority populations and the Europeanized elite, who they accused of hoarding economic opportunities.[5] Though at first condemned for their ethno-centric rhetoric by all politicians, this group of rural youth became the backbone of a new political party, namely, the Sri Lanka Freedom Party (SLFP), that swept the elections of 1955.[6] Once in power the SLFP passed the Sinhala Only Act though Parliament in 1956, which made Sinhala the only language of the State. Additionally, the government restructured the country's civil service to ensure that government resources were dedicated overwhelmingly to the Sinhala-Buddhist majority. Scholars like De Votta identify two long-term effects of the Sinhala Only Act. The first effect is that the legitimization of majoritarian discourse led to a phenomenon he names 'ethnic outbidding', where political parties are trapped in a cycle, attempting to outdo each other in pursuing ethno-centric policies in order to win elections.[7] Decades of this cycle have resulted in a deep normalization of majoritarian identities and discrimination against minority populations. From the 1950s through to the 1980s, Sri Lanka saw intermittent riots by radicalized Sinhalese, leading to a series of pogroms in the early 1980s against the Tamil minority.[8] The second effect De Votta identifies is 'institutional decay'. Legislature like the Sinhala Only Act compromised the impartiality of the State institutions,

---

[4] H. L. Seneviratne, *The Work of Kings: The New Buddhism in Sri Lanka* (Chicago, IL: University of Chicago Press, 1999). Available at: http://www.worldcat.org/oclc/924917083 (accessed on 5 March 2019).

[5] W. Rahula, *The Heritage of the Bhikkhu (Bhikṣuvage Urumaya, English) a Short History of the Bhikkhu in Educational, Cultural, Social, and Political Life* (New York, NY: Grove Press, 1974). Available at: http://www.worldcat.org/oclc/164803569 (accessed on 5 March 2019).

[6] K. M. De Silva and University of London, *Sri Lanka* (London: Stationery Office, 1997). Available at: http://www.worldcat.org/oclc/37613891 (accessed on 5 March 2019).

[7] Neil De Votta, *Blowback: Linguistic Nationalism, Institutional Decay, and Ethnic Conflict in Sri Lanka* (Stanford, CA: Stanford University Press, 2004). Available at: http://www.worldcat.org/oclc/799591573 (accessed on 5 March 2019).

[8] S. J. Tambiah, *Buddhism Betrayed? Religion, Politics and Violence in Sri Lanka* (Chicago, IL: University of Chicago Press, 1992). Available at: http://www.worldcat.org/oclc/468492140 (accessed on 5 March 2019).

including the judiciary, legislature, police, healthcare and education.[9] As majoritarian sentiments have swept through these sectors, minority populations find the resources of the State to be either inaccessible or harmful to them.

The Janatha Vimukthi Peramuna (1960s–1980s)

Left-wing radicalization in Sri Lanka emerged in two phases through the Janatha Vimukthi Peramuna (JVP), which is now a reformed electoral party in Sri Lanka. Professing Marxist–Leninist ideologies, JVP began as a group of Sinhala youth who had received their higher education through local universities and were trained for middle-class jobs. Unfortunately, this group of youth graduated during a time when Sri Lanka's economy was stagnant. The State and the Europeanized upper-caste ruling elite remained indifferent to the plight of these educated and frustrated rural youth.[10] Under the politics of the Cold War their anger flowed into radical leftist movements. In 1971, the JVP rallied youth across ethnic lines in an insurrection that spread throughout parts of the island. This insurrection took the State by surprise but was finally suppressed by military force. In the late 1980s there was a second attempt under a different leadership. Launched in a political space mired in ethno-centrism, the JVP's second insurrection involved solely the Sinhala majority and was also suppressed by military force. Between the brutality of the JVP and the State around 60,000 Sri Lankans lost their lives.[11] However, since their defeat the JVP has denounced violent action and is now a well-represented party in Sri Lankan politics.[12]

---

[9] Neil De Votta, 'Control Democracy, Institutional Decay, and the Quest for "Eelam": Explaining Ethnic Conflict in Sri Lanka', *Pacific Affairs: An International Review of Asia and the Pacific* 73, no. 1 (2000). Available at: http://www.worldcat.org/oclc/717354809 (accessed on 5 March 2019).

[10] Gananath Obeyesekere, 'Some Comments on the Social Backgrounds of the April 1971 Insurgency in Sri Lanka (Ceylon)', *The Journal of Asian Studies* 33, no. 3 (1974): 367–384. Available at: http://www.worldcat.org/oclc/6015208566 (accessed on 5 March 2019).

[11] Ibid.

[12] T. Hill, 'The Deception of Victory: The JVP in Sri Lanka and the Long-Term Dynamics of Rebel Reintegration', *International Peacekeeping* 20, no. 3

The LTTE (1976–2009)

For over 30 years, the Liberation Tigers of Tamil Eelam (LTTE) fought a bitter war against Sri Lanka's armed forces. The LTTE aimed to create a separate and independent state comprising Sri Lanka's north and east exclusively for the country's Tamil minority. The LTTE emerged as the primary militant opposition to the State in the immediate aftermath of a series pogroms in the early 1980s targeting Tamil businesses and households. Three decades of ethno-centric political practices and 'institutional decay' had marginalized an entire generation of Tamil youth. They were exempted from economic opportunities, and faced open discrimination and public violence. Marginalization along ethnic lines created fertile ground for the seeds of radicalization that inspire violence. The LTTE therefore actively engaged in recruiting the Tamil populace, particularly youth, and in their later years, they even radicalized and recruited children into their ranks. Indeed, UNICEF revealed that in the last six years of the war alone, the LTTE had deployed over 6,000 children as combatants.[13] Given this radicalization, after the war ended, the government set up a rehabilitation programme to serve former LTTE combatants, including youth.[14]

The Bodu Bala Sena (2012–Present)

The most recent spate of right-wing nationalism is the depiction of the Muslim minority as a threat to the Sinhala–Buddhist majority. This depiction has been led by a collection of new organizations, primarily the Bodu Bala Sena (BBS). Its leader espouses radical majoritarian rhetoric and has strong support among younger Buddhist clergy.[15]

(2013): 357–374.

[13] *UNICEF*, 'Sri Lanka: More Children Victims of the Conflict, Says UNICEF', 2009. Available at: https://www.unicef.org/media/media_48044.html (accessed on 5 March 2019).

[14] *Bureau of the Commissioner General of Rehabilitation*, 'Details of Reintegrated Child Ex-Combatants', 2014. Available at: http://www.bcgr.gov.lk/reintegra-tred_ex_child.php (accessed on 5 March 2019).

[15] N. Dewasiri, *New Buddhist Extremism and the Challenges to Ethno-Religious Coexistence in Sri Lanka*, 1st ed. (Colombo: International Centre for Ethnic Studies,

Following the LTTE's defeat in 2009 by Sri Lanka's armed forces,[16] the primary 'other' in Sinhala-Buddhist nationalism, Tamil Sri Lankans, could no longer be considered an urgent threat. The Muslim populations of Sri Lanka were reimagined as the new threatening 'other' with dangerous global ties by resurgent nationalist radicals. The BBS and a coterie of related organizations have been accused of orchestrating violence against Muslim businesses, mosques and individuals.[17] The worst of these erupted in 2014 along the south-western coast of the island and left three dead.[18] The BBS rhetoric uses a perceived erasure of distinct cultural identities under increasing globalization[19] However, it is a manifestation of deeply entrenched majoritarian sentiments that have pervaded the society, the institutions of the State, the media and public discourse.[20] Though their violent activities were widely condemned, the sentiments they espoused were shared and defended across the public space, even receiving endorsement from the highest levels of ecclesiastical authority.[21] Stemming from a long history, majoritarian radicalization remains a problem in Sri Lanka.

EFFORTS TO TACKLE RADICALIZATION IN SRI LANKA

To identify the way forward, it is worth considering how Sri Lanka has tackled radicalization thus far. Notably, the government has only sought to address the radicalization carried out by the LTTE, and that

---

2016). Available at: http://ices.lk/wp-content/uploads/2016/12/New-Buddhist-Extremism-and-the-Challenges.pdf (accessed on 5 March 2019).

[16] Ibid.

[17] D. Bastians and G. Harris, 'Buddhist–Muslim Unrest Boils Over in Sri Lanka', 16 June 2014. Available at: https://www.nytimes.com/2014/06/17/world/asia/deadly-religious-violence-erupts-in-sri-lanka.html?_r=0 (accessed on 5 March 2019).

[18] J. Crabtree and M. Peel, 'Buddhist Militancy Triggers International Concern', *The Financial Times*, 28 December 2014. Available at: https://www.ft.com/content/dd32491e-8b2b-11e4-be89-00144feabdc0 (accessed on 5 March 2019).

[19] R. Jones, 'Sinhala Buddhist Nationalism and Islamophobia in Contemporary Sri Lanka' (Honors Theses, 126). Available at: http://scarab.bates.edu/honorstheses/126 (accessed on 5 March 2019).

[20] Dewasiri, *New Buddhist Extremism*.

[21] Jones, 'Sinhala Buddhist Nationalism'.

effort has taken two major forms: practical engagement and normative engagement.

Practical Engagement

Following the end of the war in May 2009, Sri Lanka's government had over 12,000 LTTE cadres in its custody,[22] of whom around 500 were youth.[23] In an effort to de-radicalize, rehabilitate and reintegrate ex-LTTE combatants into society, Sri Lanka developed a process informally known as the '6 + 1' model. This model closely followed a Singaporean precedent involving counselling, education and vocational training,[24] but also combined elements of other similar efforts developed by countries across Asia and Africa.[25] Sri Lanka's 6 + 1 model is composed of six key programmes: psycho-social counselling, vocational training, spiritual activities, education, exercise and recreation, and engagement with civilian life, culture and family.[26] The '+1' component is related to preparing local communities to accept and help former combatants to reintegrate into society and find employment without discrimination.

The University of Maryland conducted research in an attempt to understand and quantify the impact of Sri Lanka's 6 + 1 model. Using two control groups,[27] researchers from the University assessed changes

---

[22] *Bureau of the Commissioner General of Rehabilitation*, 'Rehabilitation of Ex-Child Combatants', 2014. Available at: http://www.bcgr.gov.lk/child-intro. php (accessed on 5 March 2019).

[23] *Bureau of the Commissioner General of Rehabilitation*, 'Details of Reintegrated Child Ex-Combatants'. Available at: http://www.bcgr.gov.lk/reintegratred_ex_ child.php (accessed on 5 March 2019).

[24] M. Hettiarachchi, 'Sri Lanka's Rehabilitation Program: A New Frontier in Counter Terrorism and Counter Insurgency', *Prism* 4, no. 2 (2013): 105–122. Available at: https://search.proquest.com/docview/1441429436?accountid=11752

[25] Ibid.

[26] *Singapore Prison Service*, 'Rehabilitation Process', 2016. Available at: https:// www.sps.gov.sg/connect-us/rehabilitation-process (accessed on 26 April 2019).

[27] A. Kruglanski, M. Gelfand, J. Bélanger, A. Sheveland, M. Hetiarachchi, and R. Gunaratna, 'The Psychology of Radicalization and Deradicalization: How Significance Quest Impacts Violent Extremism', *Political Psychology* 35, no. S1 (2014): 69–93.

in habits and attitudes of the programme's beneficiaries. One group had no exposure to Sri Lanka's 6+1 programme, while the other underwent the 6+1 programme for nine months. Results showed that the group who underwent the programme significantly changed their core beliefs concerning armed violence for the better.[28] However, while a short-term alteration was evident, researchers concluded that there was insufficient evidence to guarantee a long-term shift in perceptions.[29] Government figures state that over 11,000 former combatants and participants in the LTTE have been reintegrated into society through the 6+1 model.[30] Criticism of this programme is abounding and justified, but the development of this model does reflect an attempt by the government to address radicalization through global engagement.

Normative Engagement

Normatively, Sri Lanka has focused on specifically tackling youth radicalization. Arguably, the main reason for this focus was to gain the necessary international support required to prevent the LTTE from recruiting child soldiers. For example, the government ratified the Optional Protocol to the Convention on the Rights of the Child.[31] In doing so, Sri Lanka committed itself to ensuring that: '(a) there is no compulsory, forced or coerced recruitment into the national armed forces; (b) recruitment is solely on a voluntary basis; (c) the minimum age for voluntary recruitment into national armed forces is 18 years'.[32] This normative engagement also communicated Sri Lanka's interest

---

[28] Ibid.

[29] Ibid.

[30] *Bureau of the Commissioner General of Rehabilitation*, 'Occupation Details of the Reintegrated Beneficiaries', 2014. Available at: http://bcgr.gov.lk/ovrl_prg. php (accessed on 5 March 2019).

[31] The Office of the United Nations High Commissioner for Human Rights, 'Status of Ratification Interactive Dashboard', n.d. Available at: http://indicators. ohchr.org/ (accessed on 5 March 2019).

[32] United Nations Treaty Collection, n.d. Available at: https://treaties.un.org/ Pages/Declarations.aspx?index=Sri%20Lanka&lang=_en&chapter=4&treaty=135 (accessed on 5 March 2019).

and willingness to counter radicalization through global normative frameworks and institutions.

GAPS IN EFFORTS TO TACKLE RADICALIZATION

While, Sri Lanka has taken steps to tackle radicalization, those efforts have been temporary and narrow in scope. Radicalization is a process, and therefore, efforts to counter it should be an ongoing process too. The 6+1 programme to counter radicalization following the end of the civil war barely exists at present. By contrast, Singapore's counter radicalization programme is still ongoing, and the country is committed to strengthening it.[33]

Sri Lanka has also done little to address deep and long-term factors that lead to continuing radical upsurges among youth. As the overview has shown, there are a variety of factors that lead to majoritarian and marginalized radicalization in Sri Lanka—unemployment, disempowerment and insecurity, among others. To address these factors Sri Lanka must go beyond the 6+1 model and normative frameworks related to child soldiers. In seeking to address the issue in Europe, EU recognized that modern youth radicalization is a 'dynamic process in specific contexts in which violence is embedded'.[34] Radicalization in Sri Lanka should be analysed as such and a variety of targeted interventions must be pursued. Sri Lanka must create a dynamic national policy that draws on global resources and partnerships with regional governments and organizations to ensure a comprehensive programme to address the political, economic and cultural structural issues that lead to radicalization.

---

[33] Channel NewsAsia, '*Singapore Still Finding Right Approach to Rehabilitate Self-Radicalised Individuals: Shanmugam*', 2018. Available at: https://www.channelnewsasia.com/news/singapore/singapore-finding-right-approach-rehabilitate-self-radicalised-10039792 (accessed on 9 December 2018).

[34] *European Parliament*, 'Preventing and Countering Youth Radicalisation in the EU', 2014. Available at: http://www.europarl.europa.eu/RegData/etudes/etudes/join/2014/509977/IPOL-LIBE_ET(2014)509977_EN.pdf (accessed on 5 March 2019).

A BLUEPRINT FOR NATIONAL POLICYMAKING

Sri Lanka needs a coherent national counter-radicalization policy, given its history of radicalization that has stemmed from majoritarianism and marginalization. This policy must take into account the various histories of ethno-religious groups and the processes involved in radicalization such as systematic radicalization and fake news. This would help develop economic, political and cultural interventions that reduce marginalization and mitigate the normalization of majoritarian sentiments.

There are a variety of global resources that Sri Lanka should consider as it plans and implements a coherent and dynamic national counter-radicalization policy. Norway[35] and Denmark[36] have comprehensive sectoral action plans involving education, religion and justice to address radicalization. For example, the Ministry of Justice and Public Security in Norway coordinates their action plan and has the right to oversee specific responsibilities allotted to other ministries, creating a centralized ownership that has improved effective implementation.[37] Similarly in the developing world, Indonesia has developed a blueprint for de-radicalization, as it deals with widespread outbursts of violence inspired by radical religiosity.[38]

When developing a national policy to counter radicalization, Sri Lanka must prioritize employment for youth, education, language and urban planning. Those four areas would enable the government

---

[35] Norwegian Ministry of Justice and Public Security, 'Action Plan against Radicalisation and Violent Extremism', 2014. Available at: https://www.regjeringen.no/contentassets/6d84d5d6c6df47b38f5e2b989347fc49/action-plan-against-radicalisation-and-violent-extremism_2014.pdf (accessed on 5 March 2019).

[36] The Danish Ministry of Immigration, Integration and Housing, 'Preventing and Countering Extremism and Radicalisation National Action Plan', 2016. Available at: https://ec.europa.eu/home-affairs/sites/homeaffairs/files/what-we-do/networks/radicalisation_awareness_network/docs/preventing_countering_extremism_radicalisation_en.pdf (accessed on 5 March 2019).

[37] Norwegian Ministry of Justice and Public Security, 'Action Plan'.

[38] Ministry of Foreign Affairs Republic of Indonesia, 'Indonesia and Counter-Terrorism', 2016. Available at: http://www.kemlu.go.id/en/kebijakan/isu-khusus/Pages/Combating-Terrorism.aspx (accessed on 5 March 2019).

to effectively counter radicalization rooted in majoritarianism and marginalization. To do this, the government could gather multiple stakeholders—from the public sector, civil society, academia, think tanks and cultural institutions—to study the issues unique to the island's context, explore global solutions and resources to create a comprehensive action plan.

Employment for Youth

Various international actors, such as the International Labour Organization (ILO), have long recognized that generating employment opportunities is crucial to building sustainable peace—particularly in post-conflict situations. However, job creation alone is insufficient to prevent youth from taking to violence.[39] For example, policy interventions that only focus on openly unemployed youth risks ignoring young people who are underemployed and/or marginalized within the labour market.[40] Such youth are just as likely to take to violence and rebellion as a means of expressing their frustration. Additionally, unemployed youth are generally likely to be more educated, better-off individuals who can depend on family networks for financial support while searching for 'good' jobs in the labour market.[41]

Instead of focusing on overall unemployment rates, Sri Lanka should devise a comprehensive strategy that considers all forms of labour market exclusion and provides responses to increase inclusion. Such a policy should improve biases in the demand for labour, while simultaneously increasing youth's ability to integrate into the labour market. While there is no precedent of a country that has implemented such a holistic approach, there are nevertheless useful measures adopted

---

[39] O. Walton, 'Youth, Armed Violence and Job Creation Programmes: A Rapid Mapping Study' (GSDRC research papers, 2010). Available at: http://www.gsdrc. org/docs/open/eirs11.pdf (accessed on 5 March 2019).

[40] F. Stewart, 'Employment in Conflict and Post-Conflict Situations', *UNDP Human Development Report Office Think Piece*, 2015. Available at: http://hdr.undp. org/sites/default/files/stewart_hdr_2015_final.pdf (accessed on 5 March 2019).

[41] M. Rama, 'The Sri Lankan Unemployment Problem Revisited' (working paper no. 2227, World Bank, Washington, DC, 1999).

by various countries that cumulatively could indicate a blueprint for such a policy.

For a developing economy like that of Sri Lanka, public works—infrastructure building—provide an opportunity for short-term employment and skill development. To maximize this opportunity India's National Rural Employment Guarantee Scheme is a viable option.[42] This would enable youth to find employment for the duration of a project, apply skills learned beyond the project's lifespan and benefit from subsequent increases in productivity that the project would bring to their locality. Nepal has also successfully adopted such a programme following the end of its civil conflict in 2006. Through this programme, the government guaranteed 100 days of employment per household per year for the districts worst affected by the conflict.[43]

However, the long-term goal should be to move youth into regular wage employment in the private sector. This is particularly necessary in Sri Lanka since youth aspire to eventually work in the white-collar sector rather than accept long-term employment in labour-intensive, unskilled jobs.[44] This aspiration could be facilitated by the adoption of a targeted wage subsidy programme that incentivizes employers to provide employment and training to youth from disadvantaged backgrounds. Argentina's Proempleo programme successfully targeted low-income workers in the State's public works programme to benefit from wage subsidies.[45] In Sri Lanka eligible youth for such a programme

---

[42] S. Sukthankar, 'India's National Rural Employment Guarantee Scheme: What Do We Really Know about the World's Largest Workfare Program?' National Council of Applied Economic Research, India, 2016. Available at: http://www.ncaer.org/events/ipf-2016/IPF-2016-Paper-Sukhtankar.pdf (accessed on 5 March 2019).

[43] F. Stewart, 'From War to Work', *UNDP Human Development Reports*, 2016. Available at: http://hdr.undp.org/en/content/war-work (accessed on 5 March 2019).

[44] N. Arunatilake and P. Jayawardena, 'Labour Market Trends and Outcomes in Sri Lanka', in *The Challenge of Youth Employment in Sri Lanka*, eds. Ramani Gunatilaka, Markus Mayer and Milan Vodopivec (Washington, DC: World Bank, 2010).

[45] E. Galasso, M. Ravailon and A. Salvia, 'Assisting the Transition from Workfare to Work: Argentina's Proempleo Experiment', *The World Bank,* 2001.

could be identified through the existing Samurdhi programme that aims to alleviate poverty.

Sri Lanka needs a sustainable mechanism for vocational training. To facilitate this, a skills development levy system could be established like in Singapore[46] and South Africa. Through such a system, employers would contribute a share of all employees' compensation into a common skills development fund, which then allocates those funds as training grants. There are other systems—like Germany's corporatist dual system and Japan's company centric model—which despite their success, are rooted in unique national contexts and are difficult to transpose directly.[47] Nonetheless these comprehensive systems can provide ideas for a programme suited to Sri Lanka. Such systems would help address the significant skills gap in Sri Lanka's labour market by mobilizing funds to assist private sector-driven training for youth, which in turn would ensure that the training they receive is in line with the current demands of the labour market.

Educational Reform

The normalization of majoritarian discourse has deeply affected educational infrastructure in Sri Lanka, which remains a primary mode of disseminating ideas and identities. Though educational institutions are far from radical, some aspects of their discourse easily lend themselves to ethno-centrism, and hence to more radical interpretations.[48] Primary and secondary education is often segregated by language, and by extension ethnicity and religion. Youth from different cultural backgrounds

---

Available at: http://siteresources.worldbank.org/INTISPMA/Resources/argentinaLaborEval.pdf (accessed on 5 March 2019).

[46] Government of Singapore, 'Skills Development Levy (SDL) System', SkillsFuture Singapore Agency, 2018. Available at: https://sdl.ssg.gov.sg (accessed on 5 March 2019).

[47] M. Godfrey, 'Youth Employment Policy in Developing and Transition Countries: Prevention as Well as Cure' (World Bank Social Protection discussion paper series, 2003). Available at: https://www.researchgate.net/profile/Pauline_Nelson/publication/254781427_The_Eurocleft_Project_1996–2000/links/53e2002f0cf24f90ff65ad10.pdf (accessed on 5 March 2019).

[48] Tambiah, *Buddhism Betrayed?*

rarely intermingle, form strong social bonds or explore tolerance and diversity. Educational instructions should be restructured to both enable education in Tamil and Sinhala and end linguistic segregation. While this would involve large-scale education readjustment, desegregating schools is a necessary first step to create cohesion among Sri Lanka's diverse social groups. Furthermore, research indicates[49] that historical and social narratives in State funded textbooks inculcate ethno-religious divides. Radical nationalist discourse often builds on this common vision of an ethnically divided island. A reform of education must address the physical segregation of students, as well as the discursive divides inculcated through syllabi.

The American Institute of Cairo presented research comparing STEM-centric education and liberal arts instruction that found the former amenable to radicalization.[50] A well-designed liberal arts model of higher education encourages multi-dimensional thinking and an appreciation for a variety of perspectives. A study, *Engineers of Jihad*, released by the University of Oxford, illustrates the large presence of engineers in violent radical movements.[51] A liberal arts education, based on history, literature, sociology and a core STEM component[52] trains students to engage varied opinions and think laterally drawing on multiple-disciplines. Training in critical, humanistic thinking strengthens tolerant, liberal views in cultural communities, making the descent into radicalization less likely.[53] Singapore partnered with Yale

---

[49] A. Gaul, 'Security, Sovereignty, Patriotism—Sinhalese Nationalism and the State in Sri Lankan History Textbooks', *Ethnopolitics* 16, no. 2 (2015): 161–178.

[50] T. Purinton and A. Hodgkins, 'The Liberal Arts as Antidote to Political Extremism in Mideast', *The Jordan Times*, 2016. Available at: http://www.jordantimes.com/opinion/ted-purinton-and-allison-hodgkins/liberal-arts-antidote-political-extremism-mideast (accessed on 5 March 2019).

[51] D. Gambetta and S Hertog, 'Engineers of Jihad' (Paper no. 2007-10, 2007). Available at: https://www.sociology.ox.ac.uk/materials/papers/2007–10.pdf (accessed on 5 March 2019).

[52] P. Lewis, 'Innovation in International Higher Education: Yale–NUS Experience', 2016. Available at: http://www.ft.lk/article/540942/Innovation-in-international-higher-education–Yale-NUS-experience (accessed on 5 March 2019).

[53] R. F Gombrich and G. Obeyesekere, *Buddhism Transformed: Religious Change in Sri Lanka* (Delhi: Motilal Banarsidass, 1990). Available at: http://www.worldcat.

University in 2011 and began Yale–NUS, a liberal arts based college. Japan and South Korea have also focused on establishing this model of education to advance critical thinking.[54]

Primary and secondary schools, along with universities that make up the secular education system, are not the only institutional network that cultivates thought in Sri Lanka. Religious institutions of different faiths, with their places of worship and centres for instructing clergy, constitute another system of education.[55] In the case of Sri Lanka several such spaces already exist, such as the Ecumenical Institute for Study and Dialogue and the Walpola Rahula Institute for Buddhist Studies. These institutions continue to thrive and influence public discourse. Sri Lanka should, therefore, focus on developing an initiative that brings together different religious institutions into conversation with each other and with the secular education system. This effort could lead to a religious education that is held accountable to a diversity of perspectives and values.

Encouraging dialogue between the secular academy and religious institutions could also lead to transformative intellectual projects. This is not uncommon in Sri Lanka. The work of Asanga Tilakaratne, a scholar and instructor, is instructive. His work meticulously explores the social teachings in Buddhist thought and he presents a vision of life where individuals balance self-cultivation with the pursuit of economic prosperity and the use of their wealth for social projects that encourage learning, critical thought and creativity.[56]

---

org/oclc/25079945 (accessed on 5 March 2019).

[54] S. Klebnikov, 'The Rise of Liberal Arts Colleges in Asia', *Forbes*, 2015. Available at: https://www.forbes.com/sites/sergeiklebnikov/2015/06/03/the-rise-of-liberal-arts-colleges-in-asia/#1b24e9537e3c (accessed on 8 December 2018).

[55] H. L. Seneviratne, *The Work of Kings: The New Buddhism in Sri Lanka* (Chicago, IL: University of Chicago Press, 1999). Available at: http://www.worldcat.org/oclc/924917083 (accessed on 5 March 2019).

[56] A. Tilakaratne, *Theravada Buddhism: The View of the Elders* (Honolulu: University of Hawai'i Press, 2016). Available at: http://www.worldcat.org/oclc/986575613 (accessed on 5 March 2019).

Language Reform

Language and its related ethnic identities underlie radicalization in Sri Lanka, and an effective counter-radicalization policy must take these issues into account. The Official Language Act of 1956, enshrined Sinhala as the country's only official language, excluding both Tamil and English, and so laid the foundations for the radicalization of Tamil youth. Tamil-speaking Sri Lankans saw their opportunities for public sector employment diminish; where in 1956 Tamil speakers made up 30 per cent of the public service, by 1970 they had been reduced to a mere 5 per cent. Tamil youth became increasingly frustrated and susceptible to the extremist ideologies of groups like the LTTE.[57]

Sri Lanka's government has taken some initiatives to rectify the issue. In 1987, the Parliament passed the 13th Amendment to the Sri Lankan Constitution affirming Tamil as an official language.[58] Since 2007 public servants must become conversant in both Sinhala and Tamil in the first five years of their appointment,[59] and since 2014 national identity cards have been bilingual.[60] Nevertheless, these measures have not resulted in significant 'on the ground' progress for the status of Tamil speakers. For example, in 2015–2016, nearly 60 per cent of civil servants passed the language test on a minimal score.[61]

Sri Lanka could take inspiration from Singapore to carry out more language reforms as part of its counter-radicalization strategy. Singapore

---

[57] *The Economist*, 'Linguistic Slights Spur Ethnic Division in Sri Lanka', 2017. Available at: http://www.economist.com/news/asia/21717987-monoglot-officials-are-impeding-post-war-reconciliation-linguistic-slights-spur-ethnic-division (accessed on 5 March 2019).

[58] The Parliament Secretariat, 'The Constitution of the Democratic Socialist Republic of Sri Lanka', 2015. Available at: https://www.parliament.lk/files/pdf/constitution.pdf (accessed on 5 March 2019).

[59] Ministry of Public Administration and Home Affairs, 'Public Administration Circular 07/2007', 2007. Available at: http://www.pubad.gov.lk/web/eservices/circulars/2007/E/07–2007(e).pdf (accessed on 5 March 2019).

[60] News First, 'National ID Cards to be Changed', 2014. Available at: http://newsfirst.lk/english/2014/01/national-id-cards-changed-next-month/1482 (accessed on 5 March 2019).

[61] *The Economist*, 'Linguistic Slights Spur Ethnic Division in Sri Lanka'.

retained English as the language of the public sphere,[62] while giving official parity status to the native languages of its three major communities (Mandarin, Malay and Tamil). Malay was promoted as the national language, given Singapore's historical Malay heritage—despite Malays being a minority in modern Singapore.[63] This strategy of promoting 'mother tongues' for use in the private sphere while promoting English as the language of business and government, led to Singapore becoming a successful multicultural society that is cosmopolitan whilst remaining rooted in its traditional communal identities. This is borne out by the fact that Singaporeans literate in at least two languages rose from 56 per cent in 2000 to 73.2 per cent in 2016.[64] Furthermore, despite more and more Singaporeans speaking English at home, government surveys have demonstrated that the percentages of Mandarin and Tamil speakers and of those who profess a faith (Buddhism, Christianity, Islam and Hinduism) have stayed the same.[65]

Sri Lanka, like Singapore, is a multi-ethnic, multi-religious society, so it would be advisable for Sri Lanka to examine Singapore's language policy.[66] The fostering of inter-communal linkages via a common 'link language' can mitigate communal polarization.

---

[62] Ministry of Foreign Affairs Singapore, 'Straits Times: English for Trade; Mother Tongue to Preserve Identity', 2004. Available at: https://www.mfa.gov.sg/content/mfa/media_centre/singapore_headlines/2015/201503/headlines_20150327_4.html (accessed on 5 March 2019).

[63] Singapore Statutes Online, 'Official Languages and National Language', n.d. Available at: http://statutes.agc.gov.sg/aol/search/display/view.w3p;ident=51172c55–9597–461f-b8fb-359bf2f94def;page=0;query=DocId%3A%222cc15e67-cf27–44b1-a736-f28ab8190454%22%20Status%3Apublished%20Depth%3A0%20TransactionTime%3A%2213%2F11%2F2015%22;rec=0 (accessed on 5 March 2019).

[64] P. Lee, 'English Most Common Home Language in Singapore, Bilingualism Also Up: Government Survey', *The Straits Times*, 2016. Available at: http://www.straitstimes.com/singapore/english-most-common-home-language-in-singapore-bilingualism-also-up-government-survey (accessed on 5 March 2019).

[65] Ibid.

[66] D. Alphonsus, 'Preventing Post-LTTE Violence in Sri Lanka', *Economic & Political Weekly* (2016). Available at: http://www.epw.in/journal/2016/20/commentary/preventing-post-ltte-violence-sri-lanka.html (accessed on 5 March 2019).

Urban Planning

Sri Lanka is yet to realize—and acknowledge—the benefits of urban planning in the context of fostering social cohesion and countering radicalization. Urban planning plays a major role in tackling radicalization because residence areas defined by income, religion or ethnicity facilitate self-segregation and the spread of radical ideologies.[67] In Sri Lanka's capital Colombo, particular communities, especially of lower-incomes, dominate certain neighbourhoods.[68] One option for Sri Lanka lies in Singapore's 'social engineering' approach to public housing to encourage integration. In Singapore, public housing is distributed according to predetermined ethnic quotas to ensure diversity within a particular housing project, and sale or resale of such housing to a buyer from a particular ethnic group was not allowed if this would exceed the predetermined quotas.[69] However, altering this trend through such a system is difficult without infringing on individual rights.

Alternatively, policymakers in Sri Lanka could develop more 'third places'. Ray Oldenburg has theorized that people require a variety of third places—places where they spend time between work and home. Such places are likely to strengthen social relations and allow people to familiarize themselves with different ethnicities, cultures and religions at leisure.[70] The development of third places could greatly reduce the risk of self-radicalization in Sri Lanka. Modern suburbanized cities lack

---

[67] Nordic Council of Ministers, *The Nordic Safe Cities Guide*, 2017. Available at: https://www.regjeringen.no/contentassets/26d0dd4a4e584b19ab02a2d1e4 68c296/nordic_safe_cities_guide.pdf (accessed on 5 March 2019).

[68] L. Manawadu and N. Fernando, 'Processes Driving Ethnic Segregation in Cities: A Case Study of the City of Colombo, Sri Lanka', 2018. Available at: https://www.researchgate.net/publication/267857143_PROCESSES_DRIVING_ETHNIC_SEGREGATION_IN_CITIES_A_CASE_STUDY_OF_THE_CITY_OF_COLOMBO_SRI_LANKA (accessed on 5 March 2019).

[69] Government of Singapore, 'Ethnic Integration Policy Is Implemented: 1st March 1989', *National Library Board Singapore*, 2018. Available at: http://eresources. nlb.gov.sg/history/events/d8fea656-d86e-4658-9509-974225951607 (accessed on 5 March 2019).

[70] S. Butler and C. Diaz, '"Third Places" as Community Builders', *Brookings Institution*, 14 September 2016. Available at: https://www.brookings.edu/blog/

engaging third spaces, and therefore, youth often seek virtual spaces as a substitute.[71] A study by Dublin City University on self-radicalization on virtual platforms analysed the demographics of Muslim youth who view YouTube content that promote religious violence and found that many lived in urban and suburban spaces.[72]

One form of third space for Sri Lanka would be a multi-faith community space. Sri Lanka consistently ranks as one of the most religious countries[73]; for most Sri Lankan youth, one of the few socially acceptable spaces available are religious sites.[74] Unfortunately, such spaces are currently segregated according to religion, and could serve as catalysts for youth radicalization. However, if it was possible to create a shared multi-faith space for youth, where separate prayer/devotional spaces are accompanied by a common space for shared activities (sport, outdoor meetings, and shopping), it would facilitate positive experiences of diversity.

Urban planning needs to address the question of making public spaces accessible and welcoming to individuals from various communities.[75] Sri Lankan public space is heavily dominated by symbols that promote the Sinhalese Buddhist communal identity (statues of the Buddha, flags and sculptures of lions). Spaces in minority-dominated

---

up-front/2016/09/14/third-places-as-community-builders/ (accessed on 5 March 2019).

[71] M. Conway and L. McInerney, 'Jihadi Video and Auto-radicalisation: Evidence from an Exploratory YouTube Study', *Intelligence and Security Informatics* (2008): 108–118.

[72] Ibid.

[73] O. Smith, 'Mapped: The World's Most (and Least) Religious Countries', *The Telegraph*, 14 January 2018. Available at: https://www.telegraph.co.uk/travel/maps-and-graphics/most-religious-countries-in-the-world/ (accessed on 5 March 2019).

[74] C. Ibargüen, 'Youth in Sri Lanka: A Review of Literature', Centre for Poverty Analyses, 2004. Available at: http://www.cepa.lk/content_images/publications/documents/83fe752f3d8cb7f4dc6939f73546192f-Youth-in-Sri-Lanka.%20-%2002.pdf (accessed on 5 March 2019).

[75] B. Somers, 'The Mechelen Model: An Inclusive City', in *Resilient Cities: Countering Violent Extremism at Local Level*, ed. Diego Muro (Barcelona: Barcelona Centre for International Affairs, 2017), 57–62.

areas are at times subjected to a 'ritual stamping' using such symbols.[76] Sri Lankan public space must be redesigned with imagery that promotes the identities of all communities; inspiration can be taken from some of the shared multi-faith spaces in Sri Lanka, such as Kataragama.

Additionally, an interesting recommendation made by experts consulted on the Nordic Safe Cities project was that more eyes on the street (the presence of more people, as opposed to surveillance technology) tends to reduce the risk of crime and violence. For example, the presence of elderly citizens in public spaces, in particular, creates a 'grandmother effect' as they provide passive security purely by their presence.[77] Sri Lanka could therefore encourage more senior citizens to occupy third places. This may deter other citizens from occupying those to spread radical ideologies that lead to violence.

GLOBAL ENGAGEMENT FOR NATIONAL POLICYMAKING

Sri Lanka shares links with countries in the Indian Ocean region and in South Asia. Its ability to corporate with regional partners also provides unique opportunities for counter-radicalization efforts, in a cultural and economic context shared by all states. Creating deeper cultural and institutional links would encourage diverse and tolerant societies. These opportunities could be realized through regional frameworks, trilateral and bilateral agreements, networks for practitioners in counter-radicalization and academic networks.

Regional Frameworks

To develop clear regional frameworks for tackling radicalization, Sri Lanka could engage with Bay of Bengal Initiative for Multi-Sectoral Technical and Economic Cooperation (BIMSTEC) and the Indian Ocean Rim Association (IORA). The South Asian Association for

---

[76] A. Zuhair, 'Dynamics of Sinhala-Buddhist Nationalism in Post-War Sri Lanka', Centre for Policy Alternatives, 2016. Available at: https://www.cpalanka.org/wp-content/uploads/2016/04/Dynamics-of-Sinhala-Buddhist-Ethno-Nationalism-in-Post-War-Sri-Lanka.pdf (accessed on 5 March 2019).

[77] Nordic Council of Ministers, *The Nordic Safe Cities Guide.*

Regional Cooperation (SAARC) has come to a standstill, and therefore, BIMSTEC and IORA are better suited for results-oriented regional engagement in counter-radicalization. Both BIMSTEC and IORA have an interest in cooperating on security issues. In 2009, member states of BIMSTEC signed[78] the Convention on Cooperation in Combating International Terrorism, Transnational Organised Crime and Illicit Drug Trafficking. Now, they are attempting to sign[79] a Convention on Mutual Assistance in Criminal Matters. In March 2017, at the IORA Leaders' Summit in Jakarta member states agreed on a Declaration on Preventing and Countering Terrorism and Violent Extremism.[80] It outlined options for IORA members to coordinate on counter-radicalization in general and emphasizes the importance of empowering community leaders, teachers, parents and civil society organizations to achieve lasting change. However, it remains a preliminary declaration and has not been developed into a study of types and drivers behind radicalization and specific forms of interventions. Sri Lanka could therefore begin its regional engagement on this issue by focusing on making the IORA Declaration a binding agreement for generating action plans.

This first step must also be accompanied by a clear definition of radicalization. Both regional organizations—BIMSTEC and IORA—are yet to create a definition of radicalization and the various types and drivers of it in member states. A regional organization that has achieved

---

[78] Government of India Ministry of External Affairs, 'BIMSTEC Convention on Cooperation in Combating International Terrorism, Transnational Organised Crime and Illicit Drug Trafficking', 2009. Available at: http://mea.gov.in/bilateral-documents.htm?dtl/5070/BIMSTEC+Convention+on+Cooperation+in+Combating+International+Terrorism+Transnational+Organised+Crime+And+Illicit+Drug+Trafficking (accessed on 5 March 2019).

[79] *The Hindu*, 'BIMSTEC Leaders Vow to Jointly Combat Terrorism', 2016. Available at: http://www.thehindu.com/news/international/south-asia/bimstec-leaders-vow-to-jointly-combat-terrorism/article5749734.ece (accessed on 5 March 2019).

[80] IORA Secretariat, 'Indian Ocean Rim Association Declaration on Preventing and Countering Terrorism and Violent Extremism', 2017. Available at: http://www.kemlu.go.id/Buku/Declaration%20on%20Preventing%20and%20Countering%20Terrorism%20and%20Violent%20Extremism.pdf (accessed on 5 March 2019).

this is EU. EU has identified the types of radicalization that threaten member states.[81] This clarity would undoubtedly enable EU to guide the implementation of coordinated policies to affect various types and degrees of radicalization in member states.

However, Sri Lanka should consider two important factors when working with regional institutions to counter radicalization. The first is to ensure that as states seek to curb radical movements, legal frameworks exist at the national levels to protect fundamental freedoms and open societies. Singapore's Undesirable Publications Act[82] is an example of a piece of legislation that tries to precariously balance freedom of expression and the regulation of divisive speech, for example by banning publications linked to known radicalizing groups like ISIS.[83] The second is to outline standards and mechanisms for measuring the success of policies. Monitoring and assessment are crucial to improving design and implementation in a programme trying to achieve such a complex and subtle goal as preventing radicalization Working with regional states to share their variety of knowledge, concerning contexts, types of achievements and setbacks, and technical skills would provide more comprehensive monitoring apparatus.[84]

Trilateral and Bilateral Agreements

Given the time lag involved with developing regional frameworks based on consensus, Sri Lanka should also focus on developing trilateral and

---

[81] Radicalisation Awareness Network, 'Introducing RAN: Europe's Radicalisation Awareness Network', 2016. Available at: https://www.youtube.com/watch?v=Z8Vy7wxQ-ik&feature=youtu.be (accessed on 5 March 2019).

[82] *Singapore Statutes Online*, 'Undesirable Publications Act', 2017. Available at: http://statutes.agc.gov.sg/aol/search/display/view.w3p;page=0;query=DocId:%22260443c8-a729–40e2-ac3a-a4fe673d71bb%22%20Status:published%20Depth:0;rec=0 (accessed on 5 March 2019).

[83] L. Liang, 'ISIS-linked Newspaper Banned in Singapore', *The Straits Times*, 2016. Available at: http://www.straitstimes.com/singapore/isis-linked-newspaper-banned-in-singapore (accessed on 5 March 2019).

[84] C. Miller, 'How Do We Know if Counter-Radicalisation Programs Are Working?' 2015. Available at: https://www.lowyinstitute.org/the-interpreter/how-do-we-know-if-counter-radicalisation-programs-are-working (accessed on 5 March 2019).

bilateral agreements. These agreements are also identified as 'minilateral' mechanisms that involve a small number of states (around three to six). Minilateral efforts allow for more specific and targeted action on common issues and have become increasingly popular in Asia. In January 2018, it was reported that six south-east Asian states launched an intelligence sharing initiative called Our Eyes that is aimed at combating security issues like radicalization.[85]

With minilateral mechanisms emerging in the context of radicalization in Asia, it would be relatively easy for Sri Lanka to advocate for similar measures with neighbouring states. Sri Lanka, Myanmar and Thailand face similar issues related to Buddhist extremism. Therefore, given the strong traditional ties between their religious cultures, these three countries could work together and coordinate counter-radicalization efforts.[86] Additionally, Sri Lanka could seek to join the cross-border counter-terrorism mechanism set up by India and the Maldives.[87] This initiative is important for several reasons: Sri Lanka shares traversable maritime borders with both countries and it would be profoundly affected by radicalization in their territories, while Sri Lanka's experience in counter-radicalization could benefit both India and the Maldives.

Networks of Educational Institutions

Creating rich links between Sri Lanka's universities and its counterparts in the wider Indo-Pacific region would encourage scholars to account for multiple perspectives and engage with cultural diversity. Instituting scholarships, exchange programmes, conferences and

---

[85] T. Allard, 'Southeast Asian States Launch Intelligence Pact to Counter Islamist Threat', 2018. Available at: https://www.reuters.com/article/us-asia-intelligence/southeast-asian-states-launch-intelligence-pact-to-counter-islamist-threat-idUSK-BN1FE163 (accessed on 9 December 2018).

[86] V. Arora, 'Connecting the Dots on Buddhist Fundamentalism', *The Diplomat*, 2014. Available at: http://thediplomat.com/2014/05/connecting-the-dots-on-buddhist-fundamentalism/ (accessed on 5 March 2019).

[87] S. Haidar, 'India, Maldives to Finalise Pact to Fight Islamic State', *The Hindu*, 2016. Available at: http://www.thehindu.com/news/national/india-maldives-to-finalise-pact-to-fight-islamic-state/article8353075.ece (accessed on 5 March 2019).

facilitating publications would generate a scholarly discourse that addresses regionally shared issues related to radicalization.[88] Those working in the humanities and social sciences would have greater opportunity to explore perspectives across various religious, linguistic, spatial and political locations. Such engagement produces cosmopolitan and tolerant perspectives. Scholarship on the history of the Indian Ocean region, innovated by Sugata Bose in *A Hundred Horizons: The Indian Ocean in the Age of Global Empire* is an exemplary of academic regional collaboration.[89]

Scholarly work could be the basis of common history textbooks that emphasizes migrations, trade links, cultural exchanges and collaborations across countries in the region. Such narratives train students to see themselves as part of a wider region of cultures and peoples mixing, moving and sharing. French and German historians and teachers created a history textbook to be taught in both countries.[90] Academics in the ASEAN group[91] have attempted to compose a similar textbook for its member states, but this has yet to bear fruit. Such efforts would transform secondary education and prepare a more cosmopolitan and globally aware youth. A common history or a more holistic understanding of historical and present regional links could also contribute to connecting Sri Lanka's diverse population to the international community. This may help reduce insecurities in Sri Lanka that are related to marginalization, which in turn could lead to radical ideologies and violence.

---

[88] G. C. Gunn, *History without Borders: The Making of an Asian World Region (1000–1800)*. (Hong Kong: Hong Kong University Press, 2011. Available at: http://www.worldcat.org/oclc/770340354 (accessed on 5 March 2019).

[89] S. Bose, *A Hundred Horizons: The Indian Ocean in the Age of Global Empire*, (Cambridge, MA: Harvard University Press, 2009). Available at: http://www.worldcat.org/oclc/818882587 (accessed on 5 March 2019).

[90] *The Economist*, 'History Lessons', 2006. Available at: http://www.economist.com/node/7141381 (accessed on 5 March 2019).

[91] Y. Sharma, 'Textbook Approach to Asia's Disputes', 2014. Available at: http://www.bbc.com/news/business-26073748 (accessed on 5 March 2019).

Networks of Practitioners in Counter-Radicalization

The effective implementation of the various frameworks and agreements on tackling radicalization requires strong networks of practitioners who regularly share insights and best practices. However, Sri Lanka's regional organizations currently lack such a robust network and that is hindering the development of effective responses to radicalization at the national and regional level.

However, there are indications that regional organizations in Asia are beginning to realize the importance of collaboration and networking on tackling such issues. IORA's Declaration on Preventing and Countering Terrorism and Violent Extremism, [92] calls on members to "collaborate to successfully rehabilitate, de-radicalize and reintegrate radicalized individuals to bolster social cohesion." However, there have been few further efforts to mobilize resources and political will to achieve these goals, especially in developing a practitioner network. To advance this, Sri Lankan policymakers should study the European Commission's Radicalization Awareness Network (RAN).[93] This EU network connects grassroots-level practitioners in counter-radicalization and de-radicalization through working groups that allow them to share insights and evaluate each other's work. Sri Lanka could use its current positions as Chair of BIMSTEC and Lead Coordinator of IORA's Working Group on Maritime Safety and Security, to push for similar networks in IORA and BIMSTEC. The findings and evaluations of these networks could then inform national policy planning and implementation related to tackling radicalization.

CONCLUSION: SEIZING THE OPPORTUNITIES

This chapter has provided an overview of the complex history of majoritarian and marginalized-led radicalization in Sri Lanka, which demands

---

[92] IORA Secretariat, 'Indian Ocean'.

[93] European Commission, 'Radicalisation Awareness Network (RAN)', 2017. Available at: https://ec.europa.eu/home-affairs/what-we-do/networks/radicalisation_awareness_network_en (accessed on 5 March 2019).

a multifaceted programme of corrective measures. The measures already taken to address radicalization in Sri Lanka have been narrow and temporary. Therefore, Sri Lanka has several opportunities to expand its efforts—particularly through global resources and engagement.

Recommendations for National Policymaking to Counter-Radicalization

Sri Lanka should:

1. Develop and implement a counter-radicalization policy that is dynamic and prioritizes employment for youth, education reform, language reform and urban planning for social cohesion.
2. Devise a comprehensive strategy that addresses all forms of labour market exclusion and provides responses to increase inclusion—instead of focusing on overall unemployment rates.
3. Invest in education, with resources dedicated to liberal arts training and the study of humanities and social sciences, alongside the hard sciences. Sri Lanka must also create closer links between traditional/religious and modern/secular institutes of learning to encourage a diversity of perspectives and tolerance.
4. Create an inclusive language policy to reduce linguistic barriers taking inspiration particularly from regional partners.
5. Ensure effective urban planning, to create public spaces that provide fulfilment and encourage social cohesion.

Recommendations for Global Engagement to Counter Radicalization

Sri Lanka could:

1. Facilitate the development multilateral normative frameworks for tackling radicalization in organizations like IORA and BIMSTEC.
2. Create bilateral and trilateral agreements with regional states to address specific shared issues through military and intelligence cooperation.

3. Establish partnerships between education institutions, regionally and globally, to generate a regional academic discourse that promotes critical and innovative thinking, cultural links and shared histories.
4. Develop networks for practitioners in counter-radicalization through regional organizations like BIMSTEC and IORA, to strengthen knowledge sharing and exchange best practices on combating radicalization.

If Sri Lanka is to realize its potential as a trade and maritime hub of the Indian Ocean region, it is imperative that it develops and implements a holistic policy framework to tackle radicalization. There is strength in diversity, but to reap its rewards Sri Lanka must ensure lasting socio-political stability by tackling radicalization. This chapter has laid out a comprehensive, two-pronged policy blueprint for realizing this goal—domestic policy reform and global engagement. However, political will be imperative to achieve this.

Sri Lanka must recognize the need for a concerted effort to tackle radicalization within its own borders and in the wider Indo-Pacific region. Addressing radicalization is a shared interest for all regional states. It provides Sri Lanka with an opportunity to prove its ability to resolve its own critical challenges, while assisting and developing robust collaborations with other states. Given the experience and resources within Sri Lanka, focusing on mitigating youth radicalization gives the small island a path to gaining greater prominence in regional and global politics.

Chapter 6

Deradicalizing Militant Youth in Northern Pakistan

Raafia Raees Khan and Feriha N. Peracha

INTRODUCTION

Following the successful counter-insurgency in the Swat region of Pakistan in 2009, male youth involved in militancy was apprehended by the Pakistan Army. These young individuals, aged between 12 and 17 years, were involved, in varying degrees, with Tehreek-e-Nafaz-e-Shariat-e-Mohammadi (TNSM), now known as Tehreek-e-Taliban Pakistan (TTP).

In August 2009, the Pakistan Army requested a psychologist (Dr Feriha Peracha) from the civil society to profile the initial youth apprehended. Twelve young boys were being held at the Circuit House, in Mingora, Swat. The psychologist with her colleague (Raafia Raees Khan) extensively interviewed and assessed the youth and the following was noted:

1. The youth were school dropouts and/or illiterate.
2. They had very little religious knowledge and some did not know the basic tenets of religion (Islam).
3. They lacked critical thinking and logical reasoning to assess whether what they were being informed was accurate or not.

4. They came from low socio-economic backgrounds.
5. Majority had fathers (authority figures) who were working abroad.
6. Majority came from a relatively large family (average eight siblings) and were middle children.
7. Head injuries (treated and untreated) and lack of postnatal care were also found to be common.

One thing that was determined through their narratives was that although these young boys were involved in militancy, they were naïve to believe that the cause they were fighting for was just, righteous and worth fighting for. They were in fact involved in anti–State activities, believing that the Pakistani soldiers they were fighting against were 'Indian soldiers sent by the Western countries'.

The Pakistan Army recommended alternatives to detention and the civil psychologists advised that these youth should not be incarcerated, but rather, there needs to be a special programme for their rehabilitation, particularly in order to address the cognitive vulnerabilities, and by giving them the opportunity to develop a better understanding of religion, inculcate citizenship values and guide them towards goal direction, so they could become a productive part of the society.

In September 2009, the Pakistan Army initiated a facility for the 12 initially apprehended and profiled youth, along with another 25 young boys. They handed over the administrative controls to the civil psychologists, who initially with the Pakistan Army's help developed the programme and its parameters, as resources to operate a residential facility needed to be sought. The facility was named Sabaoon, a Pushto word, which translates into 'the first ray of light at dawn', signifying the beginning of a new day and a new life for this youth.

By November 2009, UNICEF initiated funding for this de-radicalization and rehabilitation centre for male youth. Sabaoon was initially run through an NGO called Hum Pakistani Foundation from September 2009 to May 2012, with Dr Feriha Peracha as the projector director. However, from May 2012 onwards, a new organization (SWAaT for Pakistan), with countering and preventing violent extremism as its main objective, was formed. Dr Feriha Peracha continued as the CEO and director.

DE-RADICALIZATION AND REHABILITATION

After much deliberation based on the needs while keeping in mind the narratives of a population of the initial 80 apprehended youth, the following modules were developed.

Academic Module

The aim of this module was to provide continued education to the youth that was previously academically oriented. As many young boys inducted into the programme were school drop outs, they were enrolled in classes based on their previous academic achievement, in addition to the neuropsychological profiling. That is, for example, those who had dropped out of school in the 8th grade to join the militant group were enrolled in the 8th grade. For those who were completely illiterate, they were enrolled in grade 1–3 for basic literacy.

The academic module focuses on supporting youth by assessing the previous achieved level of education instead of chronological age. Therefore, some of the youth that was 16 years old was enrolled in the basic literacy classes with others who were younger or at a similar age to them. Similarly, the age ranges within any class varied, as enrolment was based on ability and the grade that the individual had previously cleared or passed.

In order to bring many of the youth at par to the chronologically based achievement, accelerated learning modules are implemented. This allows for the intellectually above average youth of, for example, 13 years of age to exceed in learning, by completing, for example, grade 6 and 7 in a one year period.

Similarly, those who have learning difficulties or learning deficits were and are provided with remedial learning classes in order to provide them with the opportunity to improve their achievement index outside of the mainstream classes.

Sabaoon, therefore, offers academic opportunities from grade 1 to bachelors, depending on the needs of the inducted population.

Vocational Module

For youth that is above 16 years of age and had significant financial challenges (low socioeconomic status) it was deemed necessary to provide them with an opportunity to learn a vocational skill that would allow them to become a part of the labour force and contribute to their households in an efficient manner.

The initial market survey conducted indicated that the lucrative courses would include: (a) a basic electrician course and (b) refrigeration and air conditioner repair course. The courses were affiliated with the Khyber Institute of Technical Education (KITE), Peshawar in order to provide a recognized certification.

Efforts were made to introduce an additional course for agriculture and farming, however, many of the youth with farming background felt they already had sufficient knowledge about agriculture and farming.

By 2012, it was noted that the refrigeration and air conditioner repair course was not as lucrative as initially assessed, as many of the youth came from rural regions where air conditioners and refrigerators were not being used. As a result, in 2013, two new courses were initiated at Sabaoon. One course was domestic tailoring and the other was motorcycle mechanic. Both courses were 12 months of theoretical and practical education and learning, followed by a two month on-the-job training, which was made mandatory.

Corrective Religious Instruction Module

As the narratives had indicated, the youth seemed to lack the basic understanding of the tenet of Islam. Additionally, the information that led them to accept the ideology of the militant group was based on a misrepresentation of Islam as selective texts were misused to propagate the agenda for anti-State activities. While many seemed to believe in Islam as their religion and referred to their involvement in militancy as them 'serving religion and God', they lacked knowledge of what the word 'Islam' meant. In fact, some of the youth did not even know the

1st *kalma* or word of purity in Arabic. Many of those who did know the Arabic script did not know the meaning of it (There is no god but Allah and Muhammad [SAW] is His messenger).

Certain Quranic verses were misquoted to beguile the naïve population by stating that it meant 'Oh people of Swat, raise arms against the Army, Frontier Constabulary and the police', whereas the actual verse meant 'Oh you who believe...' and is repeated in various verses in different contexts.

Through this module the youth is provided a moderate and accurate understanding of religion by focusing on aspects that promote humanism and tolerance. This is done through an emphasis on concepts of God of the Universe (as opposed to God of the Muslims), jihad as a struggle to better oneself and to serve humanity and *Talib* as a positive term (for one who is a seeker of knowledge or a student). The prophet Muhammad (PBUH) is discussed as an example of an ideal Muslim and his treatment of others is proposed as characteristics a 'good Muslim' must acquire and develop. These are considered to be the epitome of tolerance and humanism and promote forgiveness and kindness as well as love for all living beings. Additionally, where promoting religion in terms of preaching it is concerned, again, emphasis is made on acquiring the qualities of a good Muslim and becoming an example for other Muslims and non-Muslims to want to aspire towards.

The religious curriculum was specifically designed by (late) Dr Muhammad Farooq (who was the Vice Chancellor of Swat University). In depth discussions are initially held between the supervising psychologists and the religious scholar to develop a basic assessment of each inductee's religious inclination and understanding as observed in the narratives reported and collated. Based on these, interactive group sessions on broader religious concepts take place, while holding individual sessions with those who are more ideologically inclined. Similar group discussions are held with family members when they visit Sabaoon, in order to correct any misconceptions that they may have about religion.

The youth (and their families) are encouraged to view each verse (or *ayat*) in the context of the wider surah or chapter of the Qur'an, by also giving emphasis to the time period of the revelation, so that they may be better understood. Religious understanding is considered essential as part of the de-radicalization process as it allows the youth to verify the religious texts for themselves rather than relying on taking such information at face value by authority figures (such as extremist groups).

At the time of reintegration, an assessment of their ability to verify quotations from religious scripture is conducted to ensure that they have developed the necessary skills for future use.

Psychosocial Intervention and Support

The psychosocial intervention and support is managed by the mental health team (MHT). This aspect or module is considered to be the crux of the de-radicalization programme. The MHT, consisting of psychologists and social workers, have been given a number of trainings from local and international experts in the field of terrorism and countering violent extremism. Trainings have focused on intake narratives, basic assessments (objective and subjective) and psychological interventions (behavioural modification procedures and cognitive behavioural therapy) as well as investigative interviewing skills, conducting community visits to gather and cross reference information with the intake narratives and risk assessment.

The MHT is responsible for establishing an initial profile, which consists of determining the mode of involvement, the extent of involvement as well as the ideological inclination. This is carried out at the time of induction when the initial or the intake narrative is taken. Basic data, including family background (parental details, number of siblings, home atmosphere) and personal data (previous formal and religious education, peer group details, interests and ambitions) is discussed. At this point, the young inductee is briefed about the facility and its aim and objectives, in terms of providing opportunities to better themselves as Muslims and as human beings. They are informed of the academic and vocational opportunities as well as improving their religious understandings and questioning aspects that they would like more clarity about. They are informed about trust in terms of what they inform their case manager, but it is highlighted that aspects related to their involvement may be shared with the security forces, especially if that can allow for other miscreant or terrorist activities to be deterred.

Following the induction into the de-radicalization and rehabilitation programme, the MHT continues to hold regular individual and group sessions with the youth. Each MHT member is considered to be a case manager, and therefore, each case manager is assigned up to 20 cases. The case manager conducts at least one individual session per week with the youth. The session focuses on clarifying the background involvement (which is initially discussed at the time of the intake narrative) as well as the motivating factors that led one to become involved, stay involved and/or disengage from the extremist group.

A comprehensive assessment format, known as the GRAIR (guideline for risk assessment, intervention and reintegration) was developed by the SWAaT organization for this particular purpose. Adaptations and derivations from established assessments, such as the Structured Assessment of Violence Risk in Youth (SAVRY)[1] and the Historical, Clinical, Risk Management–20 (HCR–20)[2] were also included in developing this tool. This assessment covers the following variables:

1. Historical risk factors: Physical abuse (to or by others), past supervision (and failures in supervision), self-harm (and suicidal attempts), history of criminality (family members), history of familial militancy, school achievement and duration at madrasa.
2. Social and contextual risk factors: Peer militancy and peer rejection due to involvement in militancy, peer rejection due to noncompliance with peer militants, financial stress, lack of personal or

[1] R. Borum P. Bartel and A. Forth, *Manual for the Structured Assessment for Violence Risk in Youth (SAVRY)* (Odessa, FL: Psychological Assessment Resources, 2006).

[2] K. S. Douglas, S. D. Hart, C. D. Webster and H. Belfrage, *HCR–20V3: Assessing Risk of Violence—User Guide* (Burnaby: Mental Health, Law, and Policy Institute, Simon Fraser University, 2013).

social support, community disorganization due to militancy and stigma (by family, peers, community members, security forces, others).

3. Individual/clinical risk factors: Negative attitudes (related to crime, State and violence), risk taking and impulsivity, substance use, anger management problems, low remorse and empathy, attention deficit or hyperactivity related difficulties, poor compliance, low interest and or commitment to academics, disruption (in the family), exposure to aggression in the home/family, childhood history of maltreatment, poor parental management, unresponsive to discipline, lack of insight (level of acknowledgment of acts/problems), citizenship awareness and compartmentalization (identification and knowledge of country, region, etc.).

4. Protective factors: Prosocial involvement, strong social support at the community level, strong attachments and bonds at school/family, positive attitude towards intervention at Sabaoon, strong commitment to academic or remedial intervention, resilient personality traits, logical reasoning (as per Standard Progressive Matrices (SPM), also known as Raven's Progressive Matrices (a nonverbal assessment of logical reasoning)), family cohesiveness, family engagement in de-radicalization and rehabilitation programme, enjoyment seeking through sports and recreational activities.

5. Additional risk factors: Soft neuropathology (structural or functional brain-based abnormalities), low socio-economic status, large family size, personality disorders, mental illnesses (anxiety, mood or psychotic morbidity).

6. Neuropsychological and cognitive assessment: consisting of a battery of tests and subjects aimed to assess verbal and non-verbal logical reasoning, emotional stability, soft neuropathology, morbid trends, as well as attention, comprehension and memory.

The details of (1)–(5) are collated to determine the problem areas and intervention is therefore tailored to the individual needs of each inductee. A psychological profile is developed as a result of these assessments.

It is important to note here, although the information is initially taken first-hand from the inductee, this information is also verified from other sources, especially the parent/s and other family members to ascertain how valid the information is. Where discrepancies are found, further investigation takes place to determine the extent of authenticity of information. This is done through verification from other sources in the community, as well as through further individual session and behavioural observations, where possible.

Where (6) is concerned, goal direction is established on the basis of the ability and the achievement index determined through the assessment battery. Although all inductees are required to continue with academic goals (whether basic literacy or continued higher education), for some of the youth it is essential to gain vocational skills so that they may work as part of the skilled work force after reintegration. The goal-based trajectory is therefore considered to be a part of the intervention for successful rehabilitation and success post-reintegration.

The variables of the GRAIR are re-assessed intermittently, so that progress of the inductee can be determined. Progress with goal directed activities is also noted, along with progress in individual sessions (especially in relation to acceptance of involvement in militancy, understanding of factors that led one towards recruitment and continued involvement, reflecting on possible outcomes if one had not been apprehended and referred to Sabaoon, etc.). Community-based relations tend to be an essential part of rehabilitation. This includes relationships within the family (parents, siblings, uncles, cousins, etc.) as well as at the larger community level. This can be crucial as many of the youth are involved at the community level and therefore either tend to face stigma from community members (due to some atrocities they may have participated in at the community level) or have a negative attitude towards the community members (for having highlighted this youth to the security forces), which causes conflict to continue, making their reintegration more difficult. Similarly some of the family members (parents, siblings or more distant relatives) are unwilling to either accept the involvement of their offspring, or are unwilling to forgive the offspring for being involved in militant activities or supporting the militant ideology.

These, often difficult, dynamics therefore create a need for individualized assessment, intervention and support for the population inducted in this programme, making the psychosocial module an integral part of the de-radicalization and rehabilitation procedures. This, then, also guides the post-reintegration monitoring and support accordingly.

Sports and Recreation

As the programme deals with providing rehabilitation to a male youth, including sports as part of the daily routine was critical. This not only allows for the youth group to dispose of or offload their excessive physical and mental energy in a positive manner, which is necessary to prevent aggressive outbursts, but also as it helps create healthy competition, allows for cooperation and teamwork on the field, and provides an avenue to achieve (especially for youth that may be below average in achieving academically or vocationally) and create bonds.

Cricket, football, volleyball and badminton are sports that the facility caters to. Sports week is held at least once a year, generally in the summer months and allows for healthy competition between the youth at the facility as well as matches with the staff members. This widens the scope of sports to include 100 meter and 200 meter races, as well as relay races, hurdle races, long jumps and tug of wars.

Other recreational opportunities provided include music class (for those who want to learn how to play the tabla and rabab, which are indigenous musical instruments), board games and television. Television or TV time does now allow for viewing the news channels, but instead encourages watching of sports channels.

Movie nights are also arranged once a month and musical nights are also arranged at half and full term. Musical nights, due to high demand, are also arranged on the day of reintegration.

Family days are also held at the facility. Families are encouraged to visit every weekend, however, not all are able to, as some belong to far-flung areas. A family lunch is usually arranged on Eid days (following Eid ul-Fitr and Eid ul-Adha).

Occasions such as Independence Day, Defence Day & Pakistan Day are also celebrated at Sabaoon. The youth tend to prepare speeches, tableaux and sing national songs to express their understanding of and commitment to the country.

Figure 6.1 explains the three phases of the process applied at Sabaoon for de-radicalization and rehabilitation of male youth referred to the facility for induction. The details of phase one (assessment) and phase 2 (intervention) have been explained in the previous section.

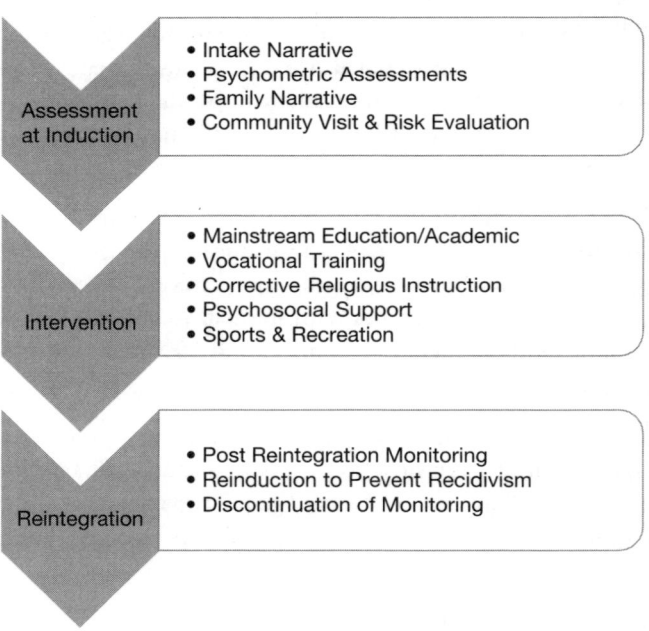

Figure 6.1 *A Model for the Process at Sabaoon*

Source: F. Peracha, R. R. Khan, A. Ayub and K. Aijaz, 'Pakistan: Lessons from Deradicalising Young Taliban Fighters', in *How to Prevent: Extremism and Policy Options*, eds. Khalid Koser and Thomas Thorp (London: Tony Blair Faith Foundation, 2015), 48–55. Available at: https://www.gcerf.org/wp-content/uploads/TBFF_How-to-Prevent_Global-Perspectives-Vol-2.pdf Figure (Model for Sabaoon on p. 50).

REINTEGRATION AND POST-REINTEGRATION MONITORING

Where the reintegration phase is concerned, youth that progresses along each of the five modules in the intervention phase and those who have accepted the extent of their involvement, as well as provided a detailed account of their role in the violent extremist group and movement, exhibit a sense of remorse for the activities undertaken (during the involvement) and an understanding of why they now think that the violent extremist groups are 'wrong', and what they should have done at that point and they should do in the future should they encounter such individuals and/or groups themselves (anti-State actors), or encounter people that support such movements (sympathizers).

Once youth has been shortlisted for reintegration, a case worker from the monitoring centre (MC)—a separate facility which also serves as a halfway house—is assigned to these cases. This case worker works to develop a rapport with the youth group to be reintegrated and is briefed about their involvement, progress, challenges and future goals.

At the time of reintegration, one of the key factors for successful rehabilitation and prevention of recidivism is goal direction. It is necessary for youth to develop long-term goals of their own choice, ones that they are interested in and that would allow them to feel useful to their families and communities at large, while also being able to contribute to sustaining their families.

At the time of reintegration, each youth is considered low risk by the Sabaoon MHT, however, he is highlighted as high risk by the MC. This is because for the first 6 to 12 month period the youth is in a transition from a controlled supportive environment (Sabaoon) to adjust to mainstream life, and is often faced with challenges that are multifold.

Seven youth have been reinducted to Sabaoon in 2012, as there were varying concerns that led to this decision. This was at the time of the general election in Pakistan and the security forces were repeatedly calling on some of these youth for questioning. Other youth, as highlighted by sources in the community, were being highlighted as becoming 'vulnerable' again, as they were seen interacting with individuals who were sympathizers to militants and or had family members who were still actively involved in militancy (and have absconded from the area). All of these youth have since been reintegrated, except one (who ran away from Sabaoon in 2014)[3]

Academically-driven youth are guided towards seeking admissions in schools or colleges, depending on the last level they have achieved. Field of study is based on their achievement index at Sabaoon as well as the career they aspire towards. For example, there are youth who are keen to become doctors, but are unable to achieve the required marks (above 80%) in science and are therefore still encouraged to pursue the field of medicine, such as diploma in nursing, health technician, or degrees in homeopathy, physiotherapy, etc. Similarly, youth inclined towards engineering may not always be able to achieve marks that would ensure admission to a BSc degree, and therefore, they are guided towards diplomas in electrical or mechanical engineering. If they are able to achieve well in these diploma's, then they can seek further admission in BTech to qualify themselves further.

Vocationally-oriented youth, depending on which vocation they have been trained in at Sabaoon and which vocation they are more interested in, are guided towards developing this further. As some youth remain at Sabaoon for extended periods of time (up to 5 years), they sometimes tend to have completed more than one vocational

---

[3] This young boy was reinducted as he was highlighted by his family as viewing videos of militants at home. He was unable to maintain his goal direction and dropped out of college. He had also taken a harsh and aggressive stance in preventing his younger sisters from going to school and was seen interacting with a local shopkeeper whose son was a suicide bomber. Once reinducted, it took him over a year to adjust to being back at the facility while still continuing to be uncooperative and resentful towards the administration and the case manager. When he exhibited some progress in academics and discipline (following routine, attending individual session in a cooperative manner), his weekend leaves (two days a month) were approved. After a few months of being allowed his weekend leave, he did not go home one weekend and absconded. A few months later, he contacted his case manager and threatened to take revenge. Having said that, he has kept in touch with other MHT members over the years, calling or messaging them on and off, sometimes sending his pictures as well. He reports to be at the border of Pakistan and Afghanistan, using an Afghani phone number, and yet not involved in a militant group.

skills course. These youth are then, depending on their achievement index in the vocational course as well as the possibility to develop this into a lucrative business, are encouraged to pursue this as a career in their local community. Initially, they are supported by a placement under supervision of a well-established tailor, motorcycle mechanic or an electrician. This is considered to be on-the-job training (OJT). This is for a minimum of 6 months, during which the youth is to refine his skills further, especially in relation to dealing with customers and clients, while also seeking active feedback on his skills. He is also guided towards how to manage operational expenses and assess profits and further investments for continued work. Once this is satisfactorily achieved, which could take up to 12 months, the case manager then solicits a location for him to open a shop, preferably in his own community, and one that his family can also monitor his work in. Tools and equipment are also provided at this point and shop rent for approximately six months is paid by the organization in order to facilitate the youth to develop his clientele and work towards assessing monthly expenses.

All youth are monitored by case managers, as part of the MHT at the MC. There are approximately 20 cases to a case worker. The case workers responsibility is to conduct follow-up visits (FUVs) with each of his cases at least once a month. FUVs entail an interaction with the reintegrated youth, his immediate family (parents and siblings), close relatives (grandparents, uncles, cousins), peer group, community members, village elders (where village councils exist) and police station or local army unit. If the youth is academically oriented, then the case worker visits the educational institution, and meets with the faculty members and classmates. If the youth is residing in a hostel, while studying outside of his immediate community, then the case worker also meets with the warden and the dorm mates. Should the youth be vocationally-goal directed, then the case worker meets with the employer and or employees as well as customers. The aim is to get feedback from the youth regarding the progress he is making as well as the challenges he is facing. The remaining sources, with whom the case worker interacts, verify the information provided by the reintegrated youth and provide an authentic account of the activities the youth is involved in. Discrepancies in information provide the case worker with an objective assessment of where intervention is required, and often times the youth is confronted with these discrepancies, in an attempt to resolve the conflicting information and better guide the youth towards more appropriate behaviours.

Issues at the community level, post-reintegration can range from conflicts within the family (due to difficult family dynamics—step families, resentment, lack of communication, authoritative parenting, etc.) to stigma at the community level (due to previous involvement or acts committed during the time of involvement). Personal issues range from difficulties in achievement (academic or vocational goals) to emotional difficulties (anger management, stress management, conflict resolution, time management, anxiety or mood difficulties, etc.).

The case worker aims to intervene where required to guide the youth, by teaching him strategies to better cope with the challenges. At times, the case worker is required to work as a mediator in familial conflicts as well as community-based difficulties, where both sides are guided prior to the discussion as to maintain a communication style that is open to understanding each other's perspective and to find ways to seek resolution.

Monitoring of each youth continues until a time where the youth is able to manage his own challenges in an efficient manner. This is determined by a two-year period where the role of the case worker has been minimized to monitoring, and not needing to provide additional support or intervention.

SABAOON'S PROGRESS: 2009–2018

To date, 192 youth have been reintegrated from Sabaoon over an approximately nine-year period. Some of the youth have been reintegrated after as little as an eight to ten month period, while others have remained at the facility for up to five and a half years. As mentioned before, the programme is individualized and each youth is reintegrated on the basis of the progress they make along each of the modules.

Sabaoon Youth

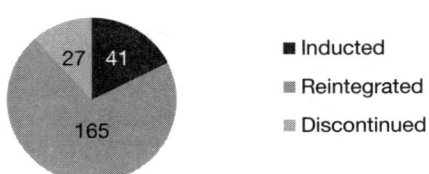

- Inducted
- Reintegrated
- Discontinued

Figure 6.2 *Sabaoon Population of 233 Youth (September 2009–June 2018)*
Source: Created by the authors and reflects the data from June 2018.

Of the 192 youth, 27 have been discontinued from monitoring in 2016. These youth are still in touch with the previous case managers and interact with them on an intermittent and informal basis. Each of the discontinued cases has been provided with an understanding that should they ever feel the need for continued support from the organization, they may approach the MC and request for the same.

At present, 41 youth is still undergoing the de-radicalization and rehabilitation process at Sabaoon. Many of these are high risk and have been involved in activities that range from being an informant, to extortion and recruitment. Of these, some have family members who have been (and are) commanders in the militant organization, while others belong to areas (near the border with Afghanistan) where recruitment to militancy and backlash from the militants is still considered a serious threat.

UNDERSTANDING GAINED FROM SABAOON

One of the most crucial challenges encountered by governments and societies around the world today is that of terrorism. The purpose of such acts is multifaceted; that is, it is essential to assess the role of political, religious and ideological as well as social factors that create an environment for terrorism to thrive in, as it is usually a vacuum in society that creates opportunities for groups to take advantage of.[4] It

---

[4] B. Saul, 'The Challenge of Defining Terrorism', *ISN ETH Zurich*, 17 September 2012. Available at: http://www.isn.ethz.ch (accessed on 2 February

is equally important to understand how and why recruitment takes place. Having said that, it is imperative to understand this particular population of recruited extremists with the qualification: As ground variables differ, the parameters of defining the recruited individual differ so do the methods of recruiting individuals. *That is, as the extremist organization continues to develop, its methods of recruitment and assigning designations and tasks also continues to develop.*

A common thesis for involvement in terrorist organizations is, 'Those who feel that society as a whole has the least to offer them are the most likely to join [the terrorist network]'.[5] However, an overabundance of factors work in contrast with poverty to have a collective effect on an individual to be susceptible towards involvement in violent extremism.

Globally, there are several projects on the de-radicalization and rehabilitation of child soldiers or militants. However, individual profiling, detailed statistics of neuropsychological, psychosocial and contextual factors are not available for most of these projects. The critical difference between Sabaoon and other de-radicalization projects as collated by El-Said and Harrigan and Horgan are as follows.[6]

1. Sabaoon is not an internment or detention centre.
2. Sabaoon is the only project that is a long-term rehabilitation and emancipation centre for adolescents where reintegration is based on the progress made at the centre on an individual basis
3. Sabaoon is managed by a civil NGO and senior programme managers, who are all psychologists from the civil society.

Sabaoon endeavoured to understand the variables or the process underlying the recruitment of children in terrorists' activities. Data has been

---

2014).

[5] M. Sageman, *Understanding Terror Networks* (Philadelphia, PA: University of Pennsylvania Press, 2004).

[6] H. El-Said and J. Harrigan, *Deradicalising Violent Extremists: Counter Radicalisation and Deradicalisation Programmes and Their Impact in Muslim Majority States* (United Kingdom: Routledge Publishing Company, 2012); J. Horgan, *The Psychology of Terrorism* (New York, NY: Routledge Publishing Company, 2005).

meticulously assessed and collated for every aspect of the narrative presented by the inducted students, enabling identification of factors that made the population vulnerable for recruitment to militancy. Vulnerable individuals have multi-causal factors, majority of which are related to issues of marginalization; including lack of employment opportunities or inability of the civil government to provide basic amenities such as education, medical/health, transportation, justice, etc. This creates a vacuum to allow for a negative sentiment to be fostered against those in power.

Over the years, it has been discerned that some (8%) of the students had also indulged in petty crime prior to being recruited. Some of the groups of adolescents who tended to join militancy together or at another's behest were already in cahoots (or collusion) with each other. This is suggestive of the same underlying factors that may promote criminal or terrorist activities, such as in gang recruitment.[7]

Why they say they joined the militant group varies. That is, some say they joined for power and status or prestige, saying that the militants had the power to 'take what they want' and 'treat people as they pleased'. These tended to be youth that had community-based conflicts that were unresolved and they felt that they were being mistreated due to their (low) status in the community. Additionally, youth that had dropped out of school became an easy target for recruitment, as they were loitering around, and were easily convinced to join the group to do something 'meaningful' or useful with their lives. Others stated that they felt that the narrative of TTP 'seemed accurate' and 'everyone else was supporting them', so they did too. Some added that they did not know the Qur'an and/or its meaning and were therefore unable to

---

[7] A. Botha, 'Factors Facilitating Radicalization in Kenya and Somalia', in *Expanding the Evidence Base for P/CVE: Research Solutions,* ed. Sara Zeiger (Abu Dhabi: Hedayah and Edith Cowan University, 2015), 73. Available at: http://www.hedayahcenter.org/activites/80/activities/511/2016/719/international-cve-rese (accessed on 5 March 2019); M. Rezende and R. Estevão, 'Juvenile Criminal Behavior and Peers' Influences: A Comparative Study in the Brazilian Context', *Universitas Psychologia* 11, no. 4 (2012): 1157–1166. Available at: http://www.scielo.org.co/scielo.php?script=sci_arttext&pid=S1657-92672012000400011 (accessed on 5 March 2019).

verify the ideological content, and therefore, took it at face value. This is especially true for the youth (although not a high number) which was madrasa going and was recruited by their religious teachers. Still others argued that as they did not know the national language (Urdu) and only spoke the regional dialect (Pushto), they were unable to discern whether the security personnel were Pakistani or even Muslim. Others stated that their family members were involved, and therefore they never questioned supporting such a group or its ideology. Still others stated that they were coerced to join by reinforcing guilt (especially those who had been sexually abused or had homosexual tendencies, or even drug addiction) to redeem himself for the 'wrong' he had previously done.

Geographic, Sociodemographic and Educational Aspects

Swat is a river valley in a difficult and hostile terrain. The upper valley of the Swat River rises up to the Hindu Kush range in the Khyber Pakhtunkhwa (KPK) province of Pakistan. The difficult topography of the place made it an attractive target for recruiting, especially the north of the Swat River, where the economic development is sparse and access is rather limited. Considering that the northern region of Pakistan, Swat in particular, shares a long and porous border with Afghanistan, this adds to the possibility of significant cross-border infiltration into Pakistan, and also allows for miscreants from Pakistan to easily slip across the border to Afghanistan as well. Many of the youth have been trained in Afghanistan and some have been caught at the border, returning from there.

Profiles of males who were inducted indicate a large family size (72.5%), being the middle child (71%), with low socio-economic status (69%) with many of the fathers working abroad or working in a different province (42%). This decreased supervision of the father at home, as well as impacting the level of bonding with fathers and thereby lacking direction from a male authority figure. Others, belonging to a large family size (and being middle children), lacked the attention and bonding with parents, creating a sense of neglect. They were seeking role models in the militant commanders who exuded power and prestige, and seemed to be willing to give these youth the attention they were not receiving from their own families.

Families themselves have low academic aspirations and achievement, which is discerned by their employment status and income, and this reflects in a lack of promotion of higher education in their offspring. 41.5 per cent of the inducted population had dropped out of school at the time of, or prior to involvement in militancy.

There is the additional factor of a low literacy rate in this region, according to the Pakistan Social and Living Standards Measurement Survey, 2014 (PSLM) in Swat among the children of 5–9 years of age overall 30.61 per cent were out of school with 23.76 per cent boys and 37.81 per cent girls. Similarly, among the age group of 10–14 years, overall 22.13 per cent children were out of the school with 8.31 per cent boys and 38.06 per cent girls. It is important to note that the standard definition of being a literate includes, 'One who can read and write a simple passage in any language and also knows basic numeracy with understanding'. It would therefore be essential to assess what kind of literacy is promoted in this region in particular. Much of the public and private education relies on rote learning as the mode of learning, where teachers read out a passage from the course/textbooks and the class repeats the same. This kind of learning aims to memorize the subject matter without taking the opportunity to gain a conceptual understanding underpinning the learning. In fact, questioning is discouraged, as with a class size of more than 50 students to a teacher (at times 80–100 students to a teacher), the aim is only to complete the course without having disruptions to impede the so-called learning. In terms of militancy, thereby causing vulnerability for the youth to be moulded in what-ever way the recruiter preferred or considered was appropriate for that concerned recruit, the dynamics of the area made for a likely recruiting ground, with a low literacy rate, the kind of literacy pro-vided and a lacking ability for critical thinking (to assess the validity of the militant narrative), they, therefore, became more vulnerable to the overtures of the militants.

These factors all together promoted vulnerability for recruitment into violent extremism (VE). Individuals as young as 7 or 8 years of age have been trained to use weapons, a little older were trained for suicide bombing; the more intelligent ones as informants, extortionists, and the rest were used for menial tasks. Furthermore, there were additional tasks an individual was assigned if they could not be clustered into the above categories which included roles like active militancy, recruiting others, spying, ambush, guard duties (with and without weapons), etc.

The type of category or task assigned to them was usually directly related to their cognitive functioning as well as their loyalty to the group. That is, the higher the intelligence, the more useful they were to the movement. Although most individuals at Sabaoon were abducted (40.5%, as per self-reports confirmed by community sources), they were threatened to cooperate with the militants or they and/or their family members would have been killed or harmed. Having said that, some joined the movement voluntarily (36.5%), believing in the ideology relayed through sermons at the mosques and the radio. Others who joined at the behest of their parents (as each family was 'ordered to give one male child from each family to the cause') and or were coerced by relatives (23%). From within these, there were some who had familial involvement and felt that their family members were doing 'nothing wrong'.

From our findings, even for the ones who were willingly recruited, the recruiters eliminated any possibility of leaving the terrorist organization. That is, there was no tolerance for a change of mind. Furthermore, if they presented with any intention to leave, the recruiters threatened their families or they were demoted to the position of suicide bombing from the holding of arms and ammunitions, as suicide bombings ranks on the lowest tier of the pyramid (refer to Figure 6.3) due to its one-off nature.

At the time of induction, whether most of the individuals had gone through such an ordeal involuntarily or voluntarily, they were significantly high risk for themselves and people around them as well, especially till the time their narratives could be verified from other reliable sources and their understanding of religion is relatively improved.

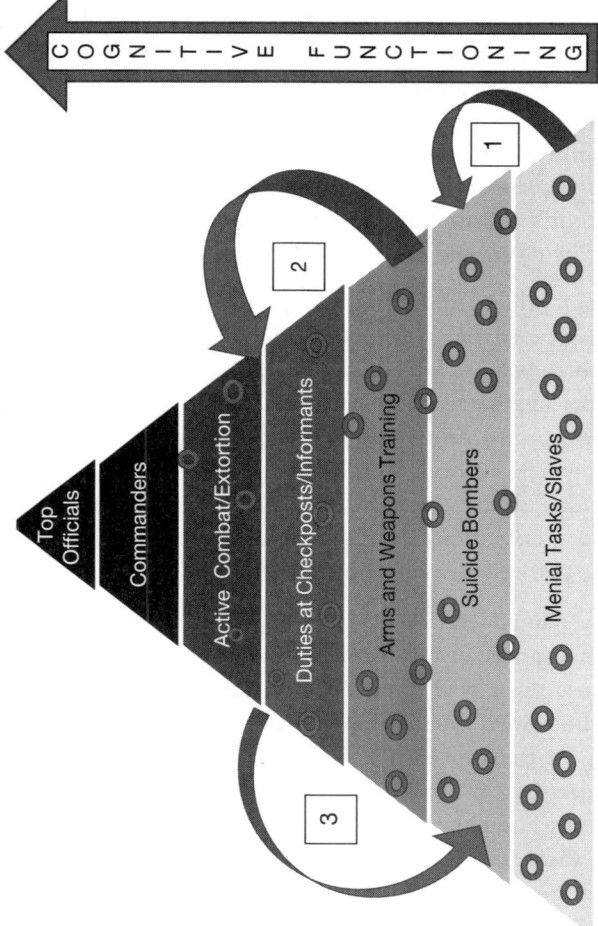

Figure 6.3 *Hierarchy of Militancy*

Source: Created by the authors.

Political and Religious Aspects

Law and order situation of Swat at the time of militancy (2007–2009) and prior needs to be taken into consideration in order to understand the vacuum in society. KPK, being under the Provincially Administered Tribal Areas (PATA), had tribal laws applicable in most communities that relied on a village council consisting of elders from that particular community, usually appointed in a non-democratic manner by the *Wali* of Swat. Generally speaking, those who were considered influential at the community level were given the authority to take decisions on legal and social matters. This process, naturally, created a sense of discrimination in the community, where many community members felt they were being treated unfairly.

The militant group, initially disguised as a religious movement, upholding Islamic law (or sharia) proposed to address these issues. The rule of law, which was implemented in the province by the extremists, and its wrongful implementation led to radicalization in the province. Initially, the extremists gained popular support by introducing laws, for example, which allowed for the people to have quick justice. Statements which attracted youth towards the movement, especially those who had a sense of perceived or actual injustice, included, 'The victim and the perpetrator will be buried the same day!'

Once they gained confidence at the community and regional level, through support in the form of charity and manpower, they began to misuse the law in their own favour. In fact, many of the individuals who joined the movement initially were petty criminals, who were given the power and authority of commanders. These supposed leaders began looting those who were financially stable, while also lashing and beheading, as punishment, when others would disagree with their stance. They termed their punishments as 'jihad' and portrayed themselves as fighting for the rights of the oppressed and the marginalized.

UNDERSTANDING RECRUITMENT AND ENGAGEMENT

Although issues of marginalization may act as push factors towards the movement, in order to understand recruitment and engagement it is important to understand the hierarchy of militancy (see Figure 6.3) as discerned from the Sabaoon population and their narratives.

At the lowest tier includes basic or menial tasks, where the recruited individuals are assigned duties related to cleaning, cooking, construction, etc. The second tier is for suicide bombers. These are individuals who are indoctrinated towards conducting suicide attacks (as indicated by 1, in Figure 6.3). Many times these individuals are also given physical and weapons training, as they may be required to carry a pistol and/or a hand grenade with them when they are assigned a target for a suicide attack. Individuals who tend to have low cognitive functioning (highlighted by confusion, forgetfulness, difficulty in concentration, learning and planning, etc.) tend to be limited to the first two tiers, as the militant group does not invest too much effort in indoctrinating them or training them for active militancy or combat. This is mainly because they would result in being a liability for the group, considering that they have limited abilities to contribute to the group and its causes.

The third tier is physical and weapons training. This level of training is usually provided after the group has been able to ascertain the loyalty of the recruit. Individuals who tend to join voluntarily tend to move to this tier swiftly, in comparison to those who may be abducted. The training in this tier is similar to gorilla training. Individuals are required to participate in rigorous physical exercise, as well as target practice (on inanimate and animate objects). During this period religious indoctrination continues, as that is considered to strengthen the resolve for individuals to sustain the extent of the training being provided. This duration can last from two weeks to three months, depending on the militant commander, the needs of the movement at the time of recruitment and the ability of the recruit.

Following the training (as indicated by 2 in Figure 6.3), some recruits are assigned to roles depending on their individual strengths. That is, those who are considered vigilant and are able to work independently are assigned duties at check posts. Some of these also work as informants and pass on information related to presence of security forces and activities of the area under their care. Those who are considered to require direction and supervision and are cooperative in team work are assigned roles in the militant army and are actively involved in combat. These individuals tend to be good marksmen and are able to sustain stressful conditions (of warfare such as excessive heat and cold, scarcity of food and/or water, living in caves or ditches, etc.). Some of these individuals who are capable of imposing force and exude strength are assigned roles of extortionists as well. Generally, those involved in active combat and extortion tend to have a greater resolve for the militant cause, are more eager to use physical force, have aggressive tendencies and are less sensitive and empathetic to others.

The next tier is of commanders. These are individuals who display leadership qualities and have higher cognitive functioning, as they are required to strategize plans in favour of the movement, take decisive action and guide others to perform functions for the group. Commanders tend to have some characteristics of charisma, in order to appeal to others and inspire devotion from those under their command. They tend to exude power and authority, as they assign roles to others within their group, and are in a position to assess the strengths and weaknesses of the recruits, while also reassessing and reassigning roles within the group, as may be required. At times, this also necessitates demoting those who question the ideology, express dissent, become disillusioned by the movement, from active combat or guard duties to suicide bombing (as indicated by 3 in Figure 6.3). This becomes a means of eliminating the threat of having the recruit pass on information.

Top officials, the highest tier in militancy are a handful of individuals. These decision-makers are considered to have a sound ideological understanding of the movement and can promote the same at the lower tiers. They act as directors for the movement, and provide administrative guidance and monitoring for the commanders that rely on them. Top officials are the most powerful, often having significant experience in militancy and having close associations with preceding leadership, tend to not interact with the lower tiers often. They, instead, send messages through other commanders, often to motivate the recruits (in active training, informants, etc.)

to keep their spirits elevated. They also tend to have the ability to negotiate within any factions their group may have, while also having the tendency to manipulate those who they lead. Very few recruits actually interact with the top officials, however, they tend to be privy to their sermons and lectures every now and then (usually circulated through videos and voice messages through mobile phones and memory cards).

Critical Thinking and Logical Reasoning

The crux of this particular aspect of the argument is deep rooted. The foundation is laid by the education system in Pakistan and how it has been structured over from independence up till now.

As already discussed in this chapter, there is a general lack of critical thinking, as for years in most public and private schools education focuses on rote learning and memorization. Culturally, questioning tends to equal disobedience and disrespect—something that is not acceptable. This holds true for many public as well as some private schools in the country. Children in the classroom are made to learn without questioning the more profound meaning of topics. Moreover, the classroom sizes of government schools, also explained earlier, is not conducive to discussions and attention. It is questionable whether it is equally conducive to learning!

The lack of critical thinking found its way to creep into the structure of religious education as well and that is where the individuals tend to become even more vulnerable where recruitment is concerned. As a result, what instead is instilled is an 'all right versus all wrong' thinking, that its either 'black *or* white', that its either 'us *or* them', without the space for any grey areas, where parts of both sides of an argument may exist.

There are only about 5 per cent of intelligent inductees, who are at or have gone through the de-radicalization and rehabilitation process at Sabaoon, who tend to have a deeper ideological inclination and commitment to the militant cause based on statements like, 'The enemies of God cannot be the friends of the State'—in reference to having a foreign policy which is open to having supportive relations with the West (who are friendly with, e.g., Israel), or 'Banks charge interest, which is against Islamic principles and the State is not doing anything to change this'.

Many (Bjørgo, 2005; Horgan, 2005; Sageman, 2004)[8] have contended that ideology is usually not the primary motivating factor, and adoption of the terrorist organization's ideology usually occurs after the individual has joined their organization. Factors such as poverty, being the middle child of large number of offspring (neglect), lack of education in the family and problematic peer group, etc., all play an integral role. This applies to a large number of our population (from Sabaoon).

Metaphoric Murder and Self-Resurrection

There is much consensus on the thesis that the human capacity to care about large and impersonal collectiveness, as if they were an extended family, is the foundation of mass politics and the prerequisite for national ethnic and religious group conflict (McCauley & Moskalenko, 2008).[9]

To achieve this sense of collectiveness as an extended family, we have found that our population at Sabaoon was assigned new names (aliases) to help create a sense of comradery in order to ease the transition into the movement and facilitate the development of a new personality. The purpose to our understanding is aimed at detaching the individual from his past life (including family members) and become a part of a greater cause (the militant movement). This has been theorized

---

[8] Sageman, *Understanding Terror Networks*; Horgan, *The Psychology of Terrorism*; T. Bjørgo, *Root Causes of Terrorism: Myths, Reality and Ways Forward* (New York, NY: Routledge, 2005).

[9] C. McCauley and S. Moskalenko, 'Mechanisms of Political Radicalization: Pathways toward Terrorism', *Terrorism and Political Violence* 20, no. 3 (2008): 415–433. doi:10.1080/09546550802073367.

as 'metaphoric murder'[10] as the individuals existing personality is removed or extinguished (de-individualization) to give way to a new identity. This loss of self-identity, in a group setting has the tendency to lead to conformity, apathy and obedience to authority.[11] In addition, it also serves the group in communication without giving away the actual identity of their recruits. This is especially so for the more senior combatants and the commanders, especially since their conversations and messages tend to get intercepted.

Sabaoon, therefore, attempts to rebuild this personality through efforts leading to 'self-resurrection'. That is, re-establishing a cohesive personality with a better understanding by reframing the experiences related to recruitment, engagement and disengagement (voluntary or forced), and using the underlying needs to identify ones' motivations, inclinations and aspirations that can pave the way for a more efficient, useful and productive lifestyle in the future. Once the youth is reintegrated, the MC, then, serves to consolidate these positive personality changes, and provides the required support to transition from a controlled environment (i.e., Sabaoon) to their communities to manage and address the issues related to post-reintegration, especially the maintenance of goal direction and the management of personal issues (as discussed in the paper above).

INDIGENOUS VARIABLES IN DE-RADICALIZATION AND REHABILITATION

Replication of Sabaoon has often been a point of interest for many organizations, especially at the international level. The model for Sabaoon has been adopted in Bara (FATA region), Pakistan, where SWAaT was requested to help with capacity building for the

---

[10] R. R. Khan and F. N. Peracha, 'Deradicalizing, Rehabilitating and Reintegrating Violent Extremists' (Peace brief, United States Institute of Peace, 2017). Available at: https://www.usip.org/publications/2017/11/deradicalizing-rehabilitating-and-reintegrating-violent-extremists (accessed on 5 March 2019).

[11] Philip G. Zimbardo, *The Lucifer Effect: Understanding How Good People Turn Evil*, 258–323 (New York, NY: Random House, 2007); S. Milgram, *Obedience to Authority: An Experimental View* (New York, NY: Harper and Row, 1974).

psychosocial team. Approximately 800 individuals surrendered during the counter insurgency in Bara, majority being adults (over 700), with approximately 70 male youth. Three separate programmes were initiated simultaneously, of which two were adult based and one was for the male youth.

The variables in Bara, which is barely 200 miles from Swat, are substantially different. That is, tribal loyalties are a priority in the culture of that region. If the leader of one tribe agrees to support any particular group (picking a side between a militant group and the State-based security agency), then the tribe remains loyal to that decision, even if they do not agree with this. Similarly, the culture requires them to participate in what the tribal elders (*masharan*) command. Having said that, some political affiliations and economic needs also drive these decisions. For example, agriculture was based around opium cultivation, which is considered a very noble profession. In order to make sales of this cultivation they needed to have connections with other groups who would process the cultivated crop, or who would be able to sell it forward to other groups. Smuggling such large shipments, in raw form, is not easy to manage in the absence of a network of support, which the tribe also understands and remains loyal to. Religious ideology was, as in the case for Sabaoon, misrepresented and misinterpreted to create sectarianism, and served to create tribal loyalties to specific militant groups, and in consequence was used to create conflict with opposing militant groups.

If we consider the case of Baluchistan, which is barely 600 miles from Swat, the level of poverty is so extreme that children are willing to place an improvised explosive device (IED) for as little at USD10. The cultural drivers may not exist as they did in terms of tribal loyalties in Bara, or religious extremism in Swat, but the political grievances indicate that the socio-economic disparity between the provinces and the obvious lack of job opportunities has led individuals to become involved in anti-State activities. Sectarianism and provincialism do play a prominent role in the conflict in Baluchistan, and issues of social and personal marginalization can easily be abused to serve the purpose of a particular conflict. In the case of children, many were easily beguiled without an understanding of the consequences of supporting or participating in such acts of terror. In fact, some youth even claimed that they were informed that placing an IED would not harm anyone and would only cause an explosion to terrorize the public and security forces. Access to media (such as newspapers and television) is limited and none of the youth was aware of the actual damage (loss of lives) their acts caused.

CHALLENGES

Although some criticism for the Sabaoon project has highlighted the expense per child per year, it is comparatively low when assessed in relation to international de-radicalization projects for Adults (as not as much information is present for those with children). Additionally, it is essential to emphasize that where the facility required USD 5,000/ per child per year to support a population of 70 youth, it required approximately USD 4,500 for supporting a population of 100 youth. This is because the operational expenses for the facility itself (staff salaries, sports equipment, general maintenance, etc.) tend to remain the same and the major changes are in the provision of meals, clothes (uniform and informal), shoes, books, etc., for each child.

Working with such a population is not without inherent challenges. First, it has been a difficult task to seek qualified staff which had experience in working with a similar population. All of the staff members, especially the MHTs (at Sabaoon and the MC) had to be significantly trained. In fact, much of the academic staff also required support in managing and dealing with youth whose academic level was not at par with their chronological age, and many who had difficulties that required additional support (remedial learning, attention and impulsive control difficulties, low frustration tolerance, etc.).

The fact that some of the youth belong to families who have absconded also creates a difficult scenario for the staff. Usually, a family absconds due to serious involvement of male members (fathers and or brothers) in the family. As a result, there are few relatives within the community or region who are willing to take responsibility to interact with the youth inducted at Sabaoon and or agree to serve as a guarantor for such youth (for weekend leave or reintegration). There is understandable reservations from the relatives, as they do not want a backlash from the security agencies (investigations, raids, undue attention and monitoring) as well as from other community members as existing community relationships can be negatively impacted, while any issues of enmity can be enhanced by additional allegations on the basis of such support. In such a situation, it creates a lot of difficulty for the MHT to gather authentic and reliable information about the youth and his family, and limits the ability to verify this to other sources.

In fact, similar challenges exist for youth that belongs to areas outside of Swat. That is, many of these regions (in Waziristan, Dir, Hangu and Bara or Tirah) are far flung, often lacking army or any security presence that may facilitate the visit. Although, in such cases, where family members are still present at home, they are encouraged to visit the facility (which they are unable to do too often themselves). Links with community members, therefore, are not established, and reliance on the family members is very excessive.

Although many of the youth who are working as an additional supporting hand to sustain their families, not all have been successful in managing to generate sufficient income. There are a few cases who have been exceptionally successful in developing their vocation in a manner that has allowed them to form partnerships with others. These are youth who have understood the importance of developing healthy interpersonal skills at the community level, and trying to assess how they can serve each other in beneficial ways. Other youth who are still academically goal directed are yet to step into the workforce and find stable footing for themselves.

A main challenge in replicating the programme in any region, within the context of Pakistan or in the international context first requires a policy framework supportive of such an initiative. Each region, as described for three areas within Pakistan, has indigenous factors that need to be assessed and understood prior to undertaking developing the content of the programme. This cannot be emphasized enough. The culture and traditions of each region drive the interaction itself, therefore, for the interaction to be a useful intervention with effective results, an understanding of 'what is important' to them is essential. The policy framework, therefore, may have to consider regional and culturally relevant aspects to support the programming needs as the requirements to make such programmes successful.

Another significant challenge is risk assessment. That is, although many risk assessment scales exist, and are rather useful, for risk to be assessed accurately, it is essential to be well trained in the use of the particular tool, using an objective evaluation, while having the risk mitigation and intervention strategies in place. Having said that, and even when all these aspects are well covered, there is always the possibility of reoffending, recidivism and or some form of violent behaviour. There is also the possibility of reviewing cases too leniently which may result in false negatives, or too strictly, which may result in false positives. Therefore, oftentimes, reintegration is a chance being taken, where calculated risks, as per the risk assessment, do exist.

Monitoring and evaluation of such programmes is only possible in the long term, and this can only be successfully achieved if contact with each of the centre graduates is maintained, or an agreement for intermittent follow up is achieved and carried out. This may not be possible for all regions, due to security based issues, however, such post-release interaction (and support) can prevent recidivism itself, by promoting continued progress in mainstream society.

Chapter 7

Countering Radicalization through Education
Global Policy Trends and the Case of Pakistan

Fatima Waqi Sajjad

Pakistan has served as a test case for education reform to counter radicalization. Following 9/11, a plethora of policy papers scrutinized curricula and pedagogies in Pakistani madrasas and public schools to identify risk factors that may lead to radicalization, and suggest reforms to counter radicalization through education. But despite excessive academic attention and heavy funding from international donors for education reform in Pakistan, the objective of countering radicalization through education remained unfulfilled, as successive studies reported growing popularity of radical ideas among educated youth in the country. Subsequently, the rise of religious extremism became a serious concern for law enforcement agencies as it triggered a series of violent incidents in the country. Following a church attack in Peshawar, the Supreme Court of Pakistan issued a special ruling for the education sector, calling for the development of appropriate curricula to foster religious and political tolerance in students. In view of the Supreme Court ruling, the government issued a directive to higher education institutions, especially those offering social, political and civic education courses, to ensure that their curricula promote respect for religious and ethnic diversity of Pakistan. Recently, the link between education and radicalization once again became a subject of debate in Pakistani media, as security agencies captured militant networks that included graduates of well-known universities holding high-level degrees. Involvement of mainstream university graduates in militant activities raised alarms and security agencies recommended greater monitoring of higher education institutions in the country. Education once again came at the forefront of the country's security policy. Drawing on a systematic review of the post-9/11 policy literature on education and security, this study re-considers the problem of education and youth radicalization by exploring three questions: (a) What is it that we call 'radicalization'? (b) What is it in education that counters radicalization? (c) What kind of education we are imparting on ground? The three questions are explored in broader global context as well as in specific Pakistani context. The study uses the lens of critical pedagogy, particularly the ideas of Henry Giroux, to evaluate global education trends and their impact on local education policies. It asserts that: (a) the way we define 'radicalization' is intrinsically linked to the way we think education can counter it. If radicalization entails resistance to unjust status quo, education should be a force fostering rather than countering it. (b) Contemporary modes of education, through their exclusive focus on economic value of education, undermine the critical and transformative function of education which can effectively counter the pull of dogmatic violent ideologies. The study evaluates contemporary higher education trends in Pakistan using a key policy document entitled 'HEC Vision 2025'. It calls for a rethinking of current economically driven policy vision and top-down approach to anti-radicalization which has been counterproductive in the past. Instead, it recommends opening up spaces in universities for peaceful dialogue and action on critical issues to channelize youth's energy in a positive direction.

THE PROBLEM

In a recent workshop organized by Pakistan Institute for Peace Studies, a Pakistani think tank, more than 40 university teachers gathered to ponder the link between education and security in Pakistan. They explored how teachers can play a role in promoting social and religious harmony in the country. A key question was raised during the discussion:

> How *well educated* individuals, especially those from applied sciences, could join militancy?[1]

This question has continued to perplex security agencies in Pakistan as they encounter well-educated terrorists for many years now. Lately, this question was actively debated in print and electronic media when a militant network called Ansarul Sharia Pakistan (ASP) was found to be operating from a leading public sector university. The group was involved in the killing of several policemen and army personnel. Its members included students holding BSc and MSc degrees in applied physics. Earlier, a suspect of an assassination attempt on a political leader from Sindh Assembly was found to be a PhD degree holder.[2]

It is to be noted that involvement of highly educated individuals in militant activities is not a recent phenomenon, neither is it confined to Pakistan. A study by Oxford University Department of Sociology entitled *Engineers of Jihad* notes that graduates from subjects such as science, medicine and engineering are strongly over-represented in extremist Islamic groups across the Muslim world. Engineers in particular, are over-represented in violent groups in the Muslim as well as the Western world.[3] The academic and policy debates, focusing on the link between education and radicalization however, have been particularly attentive to the case of Pakistan.

A plethora of academic and policy papers have scrutinized curricula and pedagogies in Pakistani madrasas and public schools since 9/11, to identify the risk factors that may lead to radicalization and suggest reforms to counter radicalization through education. But despite excessive academic attention and heavy funding from international donors for education sector reform (ESR) in Pakistan, the objective

[1] Khalid Masud as quoted by *The News*, 8 September 2017.

[2] As reported by Pervez Hoodbhoy, 'Deradicalizing our Universities', Column Section, *Dawn*, 23 September 2017.

[3] D. Gambetta and S. Hertog, 'Engineers of Jihad Sociology' (working paper no. 2007–10, University of Oxford, Oxford, 2007), 1–88.

of countering radicalization through education could not be fulfilled, as successive studies reported greater popularity of radical ideas among educated youth in the country.[4] This reverse effect of counter-radicalization policy initiatives was termed as 'signs of psychological reactance' by Sajjad, Christie and Taylor.[5]

The rise of religious extremism in post-9/11 Pakistan, fuelled by the global War on Terror milieu, not only intensified the anti-West sentiment in the country but also interfaith and sectarian clashes. A number of incidents were reported where religious minorities were targeted in different ways. The growing religious intolerance and complaints of persecution from minority communities became a grave concern for law enforcement agencies. In June 2014, the Supreme Court of Pakistan initiated suo motu proceedings for the protection of minority rights, after a suicide bomb attack on a church in Peshawar that killed 81 people. Referring to the multiple incidents of minorities' persecution reported earlier, the court emphasized the need to mitigate religious intolerance and promote interfaith harmony in the country. To this end, education once again came at the forefront as an instrument to bring about the desired social change. The Supreme Court issued a special ruling for education sector, calling for the development of appropriate curricula at educational institutions 'to promote a culture of religious and social tolerance'.[6] The Supreme Court ruling referred to the UN Declaration on the Elimination of All Forms of Intolerance

---

[4] Yusuf, Moeed, 'Prospects of Youth Radicalization in Pakistan' (Analysis Paper 14, no. 7 Brookings, 2008), no. 7 (2008): 1–27. R. Winthrop and Corinne Graff, 'Beyond Madrasas: Assessing the Links between Education and Militancy in Pakistan', Brookings Center for Universal Education, 2010. Available at: https://www.brookings.edu/research/beyond-madrasas-assessing-the-links-between-education-and-militancy-in-pakistan/ (accessed on 20 February 2019); Ayesha Siddiqa, 'Red Hot Chilli Peppers Islam—Is the Youth in Elite Universities in Pakistan Radical? Foreign-Security Policy Series', Heinrich Boll Stiftung, 2010. Available at: https://pk.boell.org/sites/default/files/downloads/Red_Hot_Chilli_Peppers_Islam_-_Complete_Study_Report.pdf (accessed on 15 June 2017).

[5] F. Sajjad, D. J. Christie and L. K. Taylor, 'De-Radicalizing Pakistani Society: The Receptivity of Youth to a Liberal Religious Worldview', *Journal of Peace Education* 14, no. 2 (2017): 1.

[6] Supreme Court of Pakistan Original Jurisdiction, 'SMC No.1/2014 etc', Suo motu action regarding suicide bomb attack, 2014, 30. Available at: http://

and of Discrimination Based on Religion or Belief, pointing out the need to foster 'a spirit of understanding, tolerance, friendship among people'.[7] In keeping with the Supreme Court ruling, a directive by the government was sent to educational institutions recommending a revision of social and political science curricula to promote tolerance of religious, ethnic and cultural diversity in Pakistan. Similar directives have been issued by successive provincial governments to check and revise curricula for tolerance and promote respect for religious diversity in the country.

This chapter reconsiders the problem of education, religious and political radicalization in Pakistan. It asserts that, to counter radicalization through education, one must consider (a) what is it that we call radicalization (b) what is it in education that counters radicalization and (c) what kind of education we are imparting on ground. Based on a systematic review of the post 9/11 policy literature on education and security, this chapter attempts to explore the aforementioned questions. Each question is explored in general global context and specific Pakistani context.

WHAT IS IT THAT WE CALL RADICALIZATION?

'Radicalization', despite being an extensively used term in policy literature, remains a fiercely contested and problematic concept. The term has been used and defined in multiple ways; quite often, it has been used interchangeably with another problematic term 'extremism'. The 'terminological complexities' of defining the two terms have been acknowledged by UNESCO's policy guide for preventing violent extremism through education.[8] UN considers the task of defining such complex notions as the prerogative of its member states. It recommends that in the absence of a consensus definition of these concepts,

---

www.supremecourt.gov.pk/web/user_files/File/smc_1_2014.pdf (accessed on 29 April 2018).

[7] Ibid., 16.

[8] *UNESCO*, 'Preventing Violent Extremism through Education: A Guide for Policy Makers', 2017. Available at: http://unesdoc.unesco.org/images/0024/002477/247764e.pdf (accessed on 29 April 2018).

they should be discussed and defined at national level.[9] Following are some definitions offered by states for their domestic policies to address radicalization or extremism.

The US government defines radicalism as, 'The process by which American citizens and residents turn to violence using Islam as an ideological or religious justification'.[10] Later, US Department of Homeland Security clarifies that it is concerned with 'violent extremism' rather than any belief system.[11] US National Counter Terrorism Centre (NCTC) emphasizes that 'radicalization is a dynamic and multi-layered process involving several factors that interact with one another to influence an individual. There is no single factor that explains radicalization or mobilization'.[12]

The British government defines extremism as 'vocal or active opposition to fundamental British values, including democracy, the rule of law, individual liberty and mutual respect and tolerance of different faiths and beliefs'.[13] While it recognizes radicalization as 'the process by which a person comes to support terrorism and forms of extremism leading to terrorism'.[14]

The Australian government defines radicalization in the following words: 'Radicalization happens when a person's thinking and behaviour become significantly different from how most of the members of their society and community view social issues and participate politically'.[15]

---

[9] Ibid., 18.

[10] F. Patel, 'Rethinking Radicalization', Brennan Centre for Justice, 2011, 1. Available at: https://www.brennancenter.org/sites/default/files/legacy/RethinkingRadicalization.pdf (accessed on 24 April 2018).

[11] Ibid., 13.

[12] Ibid.

[13] Secretary of State for the Home Department, 'Prevent Strategy', 2011, 107. Available at: https://assets.publishing.service.gov.uk/government/uploads/system/uploads/attachment_data/file/97976/prevent-strategy-review.pdf (accessed on 29 April 2018).

[14] Ibid., 108.

[15] C. Angus, 'Radicalization and Violent Extremism: Causes and Responses', *NSW Parliamentary Research Service*, 2016, 1. Available at: https://www.parliament. nsw.gov.au/researchpapers/Documents/radicalisation-and-violent-extremism-causes-and-/Radicalisation%20eBrief.pdf (accessed on 29 April 2018).

Violent extremism, on the other hand, occurs when 'a person or group decides that fear, terror and violence are justified to achieve ideological, political or social change, and acts accordingly'.[16]

Arthur notes similar distinction between radicalization and extremism. According to him radicalization can be seen as 'a process by which someone adopts an extreme position, but it may not involve violent behavior in support of the position adopted'.[17] Extreme may refer to 'holding a fixed set of views outside the norm that may prevent compromise and exclude other perspectives'.[18] The study, however, points out that there is a lack of consensus on the meaning of both terms and hence they remain open to misinterpretation. The question of who gets to define extremism or identify someone as extremist remains pertinent.

The Canadian government defines radicalization as 'the process by which individuals are introduced to an overtly ideological message and belief system that encourages movement from moderate, mainstream beliefs towards extreme views'.[19]

Macaluso points to the problematic nature of the term radicalization, arguing that historically the term 'radicalism' has been used to refer to innovative and revolutionary ideas. In this sense, radicalism has been the driving force behind the historical labour and civil rights movements in the West. Whereas, nowadays the trend is to link radicalization only with religious extremism or jihadism.[20]

Macaluso points out that the present day use of the term radicalization began with the European Commission Report which appeared

---

[16] Ibid., 2.

[17] J. Arthur, 'Extremism and Neo-liberal Education Policy: A Contextual Critique of the Trojan Horse Affair in Birmingham Schools', *British Journal of Educational Studies* 63, no. 3 (2015): 313.

[18] Ibid., 314.

[19] A. P. Schmid, 'Radicalization, De-radicalization, Counter-radicalization: A Conceptual Discussion and Literature Review' (Hague: International Centre for Counter Terrorism, 2013), 7.

[20] A. Macaluso, 'From Countering to Preventing Radicalization through Education: Limits and Opportunities' (working paper no. 18, the Hague Institute for Global Justice, the Hague, 2016), 2.

after Madrid train bombings in 2004 and London bombing in 2005. The term became instantly popular in the West as at that time there was 'a security need to identify potential terrorists before they could launch an attack'. For similar reasons, the term 'extremist' is currently used in the west to refer to Muslims 'who are perceived to radically criticize Western culture or politics'.[21]

The discourse on terrorism in Pakistan mostly borrows the terminology used in the West. In Pakistani context however, the meaning of extremism and radicalization takes a slightly different twist. Yusuf synthesizes multiple definitions of youth radicalism proposed in context of Pakistan, and describes radicalism as

> …youth perceptions/responses on religiosity, their exclusionary thinking, religious intolerance, a level of sympathy for – or at least a lack of active opposition to Islamist violence among pockets, an 'us vs. them' conception of the world and frustration with the conditions in the country as worrisome.[22]

Siddiqa defines 'latent radicalism' as, 'The tendency to be exclusive instead of inclusive vis-a-vis other communities on the basis of religious belief,' resulting in a bias against other individuals, communities or nations.[23] She warns that latent radicalism may keep youth vulnerable to extremist ideologies.

Moving towards a synthesis of the earlier discussion, one may cite the concise definition of extremism offered by Desmond Tutu[24] and the comprehensive work done by Alex Schmid on the topic. Tutu blends multiple meanings of extremism cited above by explaining the concept as: 'When you do not allow for a different point of view; when you

---

[21] Ibid., 3.

[22] M. Yusuf, 'Radicalism among Youth In Pakistan: Human Development Gone Wrong?' UNDP Pakistan, 2014, 9. Available at: http://nhdr.undp.org.pk/wp-content/uploads/2015/02/Moeed-Yusuf-Youth-Radicalisation.pdf (accessed on 15 June 2017).

[23] Siddiqa, 'Red Hot Chilli Peppers Islam', 25.

[24] As cited by R. Ghosh, W. A. Chan, A. Manuel and M. Dilimulati, 'Can Education Counter Violent Religious Extremism?' *Canadian Foreign Policy Journal* 23, no. 2 (2016): 117–133.

hold your own views as being quite exclusive; when you don't allow for the possibility of difference'.[25]

Schmid recognizes that the terms 'radical', 'radicalization' and 'de-radicalization' are based on contested, relative, politicized and problematic concepts. He, however, emphasizes the need to distinguish between the terms 'radical' and 'extremist'. He reminds that the word 'radicalism' has changed its meanings dramatically within a century. In 19th century context, it used to represent liberal and progressive forces transforming traditional social structures while in the current usage, the term stands for the opposite, that is, anti-liberal and regressive forces challenging liberal societies. Based on the historical usage of the term, Schmid offers the following definition of radicalism:

1. Advocating sweeping political change, based on a conviction that the status quo is unacceptable while at the same time a fundamentally different alternative appears to be available to the radical;

2. The means advocated to bring about the system-transforming radical solution for government and society can be non-violent and democratic (through persuasion and reform) or violent and non-democratic (through coercion and revolution)[26]

According to Schmid's definition, radicalism represents non-conformist thinking capable of imagining alternatives to the existing status quo and a firm commitment to bring the desired social, political change through whatever means available. Thinking about radicalism in this way necessitates re-thinking the role of education to counter radicalism. We need to review what is it that we are trying to counter, mitigate or prevent through education. Making a clear distinction between radicalism and extremism is therefore essential. Extremists, according to Schmid strive to create 'a homogeneous society based on rigid, dogmatic ideological tenets; they seek to make society conformist by suppressing all opposition and subjugating minorities'.[27] Schmid elaborates the distinction further by describing extremist worldview

---

[25] Schmid, 'Radicalization, De-radicalization, Counter-radicalization', 6.

[26] Ibid., 8.

[27] Ibid., 9.

as inflexible, rigid and simplistic, while radical worldview is termed as more open, rational and pragmatic.[28] Schmid contends that it is not the 'open-minded' radicalism but 'closed-minded' extremism that should be seen as the main problem.

Based on the ideas of Macaluso, Tutu and Schmid, the current chapter views extremism as a key problem that needs to be addressed through education, while the concept of radicalization needs to be re-considered and re-conceptualized. We need to consider the meaning we give to the word 'radicalism' and if it stands for resistance to the unjust status quo, education and education policies should aim to foster rather than counter it.

WHAT IS IT IN EDUCATION THAT COUNTERS RADICALIZATION/EXTREMISM?

Although a number of key policy papers emphasize the need to distinguish between radicalization and extremism, most policy literature makes little distinction between the two terms when it comes to countering radicalization or extremism and the role of education for this purpose. The terms 'radicalization', 'extremism' and 'violent extremism' have been used interchangeably in the discourse on preventing or countering these trends. As a result, there remains an ambiguity about what is it that we are trying to counter through education. This section will explore how policy literature describes education's role in countering radicalization/extremism by examining two questions:

1. What leads the young people towards radicalization or extremism?
2. How education can address what may lead the youth to radicalization or extremism?

The selected policy literature for the first question includes key policy papers that synthesize ideas and debates on possible 'drivers' of radicalization or extremism. Academic and policy papers that explain radicalization in Pakistan have also been included. A systematic examination

---

[28] Ibid., 10.

of this literature reveals at least three sets of factors that lead the youth towards radicalization or extremism.

Grievances/Sense of Injustice

According to Schmid, a sense of 'alienation, marginalization, discrimination, relative deprivation, humiliation (direct or by proxy), stigmatization and rejection' may be a significant driver of radicalization at an individual level.[29]

Neumann lists multiple recurring factors that have been identified in literature as drivers of radicalization.[30] He places 'grievance' at the top. Societal conflicts, tensions, feelings of injustice, marginalization and exclusion are considered high-risk factors that may lead young people towards radical groups and ideologies. Gosh et al. also highlight discrimination, humiliation or feelings of revenge as push factors towards extremism.[31] Specifically, Western nations' invasion of Afghanistan and Iraq are considered incidents that may justify the use of violence against the oppressive enemy to a radicalized individual.

Khan explains that in the case of Pakistan, the extremists' narratives resonate widely as they highlight the grievances of Muslims in Afghanistan, Iraq, Somalia, Ethiopia and Palestine.[32] Since Pakistanis consider their country as 'an Islamic refuge for persecuted Muslims', they remain sympathetic to narratives that condemn the past and

---

[29] Ibid., 4.

[30] P. R. Neumann, 'Countering Violent Extremism and Radicalization That Lead to Terrorism: Ideas, Recommendations and Good Practices from the OSCE Region', *Organization for Security and Co-operation in Europe*, 2018. Available at: https://www.osce.org/chairmanship/346841?download=true (accessed on 28 April 2018).

[31] Ratna Ghosh, W.Y. Alice Chan, Ashley Manuel and Maihemuti Dilimulati, 'Can Education Counter Violent Religious Extremism?', *Canadian Foreign Policy Journal* 23, no. 2 (2017): 117–133. doi: 10.1080/11926422.2016.1165713.

[32] Amil Khan, *Pakistan and the Narratives of Extremism* (US Institute Special Report no. 327, 2013). Available at: http://www.usip.org/sites/default/files/SR327-Pakistan-and-the-Narratives-ofExtremism.pdfaccessed (accessed on 18 March 2015).

present foreign exploitation of Muslim lands. The history of colonial occupation, roller coaster relations with United States during the cold war, US abandonment of Pakistan and war-torn Afghanistan after the cold war, post-9/11 US mistrust and surveillance of Pakistan and drones strikes, feed extremists' narratives in Pakistan.[33]

In addition to political grievances, socio-economic inequality is also identified as a key driver of extremism in the country. Yusuf terms relative deprivation and alienation of the underprivileged as a key cause of radicalization in Pakistan.[34] Moreover, the sense of despondence and frustration with the poor performance of government, corruption, socio-economic deprivation, concerns about the future of the state make youth vulnerable to extremist ideologies.

Looking for Meaning in Life

A second set of factors that drive young people towards radicalization or extremism, relates to their quest for 'meaning' in life. Schmid points out that ideologies and higher narratives propagated by radical groups offer individuals a sense of higher purpose and meaning in life. Religious or political ideologies catch the attention of young minds because they not only address their core concerns but also give them a feeling of empowerment.[35] Gosh et al. describe that extremists' propaganda is especially effective for individuals who seek 'significance and a reason for living'.[36] A sense of 'boredom' may also lead young people towards radical ideologies that offer excitement, adventure and thrill they seek in life.

Yusuf explains why extremists' narratives appealed to the emotions of the common people in Pakistan in post-9/11 milieu. At least since

---

[33] F. Sajjad, 'Countering Extremists' Narrative in Pakistan', *NDU Journal* (2015). Available at: http://www.ndu.edu.pk/issra/issra_pub/articles/ndu-journal/NDU-Journal-2015/04-Countering-Extremists-Narratives.pdf (accessed on 28 April 2018).

[34] Yusuf, 'Radicalism among Youth in Pakistan'.

[35] Schmid, 'Radicalization, De-radicalization, Counter-radicalization', 24.

[36] Ghosh et al., 'Violent Religious Extremism?', 'Can Education Counter.

the 1980s, the State had been pushing the idea of 'Islam in danger', at first to support the Afghan jihad, and later to support the cause of persecuted Muslims in Kashmir, Palestine and other places. The narrative promoted by the State was hijacked by the militant outfits after 9/11. The powerful militant narratives publically and loudly propagated that 'Islam is in danger due to invasion of infidel forces in Afghanistan (and elsewhere, i.e., Iraq). Jihad is a legitimate tool in this situation....'[37] This line of argument made sense in a global environment shaped by War on Terror and 'clash of civilizations' narratives. However, Yusuf points out that despite the fact that post-9/11 militant ideologies have been logically crafted and emotionally appealing, they still may not manage to convince Pakistani youth to support violence, but their connection to the cause of Islam and justice prevents the youth to create a strong counter argument.[38] A study by Sajjad et al surveys the ideas of educated youth from across Pakistan and finds that the youth tends to support confrontational ideas when they are presented in the guise of religion, for example the idea that 'war between Islam and the West is inevitable'.[39] But when presented with compassionate and liberal ideas within Islamic tradition, for example, 'there is no compulsion in religion', 'respecting the other faith traditions', a far greater number in Pakistan approve the liberal ideas from their religious tradition. The survey shows that it is not radicalism but religion which Pakistanis hold dear; hence, de-radicalization efforts should aim to disconnect the two. Peace-building efforts in Pakistan have a better chance of success when they engage with religious tradition and beliefs of the people, which offers them a more meaningful life.

Sense of Identity and Belonging

Another set of drivers of extremism or radicalization relates to individual's need for identity and belonging. Neumann terms this set of factors as 'needs', explaining that being a part of an extremist group satisfies

---

[37] Yusuf, 'Radicalism among Youth in Pakistan', 17.

[38] Ibid.

[39] Sajjad, Christie and Taylor, 'De-radicalizing Pakistani Society'.

individual's emotional need for bonding with a group.[40] Psychologically vulnerable people especially seek such protection. Using the typology of Tore Bjørgo, Schmid identifies such people as 'drifters' who join violent groups because they seek friendship, identity and protection.[41]

A number of studies report Pakistani youth's tendency to support an exclusionary, 'us versus them' worldview.[42] Youth radicalization is termed as a product of exclusively Islamic identity coupled with a broader reactive movement in shape of political, militant and missionary organizations.[43] The imposition of the State sanctioned narrative of a unified religion-based identity, through carefully crafted national curricula has been pointed out as one of the key factors that led to intolerance towards religious diversity in Pakistan.[44] However, drawing from a survey of educated youth in Pakistan, Siddiqa points out that 'a general affinity for religious identity does not necessarily indicate greater knowledge or understanding of religion'.[45] In fact, like most Pakistanis, well-educated youth was found to be rather ignorant about their religious tradition despite their support for religion-based identity.

Now let us examine which of the aforementioned drivers of extremism, education can tackle. Can education address the sense of grievance and injustice? Can it offer young minds more meaningful life? Can it empower the youth or provide them opportunities for thrill and

---

[40] Neumann, 'Countering Violent Extremism'.

[41] Schmid, 'Radicalization, De-radicalization, Counter-radicalization'.

[42] Yusuf, 'Radicalism among Youth in Pakistan'; Siddiqa, 'Red Hot Chilli Peppers Islam'; R. Haque, 'Youth Radicalization in Pakistan', USIP, 2014. Available at: https://www.usip.org/publications/2014/02/youth-radicalization-pakistan (accessed on 28 April 2018); A. Hussain, A. Salim and A. Naveed, 'Connecting the Dots: Education and Religious Discrimination in Pakistan: A Study of Public Schools and Madrassas', USCIRF, 2011. Available at: http://www.uscirf.gov/sites/default/files/resources/PakistanConnectingTheDots-Email%283%29.pdf (accessed on 18 March 2015).

[43] Yusuf, 'Radicalism among Youth in Pakistan'.

[44] A. H. Nayyar and Salim, *The Subtle Subversion: The State of Curricula and Textbooks in Pakistan* (Islamabad: Sustainable Development Policy Institute [SDPI], 2003). Available at: http://unesco.org.pk/education/teachereducation/reports/rp22.pdf (accessed on 15 June 2017).

[45] Siddiqa, 'Red Hot Chilli Peppers Islam', 85.

adventure? Can it offer them a sense of belonging and protection? So far, the education and security policies have been engaged in 'enforcing counter-radicalization measures' from the top and promoting a specific set of values and beliefs in schools. To counter extremism/radicalization through education, one has to do the opposite; that is, schools should be forums in which values and norms are questioned and openly discussed, in which critical thinking and critical dialogue between multiple perspectives are actively encouraged.[46] Hence, it is crucial for counter radicalization/counter extremism and violent extremism policies to determine what is it that they are trying to counter through education. If radicalization entails struggle against oppression and injustice, education should be a force fostering it, rather than countering it. And if extremism entails rejection of perspectives other than one's own, education can counter it by engaging with multiple perspectives and teaching respect for difference of opinion, rather than imposing 'one set of values' from the top.

The examination of the drivers of extremism identified in the literature reveals that radical ideologies pull young people through their promise of transforming the world and its injustices. Hence, I argue that education can counter extremism when it becomes the arena of transformation itself.

The policy literature on education and extremism in the West recognizes the importance of developing critical thinking skills of students to make them resilient against extremism. Ghosh et al., for example, acknowledge that 'education should aim to develop in students the ability and the disposition to arrive independently at critical and informed opinions'.[47] The study points out that the prevailing passive educational techniques in schools and universities fail to engage with real-world issues that perturb young minds, they fail to provide students critical insights to argue against extremist narratives; hence, students remain vulnerable to extremist and violent ideologies.

Earlier, a UNICEF study by Bush and Saltarelli highlights the significance of the critical function of education for building long-term

---

[46] Macaluso, 'From Countering to Preventing Radicalization'.

[47] Ghosh et al., 'Can Education Counter Violent Religious Extremism?' 10.

structures of peace.[48] It points out that authoritarian regimes deliberately suppress the critical purpose of education to maintain their hold on power, asserting that peace-building education must be critical and challenge the structures of authority, dominance and control as these structures build the foundation for intolerance in the first place. In this sense, education should be viewed as a force for social transformation or radicalization against oppressive status quo.

In Pakistan, a number of de-radicalization initiatives emphasize critical thinking for building resilience in students against extremism. Pakistan Institute for Peace Studies, a Pakistani think tank organizes regular workshops to ponder de-radicalization through education. The participants include education practitioners and religious scholars who highlight the need to encourage open dialogue on critical issues in educational institutions. They stress that a culture of enquiry must be promoted in classrooms to counter extremist ideologies in the country.[49]

On the basis of the ideas presented in literature, we can claim that in order to counter extremism we need education that engages with the real-world issues, encourages questions and reflections on most pertinent contemporary issues and which aims to transform prevailing structures of injustice.

WHAT KIND OF EDUCATION ARE WE IMPARTING ON GROUND?

Let us now examine the prevailing education policies and practices, at global and local levels. I shall first briefly discuss the history of modern schooling and the historical debates around the purpose of education. Then I shall examine contemporary global policy trends using the lens of critical pedagogy. The impact of global trends on local policies will be examined by critically reviewing contemporary higher

---

[48] K. D. Bush and Saltarelli, 'The Two Faces of Education in Ethnic Conflict: Towards a Peacebuilding Education for Children', *UNICEF*, 2000. Available at: https://www.unicef-irc.org/publications/pdf/insight4.pdf (accessed on 28 April 2018).

[49] Pakistan Institute for Peace Studies, 'Critical Inquiry in Today's Digital Age a Must for Progress and Peace', 2017. Available at: https://www.pakpips.com/article/209 (accessed on 29 April 2018).

education policy in Pakistan which has been drafted as 'Pakistan Higher Education: Vision 2025'.

Clive and Noriko point out that throughout history a conflict has remained central to modern education system.[50] There have been people who see education as a means of control or social reproduction aiming to produce politically docile, conformist and passive citizens. They advocate an authoritarian model of education. On the other hand, there have been people who see education as a means of human empowerment. They advocate education for critical consciousness, individual liberation and participatory democracy. Clive and Noriko point out that in terms of schooling, the overwhelming evidence is that the dominant or hegemonic model throughout the world is the authoritarian rather than democratic model.[51] Mass schooling systems were originally established to promote control, compliance and discipline. The purpose of public education was not only to provide new skills for industrial age but also to inculcate habits of conformity. Through colonization, the European model of schooling reached other parts of the world. To this day, the traditional authoritarian model remains dominant throughout the world. Education in democracy, human rights and critical awareness is not a principal feature of the mainstream schooling.

Mostly classrooms remain teacher centred where students have little or no control over what is taught and learned, how it is taught and learned, where and when it is taught and learned. The learning environment is predominantly controlled by authority figures such as teachers, head teachers or government officials. Development of critical thinking skills, culture of questioning authority and the goal of youth empowerment remain unattainable in authoritarian environment of majority schools.

---

[50] H. Clive and S. Noriko, 'Schooling for Violence and Peace: How Does Peace Education Differ from "Normal" Schooling?' *Journal of Peace Education* 6, no. 2 (2009). Available at: https://doi.org/10.1080/17400200903086599 (accessed on 28 April 2018).

[51] Ibid.

Contemporary Trends in Education

According to the leading American scholar of education Henry Giroux, two contemporary trends have shaped education policy, particularly higher education, since 9/11: Neoliberalism and Terrorism.[52]

The neoliberal policies in education: Contemporary education policies and practices in the West, and increasingly in the rest of the world, are being dominated by what the scholars call the 'neoliberal turn' in education. Giroux observes how the education landscape has changed dramatically since the 1980s. Teachers and schools are raided by powerful neoliberal forces. Education goals and learning outcomes are dictated by entities like International Monetary Fund (IMF), World Bank or the corporate sector. Education is now being considered a private right rather than a public good. Consumerism is the new form of citizenship offered to young people. In the new neoliberal environment, issues of social justice, equity, poverty and racism are either removed from the public discourse or reduced to 'talk show spectacle' that has no impact on public policy.[53] The vocabulary of political and social transformation remains absent in the neoliberal discourses. The laws of the market replace the laws of the State as guardians of public interest. The hegemony of the free market economy and the corporate culture turns everything, including education, into an 'object of consumption'.[54] In fact, education is one area which is most severely affected by the neoliberal tide.

The key features of the broader neoliberal agenda for education have been identified as

> … the narrowing of the curriculum to focus on market valued skills and knowledge, the closing down of humanities, social sciences and liberal arts perspectives, the imposition of high-stakes standardised assessments,

---

[52] H. A. Giroux, 'Public Pedagogy and the Politics of Resistance: Notes on a Critical Theory of Educational Struggle', *Educational Philosophy and Theory* 35, nos 15–16 (2003). doi:10.1111/1469–5812.00002

[53] Ibid., 8.

[54] Ibid.

the suppression of student dissent and recurrent attacks on academic freedom, and the overall, endless promotion of corporate interests and partnerships.[55]

Spring terms this phenomenon as 'economization of education' referring to an education model which is guided by the goal of economic growth and analysed through the lens of an economist. It reduces education to an investment in the work force, students to human capital and learning to skills-based instruction measured through standardized testing.[56]

Giroux warns that the forces of free market fundamentalism are working at a global level to reproduce a culture of privatization, commercialization and to attack social provisions provided by the State including education.[57] These forces undermine any understanding of education as an empowering practice which can transform our world in a desirable way. Neoliberalism, the discourse on terrorism, and contemporary educational policy all share a denial of politics, a redistributive economic dimension and a tendency against democratic culture and toward fundamentalist thought. Education is seen merely as a 'consumer item', not a means to change the world. Calling neoliberal brand of education as Mc Education, Giroux warns that such an education will not possibly counter radical ideologies rather it promotes radical reactionary thinking.

The hidden risks of the neoliberal, economic model of education prevalent in the West, and increasingly adopted by the rest, have been arduously pointed out by academics in United States, United Kingdom, Canada, Australia[58]

---

[55] Mayssoun Sukarieh and Stuart Tannock, 'The Deradicalisation of Education: Terror, Youth and the Assault on Learning', *Race and Class* 57, no. 4 (2015): 14. doi:10.1177/0306396815621236

[56] J. Spring, *Globalization of Education: An Introduction* (New York, NY: Routledge, 2015), 14.

[57] H. A. Giroux, 'Thinking Dangerously: The Role of Higher Education in Authoritarian Times', Truthout, 26 June 2017. Available at: http://www.truth-out.org/opinion/item/41058-thinking-dangerously-the-role-of-higher-education-in-authoritarian-times (accessed on 5 March 2019).

[58] H. A. Giroux, 'Neoliberalism, Corporate Culture, and the Promise of Higher Education: The University as a Democratic Public Sphere', *Harvard*

but the neoliberal tide continues to hold sway in education now more than ever.[59]

Educational Review 72, no. 4 (2002): 425–464; H. A. Giroux, 'Public Pedagogy and the Politics of Neo-liberalism: Making the Political More Pedagogical', *Policy Futures in Education* 2, nos. 3–4 (2004): 494–503; H. A. Giroux, 'Bare Pedagogy and the Scourge of Neoliberalism: Rethinking Higher Education as a Democratic Public Sphere', *The Educational Forum* 74, no. 3 (2010): 184–196; H. A. Giroux, *Against the Terror of Neoliberalism: Politics beyond the Age of Greed* (New York, NY: Routledge, 2015); M. W. Apple, 'Comparing Neo-liberal Projects and Inequality in Education', *Comparative Education* 37, no. 4 (2001): 409–423; M. W. Apple, 'Creating Difference: Neo-liberalism, Neo-conservatism and the Politics of Educational Reform', *Educational Policy* 18, no. 1 (2004): 12–44; M. W. Apple, 'Education, Markets, and an Audit Culture', *Critical Quarterly* 47, nos 1–2 (2005): 11–29; M. W. Apple, *Educating the 'Right' Way: Markets, Standards, God and Inequality*, 2nd ed. (New York, NY: Routledge, 2006); J. Spring, *Education and the Rise of the Global Economy* (New York, NY: Routledge, 1998); J. Spring, *The Politics of American Education* (New York, NY: Routledge, 2011); Spring, '*Globalization of Education*'; S. J. Ball, 'Performativity and Fragmentation in "Postmodern Schooling"', in *Postmodernity and the Fragmentation of Welfare*, ed. John Carter (London: Routledge, 1998), 187–203; S. J. Ball, 'The Teacher's Soul and the Terrors of Performativity', *Journal of Education Policy* 18, no. 2 (2003): 215–228; S. J. Ball, 'Performativity, Privatisation, Professionals and the State', in *Exploring Professionalism*, ed. B. Cunningham (London: Institute of Education, 2008); S. J. Ball, The Education Debate (Bristol: The Policy Press, 2008); S. J. Ball, Global Education Inc.: New Policy Networks and the Neo-Liberal Imaginary (London: Routledge, 2012); S. J. Ball, 'Performativity, Commodification and Commitment: An I-Spy Guide to the Neoliberal University', *British Journal of Educational Studies* 60, no. 1 (2012): 17–28; S. J. Ball, 'Subjectivity as a Site of Struggle: Refusing Neoliberalism?' *British Journal of Sociology of Education* 37, no. 8 (2015). doi:10.108 0/01425692.2015.1044072; S. J. Ball, 'Education, Governance and the Tyranny of Numbers', *Journal of Education Policy* 30, no. 3 (2015): 299–301. Arthur, 'Extremism and Neo-Liberal Education Policy; R. Connell, 'Good Teachers on Dangerous Ground: Towards a New View of Teacher Quality and Professionalism', *Critical Studies in Education* 50, no. 3 (2009): 213–229. doi:10.1080/17508480902998421; A. J. Means, 'Beyond the Poverty of National Security: Toward a Critical Human Security Perspective in Educational Policy', *Journal of Education Policy* 29, no. 6 (2014): 719–741. doi:10.1080/02680939.2013.876674; B. Davies and P. Bansel, 'Neoliberalism and Education', *International Journal of Qualitative Studies in Education* 20, no. 3 (2007): 247–259; Parlo Singh, 'Performativity and Pedagogising Knowledge: Globalising Educational Policy Formation, Dissemination and Enactment', *Journal of Education Policy* 30, no. 3 (2015): 363–384. doi:10.1080/0 2680939.2014.961968

[59] Ball, 'Subjectivity as a Site of Struggle'; Ball, 'Education, Governance and the Tyranny of Numbers'; Giroux, *Against the Terror of Neoliberalism*; D. Reay,

The anti-radicalization policies in education. The second trend in education since 9/11, is the anti-radicalization policies imposed on schools
and higher education institutions. In UK, the Prevent programme in
2011 led to the formation of a new unit in the education department
dedicated to preventing extremism. The policy required schools to
actively promote fundamental British values in their teaching and curricula, and keep an eye on signs of possible radicalization in students.
Similar policies were adopted by other European nations. Sukarieh
and Tannock point towards the dangers of current anti-radicalization
policies in education. The study reminds the readers that a little while
ago, the discourse on radicalization and education had a different orientation altogether.

The tradition of Paulo Freire and critical pedagogy 'embraced
radicalization as the direct goal of education'. The radical tradition of
education views education as a means of fundamentally transforming
the world, to overcome 'structures of injustice, inequality, oppression,
exploitation and exclusion'.[60]

Based on an analysis of more than 60 anti-radicalization policies in
schools and colleges across UK, the study points out three key contradictions between current anti-radicalization agenda and the alternative
radical tradition in education. First, the anti-radicalization in education
refuses to examine or address structural root causes of the problem. Any
discussion on structural causes of terrorism is considered equivalent to
justifying terrorism. The basic premise of anti-radicalization agenda is to
identify and suppress ideas, ideologies and relationships which may trigger violence. The broader context of the problem is excluded from the
analysis. Second, anti-radicalization is against learning for social change.
It upholds the claim of social reproduction theory which describes the
function of education as a means to reproduce and reinforce political,
social and economic status quo. Finally, anti-radicalization is against
the transformative educational practice. The transformative function

---

'How Possible Is Socially Just Education under Neo-liberal Capitalism? Struggling
against the Tide?' *FORUM: For Promoting 3–19 Comprehensive Education* 58, no.
3 (2016): 325–331.

[60] Sukarieh and Tannock, 'The Deradicalisation of Education'.

of education is undermined in the guise of promoting tolerance for existing state of affairs.

My contention is that if education does not engage with the deepest concerns of the students, if it brushes aside their grievances, if it suppresses the voices of dissent, if it attempts to control thinking and regulate energy that drives the young, it becomes a risk factor as it makes the child look elsewhere to seek answers to his/her deepest queries and find meaning in his/her life. Ironically, this seemingly obvious connection between the education experience of a child and the process we call radicalization remains excluded from the elaborate anti-radicalization policies of schools/colleges in UK, Europe and other parts of the world.

Summarizing the discussion till here, let us connect what has been argued so far:

1. Countering radicalization or extremism is one of the foremost challenges the world faces today. For Pakistan, in particular, it is the top most concern of the state at the moment.
2. 'Radicalization' and 'extremism' remain fiercely contested terms in policy literature. It is argued that in order to counter radicalization or extremism, we need to define these terms very clearly and make a distinction between the two. We need to be clear about what is it that we are trying to counter before we devise a policy for the purpose.
3. Education can counter radicalization when it is able address the key factors that may lead to radicalization. It has to address real-world issues that trouble the young. It has to foster critical and reflective thinking abilities of students to help them make sound judgement about a given idea or situation. Moreover, the goal of education should be transformation of oppressive structures and promotion of social justice.
4. However, around the world, education in general and higher education in particular, is being increasingly influenced by anti-radicalization policies and neoliberal or economic values of education that tend to suppress the critical function of education.

Ironically, Pakistan is catching up quickly with the global trends in education.

PAKISTAN'S HIGHER EDUCATION 'VISION 2025': A CRITICAL APPRAISAL

In the annual meeting of the Council for Higher Education Accreditation's International Quality Group (CIQG) held in Washington DC in 2014 (attended by 400 people from 30 countries), one important concern was raised: 'There is a danger that in efforts to comply with international standards, higher education systems could become less relevant to the socio-cultural needs of local communities, leaving local needs under-served'.[61]

In case of Pakistan's higher education, in a possibly 'well-intentioned' effort to follow international standards, we seem to be in danger of over-looking our local socio-cultural needs.

Using the lens of critical pedagogy that questions and challenges prevailing neoliberal or economic model of education, I examine the draft of contemporary higher education policy termed as Vision 2025; selected ideas of the leading scholar of the field—Henry Giroux are chosen to illustrate the critical pedagogy perspective. I argue that the current vision of higher education borrows heavily from the Western neoliberal/economic model of education and hence overlooks our need to promote education that helps counter extremism in the country.

Let us re-examine the key features of the economic (neoliberal) model of education, as identified by Spring:

1. Education is considered as an investment in the workforce.
2. Students are considered as human capital to be educated for work.
3. The goal of education is educating workers to compete in the global economy.

---

[61] K. MacGregor, 'National or International Quality Standards or Both?' *University World News*, 21 March 2014. Available at: http://www.universityworld-news.com/article.php?story=20140321114435506 (accessed on 28 April 2018).

4. The value of education is measured by economic growth and development.[62]

Henry Giroux highlights the values promoted by the economic model of education. He points out that neoliberalism sees competition as the key characteristic of human relations. It views knowledge as a product, schools as shopping malls, students as consumers and faculty as entrepreneurs.

A review of 'Vision 2025' shows how the global neoliberal policies and economic model of education has influenced the education policy of Pakistan. The draft measures the value of education in economic terms and uses the terminology and ideas of the dominant economic model of education. For example, the broader aim of higher education in Pakistan is described as: 'a wholesome approach for development of (education) sector through preparing knowledgeable, skilled and competent human capital that could compete internationally'.[63]

The ultimate aim of higher education in Pakistan is described as making Pakistan 'the next Asian tiger'.[64] The purpose of education is clearly linked to the aim of economic growth. Growth remains the yardstick to measure the value of education.

This vision of education places education in the framework of economic competitiveness, comparison and ranking rather than in a framework that is reflective of our peculiar social and political problems.

Elaborating neoliberal brand of education, Giroux explains that such an education confuses education with training. It undermines civic education and instead focuses on skills-based instruction. It is a system that promotes more testing and less learning, more conformity and less questioning, more dogmatic thinking and less critical enquiry.

---

[62] Spring, *Globalization of Education*, 16.
[63] Pakistan Higher Education Commission, 'HEC Vision 2025', 2017. Available at: http://hec.gov.pk/english/HECAnnouncements/Documents/Announcement/HEC-Vision-2025.pdf (accessed on 30 April 2018).
[64] Ibid., 9.

Now let us see how the system of international university ranking dictates higher education vision of Pakistan as it is unquestionably considered a measure of quality of education in the country. The Vision 2025 draft refers to a system of ranking developed by Shanghai University in 2003.[65] According to this criteria, universities are primarily ranked on the basis of research indicators in natural sciences and English.

The inclusion of 'English' as a standard criteria for judging value of education in Asian universities needs to be questioned. Also, the exclusion of social sciences, history, philosophy—the subjects that nurture human intellect, reflect on human condition and are traditionally associated with universities, needs to be questioned. Such questions are raised in universities. But in the race for economic competitiveness there is seldom a reflection on the ranking criteria and systems and how they meet our people's needs.

Another standard of quality education highlighted in the draft is the use of technology. Technology-based education has been identified as a high priority of Higher Education Commission (HEC). Transforming classrooms into smart classrooms, introducing smart assessment and learning management system (LMS) has been considered essential to 'allow better engagement among the educators and the learners'.[66] Technology embedded classrooms are supposed to provide 'state of the art technologically enabled academic environment at par with HEIs in developed world'. LMS is considered 'another major component in enhancing quality of education'.[67] To achieve this objective, HEC aims to convert as many as 350 conventional classrooms into smart classrooms. The efficacy of technology-based instruction is still a subject of debate internationally. Technology at best is a 'means' to get education *not* a 'goal' of education or 'standard of quality education'. However, the future vision for higher education puts great emphasis on making education high-tech. It vows to introduce EduCloud Services, Higher Education Management Information System (HEMIS), Edu Card, Edu

---

[65] Ibid., 13.
[66] Ibid., 46.
[67] Ibid.

TV and counselling service, standardization in course delivery, online audit of courses and online assessment. The role of higher education in developing critical consciousness and intellectual ability of students, which was once a hallmark of universities, is rarely included in the future vision of higher education.

Stephen J. Ball, a leading scholar of sociology of education points out further problems with exceedingly competitive environment of education.

In a competitive environment there is greater emphasis on 'looking good', on presentations and front impressions rather than the heart and soul of teaching. Teachers and teaching loses touch with the main purpose of education, the development and transformation of students.

Instead the emphasis remains on 'construction and maintenance of fabrications'.[68]

While recognizing that social sciences and humanities have remained under emphasized areas for HEC in the past, the Vision 2025 draft talks about now paying attention to these marginalized subject areas.[69]

But the goal of this new emphasis on social sciences is described in the following words: 'these areas need to be nurtured further to create an enlightened soft global image of our society and add value to our economy'.[70]

If 'creating an image' and 'adding value to the economy' is the role of social sciences and humanities in universities, where should we place the work of intellectual giants of the past and present including, for example, the work of Iqbal, Paulo Freire, Michel Foucault, Edward Said, Noam Chomsky to name just a few.

The value of the so far 'marginalized' social sciences is vital in developing the critical thinking skills in students which may help them

---

[68] Ball, 'The Teacher's Soul and the Terrors of Performativity', 2015.
[69] Pakistan Higher Education Commission, 'HEC Vision 2025', 14.
[70] Ibid.

evaluate extremist ideas and ideologies critically and independently. Narrowing down the scope of social sciences and the space for critical scholarship would deprive higher education of its greatest value— nurturing of human minds and improving human conditions.

CONCLUSION AND RECOMMENDATIONS

To move towards a conclusion, let us revisit the question raised at the beginning of this study: How well-educated individuals, especially those from applied sciences, could join militancy? The question raises concerns about the 'higher education' we are imparting on ground and its failure to provide young minds the ability to reason against violent ideologies. We have seen that following prevailing global trends, the policy vision of higher education for future generations of Pakistan largely views education as a means to enhance economic growth of the country, rather than nourishing intellectual ability and critical reasoning capacity of students. The aim of higher education has been linked to economic growth targets, quality of education has been defined as entering and winning the international ranking race. Instead of encouraging and empowering students to transform the world in a desirable way, education tends to restrict their capacity to engage with the world in a meaningful way. Education has been rightly identi- fied as a key factor that can help mitigate extremism and counter the pull of violent radical ideologies. But education and security policies around the world as well as in Pakistan with their exclusive focus on economic value of education, undermine the critical and transforma- tive function of education which can effectively counter the pull of dogmatic violent ideologies.

The policy vision for education in Pakistan should focus on indigenous problems in a holistic manner rather than borrowing dominant ideas from the West, without reflection. Education policy in general and higher education policy in particular, should engage with perspectives of critical studies in education and critical pedagogy that challenge the dominant business model of education around the globe.

Extremism in higher education institutions cannot be eliminated through surveillance or imposition of anti-radicalization policies from the top. The only effective way to counter dogmatic, extremist ideologies is to open up spaces for free dialogue. Universities in Pakistan should provide safe spaces for critical debates and open dialogue. Students should be encouraged to raise questions, to be reflective, critical and creative scholars. Moreover, social sciences, humanities and interdisciplinary education and research should be encouraged at all levels. These subjects should aim to empower students to undertake social enquiry for social change. It is through peaceful dialogue and action on critical issues that we can make education the arena which utilizes youth's energies for positive social change and offers them sense of purpose as well as adventure in life, which can keep them away from violent radical ideologies.

Chapter 8

Bangladesh's 'War on Terror' and Madrasa Education

Asif Bin Ali

INTRODUCTION

This chapter begins with an analysis of the question: What is madrasas' role in radicalizing Bangladeshi youth? It also suggests how the answer to this question can guide us to see the phenomenon of Islamophobia and Bangladesh's War on Terror in relation to madrasa education. Further, this chapter suggests how the distorted image of madrasas due to the Taliban led to widespread condemnation of madrasas in Bangladesh, a fact which Bangladesh State used as an opportunity to further their project of secularizing madrasas. This chapter concludes by suggesting that the contemporary reforms project in madrasa education of Bangladesh is not only the effect of the secularization project but also complemented by Bangladesh's War on Terror.

This chapter is divided into seven sections, excluding 'Introduction' and 'Conclusion'. The chapter's 'Background' section includes a brief history of terrorist attacks in Bangladesh from 2000 to 2018. It provides an overview of the home-grown terrorist organization and debate over the Islamic State's (IS) presence in Bangladesh. The 'Research Question' section starts with a short summarization of the context in which the research question regarding the madrasas' role in the radicalization of youth, the relationship between Islamophobia and Bangladesh's War on Terror, and Bangladesh State's role in the secularization of madrasas emerged.

The 'Literature Review' section mainly incorporates a review of academic literature published internationally and in Bangladesh on Islamophobia, the 9/11-related Global War on Terror, Bangladesh's war against terror and Bangladesh government's approach to secularizing the madrasa education system. It also reflects some remarks on questions like how the Taliban model was used to establish a particular image of madrasas and how these distorted images provide space for the State to mobilize their secularization project. This segment also includes a comparison of two sets of literature where one group of writers solely blames madrasas for terrorism, while another section argues that there is a doubt about it but suggests that the secularization of madrasas is an appropriate contribution to fight terrorism. It also comments on how these two sets of writers complement each other to present an image of madrasas under the influence of Islamophobia contributing to a pretentious justification for the Global War on Terror.

The 'Bangladesh's War on Terror' section provides details about the Bangladesh government's action against terrorists, with the help of America. It shows the contradiction between Bangladesh official stance on terrorism and its actions against terrorists in the field. Officially the government has denied any presence of international terrorist organizations in the country by claiming that all terrorist organizations in Bangladesh are home-grown and that only national elements are responsible for this violence. Despite this denial, the Bangladesh government is out carrying its War on Terror, which to some extent is seen to be successful in terms of controlling terrorist elements. This section also briefly focuses on how Islamophobia encouraged the State to reinforce its madrasa education modernization project.

The '9/11, Islamophobia and Madrasa at Global and National Levels' section focuses on the post-9/11 phenomenon where there grew a massive interest in deciphering the relations between Islam and terrorism by using work such as Mamdani's writings on 'cultural talk' with reference from his books such as *Good Muslim Bad Muslim* and

Citizens And Subject from a theoretical perspective.[1] It deconstructs the approach which is equating madrasa students to terrorists or potential terrorists and poses the question: Had 9/11 not happened, could we then have imagined such questions about Islam and madrasas taking its current form in public discourse? It also includes justification for this question as 9/11 did change the fate of the followers of Islam; however, to what extent could this change be subject to personal experiences? This section suggests to locate both culture and government as synchronous production of uniformly postulates, contentions and relations on the contrary to the construct that the question of fundamentalism is related with the culture and belief, particularly the Muslim culture.[2] This section states that terrorism is not an outcome of religious propensities, be it fundamentalist or secular; rather, it is born of a political encounter.

The 'Unlikely Candidates: Fall of Western Portrayals of Madrasa Students' section challenges the Western portrayals of madrasa–educated individuals. It argues that the Taliban example and its relationship with madrasa is not something which could help to understand the terrorist phenomenon of Bangladesh. Indeed, the Western portrayal is a poorly informed notion and deeply infected with xenophobia about the 'Muslim look'. Moreover, this section also includes example and present analysis by commenting that the Holey Artisan attackers are not similar to the previous Bengali Muslim terrorists who had presented their images after the Taliban look; also, they were not educated in Islamic institutions following religious model. In conclusion, it suggests that these images of typical terrorist are well past expiry.

BACKGROUND

In addition, with 141 million Muslims and 17 million non–Muslims minorities, Bangladesh is the third largest Muslim populous country. As a matter of fact, her population is more than the combined

---

[1] M. Mamdani, 'Good Muslim, Bad Muslim: A Political Perspective on Culture and Terrorism', *American Anthropologist* 104, no. 3 (2002): 766–775; M. Mamdani, *Good Muslim, Bad Muslim* (New York, NY: Pantheon Books, 2004).

[2] Mamdani, 'Good Muslim, Bad Muslim'.

population of Iran, Iraq and Saudi Arabia. Besides attaining progressive development growth in the economic sphere, this country is failing to end the corruption which has led to the prevailing unjust income distribution. It has also experienced multiple coups and counter-coups in 1947–1975, 1977–1980, 1981–1982, 1996 and 2007. Finally, all these multiple events have contributed to establish a week democracy reduced only to election and her secularizing project has systematically compromised. On top of it, since 2000, according to Ali Riaz, Bangladesh has experienced 114 Islamist terrorist attacks.[3] These attacks suggest that IS and al-Qaeda in the Indian Subcontinent (AQIS) are deliberately targeting different religious minority communities and dissents from secular as well as liberal activist groups.[4] Indeed, the situation is alarming. As a matter of fact, there are attempts to explain and understand these events by the intellectual community, but the relation between Islamist militancy and madrasa education left over as understudied.

Bangladesh has seen some 746 people killed, including 339 alleged terrorist deaths, in Islamist terrorist attacks between January 2005 and December 2017.[5] It is estimated that around 91 per cent of these terrorist attacks have been occurred since 2013.[6] Frequency of these offenses suggests that both of these organizations have on warded their operational capacity in contemporary times.[7] As a matter of fact, the IS has confessed their involvement to attack foreign citizens, LGBT community members and religious minority communities for instance Shia, Ahmadis and Sufis. Islamist militants had published an online hit list and attacked secular writers in particular bloggers. On the other

---

[3] A. Riaz, *Lived Islam and Islamism in Bangladesh* (Dhaka: Prothoma Prokashan, 2017), 227–228.

[4] S. Roy, 'Bangladesh's New Generation of Militants: Akayed Ullah, a Wannabe Jihadist, Represents a New Generation of Militants', *The Diplomat*, 29 January 2018. Available at: https://thediplomat.com/2018/01/bangladeshs-new-generation-of-militants/

[5] A. Riaz, *Undying Issues* (Dhaka: Pathak Shamabesh, 2018).

[6] C. C. Fair, 'Political Islam and Islamist Terrorism in Bangladesh: What You Need to Know', *Lawfare*, 28 January 2018. Available at: https://www.lawfareblog.com/political-islam-and-islamist-terrorism-bangladesh-what-you-need-know

[7] Roy, 'Bangladesh's New Generation of Militants'.

hand, more than dozens of Bangladeshi citizens have travelled to join the IS. Many of them died in combat. For instance in April 2016, IS English language online magazine, *Dabiq* published a news as a tribute to a Bengali militants who went to fight in Syria and died there.[8] Apart from IS and AQIS attacks, Ansarullah Bangla Team (ABT) also killed some bloggers. They have been operating since 2010 on behalf of the AQIS. Considering all these examples, Roy argues that the AQIS along with the help of some local organizations launched its own operation in Bangladesh.[9]

Beside AQIS and IS, Bangladesh has its own home-grown terrorist organizations. The Jagrata Muslim Janata Bangladesh (JMJB) is one of those groups. JMJB, a close ally to the Jamaat-ul-Mujahideen Bangladesh (JMB), is one of the most dangerous home-grown terrorist outfits. Sheikh Abdur Rahman and Siddiqul Islam 'Bangla Bhai' are the two founding leaders of these two organizations.[10] Both of the outfits overlap in terms of organizational arrangement and active personnel. Since 2013, the formation year of JMJB, all activists of JMB are members of JMJB. Besides, they had perpetrated several organized offenses since early 2000. Certainly, August 2005 attack was the most shocking attack by these groups when 63 districts of Bangladesh out of 64 were attacked by 459 bombs at a time.[11]

At present Bangladesh is not only facing potential threats from JMB, but also from the former members of Harkat-ul-Jihad-al-Islami Bangladesh (HuJI-B). This terrorist group first appeared in 1992 and helped to set up several other fundamentalists groups.[12]

---

[8] Ibid.

[9] Ibid.

[10] M. A. Islam, 'Mapping Terrorism Threats in Bangladesh', *BIISS Journal* 29 (April, 2008): 153–176; P. Cochrane, 'The Funding Methods of Bangladeshi Terrorist Groups', *Combating Terrorism Centre* 2, no. 5 (2009). Available at: https://ctc.usma.edu/the-funding-methods-of-bangladeshi-terrorist-groups/.

[11] H. Habib, '17 August 2005: Milestone of Terror', in *Bangladesh: Treading the Taliban Trail*, ed. J. Saika (New Delhi: Vision Books, 2006), 252; Islam, 'Mapping Terrorism Threats in Bangladesh'.

[12] Islam, 'Mapping Terrorism Threats in Bangladesh'.

Roy, Habib and Islam conclude that HuJI–B, which was connected with the Pakistan based HuJI, is a pro–Deobandi group.[13] Furthermore, they argue that after the end of the Afghan war, 17 Bengali mujahideen returned to Bangladesh and established HuJI–B with financial assistance from al-Qaeda. Shahadat-e al Hikma (SAH) is another group which has started activities since 2003. Sayed Kawsar Hussain Siddiki was its founding chief and it was believed that he had 10,000 commandos with 25,000 combatants.[14] In fact, there is no concrete evidence to prove these numbers; however, one objective is very common in all these terrorist organizations: They wanted to establish Bangladesh as an Islamic nation under sharia law. In order to do so these organizations sometimes jointly and sometimes independently perpetrated many terrorist attacks. Feminist writer Taslima Nasreen, poet Shamshur Rahman, and Awami League (AL) chairperson Sheikh Hasina were among some of their initial victims.

The Holey Artisan Bakery terrorist attack which happened on 1 July 2016 can be considered the deadliest offense in the history of Bangladesh. Indeed, it is important for its location as well as highest number of casualties. This bakery was very close to the US Embassy which is considered as the capital's fortified area. None of all those security arrangements were able to stop the bloodbath and therefore it would not be exaggeration if we named it as the 9/11 of Bangladesh. Compared to the rest of terrorist attacks since 1999, this single attack has generated far more intense reaction and the mass grieving to remember terrorism prey was unprecedented. In the like manner, surprise was waiting for the country while IS's news agency Amaq came with the confession news from Shaykh Abu Ibrahin Al Hanif, also known as Tamim Chowdhury, IS's emir of the Bangladesh. He had hailed the dead terrorist. Moreover, militant Nirbas Islam, Rohan Imtiaz, Andaleeb Ahmed, Meer Saameh Mubasher, Khairul Islam Payel and Raiyan Minhaj photographs were released where they were posing by holding the IS black flag. Reports claimed that these young men were 'missing' from a while. Bangladesh police stated that having

---

[13] Roy, 'Bangladesh's New Generation of Militants'; Habib, '17 August 2005'; ibid.

[14] Roy, 'Bangladesh's New Generation of Militants'.

received training during the month of missing they went to raid the bakery. Despite the pile of evidences, Bangladesh government rejected all available facts and thereby declared that these attackers as the neo-JMB militants.[15] However, Chowdhury stated that Holy Artisan is not the end, but the beginning and promised more attacks. Barely five days from the Bakery attack, the largest Eid congregation in Sholakia situated in 60 miles north-east of the capital, was attacked by another group of terrorist personnel.[16]

Some more episodes had occurred before the Holey Artisan attack. Militants attacked a police checkpoint in Ashulia, Savar and stabbed two constables leaving one spot dead.[17] An assistant inspector of police was killed in Gabtoli while there was a suicide attack in the Rapid Action Battalion (RAB) headquarters.[18] All of these fresh attacks were giving a hint of something new. Those neo-militants are not likely to the old militants. On the contrary to the previous terrorists attack patterns, these neo-militants were targeting civilians as well as attempting deliberately to attack and engage the State. Their instruments of violence had changed also. While the old terrorist group used knives and other easily available weapons to kill bloggers and minorities, neo-terrorists were using grenades, guns and ammunitions that is improvised explosive devices (IEDs) in the combat after a long time. On top of it, their medium of communication was encrypted instead of simple mobile text messages and calls. Similarly, previous terrorist would raid the targets and moved away but the neo-terrorist held their target ground until their death. Roy, considering these phenomena, suggests

---

[15] S. Roy, 'A Year of Bangladesh's War on Terror: A Year after the Dhaka Bakery Bloodbath, Counterterrorism Remains Deeply Political', *The Diplomat*, 6 July 2017. Available at: https://thediplomat. com/2017/07/a-year-of-bangladeshs-war-on-terror/

[16] S. Hammadi and J. Boone, 'Bangladeshi Militants Launch Fatal Attack on Eid Gathering', *The Guardian*, 7 July 2016. Available at: https://www.theguardian.com/ world/2016/jul/07/bangladesh-militants-exchange-fire-with-police-at-eid-prayers

[17] Staff Reporter, 'Policeman Killed in Fresh Bangladesh Attack', *The Daily Star*, 15 November 2015. Available at: https://www.thedailystar.net/frontpage/ policeman-killed-fresh-attack-167674.

[18] T. Hashmi, 'ISIS Threats in Bangladesh: Denials and Delusions', *The Daily Star*, 28 March 2017. Available at: https://www.thedailystar.net/opinion/ stranger-fiction/isis-threats-bangladesh-denials-and-delusions-1382470

that they came prepared to die.[19] However, luckily, Bangladeshi militants are incapable and worthless to cause high number of casualties. Since 2003, there were more than 114 attacks with less death casualties. They in general beat one person per raid accept the Bakery attack. Furthermore, suicide attack was very uncommon until 2017. For instance, there were only four suicides bombing in 10 years from 2005 to 2015. However, this had an upward trend in 2017 and Bangladesh had experienced more than two suicide bombing in that year only.[20] The worrying fact is that while Islamic militant group abstain them from using female suicide bombers, Bangladesh has faced female suicide attacks. This is very uncommon in comparison with South Asian suicide bombing patterns.

RESEARCH QUESTION AND METHODOLOGY

On the eve of rising terrorist activities in Bangladesh, a popular narrative developed in the national sphere affirms that madrasas chose to live in ghettos and create swamps that breed terrorists. This narrative denies and overlooks those radicalizations which occur outside the established Islamic institutions and, thus allows space to create a myth regarding the madrasa's role to radicalize youth in the post-9/11 world order. Many Bangladeshi civil society intellectuals view madrasas as the only place of radicalization.[21] The most prevailing argument is that the radicalization of society promoted terrorism, which in its turn promoted radicalization. Their perception is that none but religious and dedicated mosque-going individuals and madrasa-educated Muslims are Islamist extremists.[22] Therefore, Bangladesh was surprised to see that affluent townish young men educated in secular institutions and not penniless, miserable madrasa-trained students participated in the bakery attack. Their wonders mirror their inadequate familiarity regarding the Islamic fundamentalist groups around the world. Together they have failed

---

[19] Roy, 'A Year of Bangladesh's War on Terror'.

[20] Fair, 'Political Islam and Islamist Terrorism in Bangladesh'.

[21] T. Hashmi, 'Terrorists in Bangladesh: Why Urban Rich, Not Poor Taliban?' *The Daily Star*, 6 August 2016. Available at: https://www.thedailystar.net/op-ed/politics/terrorists-bangladesh-1265230

[22] Ibid.

to understand that these terrorist outfits are overwhelmingly carried out by rich technologically-sound upper class Muslims. Nevertheless, they were suggesting a State sponsored approach of 'indoctrination of madrasa education' system for decades.[23] At the same time in its initial stage of Bangladesh's War on Terror, policymakers ignored the threat of terrorism and countered it by saying that such statement might damage the national image.[24] Consequently, after initial terrorist attacks, the State machineries started blaming madrasa education for inflicting violence and came forward with the project of introducing a deradicalized syllabus in Bangladeshi madrasas. Considering the background, this chapter aims to address three questions. What is the madrasa's role in radicalizing Bangladeshi youth? What is the link between Islamophobia and Bangladesh's War on Terror? How does the Bangladesh State use the distorted image of madrasa, capitalizing on the wide condemnation of the Taliban, as an opportunity to further their project of secularizing madrasas. This is a qualitative research paper and to address these questions uses a content analysis method.

LITERATURE REVIEW

To comprehend the rising phenomenon of terrorism, the Bangladesh Institute of International and Strategic Studies (BIISS) organized a conference Global War on Terror: Bangladesh Perspective in 2007, which was a crucial period during which Bangladesh was experiencing emerging terrorist attacks. Prominent researchers, ministers and government officials participated in the programme and presented their papers and delivered their written speeches. This, I believe, influenced the government policymaking process and addressed the debate on madrasa education to a great extent and its relationship to terrorism in an organized form. The BISS seminar proceedings concluded with remarks on the immediate consequence of the Global War on Terror on Bangladesh.

---

[23] A. Riaz, 'Recognition of Qwami Degree: Will This Lead to Integration?' (M. Mahtab, Interviewer), *The Daily Star*, 14 May 2017. Available at: https://www.thedailystar.net/opinion/interviews/will-lead-integration-1396846

[24] M. R. Osmany, 'Chairman's Speech', in *Global War on Terror: Bangladesh Perspective*, eds. M. R. Osmany and M. H. Kabir (Dhaka: Academic Press and Publishers Library, 2007), 9.

In the seminar, Osmany posed some questions: Who is a terrorist and what acts can be called acts of terrorism?[25] He termed Bangladesh's fight against terrorism as the 'National War against Terrorism'.[26] Immauzzaman, the then Director General of BISS, delivered a written speech where he mentioned the impact of the 9/11 Global War on Terror on Bangladesh and South Asia.[27] He argued that following the 9/11 terrorist attack on the United States and its aftermath, international terrorism has been brought to the centre of attention of the global community, particularly in South Asia. Its impact has remained very high for a long period of time. He further stated that South Asia as a region has deeply experienced the impact of these developments and Bangladesh is no exception, thereby suffers the impact of these events and faced some indirect consequences. Bangladesh could not ignore the serious concern by US policymakers since America is the largest export market for the country. Considering this context, he mentioned that Bangladesh was able to successfully overcome the immediate shock of 9/11 in terms of relationship with the United States by appearing as an important confederate of America's war against terror project. This was the time when Bangladesh also had to face the attempt made in different quarters to point fingers at the country as a possible playground of Islamic fundamentalism that focused only for its own war against terrorism in its domestic space. Imamuzzaman further argues that certain forces and actors, as well as developments within the country, facilitated similar anti-Bangladeshi propaganda forcing the government to strengthen its anti-terrorist actions.[28] At the same time, to fight that propaganda and in order to prove Bangladesh's commitment to global peace, the government immediately justified their cause to join the Global War on Terror. It thus accepted the notion that terrorism is a universal opponent of all states and intimidates global, regional and national safekeeping.[29]

---

[25] Ibid., 9.

[26] Ibid., 10.

[27] A. B. Imamuzzaman, 'Welcome Speech', in *Global War on Terror: Bangladesh Perspective*, eds. M. R. Osmany and M. H. Kabir (Dhaka: Academic Press and Publishers Library, 2007), 3.

[28] Ibid., 4.

[29] Ibid., 5.

M. Morshed Khan, the then Foreign Minister of Bangladesh Nationalist Party (BNP) coalition government, was the chief guest of the BISS seminar. In his written remarks, he eluded that 17 August countryside bomb explosion and the killing of local judges proved that Bangladesh is no longer free from the extremist threat. The 17 August bombing was a wakeup call for Bangladesh. He had briefed the seminar regarding PM's declaration of zero tolerance to extremism and government action to ban several local groups for their active entanglement in the extremist violent activities. Furthermore, he mentioned the new laws which were being passed to provide strong legal structure to the domestic anti-terrorist actions and discussed State sponsored proactive role to control and end the intentional misuse of Islam as an excuse for conducting terrorist actions. Khan further mentioned that considering the 9/11 global context, Bangladesh has joined 12 UN counter terrorism conventions and protocols as well as signed SAARC Regional Convention on Suppression of Terrorism. Besides, he mentioned the US assistance to Bangladesh in building counter-terrorism capacity. To conclude his speech, Khan mentioned that Bangladesh is a victim of fundamentalism and terrorism; therefore, she has affirmed her promise to support Global War on Terror. He also added that Bangladesh will combat extremism not only to meet the global demands, but to safeguard its citizens.[30] He had ended his remarks by stating that his government will never accommodate national or international terrorist organizations to dissent the State authority. This was the entry point of Bangladesh to develop her version of the war on terror in the domestic space.

In the post-9/11 period, media campaign sought to depict Bangladesh as a militant Islamic state.[31] Bertil Lintner's articles 'Cocoon of Terror' and 'Bangladesh Breading Ground of Muslim Terrorism

---

[30] M. R. Osmany and M. H. Kabir, eds., *Global War on Terror: Bangladesh Perspective* (Dhaka: Academic Press and Publishers Library, 2007).

[31] R. Rahman, Bangladesh's Fight Against Terror: Lessons Learnt and Future Perspectives, in '*Global War on Terror: Bangladesh Perspective*', eds. M. R. Osmany and M. H. Kabir (Dhaka: Academic Press and Publishers Library, 2007), 14.

Religious Extremism & Nationalism' set the stage of this campaign.[32] Lintner asserted that some tens of thousands of madrasas exist in Bangladesh and he singled out madrasas as the breeding field of terrorists. He compared madrasas with the Taliban model and alleged that their objective was to establish Islamic rule in Bangladesh. These two articles are widely used in Bangladesh to blame madrasas as the production and assembly space of terrorists.[33] Books such as Zachary Abuza's *Militant Islam in South Asia*, Rohan Gunaratna's *Inside Al Qaeda* established the perception of alleged connection between al-Qaeda and the recruitment of Rohingya Muslims to combat in the battle of Afghanistan, Chechnya and Kashmir. This was followed by a spate of articles. However, while in reality some of Bangladeshi madrasas were run by Afghan War-returned Bengali mujahideen, this does not necessarily prove that all madrasas are potential breading grounds of terrorism. Therefore, those writers concerns are based on over-simplification of the facts and leaves scope to pose questions for further investigations.

Eliza Griswold wrote in an article entitled 'Next Islamist Revolution', published by the *New York Times*, that Siddiqul Islam 'Bangla Bhai' was leading awakened Muslim masses to Islamist revolution in several 'provinces' (Bangladesh doesn't have any provinces) of Bangladesh bordering India.[34] He accused military rulers for seeking legitimacy from Islamists, which is factual, but it doesn't prove that all Islamists are terrorists. He further stated that Bangla Bhai was linked with Osama Bin Laden and al-Qaeda, which was never proven by any

[32] Bertil Lintner, 'Bangladesh—A Cocoon Of Terror', *Asiapacificms.Com*. Available at: http://www.asiapacificms.com/articles/bangladesh_terror/.; Lintner, Bertil, 'Religious extremism and nationalism in Bangladesh,' *The Bangladesh Observer (2002)*. Available at: http://asiapacificms.com/papers/pdf/religious_extremism_bangladesh.pdf

[33] M. Sakhawat Hussain, Terrorism in South Asia: Ramification in the Internal and External Security of States, in *Global War on Terror: Bangladesh Perspective*, eds. M. R. Osmany and M. H. Kabir (Dhaka: Academic Press and Publishers Library, 2007), 87–146.

[34] E. Griswold, 'The Next Islamist Revolution?' *The New York Times Magazine*, 23 January 2005. Available at https://www.nytimes.com/2005/01/23/magazine/the-next-islamist-revolution.html.

further investigations. However, Griswold's conclusions touch on some elements of the truth, but not the sum of it.

Aravind Adiga published two articles in the *Times* magazine.[35] In his article 'State of Disgrace' on 12 April 2004, he pointed out that a brand of intolerant Islam was spreading which had pushed Bangladesh into being the most 'dysfunctional state' in South Asia. In a follow-up article published on 6 September 2004 entitled, 'A Democracy Shaken', Adiga highlighted that Islamist terrorists are operating with the tacit support to the government. This article was written in the wake of a series of grenade attacks, including the attack on Sheikh Hasina on 21 August 2004. These articles reflected a heady mix of hyperbole. They depict the segments of truth, but not the entire context. They are filled with subsistent exaggeration and were busy to establish the preconceived notions regarding madrasas role and terrorism in Bangladesh. These articles have become the hallmarks of Bangladeshi ties to terrorism. The reality all too often ignored that which leave room to question the link between militancy and madrasa education, but these questions were often ignored.

Hiranmay Karlekar writes in his book *Bangladesh: The Next Afghanistan* that madrasas were booming nationwide offering a potential space for being used as a base for various indigenous and international terrorist groups.[36] Karlekar's book makes many assumptions regarding Bangladesh's journey towards a Taliban model State. No doubt the assumption made by Karlekar that Bangladesh heading for a Taliban style Islamic uprising gained more credence due to the absence of government intervention earlier in the rise of JMJB, when the media evidence was made public and which was referred by Karlekar. A close analysis of these examples suggests that demonizing madrasas possible

---

[35] A. Adiga, 'State of Disgrace', *Time Asia Magazine*, 12 April 2004. Available at http://www.time.com/time/asia/magazine/article/0,13673,501040412-607842,00.html; A. Adiga, 'A Democracy Shaken', *Time Asia Magazine*, 6 September 2004. Available at: https://web.archive.org/web/20121026144718/ http://www.time.com/time/magazine/article/0,9171,501040906-689488,00.html.

[36] H. Karlekar, *Bangladesh: The Next Afghanistan?* (New Delhi: SAGE Publications, 2005).

links with Taliban had become fashionable for some writers within and outside the country. This fashionable propaganda approach allows new room for Western educated secular writers to come up with suggestions to secularize, functionalize and normalize madrasa education in accordance to the need of the State and market economy. M. Ataur Rahman is one of the advocates of that approach and he writes that since 9/11—even though only some madrasa-educated individuals were participated in terrorist actions—madrasas are considered to be the suspect in several Muslim countries.[37] Therefore, the madrasa education system needs total rearrangement and reorientation. He further argues that the madrasa education system requires interventions to be 'functional, modern and liberal' with an aim to create job-oriented skilled labour rather than 'an unproductive nagging and parasitical community with potential of violence and extremism'.[38] He has suggested taking appropriate measures for restructuring and interrogating the madrasa education system. Shelly follows the same line of argument and criticizes madrasa education for not building a sound base of knowledge and skills in either Bangla or English and in modern science and technology.[39] According to his argument, madrasa graduates are not equipped with education suitable for obtaining employment in a globalized world. He argues that Bangladesh and its friends are concerned that the massive pool of religiously educated and oriented madrasas graduates and students may be exploited by the extremist terrorist elements and groups. He claims that their poverty and isolation from the Western-oriented and educated segments of the society increases the possibilities of their falling prey to the terrorist organizations.[40] To support his argument, Shelly referred to the terrorist attack

---

[37] M. Ataur Rahman, Bangladesh Quest for Muslim Moderate States, in 'Global War on Terror: Bangladesh Perspective', eds. M. R. Osmany and M. H. Kabir (Dhaka: Academic Press and Publishers Library, 2007), 45.

[38] Ibid., 45.

[39] M. R. Shelley, British Engagement With Bangladesh in Counter Terrorism: Opportunities for Cooperation, in 'Global War on Terror: Bangladesh Perspective', eds. M. R. Osmany and M. H. Kabir (Dhaka: Academic Press and Publishers Library, 2007), 159–160.

[40] Ibid., 160–161.

on 7 July 2005 in the UK.[41] On that day, four home-grown Muslim British suicidal bombers had caused massive explosions in the London underground transport system and in a bus, killing more than 50 and injuring 700. The bombers were educated idle class Muslim Britons with their origins in Pakistan. The authorities report that these young men had travelled to Pakistan and received indoctrination and other types of training in Pakistani madrasas.

Hussain writes that the government education system remains poor, leaving space for the uncontrolled growth of madrasas. He argues that there is a link between these uncontrolled spaces and terrorist recruitment in the ground of socio-economic disparity.[42] However, he, by presenting his studies on the profile of three Bangladeshi suicide bombers, states that socio-economic problems may work as a strong motivating factor for terrorism. He did blame madrasas as one of the producing spaces of terrorism, but did not identify madrasas as the sole production house.[43] Even, this attitude is prevailing in organizations like Islamic Information and Research Centre (IIRC)[44] an independent group, which took an initiative in the troubled Cox's Bazar, a South Eastern district of Bangladesh, with an aim to teach 'true Islam to madrasa students and teacher community' from December 2004 to the end of 2005. They had mobilized religious leaders and teachers of the other streams to build up resistance against misinterpretation of Islam. They organized participatory dialogue where teachers of 201 madrasas of Cox's Bazar town and sub-districts participated. There are many significant points to note in their report. They claim that the madrasa education is extremely backward relative to the mainstream education system and tends to suffer from feelings of isolation and inadequacy. On account of the distance from mainstream society and the perception of discrimination, madrasa student's minds are subject to recruitment for terrorist activities. They rightfully mentioned that media often carries stories equating madrasas with extremism and religious militancy, but they use this cause to justify their reason of selecting Cox's Bazar as

---

[41] Ibid., 165.

[42] Hussain 2007, 114–115.

[43] Ibid.

[44] Osmany and Kabir, *Global War on Terror*, 174–182.

work location since it is identified as a breeding ground of terrorism because of its large number of madrasas and mosques.

Lintner, Abuza, Gunaratna, Griswold, Adiga, Karlekar located Bangladeshi madrasa as the single space of terrorist breeding and religious indoctrinations.[45] They back their hypothesis by mentioning that madrasas are operated by people who joined to fight with the 'infidel oppressor' of a Muslim land, Afghanistan. Their assumption is that since those mujahideens are in control of madrasas, therefore, they will surely use their influence to recruit and indoctrinate students and, thus they will run their campaign of establishing IS in Bangladesh. On the other hand, Hussain, Shelly, Rahman, Imamuzzaman, Riaz and Hashmi did not explicitly blame madrasa as the sole producer of terrorism, but allow space for doubt that madrasas are a potential space for terrorist recruitment, thereby, this institution needs restructuring and suggest that the government should reinforce a Western model of education in madrasas in order to establish a secular curriculum.[46]

Saika writes that volunteers from Bangladesh madrasas joined to fight with the 'infidel oppressor' of a Muslim land, Afghanistan, since Bangladesh became part of the proxy war within the US government machine.[47] It was difficult for the government to keep count of their number, after the Soviet withdrawal in 1989 and many of them returned to normal life. Many did not. It is estimated that around 3,400 Bangladeshis participated in the Afghan war and 300 never came back. The exact figure is difficult to ascertain. Many stayed on to fight Afghanistan's civil war and joined with the Taliban and worked in recruitment. Many of these Bangladeshi Taliban members fought till the last when the US assault was made on Kunduz. Some of these Afghans veterans were interested to turn their State as Islamic State. They had opposed Western concept of ruling and government system. A good number of them had joined the group known as HuJI-B under the

---

[45] Lintner 2002; Abuza 2003; Gunaratna 2003; Griswold, 'The Next Islamist Revolution'; Adiga 2004; Karlekar, 'Bangladesh'.

[46] Hussain, 2007; Shelly, 2007; Rahman, 2007; Imamuzzaman, 'Welcome Speech'; Riaz, 'Recognition of Qwami Degree'; Hashmi, 'ISIS Threats in Bangladesh'.

[47] Saika, 2006, 7.

leadership of Mufti Abdul Hannan who had tried to assassinate Sheikh Hasina in 2000. Question is who are they who joined in the proxy war in Afghanistan under the American leadership? Is not it the secular State and its Westernized minority elite who used many madrasas as solder recruitment centres for the Afghan war during the 1990s?

Ali Riaz argues that militancy is not a new phenomenon for Bangladesh and Islamic fundamentalists have been operating in the country since the mid 1990s.[48] According to his statement, there was well-established classical understanding that Islamic terrorists are the by-product of madrasas and they supposedly come from ordinary poor families. After analysing the profiles of Holey Artisan Café attackers, he argues that these terrorists background sends a blow through the Bangladeshi middle class perception, because those combatants mostly came from well-off urban middle class families, educated in mainstream secular institutions. On top of it, some of those attackers had received their education from some notable foreign institutions. This analysis is very significant in contrast to the narratives which suggest that madrasa students who are poor and deprived are prone to terrorism.[49] This is not the end of the shock but the beginning, as in the post-Café attack period newspapers reports reveal that many youth from various strata of society are missing and they are suspected of having joined militant groups. Some may travel to Syria to join ISIL. This is a difficult truth for Bangladesh to accept? John Esposito is very relevant in order to understand this contradiction.[50] He writes in his book the *Islamic Threat: Myth or Reality*, that the post imperial and post-colonial Muslim countries were led by the Westernized minority elite who shared the Western imposed concept that progress and modernization necessarily meant secularization. While the process and institutions in these societies were secularized, the mind and culture of the majority was not. The Westernized ruling elite also failed to deliver the goods in terms of sustainability, and meaningfully improving the quality of life of the masses led to disillusionment with the ways of the secularized

---

[48] Riaz, 2018.

[49] Lintner, 2002; Abuza, 2003; Gunaratna, 2003; Griswold, 'The Next Islamist Revolution'; Adiga, 2004; Karlekar, 'Bangladesh'.

[50] John L. Esposito. *The Islamic Threat: Myth or Reality?*, (Oxford University Press, 1999).

elite and paved the path of the reassertion of Islam in the politics of societies. Islam never really disappeared from Bangladesh rather under the careless ruling of secularized Westernized elite, Islam has emerged as a vibrant socio-political reality. Therefore, it is necessary to pose questions in a critical manner to understand the new reality of terrorism in Bangladesh. This changing reality's main characteristic is different compared to the earlier terrorist attacks.

The changing period of 9/11 attack carried the noteworthy variation which was the insertion of religion as a feature to comprehend inspiration to terrorism. Should religion be viewed as an ideology to motivate terrorism? If it is, then what is the distinction between political ideology and religion? These are certainly important questions in the context of Bangladesh. There, those who perceive terrorism through the prism of religion end up with a convoluted perception of terror since the issue of terrorism is blatantly politicized in the country. Bangladesh War on Terror is defiled by political expediency, exclusivity and subjectivity and at a national level this stands badly politicized and polarized. Therefore, in the attempt to explain the extremist phenomenon, many politicians, policymakers and journalist give little attention to the research findings which suggest that terrorism is not the immediate outcome of religious education, rather poverty breeds extremism and deprivation encourages individuals to join militant groups. Therefore, in attempts to understand terrorism and its relationship to madrasa education, individuals are drawing on limited evidence from Pakistan and insist that madrasas are the breeding ground of terrorists. Taliban leadership's background was supporting examples for this particular narrative. Yes, it's a fact that the Taliban leadership were educated in a few Pakistani madrasas, but still this perception is over-simplified and does not necessarily establish the link between madrasa education and terrorism. In the post-9/11 period more religious research studies were conducted and those findings suggest that neither the leadership of the international terrorist groups nor the suicide bombers came exclusively or predominantly from religious educational institutions. Their socio-economic origins did not point to poverty or deprivation as the cause of terrorism.[51] Therefore, certain narratives which suggest

---

[51] Riaz, 2018, 48.

that madrasa education is the necessary entry point to understand the terrorist phenomenon in Bangladesh need to be interrogated to bridge the gap of difference between understanding reality and preconceived notions under the influence of Islamophobia.

BANGLADESH'S WAR ON TERROR

17 August 2005 was a day when Bangladesh entered in the spotlight that grabbed international attention. On that day 459 bombs and grenade had detonated within seven minutes in 63 district towns.[52] Certainly, there was no doubt that those attacks were well coordinated and logistically impressive. Cochrane described those assaults as disciplined and deadly.[53] As a consequence of those attacks, Mrs. Zia's government was forced to change their stance on terrorism. Initially, BNP government blamed foreign elements such as Israel's Mossad and India's Research and Analysis Wing (RAW) for the attack.

They were not too late to realize that neither RAW nor Mossad were involved with the attack and it was not merely a conspiracy instigated by any other foreign agencies, but there are far more reasons to be worried. For the first time Mrs. Zia's government admitted that Bangladesh is not free from the home-grown Islamist militant threats. Consequently, the government declared JMB responsible for the attack, moreover, took prompt action to arrest 743 leaders suspect. Leaders of JMB and JMJB were arrested and executed.[54] Bangladesh authority has continued its efforts to combat and control terrorist activities and regular police raids have consistently unfolded JMB arms ammunition and propaganda books. Islam argues that JMB has developed new leadership for last 13 years.[55] Liton, Cochrane and Islam describe that there are around 100 Islamist groups remaining in Bangladesh. JMB, HuJI-B, JMJB and SAH are the major four organizations who have been banned by the State.[56]

---

[52] Habib, '17 August 2005'; Islam, 'Mapping Terrorism'.

[53] Cochrane, 'The Funding Methods'.

[54] Habib, '17 August 2005'.

[55] Islam, 'Mapping Terrorism'.

[56] S. Liton, 'Islamic Parties Boom after 1976 Ban Lifting', *The Daily Star*, 29 August 2006. Available at: http://archive.thedailystar.net/2006/08/29/

Despite the dramatic rise of violent terrorist attacks by Islamist terrorists in the contemporary periods and IS acknowledgement of many of these notorious assaults, in February 2016, PM Hasina proclaimed that there is no IS in Bangladesh. On the contrary, she suspected that it is the BNP and Jamaat-e-Islami Bangladesh who are responsible to conduct these violent attacks to overthrow her government. She refused the Syrian example and argued that there are no similarities between IS activities in the Middle East and Bangladesh. Besides PM's firm remarks, Shahriar Alam, Bangladesh foreign minister, has denied any presence of IS in Bangladesh while addressing global community concern in the awake of blogger assassinations. Furthermore, he had strongly argued that all those killings were executed by the local elements not IS.

Roy and Hashmi established that the Bakery attack had forced government to move away to some extent from their stubborn denial.[57] They have analysed the government's practical actions and crack down and formed their argument. Following the same line, Riaz argues that primarily intelligence gathering and consistent arrests are notable actions taken by the authorities.[58] Though Bangladesh lacks to end terrorist financing, but the authority is improving their capacity to deal with this challenge. Roy states that the State's actions narrate volumes regarding government seriousness in the IS threat.[59] In the context of Bangladesh Holey Artisan attack is the 9/11 and her action to combat terrorism is terminologically her intrinsic version of 'War on Terror'. The term has been coined by Roy.[60] However, in the undeclared war government has armed civilian police and provided exemption to extra judicial killing of suspected terrorist. In short, this proves Bangladesh's active affirmation of the threat and its own kind of War on Terror.

---

d6082901022.htm. Cochrane, 'The Funding Methods'; Islam, 'Mapping Terrorism'.

[57] Roy, 'A Year of Bangladesh's War on Terror'; Hashmi, 'ISIS Threats in Bangladesh'.

[58] Riaz, 2018.

[59] Roy, 'A Year of Bangladesh's War on Terror'.

[60] Ibid.

9/11, ISLAMOPHOBIA AND MADRASA
AT GLOBAL AND NATIONAL LEVELS

When al-Qaeda's chief Bin Laden asserted leadership[61] for the 11 September 2001 assault on the World Trade Centre, Huntington's thesis, *Clash of Civilizations* seemed to resonate more in the global public sphere. There grew a massive interest in deciphering the relationship between Islam and terrorism. Had the 9/11 event not happened, could we then have imagined such questions about Islam and madrasas taking its form in public discourse? It is important to ask this question as the 9/11 event did change the fate of the followers of Islam. However, to what extent could such change be subject to personal experiences?[62] Mamdani in his book *Good Muslim, Bad Muslim* locates the aftermath of 9/11 in the political and historical context, unlike the historical and biased narratives produced by either mass market media or government officials. He insists that political violence in modern club that does not observe the steps of progress is given to get discussed in what he calls 'theological terms' and observes that linking 'terrorism to Islam' is a consequence of 'culture talk'.[63] He criticized the insincere tendency which reads Islamic politics as the outcome of Islamic civilization and Western power as the result and effect of Western civilization. Furthermore he concludes by suggesting that the politics, authority and power are the upshot of their assignation and could not be cognized in isolation without the history of the confrontation and making.[64] One of the key ideas to understand the post-9/11 predicament is Mamdani's idea of 'culture talk'. In his earlier work *Citizen and Subject*, he traces the new radix of cultural talk to the colonial motive in which the colonizers justified their rule over the colonized by legitimizing their traditional

---

[61] *CBC News*, 'Bin Laden Claims Responsibility for 9/11', 29 October 2004. Available at: https://www.cbc.ca/news/world/bin-laden-claims-responsibility-for-9-11-1.513654.

[62] Mamdani, 'Good Muslim, Bad Muslim'; L. A. Peek, *Behind the Blacklash* (Philadelphia, PA: Temple University Press, 2011); A. Rabasa, *The Muslim World after 9/11* (Santa Monica, CA: RAND, 2004); J. Marguilies, *What Changed When Everything Changed: 9/11 and the Making of National Identity* (New Haven, CT: Yale University Press, 2013).

[63] Mamdani, 'Good Muslim, Bad Muslim', 766.

[64] Ibid., 766–768.

cultural resistance to modernity as an expression of cultural lag. When 9/11 happened, one found the tendency of linking the terrorists as essentially emanating from their archaic culture. Their act of terror of political significance was immediately linked to their culture of Islam and hence the birth of Islamic terrorism. Mamdani points out that, 'By equating political tendencies with entire communities defined in non-historical cultural terms, such explanations encourage collective discipline and punishment; a practice characteristic of colonial encounters'.[65] This sort of reasoning—of bypassing history for cultural explanations of political events—has basically led to equating Muslims as terrorists or potential terrorists. Such rationalization has justified America's intervention in countries like Afghanistan. Moreover, it ignores the emergence of political Islam as a result of such intervention.[66] Another aspect that is relevant to Mamdani's analysis is the propensity of imagining man (from 'traditional' cultures) in 'authentic and original' terminology, such as their self-identities have defined completely fixed culture into which they evolved. He further argues that by doing so it dehistoricizes the making of political identities.[67] Instead of understanding the issue of political Islam in the contemporary times as a result of archaic culture, it is significant to locate both culture and government as 'contemporary outcomes of equally contemporary conditions, relations and conflicts'.[68] Nevertheless, there is no denying the fact that through Islamophobia and the 'othering' of Muslim, it has led to their 'homogenization and legitimation of Islamophobia at global, national, and local levels',[69] but one demands to also hold in mind that event of 9/11 has gained its legitimacy as the event due to the massive accouchement of all kinds of literature after the event.[70] Even though, the aim was to deconstruct the modern myth of Islam to the extent that we pick up a fresh book on terrorism getting published every half dozen hours. One example to

---

[65] Ibid., 767.

[66] Ibid., 770.

[67] Ibid., 767.

[68] Ibid.

[69] B. Rustom, *Terror and Performance* (London: Routledge, 2014), 91.

[70] K. Miller, 'Transatlantic Literature and Culture after 9/11 (London: Palgrave Macmillan, 2014); A. Keniston, *Literature after 9/11* (New York, NY: Routledge, 2013).

suggest this is Omid Safi's remark on how the 9/11 event allowed the possibility for a substantial rise in the faculty recruitment and establishment of the Islamic Studies department in America which in some way led to imperial domination of knowledge production.[71]

UNLIKELY CANDIDATES:
FALL OF WESTERN PORTRAYALS OF MADRASA STUDENTS

Mostly the Western depiction of terrorist is modelled after the mujahideens of Afghanistan and Taliban who are predominantly madrasa-educated imbeciles and religious extremists coming from poor Muslim background and they stand to use arms to defend their ultra-conservative as well as dogmatic theocratic life style.[72] The similar framework has been used in Bangladesh to picture early fundamentalists since the inception of terrorist attacks. Roy argues that this is an ill-informed portrayal which is motivated by xenophobia about the 'Muslim look'.[73] In contrast with the Western notion, facts depict a different picture. Since the second half of 2016 all the terrorist attacks in Bangladesh pointed to a totally new state of indoctrination. These neo-terrorists are coming from well off socio-economic background, which had taken the country by astonishment. Indeed, they are not similar to the previous fanatics who had styled themselves following the mujahideen and Taliban. That is Holey Artisan attackers weren't coming from Islamic institutions as such madrasas but educated in secular institutions for instance schools, colleges and universities. Unlikely, religious education was not the primary focus of these establishments. On the contrary to the old classical picture of terrorists, they have modelled themselves after IS militants. For example, 27-year-old Bangladeshi migrant Akayed Ullah had tried to blow up himself in a crowded bus terminal at the New York City. Fortunately, the bomb wasn't powerful enough therefore he even failed to kill himself. Moreover, the attempt was aimed to attract attention, therefore, the

---

[71] O. Safi, 'Reflections on the State of Islamic Studies', *Jadaliyya*, 31 January 2014. Available at: http://www.jadaliyya.com/Details/30175/Reflections-on-the-State-of-Islamic-Studies.

[72] Marguilies, 'What Changed When Everything Changed'.

[73] Roy, 'Bangladesh's New Generation of Militants'.

location was chosen carefully. Hence, the incident had attracted widespread coverage. Ullah could be considered as the ambassador of the neo-Bengali Muslim terrorist and a model of new generation terrorist. A close investigation of terrorist profiles in Bangladesh will prove that he is not a single individual, but one of the many who attempted the Fedayeen format in the contemporary times. He is the member of the ever growing tribe of Jannah (heaven) hunters. The entry point of this trend is 2016 and it is consistent since then.

Except Akayed Ullah all other Bengali terrorist focused their attention on Bangladesh alone; their recruitment and political aims remained concentrated on the home only. Moreover, it may be possible that their passion is inspired by the dream of caliphate and IS war in Syria and Iraq. On behalf of IS, AQIS was leading terrorist attacks in Bangladesh. The nature of these attacks also changed and their attitude shifted towards face to face combat. Previously, a Muslim terrorist was killing in the name of religion, but the neo-Bengali Muslim terrorist intends to die for it.[74] For instance according to cooks taken hostage during the Bakery attack, Nirbas Islam and his squad came to die only. Likewise, they had no plan to leave up the ground. They also joked with their hostage that they will have their next meal in the heaven while breaking Ramadan fast. Another example is, Jebunnahar Islam, the first Bangladesh female suicide bomber, who blew herself up in December 2016. She was holding her 7-year-old daughter and chanting that she will go to haven. There were two more suicide attacks at the RAB camp and Dhaka international airport in March. These attacks happened within a span of a week and IS claimed responsibilities. It has become the consistent pattern of terrorists ever since the bakery attack. Death wish was their only goal.

The common characteristics of these young combatants are suggesting new narratives about Bengali Muslim terrorists. They are unlikely candidates. Similar to the San Bernardino attackers Farook and Orlando and Pulse nightclub attackers Omar Mateen, the Bakery attackers Nirbas Islam and his team, and New York attackers like Ullah are coming from privileged backgrounds and formed this picture of unlikely candidates. Follow up news reports had brought surprises to

---

[74] Ibid.

the readers since the attack. All national outlets continuously confirmed their surprise regarding the terrorist's profile. This shock challenged the ill-informed stereotypes of Muslims terrorist look and their background. This also proves that the previous notion on Muslim look was xenophobic generalization.

IS's operational head of Bangladesh Tamim Chowdhury who was also the designer of the Bakery attack is coming from a privileged and well-off background. On the other hand Ullah's family paid for his education and he attended two famous colleges, Rifles Public College and Dhaka City College. He had a bachelor's degree in business administration. He moved with his family and settled in America. These young Bangladeshi terrorists had access to expensive English medium education. Many of them, for instance Nirbas Islam, spent a long period of time in abroad for higher education. Nirbas studied in Monash University, Kuala Lumpur and Tamim Chowdhury had a PhD. Finally, these profiles suggest that the age-old picture of emblematic terrorist is in demise.

DEBATE: SECULARIZING MADRASAS

The secular criticism of madrasas in Bangladesh takes its precedence before the event of 9/11. This criticism starts with a debate on madrasa reform, which was about the inclusion of secular subjects (arts and science) along with religious curriculum in Bangladeshi madrasas. It is important to first understand the curriculum which is offered in madrasas and see whether the categories of secular/religious curriculum understood in madrasas matches with the concepts and categories as understood by the State. The medieval scholars used to often distinguish 'science' into two broad categories: traditionally transmitted science (naqliyyalmanqulat) and rational sciences (aqliyaamanqulat).[75] Subjects like morphology and syntax, Quranic studies, hadith, law (fiqh), principles of jurisprudence (usul-al-fiqh) and theology were traditionally transmitted sciences which were sources of knowledge which could be learnt by imitating the techniques of memorization. Subjects like

---

[75] M. Q. Zaman, 'Religious Education and the Rhetoric of Reform: The Madrasa in British India and Pakistan', *Comparative Studies in Society and History* 41, no. 2 (1999): 297.

logic, philosophy, astronomy and arithmetic were taught in rational sciences, science which needed reason to arrive at the truth. What we witness here is the difference between the revealed knowledge and gained knowledge. What needs to be stressed here is this distinction in earlier Muslim societies has little precedent in the distinction that is made now in madrasas and has changed to a new distinction (religious/non-religious [secular]). This happened due to the ulamas borrowing the concept and categories that developed in the colonial times. In colonial India, the British always inspired circumstance and organizations where no clean differentiation between the secular and the religious had been instituted. It had reminded to several of them the Europe's medieval age where similar differences were frequently obscure and served the Church's interest.

Seeing India as subjected, it allowed them to take initiative for reform. What they served was the effort to differentiate between what was 'secular' and 'religious'.[76] This according to Zaman is a modern distinction that shaped multiple debates on amendment in South Asia. He further discusses how the initiative towards the reform nurtured aspects about religion as holding a separate, exclusive and distinct sphere in society in which the ulamas also started to distinguish with the secular public sphere. Another important category which changed the notion of education and continues to persist today is the colonial analysis of 'useful instruction'. The English utilitarians invoked the idea of what was called 'useful learning' which did not consider 'religious education' to be useful. Funding to educational institutions during the colonial times was only to those which taught secular subjects. However, the Islamic tradition has also the idea of 'useful knowledge' (al-ilm al-nafi) where it directs to start with but not just to knowledge which aid in redemption.[77]

The assumption which lies at the scheme of current State policies on madrasas is based on the same colonial fact that madrasas offer only traditional subjects (religious subjects) and the so-called secular subjects which are not offered need to be taught in madrasas in order to secularize and de-radicalize the potent mind of madrasa students. What it

---

[76] Ibid., 296.
[77] Ibid.

does as a result of assuming and categorizing subjects into 'secular' and 'religious' is that the State takes autonomy over what is good and bad, what is useful and what is not?

Asad argues that the influence of enlightenment in the development of modern Europe has driven the subjugation of religion to the State authority or the captivity of the previous to the sphere of private life but also to the making of religion so far a new historical affair.[78] He concludes by stating that secularism as a political doctrine of the secular state has presupposed modern notion of religion, politics as well as ethics.[79] The distinction between the secular and religious, public and private in Bangladesh politicize this issue of terrorism and madrasas, and this is continuously invoked in the name of introducing secular subjects in madrasas of Bangladesh.

CONCLUSION

The event of 9/11 and the villainous discourse it constructed for Islam led to the emergence of new distorted hegemonic perception of madrasas in Bangladesh. It has functioned as a diabolical term for everything connected to Islam. It has also begun to be seen as the potential site of Islamic radicalism and in the popular media parlance the mere mention of the word 'madrasa' conjures up an 'us versus them' dynamic.[80] This perception, rather a misguided one, takes its cue from Taliban's misuse of madrasa for training young jihadists. Widespread condemnation began when al-Qaeda maintained close ties with the Taliban, and Afghanistan became the shelter for top leaders of al-Qaeda and engulfed more when Taliban claimed an ideological affiliation with Deoband. However, except Taliban, there has been no record of any madrasa using their institution for creating terrorists. Recent study in fact shows that Islamic terrorists tend to have no background of madrasa education

---

[78] T. Asad, *Formations of the Secular* (Stanford, CA: Stanford University Press, 2003).

[79] Ibid., 2.

[80] J. Goldberg, 'Inside Jihad: The Education of a Holy Warrior', *The New York Times*, 25 June 2000; E. Moosa, *What Is a Madrasa* (Chapel Hill, NC: The University of North Carolina Press, 2005).

and surprisingly are young men with engineering background who are trained, to everybody's surprise, in secular university spheres.[81] For instance, Osama Bin Laden, mastermind of the 9/11 was a civil engineer. One is given to wonder whether State workers and non-State actors intentionally ignore these facts so as to create the 'other' and encourage Islamophobia or is it simple ignorance? Islamophobia is not the product of Huntington's thesis *Clash of Civilizations*, instead the upshot of what Said calls 'clash of ignorance'. The rise of the Taliban as an exception, unfortunately, proved to be the rule and ever since it gained currency in the public imagination, madrasas in Bangladesh were widely condemned and more State intervention was applied. Like the Taliban, HuJI-B claimed its ideological affiliation to Deoband. Because of that link, the then Bangladeshi government bought the allegation against madrasas so much so that several leaders made provocative statements against madrasas and several attempts were made to bring all madrasas under government watch. The government proposed that modern education and pedagogy should be introduced in madrasas so as to fetch them into the mainstream. Despite deliberate attempts government has failed to attract most of the madrasas as they were suspicious of the steps and were also aware that such initiatives could snatch away the religious authority of the ulamas.

Madrasas focused on teaching Islamic rules, determinism and next wordiness, but till today accept some examples of Pakistani madrasas there are not enough evidence to make the hypothesis that madrasas appointed or induced their students into violent extremism and terrorism. Government attempt to 'reform' madrasa education to deradicalize youth as a counterpoise to terrorism shows that they are far from the truth. Terrorism is a political problem neither cultural nor a religious problem. Therefore, promoting any decontaminated madrasa education will not produce any effective sustainable change. Improvised and marginalized Bangladeshi madrasa students are too weak to organize technically sophisticated violent revolutionary Islamist movement. It is the urban, well-off, fortunate secular educated youth turn up so far to be the leading combatants of Islamist terror in Bangladesh.

---

[81] A. Riaz, *Lived Islam and Islamism in Bangladesh*, (Dhaka: Prothoma Prokashan, 2017), 242.

Chapter 9

The Gender Dimension of Extremism
The Unfolding Links between Women and Extremism in Bangladesh

INTRODUCTION: ARE WE WALKING ON THIN ICE?

Radicalization, leading to violent extremism, has become a critical security and development concern for Bangladesh. It is an issue that revolves around realpolitik, identity politics, the political economy of governance and technological dividends. Each of these statist and socio-political tools is interlinked and cannot be seen in isolation when examining and discussing the trends of and the responses against extremism. The transnational terrorist and extremist organizations have been battling to establish their presence in Bangladesh through organizational as well as ideological footprints in social, political and virtual domains. What remains as problematic is Bangladesh's compound ability, be it political or socio-economic or religious, to respond to this multifaceted and multidimensional security threat that would require more than kinetic and soft approaches. The spread of the contemporary extremist groups reflects less on their strategic prowess or military might and more on their capacity to exploit and harness the aspirations of young people—along with existing inequalities and deprivations—to their advantage. If Bangladeshi society, in inclusive and comprehensive terms, can offer more compelling roles, opportunities, and futures to men and women equally, extremism and violence it visits on women and girls, in particular, will have far less appeal.[1]

This chapter focuses on the evolving interface between gender and radicalization leading to violent extremism and the gender dimension of security in the context of Bangladesh. Hence, the chapter proposes to explain whether female, as a key development actor, a small segment of women, are emerging as a strategic target for extremist groups in Bangladesh or not. The role of gender, precisely women, has been the focus of prevention of radicalization or violent extremism discussions and policies without a deeper understanding of the drivers of radicalization linking women in the context of Bangladesh and its society.[2] Against the backdrop of the changing dynamics of extremism and the growing presence of women in extremism, it has become important to enquire into the causes and factors that determine radicalization and extremism among women.[3] There is now a need more than ever to understand the phenomenon of women's involvement in extremism, mitigate its impact and prevent its recurrence since women are often the first victims of violent extremist groups, experiencing horrific violations of their rights, including education, health care, public life and decision-making over their own bodies.[4] UN-led investigations have uncovered a range of sexual and gender-based crimes including

---

[1] Alys Willman, 'How Violent Extremism Links to Violence against Women', *The World Bank*, 2015. Available at: https://blogs.worldbank.org/voices/how-violent-extremism-links-violence-against-women (accessed on 5 March 2019).

[2] Perception-based articles and studies have been dominating the discourse and discussions with references drawn from contemporary examples, events, and specific and contextual experiences.

[3] Shahab Enam Khan, 'Bangladesh: The Changing Dynamics of Violent Extremism and the Response of the State', *Small Wars & Insurgencies* 28, no. 1 (2017): 191–217.

[4] Taqbir Huda, 'A Logical Antidote: Increasing Women's Religious Leadership to Counter Violent Extremism', *The Daily Star, 14* March *2018. Available at:* https://www.thedailystar.net/opinion/society/logical-antidote-1547707 (accessed on 5 March 2019).

rape, forced marriage, abductions and sexual slavery, highlighting the use of gender-based crimes as part of the strategic objectives of violent extremist groups. Women are also, however, impacted by counter-terrorism policies that can curtail their rights and impact their quality of life. Increasingly, they are themselves being recruited, forcibly or willingly, to these groups. This chapter, therefore, seeks to give an understanding of why women join and remain in violent extremist groups in Bangladesh, and how they are recruited.

The case of Bangladesh has emerged as an important one as the women, comprising more than 50 per cent of Bangladesh's population, are increasingly becoming targeted by the extremist organizations to carry out different levels of intervention. However, the number of detained female terrorists or extremists is minuscule, but their experience with the 'root causes' of radicalization process is large—and yet, typically, only a small fraction of individuals has turned into radical, and even a small number of them has turned into extremists. Then the question arises that what triggers this minority of individuals to become extremists? The importance of institutions, state mechanisms and humanitarian agencies in creating opportunities to frame and channel grievances in violent directions becomes important aspects to scrutinize. In addition, individual experiences, whether of injustice or other factors, may have a decisive impact. United States Agency for International Development (USAID), United Nations Development Programme (UNDP), Global Center for Counter-Terrorism, Governance, Social Development, Conflict and Humanitarian Knowledge Services (GSDRC), Hedayah, US Department of State, Department of Homeland Security, Department for International Development (DfID), Center for Security Studies (CSS), Royal United Services Institute (RUSI), Organization for Security and Co-operation in Europe (OSCE), Quilliam Foundation, Saferworld and the World Bank has conducted a number of studies to devise various frameworks categorizing and weighing different types of factors and drivers as part of the global response discourse.[5] These help to distinguish between

---

[5] UNDP, *Journey to Extremism in Africa* (New York, NY: UNDP, 2017). Available at: http://journey-to-extremism.undp.org/content/downloads/UNDP-JourneyToExtremism-report-2017-english.pdf (accessed on 5 March 2019).

'micro-', 'meso-' and 'macro-level' factors,[6] and/or 'push' and 'pull' factors.[7]

However, in the case of Bangladesh, a lack of qualitative and quantitative researches and the literature based on scientific inquiries, that is, empirical studies on the factors behind women's radicalization and extremism exist. Most research focuses on the role of women in countering/preventing violent extremism (C/PVE) rather than what triggers women to be active in the extremist network. The perception-based analysis dominates the discourses which are inadequate to capture the overall scenario. Policymakers, researchers and practitioners agree that research into the causes of extremism and its future trends are needed if governments, as well as non-state and international partners, are to achieve effective responses to the complex and multifaceted threats. The lack of verifiable evidence both about what shapes violent extremism and what works as interventions in responding to violent extremism is frequently cited as an obstacle to tangible response strategies

---

[6] According to CSS, 'micro' refers to personal motives and convictions, for instance, negative experiences of exclusion, rejection, humiliation, injustice or frustration. 'Meso' refers to the social milieu of the violent extremist, including community and the social structures in which he or she is engaged. 'Macro-level' refers to structural drivers, including chronically unresolved political conflicts; the 'collateral damage' to civilian lives and infrastructure caused by military responses to terrorism; human rights violations; ethnic, national and religious discrimination; the political exclusion of ethnic or religious groups; socio-economic marginalization; lack of good governance; and a failure to integrate diaspora communities of immigrants who move between cultures. See Centre for Security Studies, *The Concept of Countering Violent Extremism* (CSS Analyses in Security Policy No. 183, Centre for Security Studies, Zurich, 2015).

[7] 'Push' factors usually refer to locally informed structural drivers, while 'pull' factors refer to proximate incentives leading to recruitment and radicalization (USAID, *The Development Response to Violent Extremism and Insurgency*, 2011). Available at: https://www.usaid.gov/sites/default/files/documents/1870/VEI_Policy_Final.pdf). For a helpful summary based on a review of recent literature on violent extremism, see RUSI, *Drivers of Violent Extremism: Hypotheses and Literature Review* (London: Royal United Services Institute, 2015). Available at: https://assets.publishing.service.gov.uk/media/57a0899d40f0b64974000192/Drivers_of_Radicalisation_Literature_Review.pdf.

in Bangladesh since the largest share of available literature has been conceptual and perceptual as opposed to empirical.[8]

The survey of literature and opinions of the experts indicate that even though women's involvement in extremism is gaining importance in the policy circles and attracting considerable research interests, far less is known about the causes and trajectories regarding violent extremism in Bangladesh. As violent extremist recruitment and sympathy towards radical causes continue to increase in the Indian subcontinent, be it in Islamic extremism or Saffron radicalization or Buddhist nationalism, domestic as well as transnational non-actors are increasingly targeting educated women for carrying out recruitment and leadership activities in Bangladesh, and illiterate women to undertake works ranging from petty works to childbearing to suicidal acts.

Methodology

The author relied on three principal sources while preparing this chapter. The sources included the literature review including secondary documents, that is, reports, articles, public policy documents, research publications and academic publications. Then the author, given his vast experience with multiple research contributions to international organizations, used the epistemic understanding and exposures to the gender dimension of security. The author included expert opinions; views of the law enforcement agencies and the civil society; and academia. Given the nature of the chapter, the sources have been kept undisclosed.

---

[8] The author interviewed and conducted focus group discussions (FGDs) with 140 female students studying at the tertiary level in the urban cities such as Dhaka and Chittagong, and rural areas such as Tangail and Mymensingh; activists; professionals; teachers; and housewives from the aforementioned areas. The author interviewed officials working with Police and RAB officials from the Ministry of ICT, Government of Bangladesh, and Islamic Foundation. The policy of anonymity has been pursued at the request of the officials. The author held extensive discussions with eminent experts from different fields such as security sector, academia, law and IT. Similar policy has been followed.

HOW WOMEN AND EXTREMISM LINKAGES ARE FORMED?

Women's involvement in terrorism is not a new phenomenon. However, the three incidents that took place in 2016 brought the issue of women's involvement in the extremism discourse a new dimension. The women-extremism and women-radicalization interface came into the surface when the Rapid Action Battalion (RAB) arrested and detained four female students with a meritorious academic career on 15 August 2016. Three of the females studied at Manarat International University, Dhaka, and one female studied at Dhaka Medical College. RAB claimed that the arrested females were actively involved in *Dawati* and fundraising activities. Subsequently, the Police arrested female militants from Azimpur, Dhaka on 10 September 2016. The militants attacked the Police with knives and pepper spray, and three arrested female militants were claimed to be wives of Jamaat-ul-Mujahideen Bangladesh (JMB) militants.[9] On 24 December 2016, during a raid conducted by the law enforcement agencies in Ashkona, the northern part of Dhaka, a female militant carried out a suicide attack. According to the Police reports, two female militants arrested in this incident provided statements to the court claiming that the JMB was a source of their ideology, and they were inspired by their husbands to undertake such activities. Mr Monirul Islam, Chief of the Bangladesh Police Counter Terrorism Unit, mentioned that 'they try to arrange marriages among themselves to keep their activities secret'.[10] Moreover, terrorist organizations have targetted vulnerable groups such as widows, orphans, mothers of victims, internally displaced persons and refugees within their fold as part of their recruitment strategy.[11]

These interfaces expose a linkage between development deficits and insecurity in multiple forms, ranging from personal safety to human security, and compound and heighten the dynamics of

---

[9] Ashish Banik, 'Role of Women in Preventing Radicalization in Bangladesh', *Foreign Affairs Insights & Review*, 20 June 2017. Available at: http://fairbd.net/role-of-women-in-preventing-radicalization-in-bangladesh/ (accessed on 5 March 2019).

[10] Ibid.

[11] Ibid.

violent extremism and its impact. The main drivers behind women's involvement in violent extremism and terrorism are grievances with their economic and socio-political circumstances, the strong ties of relationships—family, kinship and romantic—and a commitment and indoctrinated belief to and/or the oppression by the religious or political entities. The interplay between these drivers and factors, which create the dynamics for women's involvement in violent extremism, are unique and dependent on women's socio-economic profiles. The indoctrination, which is the essential component to recruit or to motivate, takes shape on the basis of different social conditions and demographic profiles.

There is no linear model or process that can be aptly considered as universal model radical indoctrination. However, given the multilinear dynamics and the evolving socio-political environment for women to be recruited in the extremist process, extremist groups have increased their attention towards urban women through the informal network as well as social media. In the case of rural women, the activities focus on both preaching a misrepresented version of Islam and to deter them from social activities and employment. The law enforcement agencies mentioned that women are convenient individuals within the society who can act as a conveyor of messages, maintain oral networks, work as an informant, undertake analytical intelligence work, provide healthcare, food and safe houses for violent extremists and terrorists, and traffic arms and ammunition to men. Very interestingly, they are often engaged in infiltrating into communities or families through their diverse access to families. These responsibilities are considered as non-lethal duties that can define the success or failure of long-term clandestine organizational life or tactical activities of the extremist or terrorist outfits. In recent years, the enforcement agencies have been able to identify that women are also being used as the perpetrators of violence by terrorist organizations.

There are different cognitive and socio-economic motivation tools to recruit or indoctrinate women. These would range from narratives of victimhood to social justice to the lack of awareness regarding religious narratives and so on. One of the important steps in understanding women's involvement in extremism spectrum is to understand or to recognize their agency as well as their personal grievances or experiences as a victim to social or personal circumstances. It has long been perceived that women are only victims of patriarchal terrorist organizations or perhaps individual male terrorists. However, this narrow prism of view is no longer acceptable; the experts now agree that women's involvement in terrorism is a complex phenomenon that offers multiple channels for their involvement, and there is no single prism to explain women's involvement in extremism.

The law enforcement agencies mentioned that women have, so far, provided auxiliary assistance to terrorist organizations as sympathizers, supporters and mobilizers. So far, women's involvement in extremist activities has been limited as most of them came from a rural background with very limited educational exposure. During the field works in different parts of the countries, several observations were achieved. The university students as well as the law enforcement officials mentioned that the recruitment processes are different in urban and rural areas. The Counter Terrorism and Transnational Crime Unit (CTTC) of the Bangladesh Police have revealed that the extremist groups have been able to recruit female university students to carry out extremist activities in the country.[12] During interrogation, CTTC found that all the female militants claimed that they had joined militant activities as their husbands had forced them.[13]

CTTC has also found that university and college students are being recruited by terrorist organizations. There are pieces of evidence that extremist outfits have recruited female university students through marriage, family pressure and peer circle or romantic relations. Later, these females were forced into militant activities. Educated women are often given the charge to lead the female units of these extremist organizations.[14] A number of sources indicated that the *Talim* and

---

[12] Lubna Yasmin, '8 NGO Workers Held for "Funding Militancy"', *The Daily Observer*, 8 November 2018. Available at: http://www.observerbd.com/details.php?id=167496 (accessed on 5 March 2019).

[13] *Dhaka Tribune*, 'Women Being "Forced" into New JMB', *Dhaka Tribune*, 11 October 2016. Available at: http://www.dhakatribune.com/bangladesh/2016/10/11/recruiting-women-now-new-goal-terrorists/ (accessed on 5 March 2019).

[14] Ibid.

informal preaching by clandestine Islamist groups is a prime source for such extremist recruitment in the female 'hostels' in the educational institutions. Besides political rivalries or political repression by the student wings of the political parties on hostel residents, political parties often force students to undertake 'immoral' or 'unwilling' activities. If a student protests, then she may become subject to humiliation or at times may have to leave the hostel.

Alienation, depression and fear about uncertain future (in terms of financial security, employment and livelihood) are very common among the students. The active agents and recruiters of the extremist organizations carefully monitor these situations. The recruiters would make a good relationship with the target person, offer incentives based on the girl's necessity and then entrap her through indoctrination. This is a very common practice and structure. Therefore, there is a protection–reward relationship between the extremist organizations and the potential recruits. Another important component of the indoctrination process is exposing the females to teachings that are based on sharia. Through Talim and clandestine processes, fresh or potential recruits are given religious books almost exclusively, published by different groups and not essentially available in formal shops, while already recruited members are given 'manuals' to study. The process of indoctrination to purely theological texts is in line with the avowal that it as an extension of authentic Islam rather than one among the competing schools of Islamic interpretation.

Since the nature and tactics of terrorism are evolving, the reasons for involving women in terrorist attacks are also changing. A number of respondents who were involved in this research mentioned that women provide excellent cover for terrorist organizations because security personnel, as well as any other people, would make assumptions about the inherent peacefulness of women. Besides, given Bangladesh's social context, security personnel or officials will be hesitant in carrying out invasive searches on women in Hijab, or perhaps the cultural norms surrounding women will protect women from being extensively investigated by the law enforcement agencies. This is a social or perhaps natural advantage that extremist organizations would like to exploit to a great extent.

Moreover, the extremist outfits are now able to attract media coverage by projecting women as a 'brand ambassador'. Female suicide bombers are de facto brand ambassadors for their activities which receive widespread media attention as well as instil fear in local communities and the fear provides an incentive for recruitment in part by shaming young men in the community as well as at the national level. It serves two purposes, (a) it creates media hype, and (b) it creates conducive environment to recruit more young men within the system. Along with the lack of access to education, employment, legal justice and inheritance, law create multiple levels of deprivation for women within the society and family. Media enables a conducive environment that leads to create a passage for adventurism and urge to demonstrate resistance against the material world.

The enabling conditions also determine the recruitment process of women in the extremist network. The current trend shows that there is a shift from recruitment by the extremist group to self-recruitment. Recruitment refers to a process by which individuals already affiliated with a violent extremist organization enlist others into it. Where top-down recruitment is at work, it is assumed that individuals typically need at least some 'convincing' or 'nudging' before they join. 'Self-recruitment', by contrast, can be seen as a process in which individuals connect themselves with the extremist networks, physically or virtually. This is done through peer circle or the clandestine networks functional in the communities or educational institutions. They may end up carrying out extremist works on their own, or with a handful of like-minded peers. However, given the socio-economic context of Bangladesh at the moment, the trend towards a shift from recruitment to self-recruitment should not be overstated. The law enforcement agency officials indicated that there is evidence that formal recruitment is still at work. There is, however, no mistake in the tendency towards individuals, on their own, seeking others with similar worldviews, and reaching out to existing extremist networks, both domestic and transnational.

Therefore, the complexity of women's involvement in extremism depends on the individual's context, background, community, social exposure and personality. The respondents who were involved in this research mentioned that in future women would assume a leadership position in the extremist activities as a response to the suppressive nature of the extremist organizations or as a response to the overall structural failures of the society. However, many women believe that it is possible for women to assume a leadership position in Islam, which is vehemently opposed by the Muslim leadership or Islamic clergies in general.

MULTILINEAR DYNAMICS OF EXTREMISM: STRUCTURAL CAUSES OF RADICALIZATION?

The process of radicalization certainly denotes that women are vulnerable to radical preaching and susceptible to the narratives due to the multiple complex socio–economic dynamics. The following dynamics can be observed in the case of Bangladesh which is interrelated in scopes and interdependent in functional terms:

Family, Community and Extremism Dynamics

A mother can be an influential source of de-radicalization and radicalization other than just giving birth to male children. A small segment of Muslim women are being radicalized in the rural areas because they are brought up with extremist teachings and are taught to accept everything that their husbands, fathers or brothers say. In the context of Bangladeshi society, women have less tendency to complete formal education or are subject to more rigid cultural and religious norms; mothers may be considered as powerless to influence their children against extremist doctrines, even they are unable to identify when their family members are involved with extremist thought or activity. Mothers are the most difficult family members within the rural social structure to reach out to. Generally, they are surrounded by their male family members, in terms of hierarchy and accessibility, which creates a barrier to establish a functional interface between mother institutions to interact on countering extremism initiatives. This certainly creates an enabling condition for less oversight on children, the teaching of religious narratives and cultural diversity.

The Misinterpreted Narratives and Extremism Dynamics

Misrepresentation of religious ideology can be seen as an important factor behind extremism. The popular narratives often portray both extremist agenda and the key psychological driving forces behind them. That is, gender issues are the key elements in the narratives and the psycho-social behaviours of violent extremist organizations. A common thread of the extremist organizations is a strong patriarchal narrative that revolves around women's physical appearance and social role as part of both a critique of existing socio-political system and the replacement alternative that they propose to establish in the name of a distorted or Puritan form of sharia. Hence, the violence-religious nexus asserts that the progressive and democratic rights have suppressed the moral societies. The men are repeatedly reminded of their religious and social duties to protect their religion, dignity and honour, while women's bodies are offered as rewards for the pious and brave, both in paradise and as long as they are loyal to the belief or group. A number of security and gender experts argued that the commodification of female body is essential for extremist groups' appeal and survival. Therefore, narratives are the key influencing factor behind extremism in the country.

Identity as a 'good Muslim' and as a good girl are two important social constructs that explain the patriarchal structure that demands women to remain subjugated and carry out patriarchal desires. While ideology and identity are important factors in understanding extremist behaviour, these factors are not sufficient enough to explain why extremist groups succeed over other groups with moderate Islamic or secular values. Perhaps, the extremist outfits have been able to propagate religious obscurantism and economic pragmatism by taking advantage of the governance loopholes in the country. In that context, the narratives used by the extremists are a critical source to understand the women-extremism linkage. The narratives are propagated on the basis of identity, biological and socio-economic needs of women. The rural and urban socio-economic class, and literacy or education also matter in preaching religious interpretations by the religious preachers.

Thus, extremist or radical narratives do not equally target women and are based on the understanding of women's interpretations and their access to information—or lack thereof. For example, the concepts of jihad and veil vary according to localities and socio-economic backgrounds. Women, who are educated, tend to understand the meaning of jihad as a positive form of effort or struggle to live a moral life, but those who live in rural areas and clearly lacks information about the Islamic concept of jihad, tend to translate it as a method to establish religious and/or ideological causes. It was interesting to note that, narratives are often formulated on the basis of women's biological need, that is, adolescence health or mental or perhaps socially defined idea of beauty. For example, many women told that if a woman is considered as pretty, then extremist preaching would be dominated by the 'narratives of victimization', and if a woman is not pretty or confident, then the preaching will bring the 'narrative of empowerment'.

Henceforth, another key driving factor behind women's recruitment in extremism is the lack of access to religious discourse. Since religion is essentially seen as a male-dominated subject, women are generally comfortable in discussing their concerns regarding religion with their mother but not with the male members (in the family, school, community or religious institutions) in most cases. It is difficult to identify an appropriate translation of the Holy Quran and Hadith in Bangladesh. The educational institutions, community spaces, religious institutions or families are often not able to provide open space for debate or to learn religion, cultural diversity and pluralism in pragmatic and practical senses. Informal teaching or preaching through Talim, which are carried out by the educated and illiterate women, gets prominence at the family level. This creates an environment for hatred and confusion. Different versions of translations and interpretations are available in the market, which further adds confession to the public psychology. This limits people's knowledge and understanding of the true version of Islam or any other religions. That means most people are not aware of different religious concepts, terminologies and ideas. Moreover, imaginary stories, cult characters, myths and superstitions are promulgated by various religious entities.

The female radicalization is taking place in contexts where extremist ideologies are taught in mosques, madrassas and families through informal group teaching called Talim. This is particularly a fact in the rural areas as the young women receive less education there, and they have to depend on the support of elderly family members and the religious instructors for the interpretation of religious texts. This certainly leaves them vulnerable to manipulation. The women in the rural areas are also vulnerable to unscrupulous religious teachers who distort narratives and preach extremist ideology to mislead children, teach only selected aspects of Islam and misinterpret the Quran to radicalize the youth. There is also a growing trend that female madrasas are now becoming more common. This is partially to do with the rising cost of education in the country, which discourages the parents in continuing their female children's education in mainstream schools. Although schooling for female students is free up to high school, due to escalating cost related to private tuition and other ancillaries, parents feel discouraged to send the girl child to mainstream schools. This may become a potential vacuum, which can be utilized by the extremist by setting up madrasas for female students to indoctrinate female minds at a young age.

Marriage and Extremism Dynamics

Early marriage is another driver behind extremism and its linkages with women in Bangladesh. The extremist individuals choose the young wives so that the process of radicalization can be started from an early age. In that sense, the process of radicalization that we see in Bangladesh is not a new phenomenon at all. Many women who have been radicalized or involved in extremist activities or involved in preaching misrepresented or misinterpreted version of Islam got married at an early age. Extended family and the family by marriage often help in creating strong ties with radical/extremist/terrorist networks. Women, given their multiple roles as wife or mother or sister or daughter of a terrorist, may pursue a role of advocate for their family members when a family male member is arrested on the ground of extremism or terrorist activities. However, one has to understand the distinction between women who are married into extremist groups against their will, and women who are part of deliberate and strategic marriages to guarantee the cohesiveness of the extremist groups. In the case of Bangladesh, organizations such as Hefazat-e-Islam or Hizb ut-Tahrir or Tabligh are more into strategic marriages where women take part deliberately.

In the urban areas, marriage leading to divorce or separation or perhaps extramarital affairs is often identified as a driver behind radical beliefs for a small portion of the female population. This tempts towards alternative social life that can be exploited by extremist religious groups. With the pace of economic growth, families are breaking apart, parents are not able to spend enough time with their children which results into lack of oversight on child's day-to-day life, and identity crisis and lack of support for mental well-being are becoming regular phenomena. Extremists are capable of exploiting these crises and coming up with narratives of religion as a solution to women's quest for freedom from these deprivations and allow her access to heaven for eternal peace and security.

Education and Extremism Dynamics

Bangladesh has an estimated population of 161 million, with 24.3 per cent of the population living in poverty and 12.9 per cent living in extreme poverty.[15] The World Bank noted that, between 2010 and 2016, poverty fell significantly, but in recent years, the rate of poverty reduction slowed down. Poverty fell faster in rural areas. Urban poverty rates declined from 21.3 to 18.9 percent, while rural poverty declined from 35.2 to 26.4 percent.[16] The growing economy has provided suitable growth for literacy in the country too. However, since there is no agreed definition of literacy, literacy in the context of Bangladesh is seen as 'those who can both read and write with understanding a short,

---

[15] World Bank, 'Bangladesh Continues to Reduce but at Slower Pace', 24 October 2017. Available at: http://www.worldbank.org/en/news/feature/2017/10/24/bangladesh-continues-to-reduce-poverty-but-at-slower-pace (accessed on 5 March 2019).

[16] Ibid.

simple statement about their everyday life'. This does not necessarily ensure quality or skills for employment or social progress. According to UNESCO, as of 2016, the literacy rate of youth female (age 15–24) in Bangladesh was 93.54 percent while its lowest value was 27.15 per cent in 1981. In the case of male, as of 2016, it was 90.91 per cent, while its lowest value was 44.36 per cent in 1981.[17] The literacy rate for an adult female (age 15 and above) in Bangladesh was 69.90 per cent as of 2016, while its lowest value was 17.97 in 1981. At the same time, adult male literacy stood at 75.62 per cent in 2016 and 39.73 per cent in 1981.[18] Thee rate of completion of education for the female student is 70.64 per cent, higher than male (61.95%), 11.39 per cent female has access to tertiary education (as of 2014), 5.36 per cent female receives technical and vocational education and training (TVET) after completing secondary education (as of 2016), and 6.32 per cent (as of 2012) female receives tertiary education.[19]

Lack of governance in education has a direct correlation with extremism in Bangladesh. The literacy rate does not necessarily guarantee the same life skills as that of an educated individual. Basic literacy and women's lack of formal education limit the choice of employment or livelihood available to them and pushes them either to poverty or to be dependent on others. The background of some of the female extremists indicates that they chose to join extremist organizations rather than succumb to poverty. The World Bank notes that marriage is the main cause of school dropout for girls in Bangladesh. The persistence of early marriage, especially in rural areas, has a severe negative impact on girls' future prospects for employment, especially in good-quality jobs. Moreover, continuing one's education after marriage is almost non-existent, especially among working-class communities.[20] A number of experts mentioned that the politicization of educational

---

[17] UNESCO, 'Bangladesh', 2017. Available at: http://uis.unesco.org/country/BD (accessed on 5 March 2019).

[18] Ibid.

[19] Ibid.

[20] World Bank, *Bangladesh Development Update 2017* (Dhaka: World Bank, 2017). Available at: https://openknowledge.worldbank.org/handle/10986/26642 (accessed on 5 March 2019).

curriculum and corruption in the education sector had created myriad debacle in creating a pool of enlightened and knowledgeable youth. Recently, the government has compromised with the demands of the Islamist groups to reform the primary and high school level textbooks as per the demands of Hefazat-e-Islam, a Qawmi Madrasa-based Islamist organization. The Daily Star noted, 'The politics of exclusion in the textbook leads ultimately to the exclusion of the minority communities. It promotes the politics of exclusivity. It seems our young minds are increasingly becoming Laboratories for fundamentalists and extremists propagating their views and ideologies'.[21] The extremist outfits or the Islamist entities are essentially focusing on curtailing women's growing employment and education rate so that they can retain their control over the significant portion of the country's population.

Employment Scenario and Extremism Dynamics

Lack of employment has a correlation with women's involvement with extremism. Women lack a meaningful job, and the underemployed young women are receptive to the financial and other material benefits which violent extremist organizations often provide. As a result, poverty can be a powerful motivator for radicalization. Bangladesh's employment sector for women shows that poverty-stricken young women have few livelihood options, which can be exploited by the militant groups. In the absence of a male, women are often forced to assume the role of the head of their households, but that comes with a great cost. These include responsibilities to provide support for expenses for their immediate (and often extended) families which at times become difficult due to the lack of a regular income, and often it results in a cycle of poverty. The economic and social scenarios of women employment show a mixed picture in Bangladesh.[22] The

---

[21] Shamsuddoza Sajen, Moyukh Mahtab, and Nahela Nowshin, 'Disturbing Deviations in Children's Books', *The Daily Star*, 21 January 2017. Available at: http://www.thedailystar.net/opinion/the-big-picture/disturbing-deviations-childrens-books-1348375 (accessed on 5 March 2019).

[22] Rejaul Karim Byron and Md Fazlur Rahman, 'Women Workforce Growing Fast', *The Daily Star*, 11 October 2015. Available at: http://www.thedailystar.net/frontpage/women-workforce-growing-fast-155149 (accessed on 5 March 2019).

World Bank notes, 'despite significant progress in recent decades, the labour market remains divided along gender lines, and progress towards gender equality seems to have stalled'. In Bangladesh, women account for most unpaid work, and when women are employed in paid work, they are overrepresented in the informal sector and among the poor.[23] The Bank further notes, 'While growth and stability are necessary to give women the opportunities they need, women's participation in the labor market is also a part of the growth and stability equation'.[24]

However, there are a number of barriers to employment that prevent women from participating in the labour market or entering from formal business sectors as entrepreneurs or industrialists. These barriers are both formal such as discriminatory inheritance laws or regulatory frameworks or administrative barriers, and informal barriers such as unwritten social norms and cultural practices restricting female participation in activities traditionally considered as the exclusive domain of men. Besides, the religious barriers or misinterpretation of religious scriptures often work as a barrier to employment for women. Moreover, the property law of inheritance often acts as a barrier to freedom. This acts as a social impediment to freely work or to choose profession. As such, lack of access to formal employment is another major concern that enables the end extremist to exploit the financial and economic situations of a woman. Lack of access to employment is equally a problem for the woman from rich and poor classes. These factors lead to extreme resistance, which is manipulated by the extremist entities. As a result, women become a weapon for extremist organizations. This is another cognitive space where extremists can play well. Moreover, extremist narratives are based on biological and mental needs. Extremist leaders exploit frustration, anxieties and grievances. These vary according to gendered needs. Furthermore, families often fail to provide emotional security that results in psychological volatility that may influence a person to become attracted to extremist narratives.

---

[23] World Bank, *Bangladesh Development Update*.
[24] Ibid.

Media and Extremist Dynamics

The perceived injustices against Muslims, as well as media profiling, create a socio-cognitive environment to give a feel of oppression among Muslim women, especially through their husbands and sons. This feeling of oppression and visuals of persecution has resulted in Bangladeshi Muslim women and men becoming defensive of their faith, and of themselves, given that their sense of faith is under attack. Although the appreciable role of media in mainstreaming gender has no alternative, nevertheless grievances regarding the projection of women as a source of discrimination between those who wear the veil and who endorses Western values are becoming more visible. Ultimately, the 'Western' culture is seen as a source of tension between the ethos and values of the Muslim tradition, and the projection of visual contents determined by the West which is diametrically opposite than Islamic traditions preached by the extremist entities. Ironically, the commodification of women and children as 'product' and 'sexual object' has become a part of both feminist and extremist narratives.

Public Security and Safety and Extremism Dynamics

The law and order scenario across the country remains a serious problem in Bangladesh. This has created psychological stress as well as a social problem among the public. The public confidence on the law enforcement agencies as well as political institutions has significantly deteriorated for which the personal safety and security of individuals have become a fundamental concern. Political rivalries, political-criminal nexus, criminal-political-religious ideologies nexus, religious violence, extremism and violence relating to ethnicity have created multidimensional insecurity narratives and rhetoric within the society. Although Bangladesh has been experiencing a number of forms of domestic security threats, violence related to elections is another concern that is helping people to find an alternative to existing ideas relating to democracy or governance. This is exactly where the extremist ideologies are coming into play.

Despite the government development works, issues related to corruption, quality of education, bad governance, lack of justice, access to health, adolescent health, decline in family values, decline in family as institution, eroding value system, failing social justice, digital divide, misuse of social media, inability to judge good news or fake news by the mass population, and lack of good media have compound effect on the society where economic inequality and marginalization of women are increasing. However, in several FGDs, conducted for this chapter, it was observed that the participants reiterated four common concepts related to women—respect, rights, revenge and relationship. Declining women's safety including allegations of law enforcement agencies' involvement in criminal activities and human rights violation against women has a significant effect on public psychology. It is believed that the heavy-handed tactics employed by the Bangladesh security and government apparatuses are in fact resulting in an increased radicalization among the youth as well as the senior populace in the country. Therefore, one of the law enforcement agency officers mentioned, 'underground politicians are engaged in a dangerous cycle of violence because of blunt and hardened security responses. This is generating more recruits, which in turn is further polarizing the communities in the country. For them, women will always be a natural target'.

The Bangladesh Bureau of Statistics (BBS) surveys indicate that domestic violence is one of the motivating factors behind woman's inclination towards extremism.[25] The surveys conducted in 2015 indicated a high prevalence of child marriage and domestic violence against women and girls. More than 10 million Bangladeshi women have experienced physical or sexual violence every year.[26] The survey further revealed that around 50 percent of women claimed that they were physically tortured while 27 percent said that they were sexually abused.[27] The surveys further show that in 15 percent of the cases,

---

[25] Bangladesh Bureau of Statistics, Statistics and Informatics Division, Ministry of Planning, Government of the People's Republic of Bangladesh, *Report on Violence against Women Survey 2015* (Dhaka, Bangladesh: Government of the People's Republic of Bangladesh, 2016).

[26] Ibid.

[27] Ibid.

men abused their wives both physically and mentally to 'control their behaviour'.[28] Moreover, women, aged between 15 and 34, tend to be at greater risk of being tortured.[29] The situation is a bit more disheartening for the women living in rural areas. The surveys indicated that 51.8 per cent of the rural women claimed that they are subject to regular abuse.[30] The rate of abuse is 48.5 per cent and 49.6 percent at the urban and national levels, respectively.[31] In the case of economic exploitation, less difference was found between the women living in urban and rural areas. In the case of rural women, it is 12 per cent, while in urban areas it is 10.2 per cent.[32]

The same BBS study shows that the prevalence of abusing wife tends to be less among the educated couples across the country.[33] The issue of reporting abuse to the Police is also a problem due to a number of factors, including social stigma related to rape, lack of confidence or access to avail legal support, and the fear of social and family pressures against the victim. The corruption of law enforcement agencies has also been identified as a major source that discourages women to reach out for legal support and physical safety. Between 2010 and 2012, the Bangladesh Police received 109,621 complaints regarding violence against women. Most of the women did not receive the justice they deserve because of the stigma surrounding violence against women.[34] A report produced by a local NGO, Odhikar, found that in 2017, 783 women were reported to be raped, out of which 225 women were above the age of 18 and 553 were below the age of 18.[35] The post-rape suicide rate is alarming too. The same report found that four women

---

[28] Ibid.

[29] Ibid.

[30] Ibid.

[31] Ibid.

[32] Ibid.

[33] Ibid.

[34] Ibid.

[35] Odhikar, 'Rape: January 2001–December 2017', Odhikar, Annual Human Rights Report 2017, (Dhaka: Odhikar), Available at: http://odhikar.org/wp-content/uploads/2018/01/Annual-HR-Report-2017_English.pdf (accessed on 7 May 2019).

and five children committed suicide after being raped in 2017.[36] It will not be unlike to find the link between the social stigma and the fact that a woman can consider the act of martyrdom as a path to eradicate her shame. A student of Jahangirnagar University said, 'it is not new that women are committing suicide after killing their children. There are a number of incidents in the society where the mother killed her children first and then committed suicide because of domestic violence or poverty. Extremists will use religious narratives to use the same vulnerabilities of women but give a new branding to the public'.[37]

Moreover, the narrative of, particularly in light of recent events in terms of politics, law, and order, as well as global politics, very much at play. These narratives represent a powerful asset for extremists. The appeal and credibility of this narrative stem, in part, from its internal coherence and logic: past and present victimization blend into a single, old but still unfolding drama, with past oppression making current one more tangible and deeply felt, and vice versa. Meanwhile, collective humiliation and the sense of a direct threat to personal honour and integrity are inherently connected and mutually reinforcing as well. The tremendous power of these processes and relationships—rooted, as they are, in history, current events as well as individual and group psychology—would appear to overshadow many 'underlying socio-economic conditions' in their importance.[38]

Public Health and Extremism Dynamics

The issues of adolescence health and emotional health have become another contributing factor in extremism. A study conducted by the Universiteit Utrecht found that adolescent age and violent extremism can have causal linkages. Four traits were identified if adolescent mental healthcare is not provided: (a) support for violent extremism is an extension of the underlying propensity for aggressiveness and lack of impulse control; (b) support for violent extremism is a response to poor

---

[36] Ibid.
[37] Personal conversation with the author.
[38] USAID, *Guide to the Drivers of Violent Extremism* (USAID, 2009). Available at: https://pdf.usaid.gov/pdf_docs/Pnadt978.pdf (accessed on 5 March 2019).

parenting and weak bonds to social institutions; (c) support for violent extremism is learned from the exposure to political violence and violent media; and (d) support for violent extremism is the result of negative coping with stress.[39] Religion would not become associated with support for violent extremism once the other factors are controlled at that age. Bangladesh society often exposes children to the aforementioned four scenarios. Bangladesh has an adolescent and youth population of approximately 52 million that constitutes one-third of the population.[40] This demographic structure is projected to remain for a long time while it is projected that by 2050, around 10–19 per cent of the population will include young people below the age of 30.[41]

The issues of child marriage and gender-based violence, which constantly pose a health risk, remain a critical factor in putting cognitive pressures on women to resort comfort and find refuge in misinterpreted versions of religion. A report produced by a government agency, National Institute of Population Research and Training (NIPORT), found that the age of first marriage among women has increased at a very slow rate over the past decades. The report showed that the median age at first marriage among women increased from 14.4 years in 1993–1994 to 16.1 years in 2014.[42] Fifty-nine per cent of women marry before the age of 18.[43] The birth rate among the girls between the age of 15 and 19 stands at 11.8 per cent.[44] The issue of mental health of the adolescent children as well as adolescent wives is

---

[39] Amy Nivette, Manuel Eisner, and Aja Murray, *Adolescent Risk Factors for Violent Extremism* (Cambridge: Universiteit Utrecht, Institute of Criminology Seminar, 2016). Available at: https://www.vrc.crim.cam.ac.uk/PDFs/amynivette-presentation (accessed on 5 March 2019).

[40] *The Daily Star*, 'Adolescents and Young People of Bangladesh', 2015. Available at: https://www.thedailystar.net/adolescents-and-young-people-of-bangladesh-54257 (accessed on 5 March 2019).

[41] Ibid.

[42] National Institute of Population Research and Training (NIPORT), Mitra and Associates, and ICF International, *Bangladesh Demographic and Health Survey 2014* (Dhaka, Bangladesh, and Rockville, MD: NIPORT, Mitra and Associates, and ICF International, 2016). Available at: https://dhsprogram.com/pubs/pdf/FR311/FR311.pdf (accessed on 5 March 2019).

[43] Ibid.

[44] Ibid.

virtually absent in Bangladesh. This is one area which has received the least priority despite the educational institutions, by law, are required to provide psychological counseling to both male and female students. Access to mental support or psychological counseling remains a major bottleneck for the women who are compelled to get married before the legal age of 18.[45]

Technology and Extremism Dynamics

The internet is another dynamic feature of technology that has remained under-researched. This is a tool that brings economic and cultural globalizations closer to society. While the use of technology by women is of paramount importance for development and gender empowerment, the extremist-women dynamics of information and communications technology (ICT) has not been taken into cognizance by the government. During this research, many participants mentioned that extremist online platforms provide almost 'fairy tale' like visual about women empowerment which is tempting for the marginalized or alienated women. The internet and dark web (DW) give a strong sense of empowerment to those who are suffering from multiple trauma, grievances and alienation. The idea of DW, as an emerging issue, is just intriguing to many urban and educated women. With the growth of technology and the availability of user-friendly intuitive apps, encrypted social messaging will continue to grow as 3G penetration increases and data rates drop. As a result, women's access to information technology will rise. What is missing here is the necessity to build the capacity of women to deal with online extremism and platforms such as the internet and DW. With the availability of easier intuitive software and familiarity with encrypted applications, access to DW will become much easier for women in rural areas in the future. A responsible officer mentioned that 'the detained female extremists are not technology-educated individuals. But many of them had access to Facebook and YouTube though'. 'Many contents indicate that their social networks influence vulnerable people's thought process that isn't good for society. The contents are Islamist scriptures, true as well as

---

[45] Ibid.

photoshopped visual projections of children being killed in different areas; women in distress; refugees, pornographic images of women and children, pictures of male and female Jihadists with guns, war and conflict photographs, and pilgrim locations. '65% of the news circulated on the ground of religion and social concerns are fake in social media'. 'This is an alarming trend. The rural women are not yet "trapped", but the urban women are falling into the extremist 'trap"'.

VEIL AS A YARDSTICK? IS IT A RELIGIOUS OBLIGATION OR SOCIAL COMPULSION?

The issue such as veil or hijab can be considered as a classic case study to examine women's inclusion in the extremist process. The issue of the veil has to be seen differently from the society such as Saudi Arabia and numerous other Muslim countries where the wearing of the hijab is not a choice but a compulsion. Perhaps, the veil is a contested concept and has long been associated with religious orthodoxy. Over the past few decades, radical thoughts preceded by an increase in the prevalence of the veil. However, along with ideological and religious compulsions to wear a veil, identity and recognition as 'good Muslim', and the fear of social exclusion and sexual harassment have emerged as important parts of the 'hijab phenomenon'. This sense of fear backed by deprivation, lack of justice and the narratives of victimization can well be a strong motivation behind violent extremism. Interestingly, Muslim women are not the ones who cover their heads in Bangladesh, but women from other religions wear the cover to avoid harassment in public places. However, at the perception level, women in the veil are stereotyped and often become subject to discrimination. The issues of harassment and gender violence alone tell how the social and political institutions help in creating an environment that fuels extremism. However, that does not mean veil has a direct connection with extremism.

The concerns regarding veil or Islamic dress code have become an important factor in the Islamic and extremist discourses in Bangladesh.[46]

---

[46] For the purpose of this study, 'the veil' can be understood as a generic term that may denote niqab, hijab, *burqah*, chador and dupatta.

This has become a subject that has been interpreted in various ways and has created a number of interpretations that has, directly and indirectly, influenced the processes related to prevention and countering violent extremism. A study conducted by the author has found that the Muslim women's manifestation of their Islamic denomination through veil and wearing appropriate clothes (in the case of men through growing beards and wearing clothes considered appropriate for them) signifies not only an expression of a new, Islamic shaped identity, but an expression of fear of insecurity posed by the society in terms of psychological and physical harms.[47] This is a complex identity based on multiple factors including ideologies, choice and social compulsion, rather than a fundamental reaction to modernity. The veil, a public symbol of Muslim identity, is often given a different meaning by its observers than the person actually wearing it. Therefore, this case is intended to explain Hijab's linkages with extremism and to identify the factors behind a Muslim woman's veil.

The security experts tend to believe that the proliferation of the veil or hijab is happening due to the lack of understanding of the Quranic verses and manipulation of women's weaker position in the society. The ideological interpretation of the veil appeals to many alienated young Muslims, which, in part, explains the growing popularity of the veil in the country. Religious misinterpretation is another important cause that has been a major factor behind the proliferation of veil among women. Many women are forced to be accompanied by a male guardian, known as a *mahram*, at all times, and are compelled to wear double-layered veils, loose abayas and gloves. In the absence of good governance and the rise of extremist narratives in the rural areas, the male members of the family, backed by conservative and radical individuals, impose the veil on women regardless of the age or socio-economic background. The radical and extremist organizations work hand in hand with the local Imams and religious groups. These groups have acquired enough sophistication to operate smoothly with the local communities, political parties and families. They are able to convince the local people to let their daughters get married even at

---

[47] A study conducted for the UN Women between 2017 and 2018.

the age of below 10, and create an atmosphere that women should only leave the house in exceptional circumstances and should remain 'private and veiled'.

The Imams and the family members often cast women as sinners and temptresses. Conservative Islam has revived the slander for contemporary times. Women have to be sequestered or contained lest they raise male lust and cause public disorder. One must note that the Bangladesh society considerably focuses on women's 'beauty' as an important standard for her marriage and social entitlements. This is one racial component that has been prevailing thorough multiple mediums—families, communities and media—which creates a clear social demarcation between 'pretty' and 'not pretty', and 'fair' and 'not fair.' Some young Muslim women endorse veil to liberate themselves from a modern culture that objectifies and sexualizes females. And for some young women, the veil is considered as a trend in fashion.

Women across society also believe that veils represent both religious arrogance and subjugation; they both desexualize and fervidly sexualize. Women are primarily seen as a sexual entity whose hair and body incite desire and disorder in the public space. The claims that the veil protects women from lasciviousness and disrespect carries an element of self-deception. What is even more concerning are young Muslim women. The minor children are being asked to wear veils, turned into sexual beings long before puberty.

Many scholars argued that the veiled women had provoked confrontations over their right to wear veils in courts, schools, colleges, shopping centres and workplaces. Many veiled women mentioned that the veil had become a source of discrimination in the workplace, which can be easily exploited by the extremist groups. This is a grey area that has to be addressed by the society. Several participants of this research mentioned that the idea of secularism had been misused in this country and it has become synonymous to anti-Islam. Liberalism is being tested by the new Islamic ardency. Overemphasizing on veil may become counter-productive. A student argued that a bank employee or a corporate employee could not dress the way he or she wants in an office environment. Therefore, following a religious dress code should not be a concern. One may wear it because of her choice or because of social compulsion. It has been found that some women choose to wear the veil because it is a family tradition or because it is the norm in their local area. The earlier studies conducted by the author also indicate that many women would wear hijab or niqab to demonstrate their belief and commitment to social modesty and religion. Some women tend to wear hijab for specific occasions, for example, family gatherings or social events; prayers or religious events; and to attend schools or work. A number of women with hijab tend to see hijab as a source of empowerment rather than as a symbol of patriarchal or parochial suppression. One of the main arguments here has been that the veil offers a social instrument and physical projection to take control of their body and to reject the social structure that marginalizes women. However, no correlation could be established between hijab and sexual empowerment in the context of Bangladesh. Nevertheless, some university students mentioned that hijab would give them social space and enable them to have partners, as they can remain socially sanctified, and to participate in a sexual relationship.

A recently published report by the ActionAid found that the atmospheres in public service-oriented places are not very women-friendly. Different forms of harassment including rude behaviour, inappropriate remarks, touching and catcalling are quite commonplace. Of the people interviewed, 80 per cent acknowledged that women are sexually harassed in marketplaces. Inappropriate touch in marketplaces is a common form of harassment in marketplaces as 50 per cent of women, and 35 per cent of men responded. The survey finds that another form of harassment in marketplaces includes bad comments, insults, forcefully sexual harassment, tug at women's clothes, physical torture, kidnap and even rape.[48] The fast-declining security situation and lack of cooperation of the law enforcement agencies are compelling

---

[48] Nawaz Farhin, 'Report: Sexual Harassment Is Commonplace in the Public Sector', *Dhaka Tribune*, 16 July 2017. Available at: http://www.dhakatribune.com/bangladesh/law-rights/2017/07/16/sexual-harassment-common-public-sector/ (accessed on 5 March 2019).

women to wear a veil in the public places. This is the thin line between security and compulsion. Women have fewer options to ensure their personal security in public places as well as in the private domains. As a result, the veil somehow protects women against sexual harassment and/or violence is by no means a minority view. As a result, to a significant segment of women, wearing the veil would remain as a source of empowerment rather than it being a tool that suppresses rights and freedom. So rather than being feared, it's more likely that women wearing hijab might fear others.[49]

During the research for this chapter, it has been found that not only the Muslim women wear a veil but also the minority women from Hindu and Buddhist communities wear the veil. Certainly, they wear a veil not because of religious compulsion but because of the logic that is related to public security and personal safety. However, several experts mentioned that it is a myth that there is a correlation between the veil, and a low incidence of sexual harassment and violence against women. The extremist and the fundamentalists propagate the idea of the veil so that they can blame women who do not cover themselves, as well as they insinuate that a woman who has been a victim of sexual harassment while wearing a headscarf must have done something to deserve it. As has been observed in all victim blame games, this prevents women from speaking up about sexual harassments or the violence they face. After all, stigmatization and stereotyping of women matter the most. Extremism ideologies are grounded on the stigmatization structure that Bangladeshi society often presents. Prevention of extremism will require a focus on women's capacity building to meet these challenges and their access to law enforcement and justice. Unless women are safe and secured, they will always be vulnerable to extremist recruitment. Therefore, the veil can be seen as a symbol that shows a fragile atmosphere where women can control herself to remain within the mainstream society or push herself into the extremist process as a revolt against the social and legal injustices.

---

[49] Peter Hopkins, 'Five Truths about the Hijab That Need to be Told', *The Conversation*, 12 November 2018. Available at: http://theconversation.com/five-truths-about-the-hijab-that-need-to-be-told-63892 (accessed on 5 March 2019).

The security dimension of the veil demonstrates the potential of the transformation of the mindset of women that can be easily tapped by the extremists. This transformative potential of mindset not only demonstrates how the adoption of the veil acts as a moment of metamorphosis in the lives of wearers but also has significant effects on the perceptions and actions of others. As a result, the veil-wearing women tend to project their garment as a self-verifying symbol of their religious identity. Religious identity allows them to seek recognition for their perceived identity against the reactions of 'modern people', whether those are elder relatives, or secular or non-Muslims outside of the family. Therefore, an indirect linkage between the veil and the growing extremism phenomena can be found. However, it is far too simplistic to identify the veil as a driver or enabling factor behind extremism in the country.

Extremist organizations offer rewards for loyalty and identity for women who feel left out in different social structures for multiple reasons. In the urban areas, the levels and causes of frustration are more linked with social fabric, and in the rural areas, it is economic and social weaknesses. Thus, these organizations create incentives, based on necessities, to work across society. They offer ready-made religious legal system and sharia law which can be used as an informal mechanism to govern and regulate social and economic lives.[50] The perceived personalized versions of Islamic laws and institutions, through male members or mothers in the family or through peer circles, thus offer a set of religious rules and regulations that can reduce uncertainty, create an environment for reputational benefits against humiliation, and ensure social capital to overcome social or personal injustice.

It has been observed that the extremist organizations cannot rely on university educated as well as young women who are involved with various religious groups solely on the fear to rule, and it must bring in new recruits all the time, so indoctrination is a major part of its agenda. The educated and urban women are the prime targets for managerial, planning and recruitment roles, while less educated and rural women

---

[50] Aisha Ahmad, *Jihad & Co.: Black Markets and Islamist Market* (Delhi: Oxford University Press, 2017).

are the prime targets for lower-tier activities, and to carry out field-level tactical activities including suicidal acts. Patriarchy, madrasas, local Imams, informal preaching and religious teaching such as Talim, hate propaganda, failures in local governance and social frustrations act as a conduit for their recruitment activities. Since the extremist organizations want to create future generations of willing members, they are careful about educating the young women as well. Female madrasas are on the rise, Talim is spreading all over the country including in the tertiary-level institutions, and the organized Islamist political parties are creating a conducive environment for changes in public school curriculum.

WHERE TO GO FROM HERE? COMPLEX STRUCTURAL INTERVENTIONS PREVENTING VIOLENT EXTREMISM

Given these dynamics, a broad set of recommendations can be proposed against extremism which would require multiple interventions taking different levels of needs of urban and rural women, and vulnerabilities faced by women of different age groups into consideration. Programmes should also be community-specific to address the structural causes of violent extremism. It has been found that the PVE programmes may lead to the stigmatization of communities. The interviews conducted by the author exposes that the women from the rural areas, in particular, often feel as a victim of parochial subjugation, but they would also view PVE programmes as pretexts for surveillance, intelligence and political activities carried out by the government of the day. This is a valuable lesson that must be factored into PVE programmes in Bangladesh. It is important that programmes should be responsive to the specific local context and ground realities contrary to the popular beliefs and urban perceptions.

Given the existing social capital and fabric, perhaps, Bangladeshi women play multiple roles when it comes to violent extremism: they can act as enablers and actors or they can play a key role in countering radicalization and extremism. Given the trends of extremism in Bangladesh, women's roles in violent extremism have been of four distinct types: (a) enforcers and informants, (b) recruiters, (c) influencers in their communities and families, and (d) executors or suicide bombers. These types of engagement mirror those in competing strategies to advance and counter violent extremism. The extremist profiles mentioned by the law enforcement agencies indicate that educated women are being recruited by extremist organizations, namely neo-JMB, to carry out recruitment and maintain organizational networks. There is a sharp division between the roles of extremist women from rural and urban areas. One law enforcement officer mentioned that urban women are tech-savvy and perform multiple roles, while rural recruits with no education would act more as foot soldiers or undertake suicidal activities.

Moreover, on the one hand, the multiple roles of women in society can help in creating an environment for violent extremism, and, on the other hand, their role can ensure deterrence against violent extremism too. Hence, it is important to consider women's role as the fundamental strategic tool for the prevention of violent extremism or any national strategies against violent ideologies. It is important to integrate women's roles in conflict prevention and to improve extremist early-warning and response systems through the integration of gender perspectives.[51] Specific focuses should be given on women and girls' health, education, and economic opportunity to create conditions for stable societies and lasting peace. This would require multiple gendered approaches and collaborative government and civil society activities that would provide impetus and framework for supporting the roles that women play in the prevention of violent extremism.[52] There is a need to promote dialogue and participation of women and women's organizations in discussions about the prevention of violent extremism practices, policies and strategies. The dialogues and community programmes should include the gender dimension of PVE, and then the civil society and the security sector should focus on creating multiple interfaces for engagement of women in the greater PVE framework.

---

[51] USIP, 'Engaging and Educating Women and Girls in the Prevention', USIP, 2014. Available at: https://www.usip.org/publications/2014/04/engaging-and-educating-women-and-girls-prevention-violent-conflict-and-violent (accessed on 5 March 2019).

[52] Ibid.

The PVE initiatives are likely to overlook many drivers of violent extremism, for example, influences within families pushing young people to radicalization or family-related factors or religion-related issues drawing women to violent extremism.[53]

The focus should further remain to facilitate mother-institutions interface to sensitize mothers regarding extremism. Reaching out to mothers is a difficult task since invisible barriers created either by the male companions or the society itself surround her. Therefore, mothers should have access to society and institutions through schools, teachers, community leaders, local government, NGOs and civil society to learn religion, participate in religious debates or gain access to knowledge regarding social transformations. One issue has become a major flashpoint—the issue of religious narratives. This has a profound implication on women regardless of class and localities. Women lack access to knowledge to counter-extremist narratives. Extremist narratives generally rely on disputable interpretations of facts and religious tenets, which, if left uncontested, might appear as the only truth. Multiple initiatives, thought holistic approach, need to be facilitated to promote the ideas of tolerance and pluralism. These programmes should not be designed to impose one narrative as the only truth but rather to provide women with a basket of ideas from which they can construct and choose the narratives they believe in. An atmosphere has to be fostered in which different opinions and critical views can be expressed and alternative narratives put forward, challenging terrorist and violent extremist ideologies from different angles.[54]

So far, th level of inclusion of women in extremism has NOT reached to an extent where prevention is not possible. However, the trend shows, ceteris paribas, the situation may become alarmingly threatening in a short space of time. Henceforth, the society is walking on thin ice. As seen in the earlier segments of this chapter, women's

---

[53] Iffat Idris and Ayat Abdelaziz, *Women and Countering Violent Extremism* (GSDRC, 4 May 2017). Available at: http://www.gsdrc.org/wp-content/uploads/2017/05/HDR_1408.pdf (accessed on 5 March 2019).

[54] OSCE, *Women and Terrorist Radicalization Final Report*, 2012. Available at: http://www.osce.org/atu/99919?download=true (accessed on 5 March 2019).

engagement in violent extremism manifests itself in myriad roles, and these contributions tend to ebb and flow over time, and vary between movements. Ultimately, the lines of logic defining women's roles within extremist groups tend to derive from context-specific ideological, religious, social and personal considerations. Women were participants in radical activities long before it became popular to pay attention to them. Women's supporting roles in terrorist organizations are often ignored due to the overemphasis on combatants within prevalent security discourse. This makes the young women vulnerable to structural exploitation by the extremist entities. The uncertainties related to career or financial future and insecurities related to physical safety or social justice tend to dominate their thought process that, in turn, creates fear regarding their identity and social acceptance. Therefore, providing accelerated learning programmes regarding religion, strengthening of education and skills training providing psychosocial support through qualified professionals, and access to justice should remain as the core PVE components and tools to unlock the potential of the women as an enabler for peace and stability.

Chapter 10

Perception of the Pathways towards Radicalization among Urban Youth in Bangladesh

Bulbul Siddiqi

Radicalization has become a contested phenomenon in academia in recent times. However, it became a concerning issue in Bangladesh since the last decade when series of bombs blasted in various places in Bangladesh and lately after the attack at the Holey Artisan restaurant in the diplomatic zone of Dhaka city. Recent attacks in Bangladesh indicate that many of these radicalized youth were from diverse socio-economic classes with an elite educational background. Under this backdrop, the chapter aims to understand and explore the youth's perception on the exposure and expression of radicalization in the urban space of Bangladesh. By applying a qualitative research method, this chapter shows that the process of radicalization takes place in various forms. It may begin at a very earlier age of a person. It also argues that gradual isolation, a 'self-feeling' notion of alienation from family and society, and the crisis of identity force people towards a globalized Islam. The chapter also shows that 'religious globalization' provides an easy access to various forms and practices of Islam, which may direct them in radicalization.

INTRODUCTION

Radicalization has become a global and contested term in the new millennium because of various terrorist attacks worldwide. However, lack of scholarly consensus of defining radicalization[1] put academics in a complex situation in the study of radicalization. There also remains a sense of ambiguity in the definition of radicalization[2] and sometimes it is poorly defined.[3] Despite the definitional aspect of the concept, another challenge arises due to the nature of the subject that makes studying terrorism and radicalization difficult.[4] In addition, seeing radicalization primarily connected with terrorism makes the concept problematic.[5] The term has been defined in the academia in various ways. One of the definitions is to see it by associating it vaguely with ideology, although ideology is not a pre-condition for terrorist acts; rather, it has to be seen as a political expression of religion.[6] Therefore, there is a need to identify and define what ideology is and what roles does it play in the context of radicalization among its followers.[7] Furthermore, there is a lack of qualitative data, for example, ethnographic account of radicalization.[8] Thus, scarcity of empirical evidence also makes the concept difficult. Despite all these difficulties, the notion of radicalization itself is a very complex phenomenon to understand; therefore, academics need to deal it with a highest caution. If we do not understand the

---

[1] M. Crone, 'Radicalization Revisited: Violence, Politics and the Skills of the Body', *International Affairs* 92, no. 3 (2016): 587–604.

[2] P. R. Neumann, 'The Trouble with Radicalization', *International Affairs* 89, no. 4 (2013): 873–893.

[3] R. Borum, 'Radicalization into Violent Extremism I: A Review of Social Science Theories', *Journal of Strategic Security* 4, no. 4 (2011): 7–36. doi:10.5038/1944-0472.4.4.1.

[4] P. Neumann and S. Kleinmann, 'How Rigorous Is Radicalization Research?' *Democracy and Security* 9, no. 4 (2013): 378.

[5] M. Hornqvist and J. Flyghed, 'Exclusion or Culture? The Rise and Ambiguity of the Radicalisation Debate', *Critical Studies on Terrorism* 5, no. 3 (2012): 319–334.

[6] Crone, 'Radicalization Revisited'.

[7] Ibid.

[8] A. Silke, 'The Devil You Know: Continuing Problems with Research on Terrorism', *Terrorism and Political Violence* 13, no. 4 (2001): 1–14. doi:10.1080/09546550109609697, cited in Crone, 'Radicalization Revisited'.

boundary between 'extremism' of thoughts and 'extremism' of method, it may create a confusing situation while developing counter-terrorism policies.[9] The situation in Bangladesh is not very different, as the study of extremism and radicalization has derived, motivated and influenced by the Western academic perspectives and approaches.

The concept has recently become a concerning issue in Bangladesh since the last decade when a series of bombs blasted simultaneously in various places in Bangladesh.[10] Moreover, the situation has become worse after the attack at Holey Artisan restaurant located in the elite diplomatic zone of Dhaka city on 1 July 2016.[11] The entire country was shocked witnessing this disastrous attack where a number of people were killed by a group of radicalized youth. Therefore, it requires an effective mechanism of counter-violent extremism in Bangladesh.[12] It was assumed in the past that some '*qawmi* madrasa' (traditional Islamic education system who are independent of the government and determine their own curriculum) educated students or affiliated people were only responsible for such terrorist attacks in Bangladesh. However, recent attacks after July 2016 in Bangladesh indicate that many of these radicalized youth were from diverse socio-economic classes with an elite educational background. The study conducted by Riaz and Parvez show that the recent militants in Bangladesh were from better-off family with higher educated background.[13] This shows the diversity and complexity around the radicalization discourse in Bangladesh.

---

[9] A. Richards, 'From Terrorism to "Radicalization" to "Extremism": Counterterrorism Imperative or Loss of Focus?' *International Affairs* 91, no. 2 (2015): 371–380.

[10] See more at: http://archive.thedailystar.net/2005/08/18/d5081801011.htm (accessed on 8 December 2018).

[11] See more at: https://www.bbc.com/news/world-asia-36692613 (accessed on 8 December 2018).

[12] S. E. Khan, 'Bangladesh: The Changing Dynamics of Violent Extremism and the Response of the State', *Small Wars & Insurgencies* 28, no. 1 (2017): 191–217. doi:10.1080/09592318.2016.1266127

[13] A. Riaz, 'Who Are the Bangladeshi "Islamist Militants"?' *Perspectives on Terrorism* 10, no. 1(2016). Available at: http://www.terrorismanalysts.com/pt/index.php/pot/article/view/485/html (accessed on 8 December 2018); A. Riaz and S. Parvez, 'Bangladeshi Militants: What Do We Know?' *Terrorism and Political Violence* 30, no. 6, 944–961 (2018). doi 10.1080/09546553.2018.1481312

In this chapter, radicalization has been used as a way of adopting or following radical thoughts and transformation of lifestyle that may not necessarily lead towards extremism or terrorism. This definition is partly adopted from Borum.[14] In order to explore this complex phenomenon, the chapter is an attempt to understand the perception of urban youth in Bangladesh on various forms of radicalization. The chapter also aims to explore their perception of primary pathways of radicalization among the youth in the urban space of Bangladesh. The chapter shows that the process of radicalization takes place in various forms. It may begin at a very earlier to later age of a person, which follows a very complex path. In such a complex context, first the chapter argues that the gradual isolation and 'self-feeling' notion of alienation from the both family and society expose many youth into radical ideology and they use religion to justify their acts. Sometimes these youth become an easy target by various religious groups who may have radical views. Second, crisis of identity someway forces people towards a globalized Islam that provides them a sense of belongingness to a wider Muslim community. Thirdly, 'religious globalization' is a new way to know about various forms and practices of Islam that has become easier for many youth in the country, which may expose them to radicalization. These three conditions may direct them in the primary phase of radicalization among many urban youth in Bangladesh.

METHODS

A qualitative method was adopted to understand the perception of the pathways of radicalization among the youth. First, one-to-one in-depth interview (IDI) was conducted in a private setting to get more detailed information from university going students, media personnel and security analysts on radicalization. Second, desk review of contents published in various leading newspapers on radicalization and extremism in recent times after heinous terrorist attacks at Gulshan and other places in Bangladesh were conducted in this research. In relation to this method, selected cases of alleged radicalized youth published in various newspapers were analysed to explore the trigger points of radicalization.

---

[14] Borum, 'Radicalization into Violent Extremism'.

ALIENATION FROM THE SOCIETY AND FAMILY

Social isolation is seen as one of the key factors to understand poverty and well-being of the community people.[15] However, this phenomenon is also very relevant to understand the process of radicalization among many youth as the notion of isolation was evident among many alleged terrorist attackers.[16] The idea of isolation in the context of radicalization works in two different ways. First, sometimes people withdraw themselves deliberately from everyday interactions from their family members, society and friends out of frustration. This sense of isolation acts as a trigger point for many to be attracted by various radical preachers both online and offline. It was evident that people with extreme isolation seemed to be an easy target of many radical Islamic groups in many educational institutes. Hug also argues that isolation from family and peers plays a vital role in radicalization.[17] Second, when a radical group gradually influences and motivates a targeted person towards their way of life by isolating him or her from family and social life. Isolating them from social and family sphere acts as an important factor to radicalize and 'brainwash' them in an easy way. Thus, it creates an easy access to offer a good companionship as friend and gradually a close friend.

A father of an alleged terrorist attacker, who was killed in a gunfight with the police at Sholakia (a small town located in another district close to Dhaka) in 2016 while plotting a terrorist attack in a mass gathering of Eid congregation, claimed that he hardly had friends.[18] After analysing

---

[15] D. Zavaleta, K. Samuel, and A. C. Mills, *Social Isolation: A Conceptual and Measurement Proposal* (Oxford: Oxford Poverty & Human Development Initiative [OPHI], University of Oxford, 2014).

[16] *Prothom Alo*. (2016, July 28). *They Were Isolated from Family (in Bengali)*. Retrieved December 8, 2018, from Prothom Alo: https://www.prothomalo.com/bangladesh/article/928180

[17] E. C. Hug, *The Role of Isolation in Radicalisation: How Important it is?* (MA thesis, Monterey, CA: Naval Postgraduate School, 2013).

[18] S. Mollah and J. Mahmud, '"He Cannot Be My Son" Says Slain Sholakia Attacker's Father', *The Daily Star*, 10 July 2016. Available at: https://www.the-dailystar.net/frontpage/he-cannot-be-my-son-1251436 (accessed on 5 December 2018).

reports published in newspaper, a similar pattern was found where convicted youth either did not have friends and at some points of time they gradually became isolated from their friends, family and started to mingle with a new circle of friends who thought to be Islamists. The leading Bengali daily newspaper *Prothom Alo* (2016)[19] reports after the raid known as 'Storm 26'[20] that all of the killed 'militants' were isolated from the family for a longer time.

Family crisis, too much exposed into Westernized life, complexity in relationship and depression were the frequently mentioned issues in a discussion with a female university student. In her discussion, she mentioned that

> Many students in highly reputed English medium schools have problems with their family members. They have less cohesive relationship with others, and tendency of spending less time with their family on a regular basis is also a big problem for them, which left them living an isolated life. Everyone is busy with their own life. Heavy dependency in Westernized lifestyle, low family bonding with less interaction and lack of 'true' friends sometimes put them in a serious depression. These are some of the reasons why many people are getting into religion for peace [...] Sometimes they were associated by some wrong people with wrong interpretation of Islam that force them to think about to bring a radical change in the society by their action. (A university student, female)

Sense of feeling left out, less important in the family and isolation from friends sometimes creates depression. Her entire discussion refers to the process of how isolation or feeling of alienation could be a serious problem for many youth. Sometimes, inability to express views also creates a sense of alienation. A respondent mentioned about the young members of Jamaat-e-Islami that their inability to express their political thoughts and activities in public sphere leaves them in isolation. An international media professional and journalist expressed that

---

[19] *Prothom Alo* 2016.
[20] See more at: https://www.thedailystar.net/city/9-militants-killed-joint-drive-kalyanpur-1259647 (accessed on 5 December 2018).

If youth with Islamic political ideology feel that they do not have the option or choice of expressing their political ideology; they would certainly look for an alternative platform to express their views. This may create the environment for many to work in a different form. People from Jamaat or Shibir could join in another radical platform to bring changes, which you can say, a type of resistance. Bangladesh is a predominantly Islam majority country, we would not be able to deny the existence of many political parties based on Islamic ideology. The State should think about these people. Arresting them and bringing them into the judicial process would not bring a solution of this problem of radicalization in the long run. They have to be accommodated into the political and democratic framework. (An international media professional, male, Dhaka)

Adopting Westernized culture is seen as one of the ways of creating differences between parental and the younger generation that also leads towards a sense of isolation from the traditional social sphere. At some point, the younger generation may feel living in a situation of 'in-between' two cultures that creates a sense of conflict in their minds. Another respondent, who is also a journalist, mentioned that

Scarcity of cultural activities is a problem. In Dhaka city people do not have much options to take their children for cultural activities [...] There was a time in the 1980s and 1990s where in every neighbourhood used to have clubs or society for the younger people, where they used to cultivate and practice Bengali culture. They used to learn songs, dance and stage drama. But now a days, we do not have such activities, thus the youth are moving towards a life of less social activities in their everyday lives. Adopting radical thoughts or even participating in a so called jihad looks very heroic for them. (A journalist, female, Dhaka)

The government of Bangladesh also took various measures at the university level to motivate students to learn the history and culture of Bengal. One of such initiatives is to offer a mandatory course on 'emergence of Bangladesh' at the university level arguing that if the youth are to be taught about the history and culture of Bangladesh, they probably won't be attracted by radical ideology. The representatives of the government also propagate this idea in many public events[21] as well. However, the entire idea is to keep the youth engaged in a 'secular' environment. The whole idea of 'Bengalines' is seen as 'secular' as the creation of Bangladesh was based on the idea of 'Bengalines'.[22] However, the debate of being Bengali and Muslim at the same time is still an issue among the youth in the current time. Staying 'in-between' two cultures is another example of such dilemma that leads towards the crisis of identity among many youth. For example, the journalist talked about an alleged radical person who confessed that it was a dilemma for him whether he is Muslim first or Bengali, then he decided to consider himself a 'true' Muslim and transformed his entire life in an extreme path. He believed that he felt connected with the global Muslim *ummah* who are vocal against the 'oppression against the Muslim' around the world.

The crisis of identity has been an important issue for many Muslim youth globally. This is particularly evident in the diasporic situation.[23] This is also very important aspect for the youth in Bangladesh. Siddiqi, shows how Ijtema[24] in Bangladesh has become a symbolic congregational gathering of the Tablighi Jamaat[25] that reflects the connectedness with the global Muslim community.[26] Many other researches show that crisis of identity forces people to think to be connected with a wider

---

[21] Author was also present in many public events that were organized to create awareness against extremism and radicalization among the youth, where they propagate this.

[22] S. Rozario, *Purity and Communal Boundaries: Women and Social Change in a Bangladeshi Village* (Dhaka: UPL, 2001).

[23] B. Siddiqi, *Becoming 'Good Muslim': The Tablighi Jamaat in the UK and Bangladesh* (Singapore: Springer, 2018).

[24] *Ijtema* refers to annual congregation of the Tablighi Jamaat.

[25] Tablighi Jamaat is a piety movement that claimed to be an 'apolitical' movement, although the idea of being 'apolitical' notion of the movement was contested by many researchers, for example, Y. Sikand, 'The Tablighi Jama'at and Politics: A Critical Re-Appraisal', *The Muslim World* 96, (2006): 175–195; A. Alexiev, 'Tablighi Jamaat: Jihad's Stealthy Legions', *Middle East Quarterly* 12, no. 1 (2005). Available at: http://www.meforum.org/686/tablighi-jamaat-jihads-stealthy-legions (accessed on 22 July 2017).

[26] B. Siddiqi, 'Purificaiton of Self: Ijtema as a New Islamic Pilgrimage', *European Journal of Economic and Political Studies* 3, SI (2010): 133–150.

Muslim *ummah*. In the context of Bengali urban youth, the tendency of prioritizing Islam over the idea of Bengalines sometimes forces people to think to be part of the wider Muslim community. Furthermore, this is also evident that the urban youth sometimes feel a sense of belongingness to the wider and global Muslim community who are suffering. Imagination of belonging to a global community is seen as one of the key aspects of identity formation.[27] Crisis of identity often leads towards the path of radicalization.[28] Identity issue comes from two points. Many youth feel connected with the Muslim *ummah* as part of their Islamic piety. The sufferings of Muslims in various places in the world create a sympathetic psychological state of mind among many youth. Thus, many feel that they should translate their radical thoughts in radical action. In this context, a case from Bangladesh is quite relevant to understand how the sense of sufferings of global Muslim has been used to motivate people to act upon jihadi ideology. A young engineer was motivated by the members of an online Islamic group about moving to Syria for helping oppressed Muslims. Finally, he moved to Syria to help liberate those oppressed Muslims, although he came back with a realization that his act was not right.[29] Such situations can also be seen as cultural identity shift of an individual.[30]

---

[27] B. Anderson, *Imagined Communities: Reflections on the Origin and Spread of Nationalism* (London: Verso, 2006); A. Appadurai, 'Disjuncture and Difference in the Global Cultural Economy', *Theory, Culture & Society* 7 (1990): 295–310; G. Baumann, *Contesting Culture: Discourses of Identity in Multi-Ethnic London* (Cambridge: Cambridge University Press, 1996).

[28] T. Choudhury, *The Role of Muslim Identity Politics in Radicalsiation: A Study in Progress* (London: Department for Communities and Local Government, 2007).

[29] S. S. Alam, 'Self Realisation of Kamrus Salam after Going to Sirya (in Bengali)', 5 February 2017. Available at: https://www.prothomalo.com/bangladesh/article/1074713 (accessed on 5 December 2018); Z. Ahsan, 'Dhaka–Syria–Dhaka: Narrative of a Bangladeshi Engineer Reveals How He Reached Raqqa to "Fight for Muslims" and Returned Home "Disillusioned"', *The Daily Star*, 3 February 2017. Available at: https://www.thedailystar.net/frontpage/dhaka-syria-dhaka-1355287 (accessed on 8 December 2018).

[30] T. Abbas and A. Siddique, 'Perceptions of the Processes of Radicalisation and De-radicalisation among British South Asian Muslims in a Post-industrial City', *Social Identities* 18, no. 1 (2012): 119–134.

ISLAM AND GLOBALIZATION

Globalization is de-territorializing the world in many ways where people feel connected with many expressions of the global practices going beyond the local boundary.[31] In such context, Oliver Roy used the term of 'globalized Islam' to understand the contemporary expression of Islam.[32] Global version of Islam has particular appeal among the urban youth in Bangladesh in a different and attractive way. Thus, many youth in Bangladesh have been adopting the elements from global Islam. Furthermore, South–South migration is also seen as a potential threat of transmitting radical thoughts and acts.[33] While observing the impacts of Westernized cultural element among the lives of the youth, it is evident that many times, the younger generation reject Westernized cultural element as this creates conflict in one's own mind.[34]

But at the same time many youth passionately follow global scholars on Islam, for example, Mufti Menk,[35] Nouman Ali, Dr Bilal Philip[36] and others. Many respondents reported that they are very much 'trendy' to follow. This shows how personal quality or 'charisma' may have impacted many youth to turn to Islamic practices. Many youth go beyond just practicing Islam and they believe that taking action is the next step. Many of the cases of radicalized youth in contemporary Bangladesh were revealed who initially had doubt in their mind about the Westernized culture that forces them towards the global Islam and then decided to act upon their learning that they often justified and called 'jihad'. It was reported that some attackers of Holey Artisan

---

[31] A. Appadurai, 'Global Ethnoscapes: Notes and Queries for a Transnational Anthropology', in *Interventions: Anthropologies of the Present*, ed. R. Fox (Santa Fe: School of American Research, 1991), 191–210.

[32] O. Roy, *Globalized Islam: The Search for a New Ummah* (Columbia: Columbia University Press, 2006).

[33] M. Hasan, 'South–South Migration and Security Risks: Political Islam and Violent Extremism in the Shadow of Globalisation in Bangladesh', *India Quarterly* 73, no. 3 (2017): 1–15.

[34] B. Siddiqi, 'Tablighi Jamaat: Why This Conflict and Dividation (in Bengali)', Prothomalo, 6 December 2018. Available at: https://www.prothomalo.com/opinion/article/1568609 (accessed on 8 December 2018).

[35] See his personal website: https://muftimenk.com/

[36] See his personal website: http://bilalphilips.com/

restaurant used to listen to the 'hate preach' of Anjem Chowdhury.[37] According to *The Guardian*, Anjem Chowdhury was accused of influencing at least 100 British jihadis.[38] In such context, internet materials, for example, web text, online articles and videos (YouTube and others) of many international Islamic scholars are now easily accessible, which were not very available in the past. These new technologies have been used to develop a global network or to be part of a global network. Sometimes, many youth become a part of local, national and even international Islamic study circles that may motivate many towards a radical thought. First, it creates a doubt in their previous ideology and in the end justifies the radical thoughts.

The following discussion with a female university student would be relevant and clarify further. Back in her college life, she used to watch videos, which were shared by her friends on Facebook. She liked the way of Mufti Menk and Nouman Ali. She thought their way of preaching was more youth centric and they were more liberal and precise. Their teachings influenced and helped her a lot. In answering the question, whether these contents are beneficial, she thinks these are very beneficial. She added that these contents helps people a lot to understand the Quran and the teachings of the Prophet more clearly. She also added that 'however, there are malcontents on the internet, so people need to identify good contents as well'. In her entire discussion the later part is very important to understand the radicalization process in this digital age, where she added that people should be more careful about what to listen and what not to, because sometimes recruiters wait to trap people online for radicalization in their own ways.

---

[37] K. Ahmed, 'The Issue of IS in Politics (in Bengali)', Prothomalo, 19 August 2016. Available at: https://www.prothomalo.com/opinion/article/950620 (accessed on 8 December 2018).

[38] V. Dodd and J. Grierson, 'Revealed: How Anjem Choudary Influenced At Least 100 British Jihadis', *The Guardian,* 16 August 2016. Available at: https://www.theguardian.com/uk-news/2016/aug/16/revealed-how-anjem-choudary-inspired-at-least-100-british-jihadis (accessed on 8 December 2018).

In this context, another university going male student expressed his views where he thinks that these contents are in general dangerous for practitioners. He further stated

> Anyone can broadcast on YouTube with Islamic content but sometimes they can be misleading. It is the viewers' discretion to cross-check that if the content have proper referencing then it is fine. But if the content is misleading and if people believe in them then it is harmful for them [...] if anyone refers to the *Quran* or *Hadith*, people should double check before acting on anything believing online preaching. (A university student, male)

Another male student expressed a similar opinion.

> Usually, in mosques, after prayers, there can hardly be any scope for the preachers to say something wrong about Islam but that is very much possible on YouTube and other platforms. It is difficult to protest against the wrong interpretations at that moment. So there should be a check and balance system in online method of preaching Islam. There should be censoring in case of this type of contents on social media platforms. The censoring system of the social media platforms does not cover anything apart from hate speech. (A university student, male)

If we examine these comments carefully, one thing would be very clear that people have to be very cautious if they want to believe and keep practicing these in their lives. Another young female student (Dhaka) emphasizes on having a censorship in internet content as this could easily confuse people with a different interpretation of religious texts. She mentioned that

> From the philosophy of *Qiyas*[39] people preach Islam. It is beneficial indeed. However, it is evident that a censorship on the contents needs to be there because mostly people do not verify the sources and in

---

[39] *Qiyas* refers to the process of reaching in a decision on a particular issue that does not have straightforward directive based on the Qur'an or *Sunnah* through an analogy according to the Islamic law. See more at: http://www.oxfordislamicstudies.com/article/opr/t125/e1936 (accessed on 8 December 2018).

general the practice in our society is not such. People have to be very careful to take in those contents. (A university student, female, Dhaka)

Furthermore, the practice of adopting a different lifestyle by many young people is not pleasant in her eyes at all, because in her opinion most of the people do this because of radicalization. They do not understand Islam and its teachings; rather, they just do this to be socially acknowledged. They do not understand it properly and it opens up a horizon where radicalization of many sorts comes up. She thinks if people understand this religion and take it up, that is okay. If people just do this because of social recognition, especially to satisfy a particular group, it is alarming and we see the rise of extremism. So this is clear that online preaching could be very dangerous. It was found that a significant number of radicalization in Bangladesh took place using online platform.[40]

RADICALIZATION AS A PROCESS

Radicalization is a process,[41] where a targeted person transforms gradually. It does not happen overnight.[42] In addition, radicalization could happen among individuals, group and even at the mass level.[43] This is not a sudden change or transformation. In many cases parents, relatives or even other close family members are unable to interpret changes among a radicalized person, therefore, they cannot act upon logically to deal with such situation at an early stage. A similar context was evident when a sister of a radicalized student was expressing her and the family's frustration at a public event against extremism afterwards the death of her brother during a police raid. She said that

> I noticed that my brother was changing slowly, but unfortunately other family members and I could not predict what exactly was going on their beloved brother. When we saw the death news of my brother and his

---

[40] Riaz and Parvez, 'Bangladeshi Militants'.

[41] Crone, 'Radicalization Revisited'.

[42] Neumann, 'The Trouble with Radicalization'.

[43] C. McCauley and S. Moskalenko, 'Mechanisms of Political Radicalization: Pathways toward Terrorism.', *Terrorism and Political Violence* 20 (2008): 415–433.

connection with extremist group, we could connect his changes and transformation. (An undergraduate student, female, Dhaka)

This statement shows that the impacts of the process of radicalization could be visible in some cases. In some cases it could have a drastic change. Sometimes it could have a very slow and gradual shift into a different lifestyle. However, in most cases people see someone transform their activities, behaviour and attire towards religion that is generally seen as becoming a practicing Muslim in a good way. Family members could hardly identify at this early stage whether he or she is in the process of radicalization. This is really a challenging issue not only for the parents but also for academic and researchers as how should they define the process of radicalization at this early stage. If we need to understand the early stage of radicalization, we also need to understand how radical groups target schools, mosques and the neighbourhood to recruit new members.

Schools and mosques are the two important spaces found to be evident in various cases where seniors target exceptionally brilliant and religious students.[44] One of the alleged members of Jamaat-ul-Mujahideen Bangladesh (A Islamist group known as JMB) stated that he was recruited when he was in his 9th grade at school. He was also known as a member of Ahle Hadith[45] at the university.[46] Going to mosque at a very earlier stage is seen as a very good practice, and is appreciated by family members and the society as well. Furthermore, participation in mosque-based religious discussion is not seen as a suspicious activity. Therefore, students or young people generally become an easy target and stay under long observation of many recruiters. The following case shows how students are being targeted at their neighbourhood while praying or going to mosque regularly.

---

[44] In this context, the term has been used to refer practising Muslim.

[45] Ahle Hadith is an Islamic movement who claims to be the followers of *Sunnah* of the Prophet Muhammad; they highly prioritize the *Sunnah* in their everyday lives as practice.

[46] Prothom Alo. (2016, August 19). *Information of 10 more Female Militants were Found (in Bengali).* Retrieved December 8, 2018, from Prothomalo: https://www.prothomalo.com/bangladesh/article/951010?print=1

A grown up man told about a story of his life how he and his close friend was approached and targeted by an Islamist group when he was at school in the mid-1990s.

I was a very good student, so was my friend. We both were serious about our education and thought that we should pray regularly and make *dua* to God for a better result. We used to go to the mosque regularly to pray, especially in the afternoon and evening prayer. The mosque was not too far from our house. We used to live near Gulshan. We used to take a walk every day in the afternoon and prayed at the same mosque near our school. We hanged out together and went back to home after the evening prayer at the mosque. One day, a university-going student, we used to call him *bhaiya* (brother), came to us and introduced himself in a humble and nice way by appreciating us that we are too young but very serious about praying at mosque. Later on I realized that he had been observing us for a long period of time prior to approaching us. We were so excited that a university-going student was praising us. He started to spend a little time with us almost every day. I could not say how long he used to talk to us, but after some days, he proposed us that we should start reading some books after school and discuss these after the prayer. We did not find any problem with that proposal. He also told us that after reading books we could organize a quiz and that he would give a prize to the winner. We were surprised one day by seeing many other school going kids with him. We started to read books on Islam especially the life history of the Prophet and *sahabi* [companions of the Prophet]. Reading through such history gave us a detail perspective of the rich heritage and history of Islam. I now could realize that he deliberately referred those books to ignite feelings about Islam among us and to work for the Islamic *ummah*. The competition ended very well and we were surprised to see that both of our friends were the top scorers. I now realize that he deliberately did to develop a soft corner of Islamic movement among us. He still did not say anything about his mission even it was after a month or two. I can remember that our exam would be starting soon and we were not regular at the mosque. At some point, we stopped going to mosque as we wanted to concentrate more on the studies. One afternoon, I heard that my dad was shouting at a man. I came out from my room and saw that my dad was telling that *bhaiya* to not contact my friend and I further. That was the last time, I saw him. My friend and I were very fortunate those days that he did not follow us further. I could clearly remember the day when my dad's bold role protected me and my friend from being radicalized. After all these years, I could not share this story with anyone. I was afraid to share it, but I would surely be watchful about my children and their friends as well. This was learning for me. But, I know that this would be much more challenging for me in this millennium where everything happens online as we are living in the time of a digital era. I think every parent should be watchful and careful about raising their kids. If you look into the recent radicalized cases, most of the parents were not very careful and were very reluctant about the 'privacy' of their children. I see many parents who encourage their kids to live in isolation from the family by forcing them to study. But no one knows if anyone exposes to a radical thoughts or groups online using their so-called privacy. (A middle-aged man, Dhaka)

A similar attempt of was made to a university student when he was at school. He told that .people who were actively looking for students to recruit from school also wanted to nurture a master–disciple relationship for grooming their targets for a longer period for an effective conversion into their ideology. He was targeted by few members of Hizb ut-Tahrir (HT) as he could remember as it was back in 2008. He remembered that HT talked about armed jihad and wanted to recruit people for war against *Jahiliyaa*.[47] As he stated further,

When I was in class eight in 2008, my university-going house tutor (did not mention the name of the university) wanted to motivate me with his personality and benevolent behaviour to join their so-called 'religious circle'. I was also targeted at the school as well by some big brothers (students from senior sections of the school) who are into some radical groups and I denied joining them with a fear. (A university student, male)

He could not remember the name of the student-based organization that was working actively in the school, but he was very suspicious with their approach and decided not to join. He later on assumed that as he was very religious from the school, this made him an easy target. He further talked about his perception on how people were being targeted

---

[47] *Jahiliyaa* refers to a time of ignorance classically understood as the pre-Muhammad age in Arabia (Siddiqi, *Tablighi Jamaat,* 175).

and finally motivated to act upon radical ideology. He mentioned that many people who are into Westernized life, for example, exposed into 'clubbing', 'drinking' and physical relationship that is prohibited in Islam, are also targeted in urban areas by creating a sense of fear of the life hereafter as they are not doing right. As he stated, 'you would go to the hell fire due to your Westernized lifestyle. However, there is a way to rectify this only if you commit yourself to be engaged in jihad for good'. This could be a very early stage of motivating people as my respondent used the term 'brainwash'. It is their deliberate approach to inject the idea of doubt in the mind of the targeted person explaining that the Westernized life is forbidden and is not appreciated in Islamic context.

In another instance, a young student told me that he joined in a student wing of a particular Islamic group because of two reasons: one is for the peer pressure, where most of his friends joined in; and the second is to getting spiritual benefit. He was also influenced and motivated by one of his cousins who was a teacher in a college at Dhaka. As he mentioned that

> Most of my friend circles are very religious and they were the members of Chatro Shibir (student wing of Jamaat Islami Bangladesh: a religion-based political party). In that case if I remain separate and don't join Chatro Shibir, I would be isolated. As I spent most of my time with them, that's why if I don't follow them I would have to lead an isolated life, which would be very difficult for me. If I lead a separate life, it won't bring me any positive thing on the other hand if I follow them it will bring me a pious life and I would be benefited from that. That's why I have joined them and I feel that it's not a fruitless thing. It's a good way of getting peace. But now at this stage I am not doing the tasks they are asking me to do because of my busy life now. (A 25-year-old engineering student, Dhaka)

Sometimes, many youth deliberately search for the 'true' Islamic movement to cultivate their religiosity and to achieve a 'pious' life. Many of my respondents mentioned that they looked for many Islamic organizations and movement and some of them finally convinced that they have found their desired group. Some are still searching for their desired destination. In this context a follower of a Tablighi Jamaat told that he joined the Tablighi Jamaat to stay away or avoid conflict in the society and to lead a religious (practicing) life. As he stated,

> I came from a small town where parents send their children to *maqtab*[48] in the morning. You can still find this kind of informal institution at the village level. I got my religious orientation from there. When I started to go to the university, I realized that there are many conflicts between students, especially among the students who are involved in student's politics, and then I decided to join the Tablihi Jamaat. They do not have such political ideology that may create clash. I want to see this society to be a better society and to receive reward in the life hereafter. (A young university teacher, male, Dhaka)

He clearly defines his agenda and ideas of getting involved into this Tablighi movement. Although the Tablighi Jamaat claims to be an 'apolitical' movement with focus on the piety of Muslim, which aims to make Muslim true Muslim,[49] some academics and scholars identify this movement with radical thoughts and ideology. Roy levels the Tablighi Jamaat as a 'neo-fundamentalist' Islamic movement with different political manifestation[50] and Alexiev claims that the Tablighi Jamaat is more of a political movement than religious,[51] while Sikand sees this particular Islamic movement as a breeding ground for many Islamists.[52] However, the counter argument is also evident among many scholars. Metcalf shows that these types of argument is made with reference to Pakistan, although in the question of jihad, she further claims that

---

[48] In general term, *maqtab* refers to an education/learning institution based at mosque. The imam of a particular mosque used to run a short session every morning only for children to help them learn reading the Quran.

[49] M. K. Masud, *Travellers in Faith: Studies of the Tablīghī Jamā'at as a Transnational Islamic Movement for Faith Renewal* (Leiden: Brill, 2000).

[50] Roy, 'Globalized Islam'.

[51] Alexiev, 'Tablighi Jamaat'.

[52] Sikand, 'The Tablighi Jama'at and Politics'.

Tablighi jihad refers to personal purification than warfare.[53] In contrast, the ethnographic account of Siddiqi shows that the Tablighi Jamaat primarily contributes on making its followers as 'good Muslim'.[54] He shows in another article that although the Tablighi Jamaat is an Islamic piety movement, it has a high potential of engaging into democratic politics in Bangladesh.[55] Furthermore, there has been a growing tension between two groups of the Tablighi Jamaat in Bangladesh[56] that also indicates that the Tablighi Jamaat is not entirely an 'apolitical' movement.

This section shows that youth are particularly eager to know more about Islam and transform their lives towards religious practice to increase their religiosity. But interestingly, the process of radicalization and increased religiosity at the very early stage is not very different, which is the challenging part for the researchers on this area.

CONCLUSION

The chapter was an attempt to problematize the discourse of radicalization by exploring the views and perception of the youth. The chapter argues that there have been various ways by which the youth are targeted by recruiters in the process of radicalization. In such context, alienation, isolation from the family, crisis of identity and influence by the so called global Islamic scholars play important role in the process of radicalization. The findings also suggest that many youth have been targeted at the school level in the name of *dawah*. However, in the contemporary time, easy accessibility of various materials (especially video and articles) by global preachers also influence many youth to act upon their radical ideology that also has to be seen as a political

---

[53] B. D. Metcalf, *Traditionalist' Islamic Activism: Deoband, Tablighis, and Talibs* (Leiden: Institute for the Study of Islam in the Modern World [ISIM], 2002).

[54] Siddiqi, *Becoming 'Good Muslim'*.

[55] B. Siddiqi, 'Reconsidering Politics: The Case of the Tablighi Jamaat in Bangladesh', *Bangabidya: International Journal of Bengal Studies* 10 (2018): 278–291.

[56] B. Siddiqi, 'Tablighi Jamaat: Why This Conflict and Dividation (in Bengali)', Prothomalo, 6 December 2018. Available at: https://www.prothomalo.com/opinion/article/1568609 (accessed on 8 December 2018).

manifestation of their ideology where they use religion to justify their acts. Findings of this research suggest that there are many common patterns of radicalization that show early signs through the gradual and sudden changes, and transformation in the lifestyles. The transition of a person's radical ideology is noticeable at the early stage, where parents should intervene right after they could notice.

Therefore, it is very important to understand the psychology of such changes. More importantly understanding the psychological aspect of the youth is particularly essential. In this context, Borum suggested three social science theories would be ideal to understand radicalization further, among them social psychology theory is very relevant.[57] In many cases academics, professionals and experts from older generation fail to understand the way the youth see the world in the time of globalization. Inability to understand them may result in creation of a psychological separation between the two generations. In Western academia, there have been many studies by social psychologists to understand the radicalization among the youth in a better way; Bangladesh situation also requires such an approach.

Heroism is a frequently reported concept in the discussion by many youth. These urban youth interpret many radical activities as acts of heroism. According to them these radical people wanted show their heroism and they wanted to prove their ability of doing something. Scholars also argued that heroism is one of the key motivations for many youth to act upon their thoughts. Although it looks like that people consciously decide to join a radical group or motivate into a radical ideology, the process is mostly unconscious and depends on individual circumstances.

We also need to be clear that even though radicalization takes place in many forms, but not all forms of radicalization end up in violent acts. Same goes with the idea of ideology. Some also explain that the idea of ideological radicalization may not necessarily be translated into a terrorist attack or extreme behaviour. Then again, this is also important to identity what types of radical ideology is responsible for extreme

---

[57] Borum, 'Radicalization into Violent Extremism'.

behaviour or activities. Knowing about Islam is not a problem and many urban youth believe in this. Therefore, academics and researchers in the field of radicalization have to be very clear about the boundaries of radicalization, otherwise problematic and generalized understanding of the radicalization discourse would put practices of many faithful youth in question and doubt. Therefore, it requires holistic approach initiating an interdisciplinary team research to understand the complex phenomenon of radicalization.

Chapter 11

Developing Counter-Narrative for De-radicalization in Bangladesh
Issues and Challenges

Mahbubur Rahman

INTRODUCTION

'It is difficult to defeat ideas by force alone.'[1]

Terrorists commit crimes against humanity and their brutality is beyond comprehension, and yet they portray themselves as 'victims of injustices' and try to 'legitimize' their actions through their narratives.[2]

---

[1] Kruglanski et al., *Aspects of Deradicalization* (NC: Institute for the Study of Asymmetric Conflict, 2011). Available at: http://www.asymmetricconflict.org/articles/aspects–of–deradicalization/ (accessed on 12 November 2018).

[2] Referring to the research findings, A. Barzegar et al. have mentioned that the rhetorical power of extremist narratives often first comes by way of their appeal to a widespread, legitimate and long-set political or social grievance. The second step then involves building a series of arguments legitimizing and promoting violent behaviour aimed at offering redress to this widely recognized, but unresolved, protest. See Abbas Barzegar et al., 'Civic Approaches to Confronting Violent Extremism', Institute for Strategic Dialogue, 2016, 28. Available at: https://

They sometimes do so in the name of religion.[3] Bangladeshi terrorists are no exception to this. On the fateful night of 1 July 2016, when the perpetrators burst into the Holey Artisan Café and killed two dozen innocent people (mostly non-Muslim foreigners), they shouted 'Allahu Akbar', which means 'God is Great'. We also learnt from the media that after entering the bakery, the terrorists asked every hostage to recite one or two verses from the Qur'an and whoever was unable to do so was killed.[4] While there is no single factor which gives birth to this phenomenon, and religion is not always the guiding 'mantra' of the radicals either,[5] the fanatic behaviour of the Bangladeshi terrorists is nevertheless indicative that religious reference and rhetoric are very much part of their discourses and narratives. This is applicable to many prominent international terrorist organizations also. For fighting this global menace, many States have justifiably used all kinds of 'hard power'. But, as it became increasingly clear that 'the use of kinetic force against the terrorists in the War on Terror has in many cases been unproductive and downright counter-productive in other cases',[6] strategic analysts have started emphasizing the use of 'soft power instruments' to face this ever-growing global challenge. One such 'soft power instrument' is 'counter-narrative' which seeks to 'deconstruct, delegitimize and demystify extremist propaganda in order to achieve a number of aims, from de-radicalization of those already radicalized to sowing the seeds of doubt among 'at risk' audiences potentially being exposed to or seeking out extremist content'.[7] The argument

---

www.isdglobal.org/wp-content/uploads/2016/10/civic_approaches_to_confronting_violent_extremism_-_digital_release.pdf (accessed on 12 November 2018).

[3] See Mahbubur Rahman, 'Terrorism in the Name of Religion', *The Daily Star*, Dhaka, 25 July 2016. Available at: https://www.thedailystar.net/op-ed/politics/terrorism-the-name-religion-1258654 (accessed on 6 November, 2018).

[4] Rashidul Hasan, 'A 12-hour ordeal,' *The Daily Star*, 3 July 2016. Available at: https://www.thedailystar.net/frontpage/militants-prisons-deradicalisation-call-falls-deaf-ears-1523215. (accessed on 6 November, 2018).

[5] El Said writes, 'Evidence shows that most violent extremists have weak or no rigorous religious knowledge.' H. El Said, *New Approaches to Countering Terrorism: Designing and Evaluating Counter-Radicalization and De-Radicalization Programs* (London: Palgrave Macmillan, 2015), 27.

[6] See Alex P. Schmid, 'Challenging the Narrative of the "Islamic State"' (research paper, ICCT, June 2015), 1–15.

[7] M. Fayez, 'Why Pakistan Does Not Have a Countering Narrative', *Journal of Strategic Security* 8, no. 1 (Spring/Summer 2015). Available at: https://

is straightforward and plausible: Just as a variety of actors can produce and distribute narratives intended to bring others to adopt their radical viewpoints and/or engage in violence, it is similarly possible to produce and disseminate narratives to achieve a key objective associated with countering violent extremism (CVE)—dissuading support for terrorism.[8] To put it succinctly, counter-narratives aim to challenge and contradict the themes intrinsic to the terrorist narrative and, in turn, discourage the support for terrorism.

Developing counter-narrative for de-radicalization is not easy or without challenge, however. Several factors could be attributed to this. First, there are no comprehensive guidelines on how to develop and distribute counter-narratives to effectively reduce support for terrorism.[9] As a matter of fact, there is limited awareness and lack of understanding about what makes a counter-narrative campaign effective. Second, as Briggs and Feve have pointed out, 'There is a wealth of extremist material and product that is slick and professionally produced, but the same often cannot be said for their counter-narrative equivalents'.[10] Third, whether piloted by the government or implemented by the civil society organizations, counter-narrative efforts are 'tough to measure and evaluate, making appraisals of success and failure hard to gauge'.[11] Moreover, some are of the opinion that 'counter-narrative strategies may, if they fail to gain traction, do more harm than good and prove to be counter-productive, reinforcing rather than contradicting the terrorist narrative'.[12]

---

henley-putnam.national.edu/wp-content/uploads/2016/12/Counterterrorism-Narrative-Pakistan.pdf (accessed on 15 November 2018).

[8] K. Braddock and John Horgan, 'Towards a Guide for Constructing and Disseminating Counter-Narratives to Reduce Support for Terrorism', *Studies in Conflict & Terrorism* 36, no. 5 (2016): 381–404.

[9] Ibid.

[10] See R. Briggs and S. Feve, 'Review of Programs to Counter Narratives of Violent Extremism', Institute for Strategic Dialogue, 2013. Available at: http://apo.org.au/node/37101 (accessed on 15 November 2018).

[11] A. Meleagrou-Hitchens and L. Vidino, 'The Challenges and Limitations of Online Counter-Narratives', 2018. Available at: https://blog.prif.org/2018/06/04/the-challenges-and-limitations-of-online-counter-narratives/ (accessed on 16 November 2018).

[12] See Liam Byrne, *Counter-Narratives to Terrorism*, (Parliamentary Assembly Report, Council of Europe, 2018). Available at: http://website-pace.net/

Notwithstanding these challenges and limitations, the importance of counter-narrative cannot be undermined, let alone denied. As Davies et al. have mentioned, 'There is an emerging consensus that ideologically-based narratives play a central role in encouraging and sustaining radicalization to violence, and that preventing, arresting, or reversing radicalization requires some means by which to address the effects of these narratives.'[13] In order to defeat radicalization and violent extremism, there needs to be as much emphasis placed on fighting the 'War on Ideas' as there is on fighting the 'War on Terror'.[14] The purpose of this chapter is to identify the challenges that counter-narrative campaign in Bangladesh is facing today and come out with some policy suggestions for future.

To put it in perspective, while violent extremism first made its inroad in Bangladesh in the late 1990s and came to the surface more in 2004–2005, it was not until 2016 (when the Gulshan café attack took place) that the authorities recognized the importance of using soft power or counter-narrative for meeting this challenge. Even after that large-scale attack and its resultant fallout, official recognition and launching of counter-narrative campaign took longer than expected (the initiative started only recently, in the beginning of 2018). This is not very unusual though, as the usage of counter-narrative as a tool of de-radicalization is still in its infancy.[15] The very concept is contested and so its application in individual cases.

It is important to mention that Bangladesh's success regarding 'kinetic operations' for countering violent extremism has been quite noteworthy. For instance, its security agencies have been relentless in the pursuit of extremist suspects belonging to neo-Jamaat-ul-Muslimeen

---

documents/19838/4246196/20180314-TerrorismCounterNarratives-EN. pdf/8109958c-e4fc-4ee0-bb2b-41a43d6739f8 (accessed on 16 November 2018).

[13] G. Davies et al., 'Toward a Framework Understanding of Online Programs for Countering Violent Extremism', *Journal for Deradicalization* 6 (Spring 2016): 51–86.

[14] G. Hoeft, '"Soft" Approaches to Counter-Terrorism: An Exploration of the Benefits of Deradicalization Programs', *International Institute for Counter Terrorism,* 2016. Available at: https://www.ict.org.il/Article/1620/Soft-Approaches-to-Counter-Terrorism#gsc.tab=0 (accessed on 5 March 2019).

[15] Briggs and Feve, 'Review of Programs'.

Bangladesh (neo-JMB) or Ansar al-Islam, the two major terror groups of the country with the former having suspected links to Islamic State (IS) and the latter with al-Qaeda in South Asia.[16] Since July 2016, more than 100 terrorists have been killed, including Tamim Ahmed Chowdhury, neo-JMB's mastermind behind the Dhaka café attack. In addition, almost all the top leaders of the terror groups have been either killed or captured by the law enforcement bodies.[17] Despite all these notable successes, there is, however, a growing realization at the highest level of law enforcement authorities in Bangladesh that in one key area the country has fallen short and that is in countering the 'extremist narratives' which inspire individuals to join such groups in the first place.[18] This realization is indeed the reflection of the realities. For, as it appears time to time through the military operations and arrests, terror cells seem to be still alive and active in different parts of Bangladesh and both male and female, including university students and graduates, are joining these groups. They are spreading their messages day and night by all means, including the latest technology and highly discreet apps. As the *Annual Threat Assessment Report on South Asia* by the Counter Terrorist Trends and Analyses (January 2018) points out:

> The rebuttals by IS propagandists of the counter-narratives given by the local Muslim scholars against extremist ideologies, is another noteworthy trend in 2017. This means that IS ideology will have long-term implications for Bangladesh's internal security. It underscores the need

---

[16] F. Sobhan, 'The Need for an Action Plan', *Dhaka Tribune*, 10 July 2018. Available at: https://www.dhakatribune.com/bangladesh/2018/01/29/additional-igp-patwari-deradicalizing-youths-correct-interpretation-religion (accessed on 10 November 2018).

[17] See Binod Kumar Singh, 'Bangladesh's War on Terror Won't End Soon', 2017. Available at: http://www.rediff.com/news/column/bangladeshs-war-on-terror-wont-end-soon/20171221.htm (accessed on 10 November 2018).

[18] Arifur Rahman Rabbi, 'Additional IGP Patwari for Deradicalizing Youths with Correct Interpretation of Religion', *Dhaka Tribune*, 29 January 2018. Available at: https://www.dhakatribune.com/bangladesh/2018/01/29/additional-igp-patwari-deradicalizing-youths-correct-interpretation-religion (accessed on 10 November 2018).

for a more pro-active counter-ideology strategy and investment in building social awareness against violent-extremism.[19]

It is obvious that as long as extremist narratives continue to inspire new recruits to join these groups, the battle will continue for generations to come. It is because of this appalling scenario that the law enforcement agencies of Bangladesh have urged for developing counter-narratives. Recently, while launching a television commercial on anti-militancy campaign, the home minister said it very frankly: 'We cannot eradicate the militancy, just with coercion'.[20] Underscoring the importance of carrying out this campaign through 'poetry, books and songs', the minister said that this type of anti-militancy campaign would help reduce the youth motivation from joining militancy.[21] The new police chief, Dr Mohammad Javed, has also said, 'The anti-militancy drives must incorporate deradicalization strategies involving the orientation of youth to the correct interpretation of religion.'[22] He added that the youth or the ones who feel like joining militant activities need to know the proper and correct interpretation of religion and the Qur'an. Otherwise, they will lose their ways in the dark.[23] Echoing the same, the Chief of the Rapid Action Battalion (RAB) Mr Benazir Ahmed said that counter-narratives campaign would help reduce the motivation of the youth for joining militancy.[24] He also informed the audience that the elite force, that is, RAB, has been publishing counter-narratives through anti-militancy books, posters and leaflets to create mass awareness.[25]

---

[19] Annual Threat Assessment Report on South Asia, *Counter Terrorist Trends and Analyses* (January 2018). Available at: https://www.rsis.edu.sg/wp-content/uploads/2018/01/CTTA-Annual-Threat-2018.pdf (accessed 17 December, 2018).

[20] Arifur Rahman Rabbi, 'Additional IGP Patwari for Deradicalizing Youths with Correct Interpretation of Religion', *Dhaka Tribune*, 29 January 2018. Available at: https://www.dhakatribune.com/bangladesh/2018/01/29/additional-igp-patwari-deradicalizing-youths-correct-interpretation-religion (accessed on December 15, 2018).

[21] Ibid.
[22] Ibid.
[23] Ibid.
[24] Ibid.
[25] Ibid.

Accordingly, 'counter-narrative, de-radicalization and social reintegration initiative' has been officially declared as one of the targets of the Bangladesh Police in its 'Strategic Plan (2018–2020)'.[26]

This is certainly a sign of good progress towards a counter-narrative campaign in Bangladesh, but how good is this for achieving its objectives, that is., de-radicalizing the people who are on the terror path and discouraging vulnerable youth or 'would-be recruits' from joining this path? This chapter therefore has two objectives: First, it seeks to explore the counter-narratives to Islamist extremist agenda in Bangladesh, and second, it would provide some policy inputs for designing an effective counter-narrative campaign in the country. For that purpose, the questions that have been sought to be answered here are as follows.

1. What are the major themes of the extremist ideology in Bangladesh and how do the perpetrators disseminate their narratives?
2. What is the current status of counter-narrative campaign in Bangladesh?
3. Is there anything missing in this campaign? If so, what is that?
4. In the present context, what should Bangladesh do in order to develop an effective counter-narrative campaign?

For the convenience of analysis, we have first provided the conceptual perspective of de-radicalization and counter-narrative. Given that narratives do not evolve in a vacuum, we have discussed the emergence of terror network in Bangladesh and their ideological narratives. Then we have tried to explore the state of counter-narrative campaign in Bangladesh and identified its challenges, especially the missing points in this campaign. Finally, we have suggested some policy guidelines for designing an effective counter-narrative campaign in Bangladesh.

METHODOLOGY

Given that this is an exploratory study, data has been collected from both primary and secondary sources that include two primary

---

[26] Bangladesh Police, *Strategic Plan (2018–2020)*. Available at: https://www.police.gov.bd/storage/upload/announcement/bRKQRrM5Qr41qC7tniHQh-dKUJiIJmYewNt4IFf0g.pdf. (accessed on 17 December 2018).

documents prepared under the auspices of RAB and Bangladesh Jamytat-ul-Ulama. In addition, critical input was collected through key informant interviews (KIIs) and newspaper surveys. The deliberations of a workshop organized by the Democracy International (DI) and Bangladesh Enterprise Institute (BEI) on The Role of Civil Society in Preventing Extremism in Bangladesh which was held on 3 March 2018, were also extremely beneficial to this study.

KIIs included extensive interviews of 20 selected experts in the field. The interview method for this category was both structured and open-ended. Two focus group discussions (FGDs) were also organized in the Department of Political Science and Sociology of North South University wherein the faculty members from various departments participated and contributed their inputs.

The sources of secondary data included consulting research reports, journals, books, news reports and analyses published in print and electronic media websites. Data collected from one source was cross-checked by other sources to ensure their accuracy, authenticity, and corroboration.

SIGNIFICANCE OF THE STUDY

The significance of this study lies on several grounds. First, it is a fact that compared to the study of radicalization, de-radicalization, that is, the process of how individuals and groups move away from violent extremism has received much less attention in the academic discussion. Second, despite the considerable attention that counter-narrative approach has received and continues to receive worldwide, lately it is still an under-researched area globally as well as in Bangladesh. Third, in Bangladesh, a large segment of the intelligentsia is not even aware of the importance of counter-narrative. There is hardly any academic study available in Bangladesh on this subject.[27] Fourth and most importantly, the study aims to fill in the knowledge gap in the academia and seeks to provide critical inputs to policymaking in Bangladesh.

---

[27] According to our knowledge, only one such study was conducted by the Bangladesh Enterprise Institute in 2016 which was published under the title of 'Towards Developing Counter-Narrative to the Islamist Extremist Narrative in Bangladesh' (Dhaka: BEI, 2016).

COUNTER-NARRATIVE AND DE-RADICALIZATION: CONCEPTUAL PERSPECTIVE

What Is De-radicalization?

Defining 'de-radicalization' is problematic, as there is no consensus on its meaning and purpose. Tore Bjorgo, John Horgan and Alex Schmid, who have dealt with this subject quite extensively, have also pointed out that there exists an ambiguity and lack of conceptual clarity about de-radicalization in the existing literature.[28] The term 'de-radicalization,' for example, is sometimes viewed as 'any effort aimed at preventing radicalization from taking place,'[29] but others suggest that de-radicalization programmes should be designed particularly for those people who are already radicalized.

Peter Neumann agrees with those who suggest that de-radicalization is aimed at radicalized individuals.[30] He, however, made a distinction between what he calls 'cognitive de-radicalization' and 'behavioural de-radicalization'. According to him, the objective of de-radicalization is to stop the radicals' use of violence (behavioural de-radicalization), or change their mindset and ideological assumptions (cognitive de-radicalization). He further notes, 'Just like radicalization, de-radicalization is a process which plays out over time and draws on a combination of instruments, including—but not limited to—psychological counselling, ideological re-education, vocational training, re-socialization and job opportunities'.[31]

---

[28] See Alex P. Schmid, 'Radicalization, De-Radicalization, Counter-Radicalization: A Conceptual Discussion and Literature Review' (research paper, ICCT, 2013).

[29] Dianna Barrantes and Carola Garcia-Calvo, 'Exit Strategies', in *EU RAN CoE Paper on Current Radicalization Research* (Elcano Royal Institute, RAN Centre of Excellence). Available at: http://www.realinstitutoelcano.org/wps/wcm/connect/8d857357-8b96-4721-85e3-0b80ee3cce82/3_Exit_Strategies_Elcano.pdf?MOD=AJPERES. (accessed on 18 December, 2018).

[30] Peter Neumann, 'Countering Violent Extremism and Radicalization That Lead to Terrorism: Ideas, Recommendations, and Good Practices from the OSCE Region', 2017. Available at: https://www.osce.org/chairmanship/346841?download=true (accessed on 18 December 2018).

[31] Ibid.

John Horgan and Mary Beth Altier have attempted to synthesize the aforementioned viewpoints, and said: 'Deradicalization includes any effort to change or redirect views that are supportive of—and thereby...conducive to—violent action.'[32]

Froukje Demant and her colleagues have sought to provide further clarity by saying that de-radicalization 'is the process of becoming less radical. This process of "becoming less radical" applies both to behavior and beliefs'.[33] Indeed, changing the behaviour of an individual requires changing his/her ideology that motivates that behaviour in the first place. As Angel Rabasa et al. have pointed out, 'A true (or successful) de-radicalization programme should produce a change in an individual's underlying beliefs, not simply a change in behavior'.[34] The ultimate goal of de-radicalization programme is making the radicalized people and the 'would-be-radicals' recognize that violence is not only immoral and illegitimate but also ineffective. This programme therefore aims at dismantling extremist narratives through a social and psychological process whereby an individual's commitment to, and involvement in, violent radicalization is reduced to the extent that they are no longer at risk of involvement and engagement in violent activity.[35]

There are several different ways that narratives can displace or counter extremist narratives. The Institute for Strategic Dialogue (ISD) has described a 'messaging spectrum' that include three types of messaging activities: (a) government strategic communications; (b) counter-narratives; and (c) alternative narratives.[36] This study focuses on how counter-narratives can help facilitate de-radicalization.

---

[32] John Horgan and Mary Beth Altier, 'The Future of Terrorist De-Radicalization Programs', *Georgetown Journal of International Affairs* (Summer/Fall 2012): 86.

[33] See: Schmid, Radicalization, De-Radicalization, Counter-Radicalization'.

[34] A. Rabasa, S. Pettyjohn, J. Ghez and C. Boucek, *Deradicalizing Islamist Extremists* (Santa Monica, CA: RAND, 2010).

[35] J. Horgan, *Walking Away from Terrorism: Accounts of Disengagement from Radical and Extremist Movements* (London: Routledge, 2009), 153.

[36] Briggs and Feve, 'Review of Programs'.

What Is Counter-Narrative?

Counter-narrative is basically presenting a story that aims to undermine the appeal of the dominant story or narrative by providing new information or arguments.[37] *The Handbook of Counter-Narrative* defines it as a message 'that offers a positive alternative to extremist propaganda, or alternatively aims to deconstruct or delegitimize extremist narratives'.[38] This involves, among others: (a) highlighting how extremist activities negatively impact on the people they claim to represent; (b) demonstrating the hypocrisy of extremist groups and how their actions are often inconsistent with their own stated beliefs; and (c) emphasizing factual inaccuracies used in extremist propaganda and setting the record straight.[39]

As already mentioned, as a field of inquiry, counter-narrative is in the infancy and there is no common understanding about this concept.[40] In fact, a debate is still going on 'about what a counter-narrative actually is (or should be and do)'.[41] According to Grossman (2015), counter-narrative refers to a 'variety positional or relational discourse, at once overtly constructed and implicitly normative, that seeks to disrupt, dismantle, or speak back to other narrative trajectories that exert discursive power'.[42]

---

[37] B. Doosje and J. J. Eerten, '"Counter-Narratives" against Violent Extremism', in *De-radicalization: Scientific Insights for Policy*, ed. Colaert, L (Brussels: Flemish Peace Institute, 2017), 83–100.

[38] Henry Tuck and Tanya Silverman, *The Counter-Narrative Handbook*, Institute for Strategic Dialogue, 2016, 4. Available at: https://www.isdglobal.org/wp-content/uploads/2016/06/Counter-narrative-Handbook_1.pdf. (accessed on 16 November, 2018).

[39] Ibid.

[40] Kate Ferguson, 'Countering violent extremism through media and communication strategies,' 1 March 2016, p. 9. Available at: http://www.paccsresearch.org.uk/wpcontent/uploads/2016/03/Countering-Violent-Extremism-Through-Media-and-Communication-Strategies-.pdf (accessed on 16 November 2018).

[41] B. Doosje and J. J. Eerten, '"Counter-Narratives" against Violent Extremism', in *De-radicalization: Scientific Insights for Policy*, ed. Colaert, L (Brussels: Flemish Peace Institute, 2017), 83–100.

[42] Quoted in ibid.

Briggs and Feve have provided a comprehensive and yet very concise definition. According to them, counter-narrative programmes seek
to deconstruct, delegitimize and demystify extremist propaganda in
order to change the hearts and minds of those who are already radicalized or the 'at risk' audiences who may be exposed to or seeking out
extremist contents.[43] These programmes can be run both online and
offline, and many initiatives utilize both platforms.

It is worth mentioning that some scholars have expressed doubts
about the utility and efficacy of counter-narrative. They maintain
that the relationship between viewing extremist content and actually
engaging in violent extremism is not clear and from this perception,
they argue that 'actual evidence that counter-narratives are an effective
method of minimizing the impact of narratives and of preventing acts
of violence is lacking'.[44] To quote Kate Ferguson: 'Although the vast
majority of terrorist actors share and engage with extremist narratives,
suggesting a correlation, there is still little evidence to support notion
that exposure to extremist content has a causal effect on future violent
extremism activity'.[45]

Others, however, caution not to overstate this viewpoint. They
refer to the fact that messaging has an effect on consumers and that
this has been the premise of television advertising since its inception.
They also point out that the extremist groups, such as IS and al-Qaeda,
have invested heavily in propaganda efforts which is because the groups
believe that it has some impact on their recruitment prospects. On the
contrary, what we observe is that there exists sizable gap between the
volume and quality of counter-narratives and the sophisticated propaganda of the terrorist groups.[46]

---

[43] Briggs and Feve, 'Review of Programs'.

[44] Ann-Sophie Hemmingsen and Karin Ingrid Castro, *The Trouble with Counter-
Narrative* (DIIS Report, 2017), 1.

[45] Kate Ferguson, 'Countering Violent Extremism through Media and
Communication Strategies', 9. Available at: http://www.paccsresearch.org.uk/
wpcontent/uploads/2016/03/Countering-Violent-Extremism-Through-Media-
and-Communication-Strategies-.pdf (accessed on 16 November 2018).

[46] Radicalisation Awareness Network, 'Counter Narratives and Alternative
Narratives' (RAN issue paper, 2015), 4–5. Available at: https://ec.europa.eu/

Indeed, despite the reservations of the many sceptics and critiques, de-radicalization and counter-narrative programmes are gaining popularity, which is due to the fact that security measures alone cannot defeat violent extremist groups. Many States therefore have concluded that it is necessary to prevent young people from radicalizing and to rehabilitate those who are on the wrong path. Those countries have developed programmes that address both counter-radicalization and de-radicalization. Citing all these, the proponents of counter-narratives suggest that 'de-radicalization can work, but that only happens if you have a strong counter narrative'.[47]

Developing Counter-Narrative: A How-to Guide

While counter-narrative is very much talked about in the academia and policymaking arena, understanding about what makes a counter-narrative campaign effective is still very limited.[48] Moreover, de-radicalization programmes around the world are also quite different from one another in many respects. Since there is no 'one size–fits–all' solution to this case, scholars agree that 'a single, overarching, counter-narrative cannot be developed'.[49] In this backdrop, K. Braddock and J. Horgan's suggested framework titled *Towards a guide for constructing and disseminating counter-narratives to reduce support for terrorism*, which could be considered as the pioneering work on the subject.[50]

Later, some international think tanks such as Radicalization Awareness Network (RAN), the ISD and the Hedayah Centre took up the task and attempted to provide nuanced understanding of counter-narrative. The RAN was established by the European

---

home-affairs/sites/homeaffairs/files/what-wedo/networks/radicalisation_aware-ness_network/ran-papers/docs/issue_paper_cn_oct2015_en.pdf (accessed on 5 March 2019).

[47] https://www.euronews.com/2016/01/04/adam–deen–deradicalisation–can-work-if-you-have-a-strong-counter-narrative (accessed on 7 March 2019).

[48] Briggs and Feve, 'Review of Programs'.

[49] See Byrne, *Counter-Narratives to Terrorism*.

[50] K. Braddock and J. Horgan, 'Towards a Guide for Constructing and Disseminating Counter-Narratives to Reduce Support for Terrorism', *Studies in Conflict & Terrorism* 39, no. 5 (2015). doi:10. 1080/1057610X.2015.1116277

Council in 2011 with the purpose of facilitating partnerships and delivering products for aiding the practitioners of de-radicalization. Accordingly, it has produced a series of products and among them, Preventing Radicalization to Terrorism and Violent Extremism: Approaches and Practices was the most significant work in this regard. The approaches presented in this 434-page collection include the following: Training for first line practitioners; exit strategies; community engagement and empowerment; educating young people; family support; delivering counter or alternative narratives, and multi-agency approaches.[51]

ISD made a similar initiative on the design of a counter-narrative campaign called the Counter Narrative Toolkit. There are four key elements to the toolkit, which are as follows: How to plan a campaign; how to create content; how to promote a campaign and a series of case studies in which users can browse.[52]

In 2011, Global Counterterrorism Forum (GCTF)/Hedayah Centre was established by 29 founding member states, including the United States, the United Kingdom, the United Arab Emirates, the Netherlands and China, as well as the European Union in an informal environment to act on counter-terrorism efforts. In 2016, the Centre came out with another important study titled Undermining Violent Extremist Narratives in Southeast Asia: A How-To-Guide, which provides a framework for developing counter-narrative. (See the Framework in Figure 11.1).[53]

---

[51] European Union, 'Preventing Radicalisation to Terrorism and Violent Extremism: Approaches and Practices', Radicalisation Awareness Network (RAN), September 2017, 11. Available at: https://ec.europa.eu/home-affairs/sites/homeaf-fairs/files/what-we-do/networks/radicalisation_awareness_network/ran-news/docs/ran_update_42_en.pdf (accessed 17 December, 2018)

[52] Counter-Narrative Toolkit, Institute for Strategic Dialogue. Available at: http://www.counternarratives.org/html/home, quoted in Alastair Reed, Haroro J. Ingram and Joe Whittaker, Countering Terrorist Narratives, Brussels: European Parliament, 2017. Available at: https://icct.nl/wp-content/uploads/2017/11/Countering-Terrorist-Narratives-Reed-Whittaker-Haroro-European-Parliament.pdf. (accessed on 17 November 2018).

[53] Hedayah, 'Undermining Violent Extremist Narratives in Southeast Asia: A How-To-Guide', 2016. Available at: http://www.hedayahcenter.org/Admin/

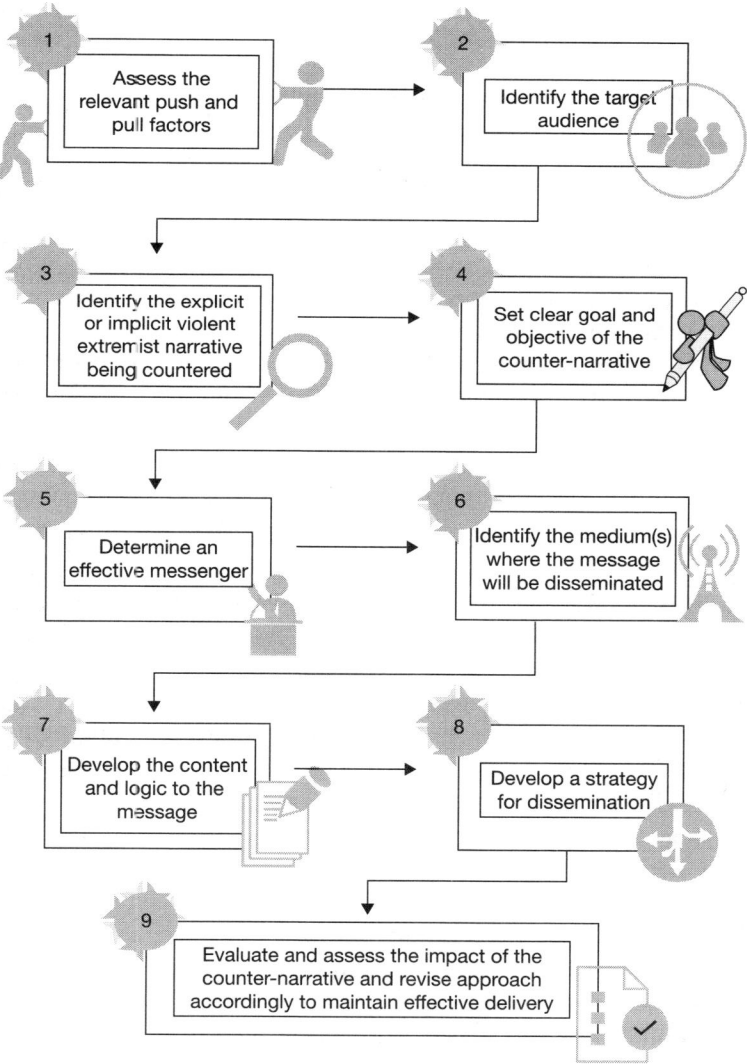

Figure 11.1 *Developing a Counter-Narrative*

Source: Sara Zeiger, *Undermining Violent Extremist Narratives in South East Asia: A How-To Guide* (Abu Dhabi: Hedayah, 2016), 3.

In developing a counter-narrative against violent extremists, there are several main steps.

The details of the framework are as follows:

1. Assessing Relevant Push and Pull Factors
   Push factors refer to 'the negative social incidents and circumstances that make it uncomfortable and unappealing to remain' in the group.[54] Pull factors, on the other hand, are defined as the positive factors that attract the person(s) to a more rewarding alternative.

2. Identifying the target audience
   It is extremely important to decide which group(s) of people will be reached through the counter-narrative campaign. For example, it could be youth, or their parents, or teachers or the entire community. Whatever the target audience is, it must be clearly defined.

3. Identify the explicit or implicit narrative that needs to be countered
   Identifying and understanding the narratives that the violent extremists use is also very important and helpful for countering their narratives successfully. It is critical to know the key arguments and logical or emotional tone and structure of the extremist agenda and discourse.

4. Set clear goals and objectives for the counter-narrative
   Defining the objectives of the counter-narrative is a pre-requisite for the success of this campaign. The objective, for example, could be changing the perceptions, knowledge, and/or behaviour of the targeted audience.

5. Choose an effective messenger
   The credibility of the messengers who convey the counter-narrative messages to the target groups can hardly be overemphasized. It is because credibility gap on the part of the messengers creates a barrier between the message and the intended recipients or audiences. Counter-narrative experts particularly suggest that governments are not the right kind of messengers, as the extremist individuals and groups look at them to be their adversaries and sources of

---

Content/File-3182016115528.pdf (accessed on 20 November 2018).

[54] Bjorgo (2016 234), quoted in D. Koehler, *Understanding Deradicalization: Methods, Tools and Programs for Countering Violent Extremism* (London/New York: Routledge, 2017).

sufferings.[55] Instead, former extremists, victims of violence, peers and family as well as civil society actors (which include but not limited to religious scholars, preachers, teachers and counsellors) are thought to be more credible and effective communicators. It is also important to note that whoever wants to act as messengers may need training and empowerment to do this specialized job and government can certainly assist and facilitate the process from behind the scene.

6. Crafting the content and logic of the message
   It is suggested that using a simple and clear message rather than a complex or complicated argument always works better. The message needs to be crafted in a way that can pull people in and make them think.[56] There is certainly need for research and using innovative approaches to counter-narrative development, particularly with creating alternative and positive narratives.

7. Identifying the right medium(s) for disseminating the message
   Selecting the right medium(s) is also important, as the platform has to be more effective and used by maximum number of the targeted audience. While doing this, consideration must be given to the platform which is similar to those used by the audiences whom the campaign aims to reach.

8. Develop a dissemination strategy
   While developing the dissemination strategy, it is important to consider the following: Does it underpin the key elements of the message? How can the target audience interact with the message? How can the target audience interact with the messenger? If there is a call to action, how can the target audience interact and respond?

9. Evaluate the impact and re-assess your counter-narrative
   Even though assessing the impact of a counter-narrative campaign is a very difficult task, it is important to apply programme evaluation methods for having a sense of what impact the campaign message

---

[55] See Byrne, *Counter-Narratives to Terrorism*.

[56] See Alexander Ritzmann, 'RAN Guidelines for Effective Alternative and Counter-Narrative Campaigns', RAN Centre of Excellence, 6. Available at: https://www.jugendundmedien.ch/fileadmin/user_upload/3_Medienkompetenz/Gegennarrative/ran_cn_guidelines_effective_alternative_counter_narrative_campaigns_31_12_2017_en.pdf

has and how and why it is having that kind of impact. It is especially important for a campaign to be sustainable and successful.

To conclude, successful counter-narrative campaigns are a complex construction, which require paying critical attention to multiple types of aspects, such as setting clear objectives, right message, credible messenger and appropriate mediums (online, offline, print, TV, radio, oration, social media, etc.), all in support of conveying and re-enforcing a central narrative that is synchronized with the realities, capabilities and expectations.

COUNTER-NARRATIVE CAMPAIGN IN BANGLADESH: APPROACHES AND CHALLENGES

As already mentioned, slowly but steadily, Bangladesh is moving towards developing a counter-narrative campaign in its quest for de-radicalization. The most encouraging development perhaps is that 'there is consensus among law enforcers and security personnel that soft measures are the new go-to'. Among the steps the country has taken so far to implement its new policy include:

1. A comprehensive fatwa against terrorism signed by over 100,000 *ulema*
2. Publishing a book by RAB titled *Jongibadider Opobyakkhya* (Misinterpretation of Verses by Militants and the Right Interpretation of the Qur'an and Hadith)
3. Revising madrasa textbooks
4. Monitoring and controlling extremism-related messaging on the internet and social media
5. Building awareness about radicalization in educational institutions among teachers, students and parents
6. Developing and broadcasting anti-militant television commercials
7. Nationwide anti-militancy publicity campaign using information and communication technology by the Ministry of Religious Affairs
8. Radicals' Rehabilitation Program and
9. Some innovative civil society initiatives

In order to understand the nature of the counter-narrative campaign in Bangladesh, it is important to discuss all of these initiatives in the light of the counter-narrative campaign framework mentioned earlier. It is particularly important to identify the potentials as well as challenges that Bangladesh is facing while formulating and implementing its campaign. However, due to space constraints, we would confine this discussion mainly on two issues, which are considered to be 'flagship programmes' on the part of the government-initiated counter-narrative scheme in Bangladesh. We would also examine the state of prison-based de-radicalization programme (which is yet to develop) in Bangladesh and its complicacies.

A 'Comprehensive Fatwa against Terrorism' Signed by Over 100,000 Ulema

The initiative of issuing fatwa against terrorism by over 100,000 Bangladeshi ulema is a noteworthy step which was shared at a press conference and published in June 2016, only a month before the Holey Artisan Café attack. According to media reports, in the wake of continued attacks on religious minorities, foreigners, intellectuals and secular writers, Maulana Fariduddin Masud, the Imam of Sholakia Eid Congregation, proposed in December 2015 that a fatwa by 100,000 ulama signatories be prepared to tackle terrorism.[57] Later, in January 2016, the signature collection for the 'anti-crime and anti-militancy peace fatwa for human well-being' started and continued until the end of May 2016, collecting a total of 101,850 signatures. It is also interesting to note that among the signatories, 9,320 were female ulema.

The fatwa titled *Shontrash o Jangibad birodhi Manob Kollanay Shantir Fatwa* (fatwa against terrorism for the peace and well-being of mankind) is a 32-page booklet which carries the names of the 1,01,850 signatories. The contents of the fatwa are presented in the form of questions and answers. It contains 10 questions and their answers from the perspective of the Qur'an and Hadith.

---

[57] https://www.dhakatribune.com/bangladesh/2016/06/18/100000-sign-anti-terror-fatwa/ (accessed on 7 March 2019).

The questions that are addressed in the fatwa contain the following:

1. Does Islam support crime and terrorism?
2. Did the prophets, particularly Muhammad (SM), take the barbaric path to establish Islam?
3. Are jihad and terrorism the same thing in Islam?
4. Does terrorism create a path to heaven or hell?
5. Will a suicidal terrorist's death be counted as martyrdom?
6. Is genocide allowed in the view of Islam?
7. Does Islam support the indiscriminate killing of people including women, children, and the elderly?
8. What sort of crime is it to kill a person while they are offering prayer?
9. Is it allowed to attack worship places of non-Muslims such as churches, pagodas and temples?
10. Is it not the responsibility of all— in the view of Islam— to create social resistance against criminals and terrorists?[58]

Through this fatwa, the message that has been conveyed is that jihad and terrorism are not the same thing. Jihad, it is said, is a key teaching of Islam, while terrorism is *haram* (forbidden) and illegal. The fatwa also made it clear that suicide and suicidal killings are not allowed in Islam. Such practices are strictly forbidden in Islam. Mass murder or killing innocent people is not allowed in Islam either. Even killing someone on suspicion is also forbidden. The fatwa further stated that anyone who kills a non-Muslim, who lives within a Muslim-majority society would never even get the smell of heaven. Attacking worship places of non-Muslims such as churches, pagodas and temples is also *haram* and illegal in the eyes of Islam. All these are considered to be sternly punishable offence and therefore everyone must stay away from this.[59]

In the preface of the fatwa against terrorism, Maulana Masud says that if, for any reason, the fatwa fails to stop terrorism completely, it will at least help reduce terrorism. He hopes that the patrons of

---

[58] Maulana Fariduddin Masoud, *Shontrash o Jangibad birodhi Manob Kollanay Shantir Fatwa* (Fatwa against Terrorism for the Peace and Wellbeing of Mankind; Dhaka: Bangladesh Jamiatul Ulama, 2016), 1–32.

[59] Ibid.

terrorism will be deterred by this. Later, when asked how much impact the fatwa might play in defeating terrorism, he said that "a fatwa is much stronger, much sharper than 100,000 weapons. A correct fatwa purifies the psychological ideals, inspires people and makes them humanitarians."

As a first step towards making a counter-narrative campaign, the fatwa could be considered a good initiative for dismantling and discrediting violent extremists' so-called religious narrative, but with all fairness, one has to admit this as well that there is hardly any scope for becoming too optimistic about it. For, apart from the fact that no empirical study has been conducted about its impact (which is also beyond the scope of this chapter), so one cannot say with certainty what exactly could be achieved through this (or any other counter-narrative measure for that matter) in Bangladesh. Second, it is not known how many copies of this fatwa were printed and disseminated. This fatwa is not available online either. Nor is it translated in English. Had it been done, the youth who were educated in English medium schools and colleges could take more advantage of this.

It is also important to mention that the topics and contents of this fatwa could have been extended and included few other issues such as Islam's position on democracy, pluralism and extremism. As we observe, as part of their narratives, the self-styled 'jihadists' of the IS, al-Qaeda, JMB, neo-JMB and Ansar Al-Islam propagate that 'democracy is shirk (associating others with God)', for it incorporates 'man-made laws'. According to them, a Muslim can and should follow only 'God's law'. To press this point, they cite a Qur'anic verse that reads, 'Rule is only for Allah'.[60] Interestingly, like the Kharijites of the 7th century, extremists' reference to the Qur'anic verse is correct, but the meaning and conclusion they draw from this is absolutely wrong. The Kharijites misinterpreted this verse to support their rejection of human arbitration in disputes, but the Qur'an states more than once that arbitration is indeed lawful and helpful.[61] By the same token, to refute the extremists' arguments against democracy, one scholar has very aptly stated: 'He who says that democracy is disbelief, neither understands Islam nor

---

[60] The Qur'an 12:40 and 6:57.
[61] The Qur'an 4:35.

democracy'.[62] To elaborate this point, the scholar has further written: 'Yes, democracy is based on the principle of the people's rule and yet this does not contradict the principle that says that the rule is only for Allah on which Islamic jurisprudence is based. It rather runs counter to the principle of the individual's rule on which dictatorship is based'. At the heart of democracy, the scholar emphasizes, is trusteeship and accountability, which is also an integral part of Islamic teaching.

In regards to disseminating this fatwa, it is said that 'the govt didn't follow up to make this fatwa public,'[63] which sounds surprising. When Maulana Farid Uddin Masud was asked about it, he said that some people took the fatwa from him on personal initiative, but he did not know if any publicity had been done at a government level for this.[64] This seems to be the result of inadequate planning, if not the lack of coordination.

RAB's Initiative for Publishing Book Titled *Jongibadider Opobyakkhya* (Misinterpretation of Verses by the Militants and the Right Interpretation of the Qur'an and Hadith)

In February 2017, the research and development wing of RAB published a book, which is first of its kind in Bangladesh that counters radical ideologies from religious perspective. The book titled *Jongibadider Opobyakkhya* (misinterpretation of verses by militants and the right interpretation of the Qur'an and Hadith) dispels many misconceptions

---

[62] Yusuf al-Qaradawi's views on democracy, quoted in *Ash-Sharq al-Awsat*, 5 February 1990.

[63] See Shaikh Sabiha Alam, 'No Concern about Counter-Militancy beyond Police Action', *Prothom Alo*, 2 July 2017. Available at: https://en.prothomalo.com/bangladesh/news/152587/No-concern-about-counter-militancy-beyond-police (accessed on 20 November 2018).

[64] Ibid.; regarding the use of the fatwa, Maulana Masud also said that imams and Islamic scholars are supposed to deliver sermons based on the fatwa before or after prayers in mosque. When asked about the implementation, he said that he has no information about it. Mr Shameem Mohammad Afzal, the Director General of the Islamic Foundation also said that the 'Fatwa against Terrorism' was solely initiated by Maulana Fariduddin Masud and he can say whether it was circulated in the mosques. See Alam, 'No Concern about Counter-Militancy'.

spread by the militants through their channels both online and offline. Describing how the idea of this book came up and why RAB has taken up the initiative for publishing this book, Mr Selim Mohammed Jahangir, the former director of the R&D cell of RAB has written, 'We confiscated a diary from a young militant with Qur'anic verses written in it. The verses were being used to justify violent jihadi ideologies. So, we decided to take out the verses from that diary and have established Islamic scholars put them in context'. He also mentioned that this book helped him connect with militants during interrogation, 'since the religious logic is foolproof'.

The 70-page book deals with following 23 topics which the violent extremists misinterpret through their propaganda machine.

1. Islam
2. The role of Islam in establishing peace and well-being of all
3. How Islam opposes terrorism and extremism
4. Why institutionally trained and universally accepted ulema should be the source of interpretation of the Qur'an and Sunnah
5. On Killing of Kafir and Mushriq
6. Rule and judgment based on the man-made law
7. Verses of the Qur'an related to jihad
8. Obligation of jihad: Misinterpretation and their correction
9. Literal and colloquial meaning of jihad
10. Qur'anic verses related to qital and combative war
11. Integrated and correct interpretation of the verses
12. Misinterpretation regarding the qital verses
13. Some misleading statements and their corrections
14. Extremist views on *Iqamat-e-Din* (establishment of religion) and their correct interpretation
15. On *Taghut* and the friends of *Shaitan*
16. Views of IS extremists about Muslim rulers and their correction
17. Extremist views on 'inil hukmu illa lillah' (Only Allah can command)
18. Extremist views on 'taking non-believers as friends'
19. Extremist views on 'a verse' and its correct interpretation
20. What is Darul Harb and Darul Islam?
21. On Gaswatul Hind

22. On suicidal mission
23. Extremist views on black flag and its refutation
24. Appendix: Killing, terrorism and jihad in the eyes of Islam

As it is evident from the contents, the book aims at de-radicalization of the youth in Bangladesh through providing religious counter-narrative. To that end, it is well written, authentic and appropriate. The religious scholars who drafted the book have the credentials and scholarship, and they have addressed the selected issues from the right perspective. The topics, however, could have been expanded and contemporary global issues like ulema's consensus on the illegitimacy of Abu Bakr Baghdadi's 'Khilafah' and ISIS could have been incorporated in this book.[65] Interestingly, only 4,000 copies of the book were distributed, which is so insignificant a number in Bangladesh where total population is more than one hundred and seventeen million. More surprisingly, like the book on fatwa against terrorism, there is no online version of this book or any mass publicity in the media.[66] As a result, mass people or youth at large have not seen the book, nor have they heard about it.

Prison-based Disengagement and De-radicalization Programme

It is a well-known fact that prisoners who had or still have terrorist ties could proselytize other inmates or they themselves could turn into more diehard radicals if they are not de-radicalized inside the prison before they are released on bail or on completion of their jail terms. What this means is that extremists even under custody remain a constant threat until and unless a well-defined and effective 'prison-based de-radicalization

---

[65] Shafik Mandhai, 'Muslim Leaders Reject Baghdadi's Caliphate: Prominent Sunny Islamic Scholars Rebuke the Islamic State Group's Self-proclaimed Caliphate, Calling It "Void" and "Deviant"', *Aljazeera*, 7 July 2014. Available at: https://www.aljazeera.com/news/middleeast/2014/07/muslim-leaders-reject-baghdadi-caliphate-20147744058773906.html (accessed on 1 March 2019).

[66] There was only one review of this book titled 'Dabiq Theory and a Publication of RAB', which was written by M. Shakhawat Hossain and was published in the *Daily Prothom Alo*, 19 April 2017.

process' is at work.[67] This also demands that the rehabilitation process needs to continue following their release too, may be in the form of 'strict monitoring' and/or 'post-prison rehabilitation programme'.

In Bangladesh, law enforcement officials maintain that 'some steps are being taken in the prisons'[68] for de-radicalization purpose. However, when they were asked to detail those 'steps', one top official responded saying: 'We do not have any measures to de-radicalize around 600 militant suspects staying in 68 prisons in the country'.[69] That top official was none other than the Inspector General of Prisons (IG, Prisons) Brig Gen Syed Iftekhar Uddin who went further suggesting that militants are motivated by their ideologies and therefore prisons must have the capacity to demotivate them with counter logic. Then, sharing the real state of affairs inside Bangladesh's prison system, he (the IG-Prison) said: 'Our manpower is insufficient even for ensuring security of the prisons. So it's not possible for us to concentrate on corrective measures or things like that'.[70] It is therefore not a surprise that radicalization in prisons in Bangladesh is increasing.[71] Since 2005, though a large number of violent extremists have been detained through various special drives, what we observe is that 'while some of them are out on bail, a good number of them are in prison carrying out radicalization from within'.[72] Among those who are released on bail, many of them have gone 'missing' and some of them have joined the extremist path again. Citing the police headquarters, *The Daily Star*

---

[67] See Marc Jones, 'Rehabilitating Islamist Extremists: Successful Methods in Prison-centred "De-radicalization" Programmes', 2013. Available at: http://www.polis.leeds.ac.uk/assets/files/students/student-journal/ma-winter-13/Jones-Rehabilitating-Islamist-Extremists.pdf (accessed on 17 December 2018).

[68] See Zayma Islam, 'Deradicalization is More Than Just Combat', *The Daily Star*, 16 March 2018. Available at: https://www.thedailystar.net/star-weekend/spotlight/counter-terror-deradicalisation-more-just-combat-1548133 (accessed on December 17, 2018).

[69] See Sahariful Islam and Rafiul Islam, 'Militants in Prisons: Deradicalization Call Falls on Deaf Ears', *The Daily Star*, 22 January 2018. Available at: https://www.thedailystar.net/frontpage/militants-prisons-deradicalisation-call-falls-deaf-ears-1523215 (accessed on 17 December, 2018).

[70] Ibid.

[71] Editorial titled 'Radicalization in Prisons', *The Daily Star*, 22 January 2018.

[72] Ibid.

reported that between January 2016 and September 2017, at least 564 militant suspects walked out of jail on bail and nine of them gone into hiding.[73] According to another report, many of the 334 JMB militants convicted in 93 cases filed over the series of bomb blasts of 2005 have been released after their jail term of 10 years, but 'the authorities are clueless as to whether they have corrected themselves or have become even hardened militants'.[74]

BANGLADESH'S COUNTER-NARRATIVE CAMPAIGN: A RECAP

Bangladesh has had success stories in terms of containing large-scale terrorist attack since 2016 by applying hard measures, but it has not yet made any meaningful progress in counter-narrative campaign and for that matter in advancing its de-radicalization objectives. While several initiatives and ad hoc programmes have been taken up by the law enforcement agencies and government, many of them have been discontinued due to a lack of coordination among agencies.[75] The good thing is that law enforcement agencies themselves have recognized the urgency of introducing counter-narrative campaign and 'the government is now focusing on de-radicalization and rehabilitation schemes for previously convicted terrorists'.[76]

In this context, certain issues need to be taken into consideration.

First, it is obvious that in Bangladesh, the major initiative of counter-narrative campaign has been taken up by the government or its affiliated agencies. However, counter-narrative experts maintain that governments are not always the most effective messengers for

---

[73] See Sahariful Islam and Rafiul Islam, 'Militants in Prisons: Deradicalization Call Falls on Deaf Ears', *The Daily Star*, 22 January 2018. Available at: https://www.thedailystar.net/frontpage/militants-prisons-deradicalisation-call-falls-deaf-ears-1523215 (accessed on 17 December, 2018).

[74] Ibid.

[75] See Syed S. B. Anik and Arifur Rahman Rabbi, 'No Coordination in Bangladesh Govt De-radicalization Program', *Dhaka Tribune*, 29 November 2018. Available at: https://www.dhakatribune.com/bangladesh/militancy/2018/11/29/experts-no-coordination-in-bangladesh-govt-de-radicalization-programs (accessed on 18 December, 2018).

[76] Ibid.

presenting the counter-narrative. As a matter of fact, counter-narrative campaigns obtain more engagement and more views when they are distributed through non-government channels. The government however can play a valuable role by facilitating grassroots and civil society actors. It is true that recently in Bangladesh some excellent initiatives have been introduced by some civil society organizations also, but those need to be strengthened and the more they are encouraged and assisted by the government, the better for the campaign and the country as a whole.

Second, as already mentioned, to develop effective counter-narrative, it is extremely important that extremist narratives are studied well, they are monitored properly and then they are responded and refuted with effective counter arguments.

Third, Bangladesh must revisit and reform its prison-based disengagement and de-radicalization programmes. As we have mentioned earlier, due to the lack of appropriate de-radicalization programme inside the prisons of Bangladesh, the prisons are being used by the radicals for spreading their own message and recruiting new 'converts' to their cause. There have been many cases—some are known and some unknown—that upon being released from the jail, the JMB activists went back to the same radical path under the neo-JMB, albeit with new zeal and commitment. This should not happen with the current inmates and therefore addressing this issue should be in the priority list of the policymakers.

Fourth, trial process of the terrorists should also be transparent and must not convey any wrong message to anyone. For instance, if the due process is absent or fair treatment of the accused is denied, it can cause lack of trust and put the credibility of the criminal justice system in question, which then can affect the counter-narrative campaign as well. As it was reported in a leading daily newspaper, *Prothom Alo*, a young man arrested under the anti-terrorism act, and later released shared his experiences by saying that: 'If the government really wants to use the youth who are involved in militancy to counter militancy, they have to take them into confidence'.[77] He complained that in most cases, things are otherwise. Elaborating his point, the young man

---

[77] Alam, 'No Concern about Counter-Militancy'.

said that sometimes "the law enforcement picks them up from their homes and keep them hidden for a long spell. Later it is said that they were arrested while in a secret meeting. Sometimes it is said they were arrested during an operation'.[78] It is possible that what is stated here is fully true or partially true. Either way, the message is clear that 'unless the trial process is transparent, the results will never be achieved'.[79]

Fifth, the focus of the campaign should be on developing a multi-layered counter-narrative strategy, incorporating many different elements designed to appeal to a wide variety of people. To quote an analyst, 'the challenge lies in developing a holistic approach to the phenomenon of violent extremism and terrorism, one that includes all stakeholders from the State, society and even beyond'.[80]

Sixth, setting clear goals and objectives of the counter-narrative is a pre-requisite of its success and therefore, at the very outset of the campaign, this needs to be delineated properly. The channels and mediums of the campaign must be multiple, including online, offline, social media, Face book, Twitter and all other contemporary and dynamic means. It is a well-known fact that extremists are using social media from the very beginning to spread their poisonous message and gain support for their organizations. Indeed, it is not only the text of the narrative that matters but also the messenger and medium that have to be compatible and, if possible, superior to the extremists' reach.

Finally, Bangladesh must formulate a National Action Plan that would combine and mobilize the various departments of the government, political parties, community organizations, and private and academic sectors and help the country devise a comprehensive and effective counter-narrative campaign. After all, counter-narrative is the means and de-radicalization is its destination. In order to reach the destination, means must be well equipped and well placed.

---

[78] Ibid.

[79] Ibid.

[80] Hamed El-Said, 'Deradicalization: Experiences in Europe and the Arab World', in (De)Radicalization and Security. Available at: https://www.iemed. org/observatori/arees-danalisi/arxius-adjunts/anuari/med.2017/IEMed_ MedYearbook2017_deradicalization_europe_arab_ElSaid.pdf. (accessed 18 December 2018).

About the Editors and Contributors

EDITORS

Mubashar Hasan is presently a research fellow at the Department of Cultural Studies and Oriental Languages at the University of Oslo, Norway. In Bangladesh, he holds the position of an Assistant Professor at the Department of Political Science and Sociology, North South University, Bangladesh.

In 2018, he was awarded an Emerging Early Career Research Award, 11th Global Studies Conference in University of Granada, Spain, by the Unites States-based Common Ground Research Network. He was previously a Bangladesh research fellow at the RESOLVE Network at the United States Institute of Peace, Washington, DC, and a short-term visiting fellow at the American Institute of Bangladesh Studies and Institute for South Asian Studies, UC Berkeley (2016).

He has a PhD from Griffith University, Australia, an MLitt in Muslims globalization and the West from the University of Aberdeen, UK, and an Msc in globalization—origin, development and contemporary impact from the University of Dundee, UK. His research on religion, politics and violence were published in leading journals such as *Australian Journal of Politics and History*, *Asian Journal of Political Science*, *Harvard Asia Quarterly*, *India Quarterly* and *South Asia Research*. He has published a chapter in the book titled *Being Muslims in South Asia*.

His brief think pieces were published in *Chicago Tribune*, *San Francisco Chronicle*, *The Quint*, *Scroll.in*, *The Conversation*, *The Wire*, *Asian Correspondent*, *Firstpost* and so forth.

He is currently writing his book *Islam and Politics in Bangladesh.*

Kenji Isezaki runs the Department of Peace and Conflict Studies, and Global Campus programme at Tokyo University of Foreign Studies in Japan. He has served in several United Nations peacekeeping missions and when Japan became the lead country for the disarmament, demobilization and reintegration (DDR) programme for Afghanistan security sector reform (SSR), he directed DDR with the support of the UN Assistance Mission in Afghanistan and successfully disarmed 60,000 soldiers of the former Afghan military forces in two years. He has also served as the chief of DDR Coordination Section for the United Nations Mission in Sierra Leone (UNAMSIL); UN-appointed governor of Cova Lima for the United Nations Transitional Administration in East Timor (UNTAET); and representative of the Japanese government to the DDR special committee by the Department of Peacekeeping Operations at United Nations Secretariat in New York. Apart from teaching, he currently serves as the Vice-President of the Association for Aid and Relief, a Japanese NGO which works in 14 post- and in-conflict countries, and also enjoys supports from Japanese imperial family.

Sameer Yasir is an independent researcher and until recently was associated with the Global Campus programme of Tokyo University of Foreign Studies. He was an assistant professor at the Centre for International Relations (Peace and Conflict Studies) at Islamic University of Science and Technology, where he taught conflict studies for five years and wrote academic and policy papers and was the youngest professor appointed by the university in its history. He is the winner of 2017 best academic article by Oxford Development Studies at Oxford Department of International Development, in the memory of late Professor Sanjaya Lall. His research focus is on armed conflict, rehabilitation of ex-combatants, and counter-insurgency (COIN) and radicalization in South Asia. He worked as Asia Programs Officer at the Information and Resource Center Asian Dialogue Society, Singapore.

CONTRIBUTORS

Noor Ahmad Baba is a distinguished academic. After his initial Education in Kashmir, Prof Baba completed his masters, M.Phil. & Ph.D. from Jawaharlal Nehru University(JNU), New Delhi. During his long academic career he has extensively travelled in Asia, Europe and North America in connection with a number of academic assignments. He has also been associated, as member, advisor and expert, with various academic and research institutes, organizations and universities both locally and internationally.

During more than thirty years experience of teaching and guiding research at the University of Kashmir, Prof. Baba has held several important academic and administrative positions in the university that include the Dean, Faculty of Social Sciences (2008–2011) and Head, Department of Political Sciences for a record period of 15 years and Chairman, Centre for Sheikh-ul-Alam Studies (2010–11). In May 2015 he joined the Central University of Kashmir to oversee the growth and academic development of the Department of Politics and Governance established in that university. Presently he holds the position of Dean, School of Social Sciences in the university.

Prof. Baba has written extensively on a range of themes dealing with the South and West Asia that have won him international level recognition and acclaim. He began with an interest in Middle Eastern and Muslim World affairs. His present focus of research is Kashmir and South Asian Affairs with a peace research perspective. However, he continues his interest in Muslim and West Asian Affairs.

Asif Bin Ali is a Lecturer (sociology) at Eastern University, Dhaka, Bangladesh and a journalist working with *The Daily Observer*, a national daily. He was a research fellow at the Co-operation in Development (Australia) Inc. affiliated with Central Queensland University, Australia. His recent book (co-edited with Sabbir Ahmed) is *Buddhist Nationalism, Rohingya Crisis and Contemporary Politics*.

Iraj De Alwis is a Research Assistant at the Department of African and African–American Studies at Harvard University, and recent graduate of the Harvard Divinity School, where his research focused on religious nationalism in Sri Lanka.

Anishka De Zylva is a global risk graduate student at Johns Hopkins University School of Advanced International Studies (SAIS). She previously held the role of research associate at the Lakshman Kadirgamar Institute of International Relations and Strategic Studies (LKI), Sri Lanka, from January 2016 to July 2018.

Maidul Islam is an Assistant Professor of political science at the Centre for Studies in Social Sciences, Calcutta, India. Previously, he has taught political science at the Tata Institute of Social Sciences and Presidency University, Kolkata, and was a fellow at the Indian Institute of Advanced Study, Shimla. As a Clarendon–Hector Pilling-Senior Hulme Scholar at Brasenose College, Oxford, he completed his doctorate in politics from the Department of Politics and International Relations at the University of Oxford in 2012. His research interests are in political theory and South Asian politics. He is the author of *Limits of Islamism: Jamaat-e-Islami in Contemporary India and Bangladesh* (2015) and *Indian Muslim(s) after Liberalization* (2019).

Shahab Enam Khan is currently serving as a Professor in international relations (IR) at Jahangirnagar University, Bangladesh. His research portfolio includes security, democratic institutions, national integrity institutions and public policy. He has served as an advisor/consultant/board member of various international organizations, that is, United Nations Development Program (UNDP) Maldives, UN Women, International Union for Conservation of Nature (IUCN), United States Agency for International Development (USAID), International Fund for Agricultural Development (IFAD), Foreign and Commonwealth Office, UK and Regional Center for Strategic Studies, Sri Lanka, and Jaago Foundation, Bangladesh. He also serves as a member of various high-level committees formed by the Government of Bangladesh. He led preventing violent extremism (PVE) research for UNDP Maldives, UN Women, and the British Foreign and Commonwealth Office. He is credited for drafting several key public policy documents for the Government of Bangladesh, including the National Broadcast Policy 2014 and the National Counter Terrorism Strategy Paper. He has completed professional courses on global security from Harvard University, and received MA degree in international political economy from the University of Manchester and Bachelors of Social Science degree in IR from the University of Dhaka. He completed fellowships at the University of Delaware, USA, and the University of Birmingham, UK. He is a Near East South Asia (NESA) Center, National Defense University, Washington, DC, USA alumnus. He is a senior fellow at the Hainan Institute of World Watch, Hainan, China.

Nazneen Mohsina is a Research Assistant at the Institute of South Asian Studies (ISAS), an autonomous research institute at the National University of Singapore (NUS). She writes on South Asia and India, focusing on politics, terrorism and extremism.

Feriha Peracha is the Director and Supervising Psychologist for the Sabaoon Project, a school in Pakistan which uses academic and religious education, psychology and other techniques to de-radicalize young boys from their Taliban indoctrination. She is also the CEO of SWAaT for Pakistan. She is a leading practitioner in the field of de-radicalization and widely interviewed by global media outlets including BBC News, ABC News Australia and the United States-based National Public Radio, among others. She holds an MSC degree from the University of Calgary and a PhD from the University College London, UK. She has worked in the United Kingdom for approximately 20 years as a psychologist in interface medicine. She is the Vice President of Lahore Mental Health Association and the Fountain House, and has been a board member of many philanthropic organizations (i-Care Foundation, Sanjan Nagar, World Wide Fund for Nature (WWF), etc.).

Raafia Raees Khan is currently the Vice CEO of SWAaT for Pakistan and oversees Sabaoon (Centre for de-radicalization and rehabilitation for militant youth) and the monitoring centre (which continues to support the Sabaoon graduates in order to prevent recidivism). She has co-authored a number of publications in relation to her work in de-radicalization. Her work has gained much respect and contributed to a deeper understanding of violent extremism internationally. She and her colleagues (at SWAaT and IC Thinking—an intervention science research group based in the Department of Psychology at the University of Cambridge, Cambridge) are currently working to inculcate critical thinking, social intelligence and empathy through developing modules based on integrative complexity.

Mahbubur Rahman is an Associate Professor at the Department of Political Science and Sociology of North South University, Bangladesh. Previously, he taught at York College of the City University of New York (CUNY). He has received several grants and fellowships, including the Fulbright scholarship, and published several articles in peer-reviewed journals.

Fatima Waqi Sajjad is an Assistant Professor, Department of Political Science, the University of Management and Technology in Pakistan. Her recent work for *Journal of Peace Education* reconsiders the problem of youth radicalism in Pakistan and suggests alternative ways to counter extremism in the country. Her work has been published in leading national and international journals, and presented in multiple forums including International Human Security Conference in Istanbul, Turkey; the Asian Education for Peace and Interfaith Congress in Hiroshima, Japan; and the International Conference on Education, Research and Innovation in Seville, Spain. She has a PhD in IR from Punjab University, Lahore. She completed her MPhil in IR from Kinnaird College, Lahore, and MSc in IR from Quaid-i-Azam University, Islamabad. She has an extensive professional experience as a teacher and teacher trainer. Prior to joining University of Management and Technology (UMT) in 2012, she worked as a teacher and trainer at Lahore Grammar School for eight years.

Bulbul Siddiqi is an Assistant Professor at the Department of Political Science and Sociology, North South University. His monograph *Becoming 'Good Muslim': The Tablighi Jamaat in the UK and Bangladesh* was published in 2018. He holds an MA in global citizenship, identities and human rights from the University of Nottingham, UK, and a PhD from the Cardiff University, UK.

Mohammed Sinan Siyech is a Research Analyst with the International Centre for Political Violence and Terrorism Research (ICPVTR), a constituent unit of the S. Rajaratnam School of International Studies (RSIS), Nanyang Technological University, Singapore. He has written on politics, conflict and security pertaining to West Asia and India.

Barana Waidyatilake is a non-resident fellow with LKI in Colombo, Sri Lanka, where he was a research fellow from February 2016 to October 2018.

Azim Zahir is a Political Scientist with the Centre for Muslim States and Societies, the University of Western Australia. He has specialized in political Islam and democratization theory, and the politics and religious issues of the South Asian country of the Maldives. He has done research in radicalization and violent extremism.

Index